Muslim Societies in the Age of Mass Consumption

Muslim Societies in the Age of Mass Consumption: Politics, Culture and Identity between the Local and the Global

Edited by

Johanna Pink

CAMBRIDGE SCHOLARS
P U B L I S H I N G

Muslim Societies in the Age of Mass Consumption:
Politics, Culture and Identity between the Local and the Global,
Edited by Johanna Pink

This book first published 2009

Cambridge Scholars Publishing

12 Back Chapman Street, Newcastle upon Tyne, NE6 2XX, UK

British Library Cataloguing in Publication Data
A catalogue record for this book is available from the British Library

Copyright © 2009 by Johanna Pink and contributors

All rights for this book reserved. No part of this book may be reproduced, stored in a retrieval system, or transmitted, in any form or by any means, electronic, mechanical, photocopying, recording or otherwise, without the prior permission of the copyright owner.

ISBN (10): 1-4438-1405-9, ISBN (13): 978-1-4438-1405-8

CONTENTS

Introduction (Johanna Pink) ix

I Spaces of Consumption in a Globalized World 1

1 Halal, Haram, or What? Creating Muslim Space in London
   (Johan Fischer) 3

2 New Transnational Geographies of Islamism, Capitalism, and
   Subjectivity: The Veiling-Fashion Industry in Turkey (Banu
   Gökarıksel and Anna Secor) 23

3 The Shopping Mall: The Enchanted Part of a Disenchanted City.
   The Case of ANKAmall, Ankara (Aksu Akçaoğlu) 53

4 Between East and West: Consumer Culture and Identity
   Negotiation in Contemporary Turkey (Tanfer Emin Tunç) 73

**II Facetted Consumer Identities: Politics and Strategies of
Consumption** 87

5 Consumers' Monarchy: Citizenship, Consumption, and Material
   Politics in Saudi Arabia since the 1970s (Relli Shechter) 89

6 The Cola Turka Controversy: Consuming Cola as a Turkish
   Muslim (Dilek Kaya Mutlu) 105

7 Consumption in Yemen: Continuity and Change (Ulrike Stohrer) . 129

8 (Un-)Islamic Consumers? The Case of Polish Tatars (Katarzyna
   Górak-Sosnowska and Michał Łyszczarz) 145

9 Marketing the Alevi Musical Revival (Ayhan Erol) 165

III Islamic Products, Islamic Brands, and Muslim Target Groups 185

10 Barbie, Razanne, Fulla: A Tale of Culture, Globalization, Consumerism, and Islam (*Petra Kuppinger*) 187

11 Islamizing the Market? Advertising, Products, and Consumption in an Islamic Framework in Syria (*Alina Kokoschka*) 225

12 Video Games, Video Clips, and Islam: New Media and the Communication of Values (*Vít Šisler*) 241

13 Representation of Fashion as Muslima Identity in *Paras* Magazine (*Firly Annisa*) 271

14 The Re-Spiritualization of Consumption or the Commercialization of Religion: Creativity, Responsibility, and Hope. The Case of Sunsilk Clean and Fresh in Indonesia (*Ragnar K. Willer*) . 281

15 American-Muslim Identity: Advertising, Mass Media + New Media (*Michael Hastings-Black*) 303

IV Epilogue 325

16 The Economic Politics of Muslim Consumption (*Patrick Haenni*) . 327

List of Contributors 343

List of Figures

3.1 An evening view of ANKAmall. 57
3.2 A dinosaur display at ANKAmall. 62

4.1 İsmail Acar's mural at Ankara's Cepa shopping mall, *Büyük Türkiye Resmi* ("Big Picture of Turkey") 78
4.2 The Mevlana display at Antares, Ankara 81
4.3 Glimpse of a food court 83

5.1 A model of Saudi citizenship 100

7.1 A woman wearing the *sitāra* in a shop for fabrics in Sanaa, 1989 132
7.2 Shops in Sanaa with colorful advertising signs 133
7.3 A "typical" Yemenite couple 136
7.4 New shop for fabrics in Sanaa 2006 137
7.5 Shop for Western-style clothing in Sanaa 2008 138
7.6 New shoe shop in Sanaa, 2008 139

8.1 Polish Tatars during a prayer at the Muslim cemetery in Warsaw 148
8.2 Mufti Tomasz Miśkiewicz, the leader of the Polish Tatars community, and Halina Szahidewicz, chairwoman of the Muslim Religious Union in Białystok 159

10.1 The multicultural doll family 193
10.2 Razanne 205
10.3 Singing Fulla and Outdoor Fulla 208
10.4 Fulah 212
10.5 Razanne, Singing Fulls, Outdoor Fulla, and Fulah (white and black dress) 219

11.1 Advertisement for Dima cookies seen in Lattakia, Syria . . . 229
11.2 Detergent ad placed on top of a building in Midan Square, Damascus 230

11.3	Wallpaper for sale in a mobile shop in Old Damascus	234
11.4	Wallpaper for sale in a mobile shop in Old Damascus	234
11.5	A typical range of bracelets for men	235
11.6	Educational computer in the style of an Apple Macintosh laptop	236
11.7	Pink for prayer	238
11.8	Coloring Fulla's world	239
12.1	Scene from the edutainment CD-ROM *Taᶜlīm al-ṣalawāt*	250
12.2	Scene from the edutainment CD-ROM *Al-Muslim al-ṣaghīr*	250
12.3	Scene from the video game *Quraysh*	253
12.4	Scene from *Second Life*	254
12.5	Video game *Quraysh*	262
12.6	Video game *Arabian Lords*	263
16.1	McDonald's advertisement during Ramadan	329
16.2	Dawahwear: An American pop culture take on Muslim identity	333
16.3	A scene from a bazaar in Le Bourget, Paris	334
16.4	Cover of a magazine devoted to veiled women	337
16.5	Advertisements for global brands during Ramadan	341

INTRODUCTION

JOHANNA PINK

Muslim Societies and Mass Consumption

I returned to Cairo in 1998 after a long absence [...]. The flow of cash had increased among certain classes, and along with it conspicuous consumption. [...] Today Cairenes can order local fast food to be home delivered [...]. With increasing consumer appetites, shopping malls [...] had proliferated in various areas of Cairo. I was fascinated by how youngsters, both poor and rich, had conquered these spaces of consumption and how these are turning into specifically gendered spaces at specific times of the day. New forms of leisure socialization are in the making among middle class Cairenes. [...] If we take into account phenomena such as the spread of McDonald's, ATMs, mobile phones, condominiums, email usage, and gated communities, then Egypt has indeed entered the age of globalization. But to jump from that premise to the conclusion that these types of phenomena are leading to a homogenization in lifestyle is too simplistic.[1]

In the course of the 20th century, mass consumption—characterized by the availability and affordability of a broad spectrum of differentiated and ever-changing commodities far exceeding the consumers' basic needs both in substance and in variety—has spread across the world. The global triumph of consumerism is affecting not only the availability and variety of consumer goods, but also the presentation, promotion and advertising of goods and the spaces in which consumption takes place. From Coca-Cola to shopping malls, consumerism is everywhere—in the Muslim world and beyond.

However, it would be too easy to assume that we are confronted with a one-directional force of homogenization, a process in which a hegemonial

---

[1] Mona Abaza, *Changing Consumer Cultures of Modern Egypt. Cairo's Urban Reshaping* (Leiden: Brill, 2006), 2–3.

Western culture of consumerism is taking over and sweeping away local structures and traditions of consumption. Although global brands and practices of consumption do have a homogenizing effect, local consumers are not merely passive victims of global consumerism. Local agents can be observed as they actively appropriate global developments, adapt commodities and spaces of consumption to their own needs and integrate them into their culture; but simultaneously, this culture is reshaped, reinvented and often folklorized in order to comply with the mechanisms of conspicuous consumption.

Most aptly, the spread of consumerism can thus be described in the framework of "glocalization"—the complex interaction between globalizing and localizing processes.

Consuming the same global products might mean very different things to people in different local circumstances. A drink of Coca-Cola might be no more than a quick and cheap refreshment to some, but might serve as a status symbol to others who offer one, and only one, glass of it as an aperitif before dinner,[2] while still others denounce it as a symbol of imperialism and call for a boycott of the soda. Similarly, the motives for visiting or not visiting a shopping mall, and the ways to spend one's time there, might differ vastly between consumers in different local contexts.

Consumption can fulfill a broad spectrum of purposes, among them the fulfillment of basic needs or of refined desires, the acquisition of status and identity formation; it can serve to express one's individuality or an association with a group or social class, and it can even function as a political statement. All these motivations have to be taken into account by producers in the way they design, sell and advertise their consumer products if they want to be successful in the global market.

This process works in two ways: On one hand, many global companies such as Coca-Cola, McDonald's or Unilever—which are, at first glance, at the forefront of the homogenizing forces of globalization—flexibly and creatively adapt their brands, products and advertising to specific target markets, taking into account the local consumers' lifestyle and expectations. On the other hand, local producers invent products that fit seamlessly into a globalized consumer culture while maintaining an impression of cultural and/or religious authenticity—modern Islamic fashion and anti-American soft drinks, headscarf-wearing Barbies and halal fast food chains, glossy magazines for the Muslim woman and shopping malls decorated with Ramses statues or displays of whirling Dervishes are all evidence of this trend,

---

[2] As experienced by the author during her stay in Jordan 1995/96 among Jordanian-Palestinian middle-class families.

and they are arguably most successful where global brands fail to meet the expectations of local consumers.

In the past decade or two, Muslim societies[3] have undergone tremendous transformations. Internet cafés and shopping malls, the increased presence of global consumer goods, new media and satellite TV have made an enormous impact on urban spaces, consumption practices and advertising. The fundamental changes caused by globalization affect not only the flow of money, but also transform social stratification, lifestyles, processes of identity formation, cultural expression, and gender roles. Consumption moreover increasingly serves as a venue of political expression.

Consumption, Identity, and Islam

Mass consumption results in differentiation. Today's consumers can choose between countless brands and varieties of products, and their decisions define their lifestyle—and not only their lifestyle but also their identity: "I am what I buy." Companies try to capitalize on this by offering products with an added cultural, ethical or religious value. This added value sometimes becomes a product's most important feature, the most compelling reason to buy this specific product over others that are supposedly less ethical, culturally authentic or religiously virtuous.

In recent years, news reports of Islamic dolls, Islamic soft drinks and Islamic garments like the *burqini* have been abundant, encouraging the impression that Muslims increasingly seek to define and express their distinct identity through the consumption of "Islamic" commodities.

As fascinating as these products are at first glance, only careful study can reveal their significance and meaning: Are they more successful, on the long run, than their 'un-Islamic' counterparts? Who consumes them and for what reasons? Are they tokens of religiousness or of cultural authenticity— or mere status symbols?

All of these hybrid products elude easy categorization. The closer one looks at them, the more questions arise.

- Is *Mecca Cola* really a soft drink geared towards a religious public, or is it rather a product that intends to make a political statement, as the success of competing products such as *Cola Turka* might indicate?

---

[3] The term "Muslim societies" here refers to countries in which the majority of the population is Muslim, without implying that all of these societies or nation states define themselves primarily in a religious sense. In the broader sense in which it is used in the title of this book, it also includes diasporic Muslim communities in Western countries.

- Is *Fulla* popular because it is an Islamic doll, or is it popular because it is closer to the lifestyle and looks that Arab girls are familiar with?
- Is the *burqini*, while arguably making a statement against "Western" decadence, in reality a distinctly Western item, geared toward a diasporic target group and completely unknown to women in Muslim majority societies—most of all in Afghanistan, the country where the much less fancy *burqa* is worn by most women? What is the exact relationship between traditional forms of clothing and new "Islamic" fashion?

How popular are these products among Muslims, anyway? Do they sell to the public as well as they do sell the media? And if they do, who buys them? Close analysis reveals that most "Islamic" products, in reality, do not appeal to Muslims everywhere, but are actually geared to a specific segment of the Muslim population in a specific environment. There is *Fulla* in the Middle East and *Razanne* in the U.S.; modern Islamic fashions compete with traditional forms of dress that are bought and sold in different outlets.

Especially when analyzing the relationship between Islamic religion and consumption, one should be careful not to define Muslims predominantly or exclusively by their "Muslim-ness;" like anywhere else, consumer behavior in Muslim societies is influenced by a large number of factors, including gender, social and economic status, ethnicit, and nationality. Muslims have always made fashion decisions that go beyond the choice for or against wearing a veil; and buying a wall picture with the Dome of the Rock is more likely to be a political than a religious statement.

The Islamization of consumer goods, as evidenced in the above-mentioned examples, does exist, but it is a phenomenon of a certain class and tied to specific local circumstances. It is particularly successful among Muslims who sympathize with what Patrick Haenni labels "Salafi Islam."[4] Diasporic communities play an important role in it; but as the case of *Fulla* shows, it is not merely a diasporic phenomenon, and as the case of the Polish Tatars shows,[5] many subgroups within "the" Muslim diaspora show no interest in it. Thus, the phenomenon is too complex to allow for a summary appraisal; rather, it merits in-depth case studies in order to elucidate the conditions under which brands and commodities are Islamized—i.e., provided with an added value that turns a consumption decision into a pious act.

However, products and brands that are framed in Islamic references can only be properly understood if the adverse tendency is also taken into ac-

---

[4] See p. 328 of this volume.
[5] See chapter 8 of this volume.

count: While banal products, like dolls or soft drinks, are loaded with religious value, Islamic products are arguably de-sacralized by turning them into commodities: the marketing of Alevi music, which is stripped of its spiritual meaning by gearing it to a non-Alevi mass market, is a good example.[6]

This Volume

The issues raised above can best be approached from a multidisciplinary perspective. Economy, sociology, political science, anthropology, geography, communication sciences, and religious studies all can contribute to a better understanding of the recent changes in the global consumption landscape. So far, however, such studies have been few and far between with respect to Muslim majority and minority societies.

While the impact of global commodities in East and South-East Asia has attracted some scholarly attention,[7] the situation in the Middle East has scarcely been the subject of extensive research; the single country that has probably been studied the most is Turkey.[8]

The relation between (Islamic) religion and consumption has mostly been discussed with a focus on veiling and modern headscarf fashions.[9] The majority of contributions have concentrated on the ideological and political context of the headscarf debate, whereas, for example, economic aspects have been understudied. "Traditional" forms of veiling have been just as marginalized as other aspects of dress, be they religiously framed or otherwise.

---

[6] See chapter 9 of this volume.

[7] See, e.g., James L. Watson, ed., *Golden Arches East: McDonald's in East Asia* (Stanford University Press, 1997); Robert Robison and David S. G. Goodman, *The New Rich in Asia: Mobile Phones, McDonald's and Middle-Class Revolution* (London: Routledge, 1996); Beng-Huat Chua, *Life is Not Complete without shopping. Consumption Culture in Singapore* (Singapore: Singapore University Press, 2003); Johan Fischer, *Proper Islamic Consumption: Shopping among the Malays in Modern Malaysia* (Copenhagen: NIAS Press, 2008).

[8] Among the few larger contributions are Abaza, *Changing Consumer Cultures of Modern Egypt. Cairo's Urban Reshaping*; Roni Zirinski, *Ad hoc Arabism: Advertising, Culture and Technology in Saudi Arabia* (New York: P. Lang, 2005); Çağlar Keyder, ed., *Istanbul between the Global and the Local* (Lanham: Rowman / Littlefield, 1999).

[9] See, e.g., Barış Kılıçbay and Mutlu Binark, "Consumer Culture, Islam and the Politics of Lifestyle: Fashion for Veiling in Contemporary Turkey," *European Journal of Communication* 17 (2002): 495–511; Jenny White, "Islamic Chic," in *Istanbul between the Global and the Local*, ed. Çağlar Keyder (Lanham: Rowman / Littlefield, 1999), 77–91; Anna Secor, "The Veil and Urban Space in Istanbul: Women's Dress, Mobility and Islamic Knowledge," *Gender, Place and Culture* 9 (2002): 5–22; Banu Gökarıksel and Katharyne Mitchell, "Veiling, Secularism and the Neoliberal Subject: National Narratives and Supranational Desires in Turkey and France," *Global Networks* 5 (2005): 147–165.

Although Islamic brands and products have evoked some scholarly interest,[10] few in-depth studies of consumer behavior, advertising strategies or the cultural places of these new products are available as yet.

This volume seeks to further the study of the impact of mass consumption on Muslim societies through a broad spectrum of contributions from a variety of academic disciplines. It presents case studies from different regions of the Muslim world as well as diasporic communities, seeking to deepen the understanding of the recent changes in consumer landscapes and of the ways in which consumers and producers adapt to them. This includes, but is not limited to, a process that might be called the "Islamization of consumption," as evidenced by Islamic dolls, shampoos, and video games. However, we do not presume to identify such a phenomenon as *the* Muslim consumer. Religion and culture are important influences on consumption habits; but their significance can only be understood when specific local circumstances are taken into account. Similar products or structures might have very different meanings in Poland or Turkey, in Saudi-Arabia or Malaysia, in London or New York. It is these concrete adaptations and appropriations of aspects of global consumerism that the authors of this volume, who come from a variety of disciplines, seek to describe in their case studies.

Spaces of Consumption in a Globalized World

The first part explores transformations of the spaces in which consumption takes place—a fundamental theme that repeatedly is taken up again in later parts of the volume.

One of the most important aspects of globalization is an increased mobility, which leads to the existence of diasporic Muslim communities nearly everywhere on the globe. In this context, **Johan Fischer** reviews the ways in which Malay immigrants create spaces for halal consumption in London, thereby elucidating the complex social, economic, cultural, and political interrelation between Malay individuals, their host country, and their country of origin.

Moving to a predominantly Muslim society, **Banu Gökarıksel** and **Anna Secor** situate the veiling-fashion industry in a geopolitical, religious, and

---

[10] See, e.g., Patrick Haenni, *L'islam de marché. L'autre révolution conservatrice* (Paris: Seuil, 2005); Ragnar K. Willer, "Dispelling the Myth of a Global Consumer: Indonesian Consumer Behavior Researched by Means of an Analytical Diagram for Intercultural Marketing. With a Case Study of Sunsilk Shampoo for the Veiled Woman" (Dissertation, Humboldt Universität, 2006), http://edoc.hu-berlin.de/dissertationen/willer-ragnar-karl-2006-07-19/HTML; Amina Yaqin, "Islamic Barbie: The Politics of Gender and Performativity," *Fashion Theory* 11, no. 2/3 (2007): 173–188.

economic context and analyze its role in subject formation, thereby transcending the usual depiction of the veil as a *topos* of ideological discourse.

Finally, **Aksu Akçaoğlu** and **Tanfer Emin Tunç** approach, from different perspectives, the single institution that is perhaps most powerfully changing the urban consumption landscape in Middle Eastern societies—i.e., the shopping mall. Both concentrate on the case of Turkey. While Akçaoğlu offers a sociological analysis of the function of shopping malls for the residents of modern Turkish cities, based on a case study of the visitors to one particular mall in Ankara, Tunç's contribution focuses on the cultural impact of the large-scale adaptation of malls from America.

Facetted Consumer Identities: Politics and Strategies of Consumption

The second part focuses on the social and political implications of consumption within various Muslim societies and minority communities, exploring the opportunities that globalization processes have created for consumers and the strategies they use to maintain a balance between continuity and change.

Relli Shechter analyzes the way in which consumerism was embedded into the already existing socio-political system of Saudi Arabia, where consumption—when linked with the notion of religious virtue—may function as a venue of political expression at times, but nevertheless contributes to the stability of the monarchical system.

In Turkey—a country that defines itself as secular but where the political role of Islam is continuously under debate—more direct ways to express political or religious preferences through consumption are available. **Dilek Kaya Mutlu** discusses the instructive case of Cola Turka, a soft drink that, unlike the more widely noticed (and arguably less successful) Mecca Cola, outwardly drew on nationalist rather than religious symbolism, thereby raising the question of the motives behind individual consumers' decisions to buy it. To answer this question, Mutlu examines the ways in which Cola Turka was marketed and the controversial debates it triggered.

Ulrike Stohrer takes us to Yemen, a country where mass consumption is only starting to gain ground, but which has a long history of participation in global trade. Yemenite fashion thus proves to be particularly interesting with respect to the local appropriation of global commodities and fashion trends. Stohrer shows that, far beyond the issue of veiling, gender roles are an important factor for consumer decisions and the transformations of urban space. While cultural norms are crucial for her findings, religious rules are much less so, despite the common perception of Yemen as a traditional Muslim society.

Similarly, **Katarzyna Górak-Sosnowska** and **Michał Łyszczarz**, in their case study of the Tatar minority in Poland, raise fundamental questions regarding the Muslim-ness of Muslim consumers and the cultural context in which certain groups of Muslim consumers identify themselves, at least partly, through their religion, while others do not. The "clash of Islams" they describe is a strong point in favor of the hypothesis that "Islamic" products are not actually targeted at Muslims but rather at specific groups of Muslims with very particular priorities.

Ayhan Erol draws our attention to an important segment of the Muslim Turkish population that does not follow the priorities of orthodox Sunni Muslims—namely the Alevis, who, throughout the emergence of mass consumption, have developed their own ways to express and market their cultural identity, especially in the field of music. His contribution raises the question of how far religious rituals or symbols are de-sacralized through their conversion into a commodity, a question that is further examined in the third part.

Islamized Products, Islamic Brands and Muslim Target Groups

The last part deals with the emergence of products, brands and advertising campaigns that are specifically geared toward Muslim target groups and are at the same time very much a part of contemporary global consumerism. There is hardly a better symbol for this than *Fulla*, the "Islamic doll," and her sisters, which **Petra Kuppinger** discusses in her contribution. These dolls, which cater to different Muslim markets and segments, position themselves as pious and culturally authentic "counter-Barbies," but are nevertheless firmly rooted in Barbie's existence.

Fulla accessories are an important part of the Syrian landscape of Islamic consumption that **Alina Kokoschka** describes in her paper, which analyzes advertisements that appeal to religious sentiments yet simultaneously convey an image of modernity, and Islamized products that are geared toward a young Muslim target group.

The convergence between religious virtue and up-to-date global products or forms of expression is even more striking in **Vít Šisler**'s paper on new media. There is an increasing number of educational media, video games and video blogs that communicate religious values or try to appeal to "Muslim identity." Šisler shows that more and more of them are just as professional and technologically up-to-date as their non-religious counterparts, which is a *conditio sine qua non* for their success among adolescent and adult audiences. They try to differentiate themselves from mainstream productions by promoting "positive values" as opposed to the perceived depravity and violence of their "Western" counterparts.

Moving to South-East Asia, **Firly Annisa** takes a critical look at *Paras*, an Indonesian glossy magazine for middle- to upper-class Muslim women that portrays Islam as a fashion trend not at all incompatible with female beauty and seductiveness. In the same vein, Unilever introduced a shampoo in Indonesia that is aimed exclusively at headscarf-wearing women. **Ragnar Willer** analyzes the branding and advertising of *Sunsilk Clean and Fresh* and the social and economic context in which the product could become a huge success.

Finally, **Michael Hastings-Black** offers a contribution from a professional perspective, discussing the significance of diasporic Muslim groups to the American advertising and media industry. In this context, he also analyzes the important role of new media in opening a space for self-representation of ethnic, religious, and cultural minorities.

The Economic Politics of Muslim Consumption

Taking up the findings of previous contributions, **Patrick Haenni**, in his conclusion, analyzes the way in which the commercialization of religion—or the Islamization of commerce—goes together with the emergence of a cosmopolitan conservative leisure class and the predominance of a Salafi discourse with its emphasis on outward piousness. He considers consumption "a prism through which we can analyze the meaning of what we call re-Islamization."[11]

In this sense, all the papers in this volume use consumption as a prism through which specific aspects of the enormous transformations that Muslim societies have undergone in the past decades can be studied and better understood.

Acknowledgments

This volume is the outcome of the conference *Contemporary Muslim Consumer Cultures. An Emerging Field of Study* which took place at the Free University of Berlin in September 2008. Neither the conference nor the publication of this volume would have been possible without the generous support of the Free University's Department of History and Cultural Studies, for which I would like to express my heartfelt gratitude. I am especially thankful to Professor Dr. Gudrun Krämer for her wholehearted support of

---

[11] See p. 329 of this volume.

this endeavor. Tonice Sgrignoli deserves my gratitude for the painstaking work of copyediting the papers. Last, but not least, I would like to thank the authors of this volume. It has been a pleasure to work with them.

Berlin, August 2009   Johanna Pink

Part I

Spaces of Consumption in a Globalized World

CHAPTER ONE

HALAL, HARAM, OR WHAT? CREATING MUSLIM SPACE IN LONDON

JOHAN FISCHER

Introduction

The 2003 book *Halal Food: A Guide to Good Eating—London*, by the Malaysian publisher KasehDia, reviews more than a hundred restaurants, take-away counters, and cafés in London. Much more than strictly traditional halal requirements are involved in guiding Muslim consumers: the spatial context (atmosphere, feel, and ambience) of food consumption as practice might be just as significant as the intrinsic qualities of the food and its ingredients. The various establishments are classified according to their halalness, e.g., whether alcohol is sold and whether food is produced and served by Muslims or non-Muslims. During my fieldwork on halal understanding and practice among Malay Muslims in London from 2005 to 2007, "spatial trajectories"[1]—i.e., stories that traverse and organize places and link them together—were prominent in halal narratives. I shall explore how my informants understand and practice these often ambiguous and confusing halal spaces (such as restaurants, butcher shops, grocery and convenience stores, supermarkets, and hypermarkets) in London. I will also discuss articulations of difference between "eating out" and "eating in" in the lives of my informants. By "eating in" I mean shopping for halal meat and other types of food in London, which would be cooked in the homes of my informants.

---

[1] Michel de Certeau, *The Practice of Everyday Life* (Berkeley: University of California Press, 1984), 115.

Thus far, scholarly attention to halal in Britain has, for the most part, focused on conflicts over the provision of halal in schools,[2] the politics of religious slaughter,[3] and the marketing of halal meat.[4] In many parts of London, such as Finsbury Park, Edgware Road, and Whitechapel Road, halal is a distinctive presence on signs and in butcher shops and restaurants. Lately, more and more types of halal-certified products are appearing in supermarkets such as Tesco and ASDA. In contemporary London halal is no longer an expression of esoteric forms of production, trade, and consumption; it is part of a huge and expanding globalized market. A Canadian government study reveals that the global halal trade annually amounts to $150 billion, and it is growing among the world's approximately 1.3 billion Muslims.[5] Based on ethnographic evidence from halal spaces in London this paper argues that the proliferation of modern halal is a particular form of urban space making.

Muslim space making is the production of "the 'social space' of networks and identities created as individuals interact in new contexts, as well as the 'cultural space' that emerges in a wide variety of ways as Muslims interact with one another and with the larger community."[6] I explore the proliferation of halal as contributing to social and cultural space making in London. Often it is certain activities that contribute to the creation of "Muslim space."[7] A central theme in this paper is the display and transmission of the Arabic word halal and its involvement in the production, recognition, and contestation of space in London. Turkish migrants in Germany take great care to prevent the moral contamination from haram (unlawful or forbidden) meat that can seem threatening to them in Germany. These concerns have

---

[2] Tahir Abbas, *Muslim Britain: Communities under Pressure* (London and New York: Zed Books, 2005).

[3] Florence Bergeaud-Blackler, "New Challenges for Islamic Ritual Slaughter: A European Perspective," *Journal of Ethnic and Migration Studies* 33, no. 6 (2007): 965–980; Roger Charlton and Ronald Kaye, "The Politics of Religious Slaughter: An Ethno-Religious Case Study," *New Community* 12, no. 3 (1985): 490–502; Ronald Kaye, "The Politics of Religious Slaughter of Animals: Strategies for Ethno-Religious Political Action," *New Community* 19 (1993): 235–250.

[4] Allam Ahmed, "Marketing of Halal Meat in the United Kingdom," *British Food Journal* 110, no. 7 (2008): 655–670.

[5] Agriculture and Agri-Food Canada, *Halal Food Products Market Report* (Ottawa: Agriculture / Agri-Food Canada, 2006).

[6] Barbara Daly Metcalf, "Introduction: Sacred Words, Sanctioned Practice, New Communities," in *Making Muslim Space in North America and Europe*, ed. Barbara Daly Metcalf (Berkeley, Los Angeles and London: University of California Press, 1996), 2.

[7] Ibid., 6.

moved to the forefront in diaspora, whereas these dietary laws are "nearly unconscious" in Turkey.[8]

Conversely, Malaysia holds a special position in the global halal market, and it will be clear why the focus in this paper is on Malays. Unlike in Turkey, dietary laws among Malay Muslims in Malaysia are both highly conscious and halal is ubiquitous as a signifier in public as well as in private spaces or domains in Malaysia. From previous periods of fieldwork in Malaysia I learned that many middle-class Malays see themselves as being quite fastidious about halal.

The methodology for this study was ethnographic—i.e., I spent an extended period of time on research in London's halal spaces, and I committed to adapt to this environment and to develop a sensitivity to the people I was learning from. At the same time, the fieldwork for this study can be said to be a multi-sited ethnography involving Kuala Lumpur, the capital of Malaysia, and London. Thus, my methodology rests on an intention to "follow the people."[9] It leads me to focus on descriptions of Malays who migrated from Kuala Lumpur to London and their migration narratives, with special emphasis on understandings and practices of halal space in these two locations. Before starting my extended period of fieldwork in London, I conducted fieldwork for one month in Kuala Lumpur. The aim of this fieldwork was to capture powerful discourses of halal in urban Malaysia. In addition, since 1996 I have also conducted fieldwork in Malaysia for a period of two years.

My exploration of the Malay Muslim diaspora in London elaborates and continues a study of what I have called Proper Islamic Consumption in Malaysia.[10] I shall discuss this study in greater detail below. The main motive for focusing on Malays in multiethnic London is that Malays hold a special position with regard to halal. In Malaysia the state has standardized, certified, and institutionalized halal since the 1980s. Thus, state institutions regulate the proliferation of halal and concentrate certification in the realm of the state. The proliferation of halal in Malaysia cannot be divorced from developments in the country over the past three decades, including its steady economic growth, the emergence of large groups of Malay Muslim middle-class consumers, and centralized state incentives that attempt to strengthen

---

[8] Ruth Mandel, "A Place of Their Own: Contesting Spaces and Defining Places in Berlin's Migrant Community," in *Making Muslim Space in North America and Europe*, ed. Barbara Daly Metcalf (Berkeley, Los Angeles, and London: University of California Press, 1996), 151.

[9] George Marcus, "Ethnography in/of the World System: The Emergence of Multi-Sited Ethnography," *Annual Review of Anthropology* 24 (1995): 106.

[10] Johan Fischer, *Proper Islamic Consumption: Shopping among the Malays in Modern Malaysia* (Copenhagen: NIAS Press, 2008).

halal production, trade, and consumption. As mentioned above, halal spaces are ubiquitous in urban Malaysia. In order for local and foreign producers and traders to enter the halal market it is necessary to obtain state halal certification and a particular halal logo issued by the state. This logo signifies that factories or shops comply with state guidelines on halal. The majority of Malay Muslims in urban Malaysia frequent certified restaurants or stores in which this logo is fully visible. Halal is increasingly subject to requirements that are not only directly related to the intrinsic qualities of products but to their handling and storage. Hence, traceability is becoming important to convince consumers that producers, certifiers, and carriers are aware of the increasing requirements in "halal spaces" or domains. This trend is also apparent in London.

London is home to a substantial number of Malays and Malaysian political and religious organizations. The focus on Malay halal consumption in London allows me to offer comparisons to previous research on halal and consumption among Malays in Malaysia—especially with regard to the understanding and practice of what I call halal spaces.

Starting in 2005, I visited London on several occasions. The extended period of fieldwork in London took place from July to December 2006, with one shorter stay in the spring of 2007. The initial stage of the research in London was quantitative in method and outlook. Informants were selected on the basis of a survey that covered 100 mainly Malay respondents. The design of the survey primarily served to map migration trajectories, broader halal consumption patterns, as well as the informants' understanding and practice of divergent types of halal certification in London. On the basis of the survey, 14 Malay informants were selected for interviewing and participant observation. Moreover, a number of background interviews and participant observations were carried out with halal producers and traders, Islamic organizations, and food authorities.

Halal Transformed

Halal literally means "lawful" or "permitted." The Koran and the Sunna exhort Muslims to eat the good and lawful food God has provided for them, but a number of conditions and prohibitions obtain. Muslims are expressly forbidden from consuming carrion, spurting blood, pork, and foods that have been consecrated to any being other than God himself. These substances are haram and thus forbidden.

The lawfulness of meat depends on how it is obtained. Ritual slaughtering entails that the animal is killed in God's name by making a fatal incision across the throat. In this process, blood should be drained as fully as possible. Another significant Islamic prohibition relates to wine and any other alcoholic drink or substance; all such are haram in any quantity or substance.[11]

In addition to halal and haram, doubtful things should be avoided, i.e., there is a gray area between clearly lawful and unlawful.[12] The doubtful or questionable is expressed in the word *mashbūh*, which can be evoked by divergences in religious scholars' opinions or the suspicion of undetermined or prohibited ingredients in a commodity.[13] Hence, far more abstract, individual, and fuzzy aspects of context and handling are involved in determining the halalness of a product. To determine whether foodstuff is halal or haram "depends on its nature, how it is processed, and how it is obtained."[14]

Muslim dietary rules have assumed new significance in the 20th century as some Muslims strive to demonstrate how such rules conform to modern reason and the findings of scientific research.[15] Another common theme in the revival and renewal of these dietary rules seems to be the search for alternatives to what is seen to be Western values, ideologies, and lifestyles. These reevaluations of requirements and prohibitions are prominent, firstly, in postcolonial Islamic cultures such as Malaysia, and, secondly, among diaspora groups for whom halal can serve as a focal point for Islamic movements and identities.[16]

My exploration of the Malay Muslim diaspora in London elaborates and continues a study of what I have called Proper Islamic Consumption in Malaysia.[17] Building on 10 months of anthropological fieldwork in suburban Malaysia from 2001 to 2002, in this study I argued that the more cultures of consumption assert themselves, the more controversies over what Islam is, or ought to be, are intensifying. As new consumer practices emerge, they give rise to new discursive fields within which the meaning of Islam and Islamic practice are being debated. One key effect of these transformations is the deepening and widening concern for halal commodities among Malay

---

[11] Frederick Mathewson Denny, *An Introduction to Islam*, 3rd ed. (Upper Saddle River: Pearson Prentice Hall, 2006), 279.

[12] Mian Riaz and Muhammad Chaudry, *Halal Food Production* (Boca Raton: CRC Press, 2004), 6–7.

[13] Ibid., 7.

[14] Ibid., 14.

[15] Johan Fischer, "Religion, Science and Markets: Modern Halal Production, Trade and Consumption," *EMBO Reports* 9, no. 9 (2008): 1–4.

[16] John Louis Esposito, "Halal," in *The Oxford Encyclopedia of the Modern Islamic World*, ed. John Louis Esposito (Oxford: Oxford University Press, 1995), 376.

[17] Fischer, *Proper Islamic Consumption: Shopping among the Malays in Modern Malaysia*; Johan Fischer, "Nationalizing Rituals? The Ritual Economy in Malaysia," *Journal of Ritual Studies* 22, no. 2 (2008).

Muslims that I label *halalization*. Halalization signifies a major preoccupation with the proliferation of the concept of halal in a multitude of commodified forms. Out of halalization have emerged new forms of Malay aesthetic communities based on different taste preferences in various middle-class fractions. This proliferation of halalization has incited a range of elaborate ideas of the boundaries and authenticity of halal purity versus haram impurity.

Similarly, in contemporary London halal is no longer an expression of esoteric forms of production, trade, and consumption, but part of a huge and expanding globalized market. In the modern food industry, a number of Muslim requirements have taken effect—e.g., an injunction to avoid any substances that might be contaminated with porcine residues or alcohol, such as gelatin, glycerine, emulsifiers, enzymes, flavors, and flavorings.[18] As an example of this, the heading of an article in the *Guardian* (26 October 2006) read "Something Fishy in Your Pasta?" The article demonstrated that in some cases gelatin, among other ingredients, is "sneaked" into a variety of foods. The problem in certifying food and other products with regard to these substances is that they are extremely difficult to discover.

Apparently, a growing number of Muslim consumers are concerned with not only traditional halal food requirements but also contamination from haram sources in products such as toiletries and medication. Moreover, for some Muslims halal sensibilities necessitate that halal products be produced by Muslims only, and this type of production must be kept strictly separate from non-halal.

The halalness of products is not easily verifiable: smell, texture, and taste cannot determine whether or not a product is halal. Consequently, understandings of halal commodities tend to hinge on the context of their everyday handling, rather than their intrinsic properties. The main point is that the effects of commodities on people and contexts depend on how the tension between its imputed properties and its handling (either mitigating or amplifying these) are played out. In this respect, ideas and practices of halal and haram are essential. In other words, the nature (intrinsic qualities), processing (production method and context), and manner of acquisition (the morality or immorality of handling and origin) of commodities all determine whether they are classified as halal, haram, or indeterminable.

---

[18] Riaz and Chaudry, *Halal Food Production*, 22–25.

A Malaysian Halal Cuisine

A large part of my fieldwork took place in halal restaurants and Malaysian halal restaurants in particular. In these restaurants I ate halal food and discussed halal with informants, restaurant owners, and halal traders. One of the most popular Malaysian restaurants in London advertised itself as "Malaysian (halal) cuisine" on a sign outside the restaurant. I was a regular guest in this restaurant during fieldwork. In this section, I show that halal as a signifier is involved in the forging of a Malaysian national halal cuisine in diaspora.

In my conversations with Hamza, the owner of this Malaysian halal restaurant, many of the central themes of this chapter came out. He stressed that halal was also about lifestyle and ethos, and not just a question about a religious injunction pertaining to food and its intrinsic qualities. Hamza explained to me that one of the main motives for starting a restaurant specializing in "authentic" Malaysian halal food was that this food was well known in the Islamic community in London. Even more importantly, alcohol was not sold in the restaurant. As a guest you were allowed to bring your own alcoholic drink, but I never noticed any guest doing so. In the eyes of Hamza, his restaurant was "100 percent halal," meaning that alcohol was not sold in this establishment and income would never be used for any haram activities, such as gambling.

Hamza employed only Malays, and one of his motivations for running the restaurant was to demonstrate to non-Muslims that Malay waitresses, all of whom wore a *tudung* (a long headscarf), were accommodating, modern, and efficient women. Hamza's vision was to serve Malaysian halal cuisine for Muslims as well as non-Muslims in a cosmopolitan atmosphere. During my fieldwork in London in 2006, several Labour ministers criticized and questioned the right of Muslim women to wear the *niqāb*, a veil that covers the face. These claims emerged in a society where powerful political discourses identify the veiling of Muslim women as an undesirable Islamic practice in public space, whereas halal is undergoing a revolution in a discursive vacuum.

Hamza put in plain words that trust was essential in the halal market in London. In Malaysia, halal spaces—restaurants, shops, and factories—are certified by the state, whereas in Britain the state is largely absent in halal. Thus, Hamza relies only on what he considers trustworthy (but also more expensive) suppliers of halal meat.

According to Hamza and my other informants, distinctions between halal, *mashbūh*, and haram are to a large extent premised on context and practices. Hamza, for example, repeated the rumor that some Malaysian ministers, and even the Prime Minister, visit a certain Malaysian restaurant in London even though it is run by a non-Muslim Chinese Malaysian. Of the Malaysian population of around 25 million in 2004, about 61 per cent are indigenous Malays (virtually all Muslims) and tribal groups, also labeled *bumiputera* (literally, "sons of the soil"), 24 per cent are Chinese, and 7 per cent are Indians.[19] Many Malay Muslims consider non-Muslims unable to prepare and handle halal food. That Malaysia's political elite would visit such a restaurant in London seemed odd to Hamza, especially when the Malaysian state is simultaneously trying to promote halal on a global scale. That particular restaurant also has a bar and serves alcohol.

The forging of a Malaysian national cuisine has fused with Malaysia's aspirations to become a world leader in halal. In fact, on November 4, 2006, BBC announced under the heading *Malaysia dishes out to raise profile* that the Malaysian government is trying to "raise the country's international profile" and offer businessmen cash incentives to open "thousands" of Malaysian restaurants worldwide:

> According to the Malaysian government, which clearly keeps a close eye on such things, there are just 376 Malaysian restaurants to feed the six billion people who live outside the country. So its government has set a target of raising that number to 8.000 by 2015.[20]

Ideally, Malaysia's "name will be more renowned globally." This ideal is inseparable from the wider halal vision, as halal has become a form of national cuisine for Muslims as well as non-Muslims in Malaysia. However, in a discussion about the Malaysian state's vision to "globalize" a Malaysian (halal) cuisine, a woman Malay trader complained that the current Malaysian political leadership was not "capitalistic" enough for this vision to be fulfilled. The point here is that these restaurants are also political spaces or contexts for halal.

The menu in Hamza's restaurant tried to represent the wealth of food in multiethnic Malaysia. The basic ingredients were imported from Malaysia in order to achieve an "authentic" Malaysian taste. Typical dishes were *nasi lemak* (rice soaked in coconut cream), *nasi goreng* (fried rice), and *rendang daging* (rich coconut beef). My informants, who often frequented Malaysian restaurants in London, considered these dishes quintessentially "national."

In Hamza's restaurant there were several tourist posters from Malaysia but no visible Islamic paraphernalia, such as plaques with Islamic calligra-

---

[19] Cf. http://www.indexmundi.com/malaysia/demographics_profile.html
[20] http://news.bbc.co.uk/2/hi/asia-pacific/6116878.stm.

phy. The atmosphere clearly indicated that this was a Malaysian restaurant. This restaurant also hosted a *Hari Raya* celebration (signifying the end of the fasting season of Ramadan) and throughout the day a large number of mainly Malays enjoyed the free food and hospitality of the restaurant.

Another Malaysian restaurant in North London likewise advertised itself as offering "Halal Malaysian Cuisine." This restaurant was part of a food court located in the Oriental City Shopping Mall. Adjacent to the food court was an Asian supermarket that also sold fresh halal meat and a whole range of other halal products, including Malaysian ones. The owner of this restaurant, Siti, argued that during the last 15 years, due to Islamic revivalism and increased political awareness of the commercial aspects of halal in Malaysia, the political leadership had equated Malaysian "national" food with halal. This transformation was significant not just for Malays but also for Chinese and Indians. This point was substantiated during fieldwork in Malaysian restaurants in London since quite a number of Indians and Chinese, in particular, frequented these restaurants. In this restaurant in North London, a plaque with Islamic calligraphy was visible behind the counter. In another Malaysian halal restaurant in Bayswater, in West London, plaques with Islamic calligraphy as well as the Malaysian national flag called attention to the focus on a Malaysian halal cuisine.

Another popular halal eatery among Malays in London was Malaysia Hall, which I visited as part of this research. This facility provides accommodation for Malaysian students who have just arrived in London and there is also a canteen where Malaysian halal dishes are served. In addition to introducing students to living in Britain, Malaysia Hall also offers guidance on proper halal food practice. One of my Malay informants mentioned that he considered Malaysia Hall a very "political" space, in which the presence of the Malaysian state and Malaysian Islamic doctrine was excessive.

In these eateries most Malay women would be wearing the *tudung*, but by no means all wore it. Based on my previous fieldwork in urban Malaysia, it was clear that comparatively more women wore the *tudung* in this Malaysian setting. This point indicates that claims for piety and Islamic identities through Islamic dress for women in particular are not necessarily stronger in a diasporic context.

To sum up, the vision to forge a Malaysian halal cuisine has fused with the way in which the state has institutionalized and regulated halal in Malaysia. The dual focus on halal and a Malaysian national cuisine seems to come together in the spaces of the Malaysian halal restaurants discussed above. In a broader perspective, there has been an increasing articulation of regional and ethnic cuisines[21] and Malaysia is an example of how halal can add to this trend. Appadurai writes that the critical features of national cuisines "are the twin processes of regional and ethnic specialization, on the one hand, and the development of overarching, crosscutting national cuisines on the other."[22] What is more, the emergence and consolidation of national food is tightly linked to diasporic culture among migrant groups.[23] My informants were regular guests in these restaurants and they enjoyed this kind of national halal food and the spaces in which it was prepared and served. My next topic is how Malays in London more generally understand and practice "eating out."

Eating Out: Halal Understanding and Practice

A Malay Imam, who had worked at Malaysia Hall since 2002, complained that it was unconvincing when restaurants in London advertised themselves as halal, when in fact only the chicken, for example, probably was halal certified. He did not recognize a restaurant as halal if it sold liquor, much in the same way that a pizzeria could not claim to be halal if it used and stored ham together with halal meat, or allowed the same utensils to be used for all types of food. In the eyes of the Imam, a restaurant that did not display a halal sign could not be considered halal. Only if a restaurant was clearly marked as halal in Arabic was it a suitable halal space. He mentioned that a Bangladeshi member of his congregation once invited him to his restaurant. This restaurant did not display a proper halal sign since it catered to non-Muslims by selling alcohol. According to the Imam, this restaurant did not qualify as halal because income was coming from a haram source. Consequently, his favorite restaurant in London was an Afghan restaurant in which alcohol was not allowed under any circumstances. This Imam can be seen to represent an authoritative Malaysian state discourse on halal.

In this section I discuss how my Malay informants in London understand and practice eating out, with particular reference to the spatial context or domains of halal.

Izura was a woman in her 20s, who moved to London in 2005 to complete her postgraduate studies in international marketing. At the same time, she worked part-time with an insurance company. In the eyes of Izura, Malay

---

[21] Arjun Appadurai, "How to Make a National Cuisine: Cookbooks in Contemporary India," *Comparative Studies in Society and History* 30, no. 1 (1988): 3–24.
[22] Ibid., 22.
[23] Richard Wilk, "Food and Nationalism: The Origins of 'Belizian Food,'" in *Food Nations: Selling Taste in Consumer Societies*, ed. Warren Belasco and Philip Scranton (New York and London: Routledge, 2002), 80.

concerns about halal can be ascribed to the relatively strict Shafi^{c}i school of jurisprudence within the Sunni division of Islam dominant in Malaysia. She argued that:

> I would always say that Malays are stricter. It is just the way that we were taught, I think. We are Sunni, Shafi^{c}i school of thought, we are the strictest. Even if you go to Mecca there is a lot of people who pray differently, or eat differently, they say that this is considered halal, but for us it is not halal. I have Pakistani friends here in London and they still go to KFC and eat the chicken; they don't care. I guess to them if you have been in a country for a long time, you can eat whatever in that country, whether it is halal or not.

This point is important in two respects. First, it reflects the particular way in which halal and halal certification have been institutionalized in Malaysia, and thus have become an essential part of everyday life for Malays. Izura was outraged that in London she could find false halal signs in Arabic that pretended to represent proper certification on restaurants and shops. She was not comfortable going to places such as KFC and McDonald's because halal options were limited, and so was the knowledge of what my informants considered proper handling of halal. Izura, like several other informants, mentioned that it was tiresome, for example, to only be able to eat the Filet-O-Fish burger at McDonald's. In Malaysia, the entire menu at McDonald's and other fast-food outlets is certified by state groups, and thus going there is not a problem from a Malay perspective. Izura would ask at restaurants if she was uncertain about the halalness of the food served. In general, she felt that her inquiries were taken seriously at these eateries. Izura brought up an essential argument for my discussion of how halal is evoked and contested in Muslim space making. All of my informants would concur that halal was a religious injunction, but at the same time they would agree that its interpretation and translation into actual practice was divergent and "depended on the person." Izura would consider an entire restaurant space non-halal because of particular non-halal ingredients in the food, or if the cutlery or the wok was not handled properly. At the same time, she acknowledged that other Muslims would frequent such establishments because they were either not concerned about halal or perhaps the craving for the food overshadowed their doubts.

Another informant, Henny, was also a single woman in her 20s. Similar to what we saw with Izura, Henny could be considered relatively fastidious about eating out in London. She moved from Kuala Lumpur to London in 2005 to start her education at London School of Economics. Henny lived with three flatmates in South London. She was aware that even though

14   Chapter One

McDonald's and KFC in London are not halal certified, more and more proper alternatives for Muslims in London are emerging. She reasoned:

> The thing in London is that McDonald's and KFC are not halal, so if I like to go to a halal fast-food place I go to the Chicken Cottage or any other fast-food place that is halal certified, [with] halal logos at their doors.

Henny had chosen Chicken Cottage, a halal fast-food chain, after checking on the internet and noticing the halal logo on the façade of a Chicken Cottage outlet. In general, she would only trust a restaurant to be halal as long as it was certified by one of the halal-certifying bodies in Britain—e.g., Halal Food Authority or Halal Monitoring Committee. Thus, understanding and practicing halal space is often determined by proper certification and marking by these authorities.[24] Henny reasoned that she would "take all of the authorities as long as it is a body, a well-known and big organization that has undergone certain processes of the law." Conversely, she would not go to a non-halal restaurant, such as Pizza Hut, except for gatherings with non-Muslim friends, because that was a time to show that you are a "flexible Muslim." In that instance, Henny would be extra careful to search for vegetarian food and drinks. In the restaurant Subway, for example, Henny argued, the meat is non-halal, but you can eat the tuna sandwich. However, friends had told her that the employees at Subway used the same gloves to prepare all different kinds of food, meaning that the food was *mashbūh*, at best. This Malay register of halal consumption is relatively fastidious about halal when eating out, but now let's consider another register that's more relaxed and pragmatic about halal consumption.

Azmi was a 29-year-old Malay man who moved from Kuala Lumpur to London in 1994 to finish his schooling as a medical doctor, and he was currently working in a hospital. Azmi was relaxed and flexible about going to non-halal restaurants to eat. If a non-Muslim restaurant was selling halal food as part of its otherwise non-halal menu, that was acceptable to him. What's more, Azmi was content with the provision of halal food in his workplace. Other informants, however, complained that the provision of halal food in their workplaces or educational institutions was quite unsatisfactory.

A Malay couple, Yusof and Altaf, who were in their 20s moved from Kuala Lumpur to London in 1998 to study, and they both worked in the financial sector. Yusof and Altaf were fairly relaxed and pragmatic about

---

[24] Johan Fischer, "The Other Side of the Logo: The Global Halal Market in London," in *The New Cultures of Food. Marketing Opportunities from Ethnic, Religious and Cultural Diversity*, ed. Adam Lindgreen and Martin Hingley (Aldershot: Gower Publishing, 2009), 73–88.

halal in restaurants. For example, Yusof traveled frequently for his job and it was not always easy to find proper halal food. Consequently, Yusof had to be flexible about his food choices—for instance, he would eat a non-halal beef burger at McDonald's. Altaf argued that in many cases halal was most important when eating out with friends or parents. If the parents noticed that pork was served in a Chinese restaurant, they would not eat there. In principle, however, most informants would prefer to go to what they considered properly halal-certified establishments, such as the chain restaurant Halal Fried Chicken.

To sum up, the two registers of modern Malay halal consumption understand and practice eating out divergently. While the first register is fastidious about halal when eating out, the second register is more pragmatic about the practice of halal space. Informants within the more fastidious register of public halal consumption often evoke Western fast-food restaurants, such as McDonald's, KFC, or Subway (all fully halal certified in Malaysia), as problematic spaces that cannot be considered compatible with increasingly strict halal requirements. However, this register of Muslim consumers recognizes that in connection with socializing or work, for example, their halal requirements when eating out cannot be fully met. A crucial insight generated during the fieldwork was that many of these Malays were relatively pragmatic about halal understanding and practice in a diasporic context. Pragmatically, they acknowledged that while living in London, "you just have to shut one eye," as one informant put it. These Malays have been exposed to powerful halal discourses in the interfaces between revivalist Islam and the state in Malaysia, but they do not translate this spatial trajectory of halal into extreme fastidiousness about eating out in public space in their everyday lives in London. In fact, the pragmatism toward halal among some Malays in London might be an indirect critique of the way in which halal has become an expression of excessive public morality and conformity in urban Malaysia.

Eating In: Importing Purification

The question I will now address is how my Malay informants understand and practice "eating in." Specifically, how halal products, such as meat, and the public spaces in which it is bought, are conceptualized. An important theme is the expanding market for halal in London and the consequent pluralization of shopping choices.

The huge Tesco Extra store in Slough, outside London, boasts that it offers the widest range of world food products—including halal—in Britain. On a trip to the store in November 2006, I found Maggi chili sauce produced and halal certified in Malaysia, a halal "Curry Special" butter chicken with no certification or logo on it, and a more traditional halal butcher shop operating as a concession selling fresh meat. Anecdotal evidence from fieldwork suggests that Tesco is using this store to enter the halal market, and this has reduced sales among halal butchers in the surrounding area. Around the same time, in an ASDA supermarket in North London, I found Halal Food Authority certified chilled chicken and mutton. It is a recent trend that halal has been lifted out of its traditional base of halal butchers to become part of the "world food" offerings at supermarkets and hypermarkets.

My survey data from London shows that most Malays prefer eating in to eating out. This survey data also indicates that Malays in London mostly shop for groceries at hypermarkets or supermarkets. These Malays, however, most often buy halal products at local grocery stores or halal butcher shops. In my conversations with food authorities and Islamic groups during fieldwork I learned that rumors of fraud and falsely certified halal meat are common. These views are supported by Dr. Yunes Teinaz, who is Health Adviser to the Director General at the Islamic Cultural Center in London. For 10 years he has worked on illegal food and brought cases to court. He explained to me that "you can easily buy certification, if you pay for it. And they get away with it because there is no control, regulation, or inspection from the state." The halal market in London is fragmented and relatively unregulated. The question is, what effect does this have on the everyday shopping of Malays for halal?

The Malay Imam I discussed above lived with his family in Cricklewood, North London. He would normally shop for halal in a grocery store near his house since this was the most convenient place in terms of location, price, and quality. Often he would also go to Shepherd's Bush Market. When shopping for halal, he would pay particular attention to the hygiene of establishments. He explained to me that it was not enough to make sure that meat was properly slaughtered: it also mattered if the meat was treated in an unhygienic manner, or if earnings were used for haram purposes, such as gambling. Even when halal was written in Arabic on the façade or on signs in butcher shops, the Imam was not always convinced about the halalness of the products. Like nearly all my informants, the Imam agreed that even though it was not an Islamic injunction that halal be produced, sold, and handled by Muslims, he would prefer to shop for halal from Muslims.

Many Muslim groups with divergent understandings and practices of halal compete in this expanding market in Britain and globally. However, my informants did not prefer to buy halal from certain ethnic groups and avoid others. Instead, as the Imam pointed out, appearance, piety, and devotion—being a practicing Muslim—were essential markers of trustworthiness when shopping for halal. For instance, if a butcher was wearing gold rings or necklaces, considered to be haram, the Imam reasoned that the butcher was probably not sufficiently knowledgeable about halal either. However, as discussed above, the Imam represents a particular and authoritative halal discourse. I will now explore how my informants went about shopping for halal in their everyday lives.

The informant Ahmad was a single man in his 20s who came to London in 2001 from Kuala Lumpur to study. He is also a councillor with an Islamic student organization. He lived with 15 other students in a residence hall. Ahmad normally shopped for groceries at halal butchers, a local grocery store, and ASDA. When we discussed the state of halal certification in London, Ahmad complained that as a general tendency in London, many shops and butcher shops simply put up a sign with the Arabic word for halal. In the eyes of Ahmad, proper halal marking of products and shops is premised on certification by a trustworthy certifying body that can be held accountable for the halalness of products. Ahmad also argued that anyone could put up a sign in Arabic that indicated halal: "I worry about local halal certification sometimes because you can see people we don't even know creating their own halal signs and putting them up." Ahmad hoped to see more shops selling properly certified halal products. As long as the certification process was ensured by a dependable certifier, he did not take the trouble to look at labels that could reveal if products contained, for instance, alcohol or gelatin. To Ahmad, proper halal certification with a convincing logo was sufficient proof that the products were fit for Muslim consumption. Thus, in the case of this informant, halal space making hinges on proper certification above everything else.

Like Ahmad, most informants observed the atmosphere and appearance of the halal butcher or shop assistant to judge the halalness of the meat or other types of products. Asking about certification in a halal butcher shop in London might suggest that one is questioning the authority of the butcher. As in the case of most other informants, Ahmad patronized a local halal butcher shop for meat, which requires trust in the Muslim butcher, because in most cases, there is no visible certification in such facilities. Local halal butchers were favorites among Malay consumers in London, because the meat is affordable compared with halal meat in supermarkets. Conversely, halal in supermarkets was normally certified by the Halal Food Authority, Halal Monitoring Committee, or another Islamic organization. Consequently, to consumers, the proper "branding" of halal commodities might represent a luxury that is not always affordable.

When we were discussing differences between eating out and eating in, Ahmad argued that in London most Malays would prefer to cook at home.

As most of my informants were students like Ahmad, it is obvious that the aspect of thrift, as Ahmad noted, was central to Malay food consumption. However, even informants high in economic capital, who would prefer to cook at home, felt that eating out was in many cases a pragmatic necessity because of a busy lifestyle of work and travels. Ahmad acknowledged that eating at home was also a preference that was related to the familiarity of certain types of dishes, such as chicken curry, that could be personalized in the home. He argued that most Malays would try to find a house near a halal butcher or grocery store selling halal products. Data from my respondents and informants indicated that most Malays in London shopped for halal because of thrift, convenience, and familiarity with a local shop, rather than going to a supermarket or hypermarket as a primary preference. Informants would tell me that the "best deals" were often discussed among Malays in London. When I was out shopping for halal with informants, we often frequented butcher shops that were said to have the "best deal" in halal meat.

The couple Yusof and Altaf, discussed above, argued that in their local halal butcher shop in Walthamstove there were extra services compared to supermarkets. Still, informants are often not quite sure about halal meat at these butcher shops, and they negotiate the affordable prices and high levels of service against the more expensive and reliable types of certification to be found in supermarkets. Comparing their local halal butcher shop to Tesco, both Yusof and Altaf would agree that Tesco was cleaner. This was a point generally held by informants.

The informant Murni was a single woman in her early 20s, who lived with two flatmates in London. She moved to London in 2005 to study, and she also worked for a phone company. Unlike the majority of my informants, normally Murni shopped for groceries in supermarkets such as Tesco Express (it was open 24 hours), Sainsbury's and Waitrose (situated close to her home), and Green Valley (good halal selection and fresh meat certified by trustworthy authorities). Consequently, halal and halal certification is to a large extent premised on the context in which it is displayed and sold, and not simply halalness as an intrinsic quality that complies with a particular religious injunction.

The informant Izura, who was discussed above as being fairly fastidious about eating out, was surprisingly relaxed about shopping for halal in butcher shops and supermarkets in London. She used Muslim websites to access information about halal and haram products, and she did not think that the current availability of halal products in London was satisfactory. In much the same vein, she was not satisfied with product labeling. However, above everything else, shopping for halal was conditioned by thrift and convenience, meaning that local halal butcher shops and grocery stores were Izura's favorites.

Izura's husband, Irfan, accompanied her to London in 2005, and he was working for a mobile phone company before starting a master's degree. Irfan did much of the couple's shopping for halal at halal butchers, convenience stores, supermarkets, and hypermarkets. Irfan found the current availability of halal products in London satisfactory. When discussing halal with Irfan, the issue of thrift dominated:

> On weekends I go to Tesco. On weekdays, normally I buy halal food in a halal butcher shop near my place, and I go to Lidl because it's cheap. They also have halal meat in Lidl, but in terms of certification I'm not so sure about this meat. I have never seen a logo. That is why I go to the proper halal butcher shop in ASDA, for example. I think they have a Halal Food Authority logo stamped on it.

The price level of properly certified halal conditions a range of shopping practices in everyday life. Like several other informants, Irfan's primary concern about halal in shops was cleanliness. Again, supermarkets were seen to be more hygienic but also more expensive. Irfan was reassured if he saw a copy of the Koran or a plaque with Islamic calligraphy displayed in a halal butcher shop. He felt that this testified to the devotion of the owner and employees.

The informant Henny, discussed above, much like Izura, was surprisingly relaxed about shopping for halal in local butcher shops compared to her requirements for halal restaurants. When I was out shopping with Henny and her flatmate in halal butcher shops near their home in South London one day, I noticed that logos of certification were rare and not overtly displayed. Henny reasoned that even though she felt that inquiring about certification in some of the butcher shops was embarrassing, she would do it anyway as many of these establishments simply "put a sign on the door when they don't have a certificate. In other butcher shops the certificate is put up so far away I can't see if it's Halal Food Authority or . . . " The central point here is that the halal butcher shops embody a certain authority and expertise that customers rarely question, even if these customers are not quite sure about the halalness of products.

To sum up, most informants would agree that over the last few years halal availability has improved greatly in Britain, and London in particular. However, many Muslim consumers are confused about the moral implications of an expanding halal market and the pluralization of shopping choices involved in halal. Belief, piety, quality, certification, cleanliness, thrift, and convenience were all keywords to describe everyday shopping for halal among Malays in London.

Conclusion

I have shown that spatial trajectories are essential in Malay understandings and practices of halal in London. Halal is now part of a huge and expanding globalized market, and this affects new forms of Muslim space making. This transformation and proliferation of halal both pluralizes and confuses everyday shopping choices. Comparatively, eating out was seen by the majority of my informants to be more complex and problematic than eating in. Malaysia and Malays hold a special position in the halal market and this has an impact on everyday halal understandings and practices in a diasporic context. The vision to forge a Malaysian halal cuisine, for example, is an attempt to "nationalize" halal as a particular form of consumption. The ethnography demonstrated that the conceptualization of halal commodities to a large extent hinges on the context of their everyday handling rather than their intrinsic properties. When the halalness of products is not verifiable based on smell, texture, or taste, the context or space in which halal is prepared, stored, handled, or sold is "what you can see," as one informant told me. Interestingly, there is a clear tendency to see that eating out is articulated as more problematic than eating in. In spite of the fact that the halal market is complex and fragmented in London, informants were surprisingly pragmatic and relaxed about shopping for halal in butcher shops, in particular, but also in supermarkets and hypermarkets. Informants would explain to me that cooking at home was mainly a question of thrift, but I contend that eating in, in the home, is also essential to the way in which halal is domesticated and purified among the Malays in London.

With reference to Claude Lévi-Strauss, it has been shown that the house as a social institution combines a number of opposing principles or social forms, thus reuniting and transcending incomparable principles, adding to an appearance of unity.[25] The house "transfixes" an unstable union, becoming "the objectification of a relation: the unstable relation of alliance which, as an institution, the house functions to solidify, if only in an illusory form."[26] The safety of this type of haven ensures that halal imports are emotionally accommodated. Halal bought outside can become imbued with the values of kinship and unity associated with the house, and above all with

---

[25] Janet Carsten and Stephen Hugh-Jones, "Introduction: About the House: Lévi-Strauss and Beyond," in *About the House: Lévi-Strauss and Beyond*, ed. Janet Carsten and Stephen Hugh-Jones (Cambridge: Cambridge University Press, 1995), 8.
[26] Ibid., 24.

the kitchen. None of my informants lived alone, and rituals of sharing in privacy seemingly purified and legitimized the understanding of otherwise doubtful halal practices in the complex, fragmented, and confusing halal market. In other words, the import of halal into homes may translate ambiguous or malevolent commodities into something benevolent that can be shared and enjoyed within families or with friends or flatmates.

Bibliography

Abbas, Tahir. *Muslim Britain: Communities under Pressure*. London and New York: Zed Books, 2005.

Agriculture and Agri-Food Canada. *Halal Food Products Market Report*. Ottawa: Agriculture / Agri-Food Canada, 2006.

Ahmed, Allam. "Marketing of Halal Meat in the United Kingdom." *British Food Journal* 110, no. 7 (2008): 655–670.

Appadurai, Arjun. "How to Make a National Cuisine: Cookbooks in Contemporary India." *Comparative Studies in Society and History* 30, no. 1 (1988): 3–24.

Bergeaud-Blackler, Florence. "New Challenges for Islamic Ritual Slaughter: A European Perspective." *Journal of Ethnic and Migration Studies* 33, no. 6 (2007): 965–980.

Carsten, Janet, and Stephen Hugh-Jones. "Introduction: About the House: Lévi-Strauss and Beyond." In *About the House: Lévi-Strauss and Beyond*, edited by Janet Carsten and Stephen Hugh-Jones, 1–46. Cambridge: Cambridge University Press, 1995.

Certeau, Michel de. *The Practice of Everyday Life*. Berkeley: University of California Press, 1984.

Charlton, Roger, and Ronald Kaye. "The Politics of Religious Slaughter: An Ethno-Religious Case Study." *New Community* 12, no. 3 (1985): 490–502.

Denny, Frederick Mathewson. *An Introduction to Islam*. 3rd ed. Upper Saddle River: Pearson Prentice Hall, 2006.

Esposito, John Louis. "Halal." In *The Oxford Encyclopedia of the Modern Islamic World*, edited by John Louis Esposito. Oxford: Oxford University Press, 1995.

Fischer, Johan. "Nationalizing Rituals? The Ritual Economy in Malaysia." *Journal of Ritual Studies* 22, no. 2 (2008).

———. *Proper Islamic Consumption: Shopping among the Malays in Modern Malaysia*. Copenhagen: NIAS Press, 2008.

Fischer, Johan. "Religion, Science and Markets: Modern Halal Production, Trade and Consumption." *EMBO Reports* 9, no. 9 (2008): 1–4.

———. "The Other Side of the Logo: The Global Halal Market in London." In *The New Cultures of Food. Marketing Opportunities from Ethnic, Religious and Cultural Diversity*, edited by Adam Lindgreen and Martin Hingley, 73–88. Aldershot: Gower Publishing, 2009.

Kaye, Ronald. "The Politics of Religious Slaughter of Animals: Strategies for Ethno-Religious Political Action." *New Community* 19 (1993): 235–250.

Mandel, Ruth. "A Place of Their Own: Contesting Spaces and Defining Places in Berlin's Migrant Community." In *Making Muslim Space in North America and Europe*, edited by Barbara Daly Metcalf, 147–166. Berkeley, Los Angeles, and London: University of California Press, 1996.

Marcus, George. "Ethnography in/of the World System: The Emergence of Multi-Sited Ethnography." *Annual Review of Anthropology* 24 (1995): 95–117.

Metcalf, Barbara Daly. "Introduction: Sacred Words, Sanctioned Practice, New Communities." In *Making Muslim Space in North America and Europe*, edited by Barbara Daly Metcalf, 1–27. Berkeley, Los Angeles and London: University of California Press, 1996.

Riaz, Mian, and Muhammad Chaudry. *Halal Food Production*. Boca Raton: CRC Press, 2004.

Wilk, Richard. "Food and Nationalism: The Origins of 'Belizian Food,'" in *Food Nations: Selling Taste in Consumer Societies*, edited by Warren Belasco and Philip Scranton, 67–89. New York and London: Routledge, 2002.

CHAPTER TWO

NEW TRANSNATIONAL GEOGRAPHIES OF ISLAMISM, CAPITALISM, AND SUBJECTIVITY: THE VEILING-FASHION INDUSTRY IN TURKEY

BANU GÖKARIKSEL AND ANNA SECOR[1]

Introduction

In April 2008, Tekbir ("God is great") Inc., Turkey's leading producer of women's Islamic dress, put on its 16th annual fashion show. Controversial as usual, the fashion show made waves in the Turkish press, with headlines reading "*Önce Namaz, Sonra Defile*"—the Turkish equivalent of "First prayer, then the catwalk."[2] The controversy this year was complex: First, Tekbir had hired a German fashion designer, Heidi Beck, to design the 2008 collection, the irony of which was highlighted with newspaper headlines such as "Taking up veiling in the hands of a Christian designer!" Secondly, the fashion show included performances of religious music, an Ottoman marching band, and whirling dervishes—an attention-grabbing mishmash of cultural and religious references. The same eclecticism marked the styles

---

[1] This article has been published as Banu Gökarıksel and Anna J. Secor, "New Transnational Geographies of Islamism, Capitalism and Subjectivity: The Veiling-Fashion Industry in Turkey," *Area* 41, no. 1 (2009): 6-18. Reprinted with permission from Wiley InterScience. Research has been funded by the National Science Foundation, Geography and Regional Science, Proposal No: 0722825. The title is "Collaborative Research: The veiling-fashion industry: transnational geographies of Islamism, capitalism, and identity."

[2] *Milliyet*, April 21, 2008. *Milliyet* is one of the major daily newspapers in Turkey. Many other newspapers, web sites, and television channels used the same title in their coverage of the fashion show, including the best-selling daily, *Hürriyet*, and the television channels Fox and Haber3 TV.

on the runway, which referenced sufism, the finery of the Ottoman court, European wedding wear, and the aesthetics of Arab and Indian dress. In the Islamic newspaper *Milli Gazete*, Tekbir was bombarded with criticism for its "sale" of Islam and its seduction of consumers through the use of young, attractive models.[3] And finally, immediately after the show the press erupted with the revelation that Tekbir's CEO, Mustafa Karaduman, was a polygamist, a practice that is banned in Turkey. Karaduman's defense of polygamy in the following days seemed to confirm the critics' worst fears about gender inequality in the lifestyle of the new Islamic bourgeoisie.

These events surrounding the fashion show catalyzed a flurry of criticism of Tekbir and, more broadly, of the relationship between veiling and fashion in Turkey. Why does the idea of "veiling-fashion" continue to pose a problem, despite its actualization in the everyday practices of Muslim women, not only in Turkey but globally?[4] Since the early 1990s, this paradox has been vividly illustrated in the pages of Islamic women's magazines in Turkey, where Islamic scholars and journalists have condemned veiling-fashion as contrary to Islamic principles, which forbid waste (*israf*) and frown upon the display involved in modeling and fashion.[5] Veiling, for Islam, is usually understood as a Koranic injunction requiring women's modest dress.[6] Yet alongside such articles, these magazines have displayed ever more sleek advertisements for veiling-fashion and have played a central role in the creation of the profitable niche market that veiling-fashion has become today.[7]

---

[3] Mehmet Şevket Eygi, "Evlere senlik tesettür defilesi [An Odd Veiling-Fashion Show]," *Milli Gazete* (25 April 2008, http://www.milligazete.com.tr/index.php?action=show&type=writersnews&id=18157, accessed 16 June 2008).

[4] Heather Marie Akou, "Building a New 'World Fashion': Islamic Dress in the Twenty-first Century," *Fashion Theory* 11 (2007): 403–422.

[5] Cihan Aktaş, *Mahremiyetin tükenişi [The End of Modesty]* (İstanbul: Nehir, 1995); İsmail Fatih Ceylan, "'Amacımız tesettürü sevdirmek' ['Our Goal Is to Make Tesettür Loved']," *Milli Gazete* (10 October 1992, http://www.milligazete.com.tr/index.php?action=show&type=news&id=53943, accessed 16 June 2008); Halise Çiftçi, "Tesettür, moda ve defile [Veiling, Fashion and the Catwalk]," *Milli Gazete* (28 April 1993); Fatma Karaosmanoğlu, *Moda ve zihniyet [Fashion and Mentality]* (İstanbul: İz, 2002).

[6] Veiling takes many forms, from simply covering the hair to loose clothing that does not reveal the shape of women's bodies, to complete covering that exposes no more than the hands and feet. While many Muslims consider veiling an essential expression of women's piety, others do not consider it necessary to express their religious beliefs in this way. Veiling-fashion involves the covering of women's hair and "modest" dress, which, of course, is open to interpretation.

[7] Barış Kılıçbay and Mutlu Binark, "Consumer Culture, Islam and the Politics of Lifestyle: Fashion for Veiling in Contemporary Turkey," *European Journal of Communication* 17 (2002): 495–511; Özlem Sandıkçı and Güliz Ger, "Constructing and Representing the Islamic Consumer in Turkey," *Fashion Theory* 11 (2007): 189–210.

The difficulty of the idea—if not the practice—of veiling-fashion can be traced out through the concept of fashion itself. Marked by cycles of rapid change, fashion is usually defined in relation to the rise of mercantile capitalism in Europe, new forms of social mobility, the abandonment of "tradition," and the rise of the individualistic modern subject.[8] For Baudrillard, fashion represents the final result of consumer capitalism, the ultimate emptying out of the sign of all reference. With no sense except its constant renewal, its up-to-dateness that consists of recycled bits of the past, fashion for Baudrillard is inherently "immoral" and subversive of meaning:

> Beyond the rational and the irrational, beyond the beautiful and the ugly, the useful and the useless, it is this immorality in relation to all criteria, the frivolity which at times gives fashion its subversive force (in totalitarian, puritan or archaic contexts) [...][9]

In short, veiling-fashion has not ceased to be controversial because it combines two systems that are seemingly incompatible: veiling, with its powerful set of religious, cultural, and political references, and fashion, an unmoored system of self-referential change associated with capitalism, modernity, and a particular kind of consumer subject. And yet, this apparent contradiction dissolves in the everyday practices of the producers and consumers of veiling-fashion.

We argue that to understand veiling-fashion as it plays out across economic, political, and cultural fields is to enter into a new understanding of the role of Islam in the global arena today. Veiling-fashion crystallizes a series of issues about Islamic identity, the transnational linkages of both producers and consumers, and the shifting boundaries between Islamic ethics and the imperatives of neoliberal capitalism. In this paper, our overarching argument is that controversies and practices surrounding veiling-fashion show how Islamic actors are adapting and transforming neoliberal capitalism at the same time as they navigate a complex geopolitical terrain in which Islam—and the iconic Muslim, headscarf-wearing woman—has been cast as a threatening "Other." Thus the rise of veiling-fashion as a transnational phenomenon positions women and women's bodies at the center of political debates and struggles surrounding what it means to be "modern" and Muslim today.

---

[8] Ted Polhemus and Lynn Proctor, *Fashion and Anti-Fashion* (London: Thames / Hudson, 1978); Thorsten Veblen, *The Theory of Leisure Class. An Economic Study of Institutions* (New York: Mentor, 1953 [1899]); Elizabeth Wilson, *Adorned in Dreams: Fashion and Modernity* (London: Virago, 1985).

[9] Jean Baudrillard, *Symbolic Exchange and Death* (London: Sage, 1993), 93–94.

Based on interviews with producers, consumers, and salesclerks, and our analysis of newspaper articles, catalogs, and web sites,[10] this article traces out how the transnational production, sale, and consumption of veiling-fashion works to order spaces of geopolitics, geo-economics, and subject formation. In doing so, we respond to calls for commodity research that bridges the divide between economic and cultural studies.[11] By situating "the fashionable veil" as a commodity at the center of a web of geopolitical, economic, and cultural relations, we go beyond previous work that has understood veiling primarily as a problem of competing ideologies, such as secularism vs. Islamism or tradition vs. modernity. To this end, after contextualizing the rise of veiling-fashion within Turkey, we present three interlocking lenses on the phenomenon and its transnationalization: 1) veiling-fashion as geopolitical, 2) veiling-fashion as Islamic practice within neoliberal capitalism, and 3) veiling-fashion as a site of subject formation.

Veiling-Fashion in Context

The rise of the transnational veiling-fashion industry in Turkey has taken place within the context of neoliberal economic restructuring and the resurgence of Islamic identities worldwide. Turkey has been at the nexus of both of these trends. In the past three decades, neoliberal economic reform has reoriented the Turkish economy from the state-led, import-substitution industrialization of the 1960s and 1970s towards open markets, liberalized financial institutions, and production for export.[12] In the wake of this broad economic transformation has followed an unexpected development: the rise of Islam as an increasingly prominent force both politically and economically in the public sphere of this secular, democratic state.

---

[10] Interviews were conducted in 2004, 2005, and 2007 with different actors in Istanbul's veiling-fashion industry, including the CEO of Tekbir, Mustafa Karaduman (four interviews), salesclerks (eight interviews, six of Tekbir), and store managers and owners in Fatih and İstanbul Manifaturacılar Çarşısı (five interviews).
[11] Angela McRobbie, "Bridging the Gap: Feminism, Fashion and Consumption," *Feminist Review* 55 (1997): 73–89; Peter Jackson, "Commercial Cultures: Transcending the Cultural and Economic," *Progress in Human Geography* 26 (2002): 3–18; Shane Gunster, *Capitalizing on Culture: Critical Theory for Cultural Studies* (Toronto: University of Toronto Press, 2004); Julie Mansvelt, *Geographies of Consumption* (Thousand Oaks: Sage, 2005); Louise Crewe, "Geographies of Retailing and Consumption: Markets in Motion," *Progress in Human Geography* 27 (2003): 352–362.
[12] Ziya Öniş, "Neoliberal Globalization and the Democracy Paradox: The Turkish General Elections of 1999," *Journal of International Affairs* 54 (2000): 283–306; E. Fuat Keyman and Ahmet İçduygu, "Globalization, Civil Society and Citizenship in Turkey: Actors, Boundaries and Discourses," *Citizenship Studies* 7 (2003): 219–34.

From this combination of economic, political, and cultural reshuffling has emerged a highly visible new Islamic culture of consumption, including an Islamic fashion industry.[13] Despite legislation against veiling in state institutions in the 1980s, a new style of Islamic dress has become increasing popular among educated, upwardly mobile young women, many of whom are active in Islamist politics.[14] This industry, which encompasses mostly everyday wear and some haute couture, is based on modest dress and head covering. It comprises an estimated 200 firms operating out of Turkey in 2004.[15] Turkish producers of veiling-fashion have begun to export their products to retail outlets in the Middle East, Europe, and North America. Tekbir, for example, has outlets in Germany, the Netherlands, France, England, Belgium, Austria, Switzerland, Bosnia Herzegovina, Macedonia, Azerbaijan, Dubai, Lebanon, Jordan, Syria, Palestine, Libya, Egypt, Sudan, Algeria, South Africa, the United States, Canada, and Australia.[16]

The veiling-fashion industry in Turkey has its roots in the re-veiling movements across a range of Muslim societies, from Indonesia to Egypt, since the late 1970s. In Turkey, a new style of women's modest dress began to appear in urban areas in the 1980s. This style, called *tesettür*[17] by its wearers and

---

[13] Nilüfer Göle, *İslamın yeni kamusal yüzleri [The New Public Faces of Islam]* (Istanbul: Metis, 1999); Yael Navaro-Yashin, *Faces of the State: Secularism and Public Life in Turkey* (Princeton: Princeton University Press, 2002); Ayşe Saktanber, "'We Pray Like You Have Fun': New Islamic Youth in Turkey between Intellectualism and Popular Culture," in *Fragments of Culture: The Everyday of Modern Turkey*, ed. Deniz Kandiyoti and Ayşe Saktanber (London: IB Tauris, 2002), 254–276; Jenny White, "Islamic Chic," in *Istanbul between the Global and the Local*, ed. Çağlar Keyder (Lanham: Rowman / Littlefield, 1999), 77–91.

[14] Cihan Aktaş, *Tanzimattan günümüze kılık, kıyafet ve iktidar [Politics and Clothing since the Ottoman Constitutional Period]* (İstanbul: Nehir, 1991); Banu Gökarıksel, *Islams, Neoliberalism and Transnationalism: The Making of Subject-Citizens and Tesettür Fashions in Istanbul*, Paper presented at the Muslim Fashions/Fashionable Muslims Workshop, University of Amsterdam and the International Institute for the Study of Islam in the Modern World, Amsterdam, 15–16 April 2005; Aynur İlyasoğlu, *Örtülü kimlik [Veiled Identity]* (Istanbul: Metis Kadın Araştırmaları Dizisi, 1994); Nilüfer Göle, *The Forbidden Modern: Civilization and Veiling* (Ann Arbor: University of Michigan Press, 1996); Anna Secor, "The Veil and Urban Space in Istanbul: Women's Dress, Mobility and Islamic Knowledge," *Gender, Place and Culture* 9 (2002): 5–22.

[15] Kılıçbay and Binark, "Consumer Culture, Islam and the Politics of Lifestyle: Fashion for Veiling in Contemporary Turkey"; Navaro-Yashin, *Faces of the State: Secularism and Public Life in Turkey*; Özlem Sandıkçı and Güliz Ger, "Fundamental Fashions: The Cultural Politics of the Turban and the Levi's," *Advances in Consumer Research* 28 (2001): 146–50.

[16] This information is from interviews with Tekbir CEO, Mustafa Karduman. Other companies, including Dicle, Hak, Selam, and Aydan, similarly export their products to the Middle East, Europe, and North America.

[17] *Tesettür* is derived from *setr*, which means "to cover up, to conceal" in Arabic. *Tesettür* by definition is an umbrella term that includes various styles of covering, from the full body cloak to just a headscarf.

producers, was neither fashionable nor an industry at this time. *Tesettür* consisted mainly of headscarf-coat combinations. A large headscarf that wrapped tightly around the face and draped down to cover the neck and the shoulders was its centerpiece. Its critics underlined the novelty of this headscarf and its threatening connections to Islamist politics by the term *türban*, while its supporters simply called it *başörtüsü*, a headscarf traditionally knotted under the chin, leaving the neck and the hairline partly exposed. The accompanying ankle-length coat was cut loosely. The whole ensemble was typically in conservative solid colors (navy, black, gray, or beige).[18] Many were sewn as special order by tailors or made at home. The advertisements of this era were very simple, consisting of a list of items available and illustrations of women, usually drawn without a face.[19]

These qualities contrast significantly with today's diverse, colorful, and constantly changing styles of veiling-fashion and a newly emergent and profitable industry that encompasses production, distribution, marketing, advertising, and sale of this fashion as part of the consumer lifestyle of a new urban Muslim bourgeoisie. In the last decade, Tekbir and its competitors (Aydan, Dicle, Hak, Hilye, Setre, Sitare, Selam, and others) became recognizable brand names with glossy catalogs, advertisements, and even fashion shows that posed attractive models in sophisticated scenes. These scenes display and construct the elements of this new lifestyle: upscale vacationing, playing tennis (an elite sport in Turkey), and using state-of-the-art camcorders. In the catalogs and web sites of several companies, such as Benna and Dicle, headscarf-wearing models appear side by side with those who are not wearing a headscarf. Islamic female consumers can now choose from a proliferation of styles, including tunic and pants combinations, suits, formal wear, daily wear, sports, bridal, maternity, and haute couture. These styles cater to different tastes, age groups, socio-economic classes, and life stages. The colors, patterns, and cuts vary greatly, from very bright colors, bold patterns, and tight-fitting clothing to more conservative ones. These styles are under constant scrutiny as to whether or to what extent they are "Islamic."[20] The collections change at least seasonally, following national and international fashion trends. The designs are adopted from the catwalks of the women's global fashion meccas of Paris and Milan. For example,

---

[18] Navaro-Yashin, *Faces of the State: Secularism and Public Life in Turkey*.

[19] Kılıçbay and Binark, "Consumer Culture, Islam and the Politics of Lifestyle: Fashion for Veiling in Contemporary Turkey"; Sandıkçı and Ger, "Constructing and Representing the Islamic Consumer in Turkey."

[20] Aktaş, *Tanzimattan günümüze kılık, kıyafet ve iktidar [Politics and Clothing since the Ottoman Constitutional Period]*; Navaro-Yashin, *Faces of the State: Secularism and Public Life in Turkey*; Nazife Şişman, *Kamusal alanda başörtülüler: Fatma Karabıyık Karaosmanoğlu ile söyleşi* (Istanbul: Iz, 2001).

Tekbir's CEO and its designers go to the conventions and shows in France and Italy every year. Tekbir's hiring of the German designer Heidi Beck in 2008 points to further attempts to integrate European design elements and techniques with the veiling-fashion industry in Turkey. Yet Europe is by no means the only source of influence for this industry. The inspiration for designs also comes from East and Southeast Asia (for example, in Tekbir's 2005 spring/summer collection and in Aydan's 2007 summer collection) and the Middle East, as well as from the Ottoman and pre-Ottoman past. In fact, Ottoman court dresses have been a style that Tekbir has continually referenced since its first fashion show in 1992. Tekbir's 2008 line prominently illustrates this eclecticism and recycling. The diverse and ever-changing styles of veiling-fashion work to create and to profit from an increasingly segmented and growing domestic and transnational Islamic consumer market while raising many questions about the relationship between Islamic ethics and practice and neoliberal capitalism.

Navigating the Geopolitical Terrain

For over two centuries, veiling has been geopolitical—which is to say, it has been practiced, represented, and regulated as part of the enactment of global and local geographies of power. Embedded in the history of European colonialism in the Middle East and North Africa, veiling has been both a symbol of "Oriental" difference and a focal point for the regulation of societies.[21] In the mid-20th century, for example, the French attempted a colonial strategy that hinged on the unveiling of Algerian women.[22] Throughout the century, unveiling was either forced or encouraged by modernizing and Westernizing Middle Eastern states, such as Egypt, Turkey, and Iran.[23] Veiled women were represented, both by Europeans and by the local modernizers, as backwards and oppressed, and this judgment was in turn extended to Islam itself.[24] The legacy of these attacks on the veil is that this item of women's

---

[21] Meyda Yeğenoğlu, *Colonial Fantasies: Towards a Feminist Reading of Orientalism* (Cambridge: Cambridge University Press, 1998).
[22] Fatma El Guindi, *Veil: Modesty, Privacy and Resistance* (Oxford: Berg, 1999); Franz Fanon, *A Dying Colonialism* (New York: Grove Press, 1967); Marnia Lazreg, *The Eloquence of Silence: Algerian Women in Question* (London: Routledge, 1994).
[23] Deniz Kandiyoti, ed., *Women, Islam and the State* (Philadelphia: Temple University Press, 1991).
[24] Leila Ahmed, *Women and Gender in Islam. Historical Roots of a Modern Debate* (New Haven: Yale University Press, 1992); Mohja Kahf, *Western Representations of the Muslim Woman* (Austin: University of Texas Press, 1999); Judy Mabro, *Veiled Half-Truths* (London: IB Tauris, 1996).

dress has become a potent cultural and political symbol.[25] As a result, the *re-veiling* of women has been a central motif of the "Islamic resurgence," or the transnational rise of movements for the Islamicization of society since the late 1970s.

Today, veiling and its regulation take place within a transnational legal context that produces "European" and "Muslim" spaces at both local and global scales. The production, sale, and consumption of veiling-fashion are part of the growing transnationalization of Muslim identity and political practice.[26] Controversies surrounding the regulation of veiling in the European Union (EU) have been a flashpoint for the tensions arising from Muslim immigration to Europe, especially since the attacks of 9/11 in 2001 and the beginning of the Iraq war in 2003.[27] Disputes around women's rights to veil in public institutions have erupted in France, and the veil (or *hijab*, as it is commonly called by Arabic-speaking immigrants in France) has been banned in schools since the State Court judgment of 1989. The strengthening of the French court's anti-veiling stance throughout the 1990s was welcomed by Turkish secularists and represented a blow to those who have tried to cast veiling as a human rights issue in Turkey.[28] In Germany, veiling has also provoked legal controversies regarding the appointment of veiled women to civil servants' posts as schoolteachers.[29] As in France, the courts have been asked to rule on whether or not veiling is inconsistent with the

---

[25] El Guindi, *Veil: Modesty, Privacy and Resistance*; Arlene MacLeod, *Accommodating Protest: Working Women, the New Veiling and Change in Cairo* (New York: Columbia University Press, 1991); Saba Mahmood, *Politics of Piety: The Islamic Revival and the Feminist Subject* (Princeton: Princeton University Press, 2005).

[26] Yasemin Soysal, *Limits of Citizenship: Migrants and Postnational Membership in Europe* (Chicago: University of Chicago Press, 1994); Patricia Ehrkamp and Helga Leitner, "Transnationalism and Migrants' Imaginings of Citizenship," *Environment and Planning A* 38 (2006): 1615–1632; Michael Samers, "Diaspora Unbound: Muslim Identity and the Erratic Regulation of Islam in France," *International Journal of Population Geography* 9 (2003): 351–364; Peter Jackson, Phil Crang, and Claire Dwyer, eds., *Transnational Spaces* (London: Routledge, 2004); Caroline Nagel and Lynn Staeheli, "Citizenship, Identity and Transnational Migration: Arab Immigrants to the United States," *Space & Polity* 8 (2004): 3–23; Rachel Silvey, "Geographies of Gender and Migration: Spatializing Social Difference," *International Migration Review* 40 (2006): 64–68; Lynn Staeheli and Caroline Nagel, "Topographies of Home and Citizenship: Arab-American Activists in the United States," *Environment and Planning A* 38 (2006): 1599–1614.

[27] Stefano Allievi and Jørgen Nielsen, eds., *Muslim Networks and Transnational Communities in and across Europe* (Leiden: Brill, 2003); Peter Mandaville, *Transnational Muslim Politics* (London: Routledge, 2003).

[28] Banu Gökarıksel and Katharyne Mitchell, "Veiling, Secularism and the Neoliberal Subject: National Narratives and Supranational Desires in Turkey and France," *Global Networks* 5 (2005): 147–165.

[29] Ulf Hausler, "Muslim Dress-Codes in German State Schools," *European Journal of Migration and Law* 3 (2001): 457–74.

state's principle of neutrality in religious matters. In the Netherlands, the government has cited reasons of "public order, security and protection of citizens" for planned legislation banning the veil in all public spaces, the most comprehensive anti-veiling legislation yet.[30] Although today the legal regulation of veiling varies across EU member states, in the long run veiling regulation must also be considered against the backdrop of the European Court of Justice and its evolving jurisprudence.[31] The regulation or deregulation of veiling has thus become bound up with debates surrounding the identity of the Turkish state, Muslim migrants in Europe, and Turkish-EU relations.

Turkey's ban on the veil in public schools, universities, courts, and state offices has become a high profile political issue. Since the headscarf ban began to be enforced in the mid-1980s, protests on university campuses have expressed popular opposition to the ban, while pro-headscarf politicians and pundits have made lifting the ban a human rights issue.[32] At the same time, secularists have defended the ban as protecting the right of women *not* to cover their heads. Indeed, the movement to lift the ban has been seen as a harbinger of an Iranian or even Taliban-style reconfiguration of space, gender, and power in Turkey. The wider geopolitical mapping of this conflict jutted to the surface in 1999 when Merve Kavakçı, the Islamic party (Fazilet Partisi) parliamentarian attempted to take her oath of office wearing a headscarf and was escorted from the premises. While many commentators and ordinary people alike decried the incident for (further) politicizing the headscarf, the mainstream Turkish press managed to accuse Kavakçı, who had both Turkish and U.S. citizenship, of being at once an American provocateur and an Iranian agent.[33] Such fears and suspicions have frequently become attached to the wearers and producers of veiling-fashion. It is within this transnational juridical landscape and the geopolitical relations that structure it that not only veiling in general but veiling-*fashion* in particular has become popular in Turkey and transnationally. On one hand, the legal regu-

---

[30] "Dutch Government Backs Burqa Ban," *BBC News* (2006, http://news.bbc.co.uk/2/hi/europe/6159046.stm, accessed 16 June 2008).

[31] W.A.R. Shadid and P.S. van Koningsveld, "Muslim Dress in Europe: Debates on the Headscarf," *Journal of Islamic Studies* 16 (2005): 35–61; Gökarıksel and Mitchell, "Veiling, Secularism and the Neoliberal Subject: National Narratives and Supranational Desires in Turkey and France."

[32] Anna Secor, "Islamism, Democracy and the Political Production of the Headscarf Issue in Turkey," in *Geographies of Muslim Women: Gender, Religion and Space*, ed. Ghazi Falah and Caroline Nagel (New York: Guilford Press, 2005), 203–225.

[33] Esra Özyürek, *The Headscarf Knot in the Turkish Parliament*, Conference paper, Workshop on gendered bodies, transnational politics, American University in Cairo, 12–14 December 2003.

lation of veiling applies equally to all Muslim women who cover their hair, whether or not their style is *à la mode*. Thus from the perspective of regulation, the rise of veiling-fashion, with its appeal to young, educated women, does not shift the terms of the debate as much as it contributes to its visibility. On the other hand, veiling-fashion directly engages with the regulation of veiling and shifting geopolitical relations. For instance, in response to the Turkish parliamentary vote to lift the headscarf ban in February 2008 (a move declared unconstitutional by the courts four months later), Tekbir publicized special ways of tying the scarf and styles for university students and projected a 30 percent increase in sales.[34]

Veiling-fashion and its design can also be seen as responding to the post-9/11 geopolitical milieu and to the intensification of anti-Islamic sentiment both in Turkey and in Europe over the past decade. In an interview in 2004, a veiling-fashion store manager explained that she chose hot pink and white polka dotted headscarves and completely white attire as the uniform for the salesclerks in an effort to avoid black and its associations with conservatism and fundamentalism. Choosing bright colors, she explained, improves the image of veiled women in society. Likewise, according to Özlem Sandıkçı and Güliz Ger:

> The events of 9/11 had a further impact on the sense of tesettür fashion in Turkey. As the media repeatedly circulated stigmatizing images of Muslims highlighting the veil and the beard as symbols of Islamist militancy, it became even more important to portray a pleasant, elegant, and modern appearance. Black and dark-colored tesettür clothes and large headscarves became less popular [...]. [T]he new "modern" style of covering rapidly spread to a larger group who did not want to appear repellent to the uncovered public or to become stereotyped as "ugly," "backward," and "threatening" [...][35]

Veiling-fashion is part of how Muslim women navigate the everyday geopolitics of "Islamic threat." With American and British leaders asserting the need to distinguish between "good Muslims" and "bad Muslims" in the global arena, veiling-fashion can potentially work on the bodily level

---

[34] Eylem Türk, "Tekbir'den üniversiteliye özel türban koleksiyonu [From Tekbir, a Special Collection for the University Student]," *Milliyet* (2 February 2008, http://www.milliyet.com.tr/2008/02/10/ekonomi/axeko03.html, accessed 16 June 2008); Sevda Yüzbaşıoğlu, "Headscarfonomics: Wig Shops Wig Out," *Turkish Daily News* (5 February 2008, http://www.turkishdailynews.com.tr/article.php?enewsid=95492, accessed 16 June 2008).

[35] Sandıkçı and Ger, "Constructing and Representing the Islamic Consumer in Turkey," 203; Özlem Sandıkçı and Güliz Ger, "Aesthetics, Ethics and Politics of the Turkish Headscarf," in *Clothing as Material Culture*, ed. Susanne Kuechler and Daniel Miller (Oxford: Berg, 2005), 61–82.

to associate oneself with the former.[36] By wearing lighter colors and more "pleasing" styles, Muslim women not only attempt to dispel the negative associations of the veil, but also to position themselves as fashion-conscious consumers, integrating in "modern" society—as a profitable niche market, no less. In short, veiling-fashion works on multiple levels— aesthetically, discursively, and in the everyday practices of both its producers and consumers—both to accommodate and to challenge global geopolitical mappings that pit "Islam vs. the West."

Islam and Neoliberal Capitalism

> Muslims of the Information Age, with their principles of High Morality, Free Market and Freedom of Thought and Belief have to build a global market based on the spirit of the Market of Medina [...][37]

> When you [only] think of how to make more money in trade, then service suffers. But if you think of how best to serve your beliefs through trade, then it will be *bereketli* [bountiful] and service will be prolific [...] [Our goal] is to make *tesettür* part of Turkey's current affairs, to have it endorsed, liked, and accepted. (Tekbir's CEO, Mustafa Karaduman)[38]

The formation and development of the veiling-fashion industry puts the producers and consumers of its "Islamic" products in a complex relationship with the rationality and imperatives of neoliberal capitalism.[39] The

---

[36] Mahmood Mamdani, "Good Muslim, Bad Muslim: A Political Perspective on Culture and Terrorism," *American Anthropologist* (2002): 766–775.

[37] MÜSİAD, *Bülten [Bulletin]* (vol. 5, no. 24, 1997), in Emin Baki Adaş, "The Making of Entrepreneurial Islam and the Islamic Spirit of Capitalism," *Journal for Cultural Research* 10 (2006): 131.

[38] Ceylan, "'Amacımız tesettürü sevdirmek' ['Our Goal Is to Make Tesettür Loved']," 1.

[39] Although the exact form neoliberalism takes varies from one context to another, it is generally characterized by the active promotion of "free market" economics and its rationality of governance worldwide; see Neil Brenner and Nik Theodore, "Cities and the Geographies of Actually Existing Neoliberalism," *Antipode* 34 (2002): 349–379; James Ferguson and Akhil Gupta, "Spatializing States: Towards an Ethnography of Neoliberal Governmentality," *American Ethnologist* 29 (2002): 981–1002; Jamie Peck and Adam Tickell, "Neoliberalizing Space," *Antipode* 34 (2002): 380–404; Stephan Gill, *Power and Resistance in the New World Order* (New York: Palgrave, 2003); David Harvey, *The New Imperialism* (Oxford: Oxford University Press, 2003); Wendy Larner, "Neoliberalism?" 21 (2003): 509–512; Richard Peet, *Unholy Trinity: The IMF, the World Bank and the WTO* (New York: Zed Books, 2003). The ideal neoliberal subject is an autonomous, entrepreneurial, competitive, self-regulating, and self-realizing individual; see Mitchell Dean, *Governmentality: Power and Rule in Modern Society* (London: Sage, 1999); Colin Gordon, "Governmental Rationality," in *The Foucault Effect: Studies in Gov-*

veiling-fashion industry has emerged and grown rapidly as part of an expanding apparel production, retail, and marketing sector fueled by Turkey's neoliberal policies and entry into Customs Union with the E.U.[40] It is part of a growing "halal" economic landscape from banking and finance[41] to online marketing and tourism.[42] Proponents of "Islamic economics" proscribe rules for the behavior of Islamic firms based on Koranic injunctions and Islamic ethical mandates regarding business transactions, workplace practices, fair wages, community benefits, and modes of profit.[43] Thus, Islamic businesses must navigate the solidarity, social responsibility, other-worldly orientation, and "high morality" of Islamic ethics, while at the same time adhering to the demands of competitiveness, global integration, profit-making in an interest-based economy, and this-worldly concerns. As the actors of the veiling-fashion industry navigate this complicated economic and ethical terrain, they formulate a highly contested Islamic neoliberal capitalism. We argue that this process involves not only the adaptation and appropriation of neoliberal capitalism but also the redefinition and transformation of Islamic practice and values.

---

ernmentality, ed. Graham Burchell, Colin Gordon, and Peter Miller (Chicago: University of Chicago Press, 1991), 1–52; Gökarıksel and Mitchell, "Veiling, Secularism and the Neoliberal Subject: National Narratives and Supranational Desires in Turkey and France"; Nikolas Rose, *Powers of Freedom: Reframing Political Thought* (Cambridge: Cambridge University Press, 1999).

[40] Binnur Neidik and Gary Gereffi, "Explaining Turkey's Emergence and Sustained Competitiveness as a Full-Package Supplier of Apparel," *Environment and Planning A* 38 (2006): 2285–2303; Nebahat Tokatlı, "Globalization and the Changing Clothing Industry in Turkey," *Environment and Planning A* 35 (2003): 1877–1894; see also Bob Begg, John Pickles, and Adrian Smith, "Cutting It: European Integration, Trade Regimes, and the Reconfiguration of East-Central European Apparel Production," *Environment and Planning A* 35 (2003): 2191–2207; John Pickles et al., "Upgrading, Changing Competitive Pressures, and Diverse Practices in the East and Central European Apparel Industry," *Environment and Planning A* 38 (2006): 2305–2324.

[41] Bill Maurer, "Anthropological and Accounting Knowledge in Islamic Banking and Finance: Rethinking Critical Accounts," *Journal of the Royal Anthropological Institute* 8 (2002): 645–667.

[42] Ala Al-Hamarneh and Christian Steiner, "Islamic Tourism: Rethinking the Strategies of Development in the Arab World after September 11," *Comparative Studies of South Asia, Africa and the Middle East* 24 (2004): 173–182; Mücahit Bilici, "İslam'ın bronzlaşan yüzü: Caprice Hotel örnek olayı [The Suntanning Face of Islam: The Case of Caprice Hotel]," in *İslamın yeni kamusal yüzleri [The New Public Faces of Islam]*, ed. Nilüfer Göle (Istanbul: Metis, 1999), 216–236.

[43] Karen Pfeifer, "Islamic Business and Business as Usual: A Study of Firms in Egypt," *Development in Practice* 11 (2001): 20–33; Syed Uddin, "Understanding the Framework of Business in Islam in an Era of Globalization: A Review," *Business Ethics: A European Review* 12 (2003): 23–32.

In the context of Turkey, the rise and development of "Islamic capitalism" has been directly associated with neoliberalization processes of the last two decades.[44] Neoliberal policies since the 1980s included market and trade liberalization, fiscal austerity measures, increased transnational capital mobility, and the privileging of small-scale businesses more adaptable to flexible markets. These policies worked to limit the secular state's role in the economy directly (through privatization) and indirectly, by undermining the support relationship it had established with the mostly secular, Istanbul-based oligarchy of large enterprises.[45] Many small- or medium-scale, mostly family-owned and Anatolian-based businesses that claim an Islamic identity were founded in this new economic environment. Most veiling-fashion companies fall into this category. The success of these new Islamic businesses, often called "Anatolian lions," is attributed to the combination of "religious discipline, ethical solidarity and entrepreneurial dynamism" in their business practices (Yavuz 2003, 82). The use of religious networks to secure investment finance from Turkish immigrants in Europe (especially Germany) has also been noted in the success of Islamic businesses.[46]

The distinction between these new Islamic enterprises and the secular business establishment was spelled out by the founding of two business associations, MÜSİAD (Independent Industrialists and Businessmen Association, in 1990) and ASKON (Anatolian Lions Businessmen Association, in 1998), as alternatives to the secular TÜSİAD (Turkish Industrialists and Businessmen Association).[47] Since their establishment MÜSİAD and ASKON have become the prominent platforms for the concerns and interests of their members while also promoting Islamic ethics and solidarity. The textiles and apparel sector and the veiling-fashion industry are well rep-

---

[44] Yıldız Atasoy, "Explaining Local-Global Nexus: Muslim Politics in Turkey," in *Global Shaping and Its Alternatives*, ed. Yıldız Atasoy and William Carroll (Aurora, Ontario: Kumarian Press, 2003), 57–80; Ayşe Buğra, "Class, Culture and State: An Analysis of Interest Representation by Two Turkish Business Associations," *International Journal of Middle Eastern Studies* 30 (1998): 521–539; Ayşe Buğra, "The place of the economy in Turkish Society," *The South Atlantic Quarterly* 102 (2003): 453–470; Öniş, "Neoliberal Globalization and the Democracy Paradox: The Turkish General Elections of 1999"; Cihan Tuğal, "Islamism in Turkey: Beyond Instrument and Meaning," *Economy and Society* 3 (2002): 85–111; M. Hakan Yavuz, *Islamic Political Identity in Turkey* (Oxford: Oxford University Press, 2003).

[45] Buğra, "Class, Culture and State: An Analysis of Interest Representation by Two Turkish Business Associations"; Yavuz, *Islamic Political Identity in Turkey*.

[46] Buğra, "Class, Culture and State: An Analysis of Interest Representation by Two Turkish Business Associations," 532.

[47] MÜSİAD has a very large presence in Istanbul and has chosen a more centrist approach, while ASKON emphasizes its Anatolian base and is more aligned with conservative Islamic politics.

resented in both of these organizations. For example, MÜSİAD's web site lists 12 members specializing specifically on *tesettür* clothing, not including its member Setre. Tekbir has membership in both ASKON and MÜSİAD and its CEO is the head of the textiles and apparel sector of the first. An analysis of these associations' rhetoric and activities provides important insights into the wider Islamic neoliberal context, of which the veiling-fashion industry is a part.

As the quote above illustrates, MÜSİAD appeals to the "Muslims of the Information Age" to form a global Islamic market. Presenting Muslim businesses as "the driving force of the Muslim rebirth," it advocates for covering "the whole world with information and business networks."[48] Like many other Islamic intellectuals and businesses, this association refers to the Market of Medina as the basis of Islamic capitalism. The Market of Medina, established by the prophet himself, represents the utopian Golden Age of Islam and is defined retrospectively as the ideal and authentic "free market" of Muslims.[49] The Market of Medina is depicted as non-interventionist, non-monopolistic, and tax-free; it attracts merchants, stimulates profits, allows for "just" prices to be reached through market mechanisms, and thus benefits the consumers.[50] ASKON differs from MÜSİAD in its critique of "globalization" (as benefiting large Western corporations and eroding local cultures), the IMF, and U.S. involvement in the Middle East.[51] Nonetheless, ASKON is a proponent of the "free market" redefined within an Islamic framework. Its motto "Haklı Zenginlik" (sanctified wealth) sends the message of Islamic capitalism; its principles are listed as commercial ethics, honesty, freedom (particularly free enterprise), virtue, quality, non-wasteful consumption, and fair income distribution.[52]

This Islamic neoliberal ethic is embodied by *Homo Islamicus*, a figure repeatedly put forward by MÜSİAD. *Homo Islamicus* seeks wealth and economic success not only for personal reasons but also for the greater good of Islam and community.[53] Presenting free market capitalism not only as compatible with Islam but as already Islamic, MÜSİAD and ASKON demonstrate the Islamicization of neoliberalism to justify and to promote Islamic entrepreneurialism. Yet this rhetoric often reinterprets Islamic convention and rarely includes a comprehensive and consistent schema. In practice,

---

[48] MÜSİAD, *Bülten [Bulletin]*.
[49] Adaş, "The Making of Entrepreneurial Islam and the Islamic Spirit of Capitalism."
[50] Ibid., 133.
[51] ASKON 2008, *Movie: Haklı zenginlik [Sanctified Wealth]*, http://www.askon.org.tr/mov.asp\#, accessed 6 June 2008.
[52] ASKON 2008, *Home page*, http://www.askon.org.tr/, accessed 6 June 2008.
[53] Adaş, "The Making of Entrepreneurial Islam and the Islamic Spirit of Capitalism," 130.

even the most fundamental principles of Islam, such as interest rates, are flexibly redefined to suit business needs and working conditions are often not better for workers in terms of wages, safety, hours, etc. In fact, Islamic brotherhood can be mobilized to suppress dissent in the workplace.[54]

The veiling-fashion industry is one of the key areas where Islamic entrepreneurialism and *Homo Islamicus* become prominently visible. Many of the companies in this industry construct an Islamic identity through such means as their choice of names for the company and its products and the messages they publicize through their web sites, catalogs and fashion shows. The ones that do not do so, including stores that include *tesettür* among their product mix to appeal to the widest possible segments of the market, such as Özbil and Eser (interviews June 2004), remain invisible in the contemporary economic and cultural landscape. The largest and leading company of this industry, Tekbir, has used its constructed Islamic identity as a successful marketing and branding strategy. This company demonstrates vividly the many issues related to Islamic neoliberal capitalism.[55]

Tekbir's Islamic identification is articulated in the name of the company (target of a recent lawsuit[56]), its stated mission, its products, and its personal and professional ethics—most of which are contested, as our opening story about the aftermath of the 2008 fashion show illustrates. Tekbir is a family corporation, founded and run by eight brothers who migrated from rural East Anatolia to Istanbul at an early age. The oldest brother and CEO, Mustafa Karaduman, started a very small scale tailoring business which began focusing on *tesettür* clothing in 1982. After the establishment of Tekbir in 1990 and following the global interest and national controversies following its first fashion show in 1992, the company started to grow into a brand name with numerous chain stores and franchises and its recently opened state-of-the-art garment factory. As of June 2008, Tekbir has a total of 31 stores throughout Turkey; 16 of these are located in Istanbul, 2 in the capital Ankara and 13 across the country. In addition, the company has 39 outlets/franchises domestically and 11 internationally. Its goal is to have a total of 100 stores and franchises by the end of 2008.

---

[54] Ibid., 124.

[55] Unless otherwise indicated, the authors' interviews with CEO Mustafa Karaduman (in 2004, 2005 and 2007) are the primary source for all views attributed to Karaduman and the information about Tekbir presented below.

[56] Two Islamic intellectuals of the magazine *Islamiyat* have brought a case against Tekbir, arguing that this name is distinctively Islamic and as a sacred name, it is not appropriate for use in commerce; see "Islamic Fashion Designer Sued for Islamic Name," *Turkish Daily News* (2008, http://www.turkishdailynews.com.tr/article.php?enewsid=103728, accessed 16 June 2008).

CEO Karaduman attributes the success of the company to the hard work and Islamic devotion and mission of its founders. In his words, this mission is to "get as many women as possible to wear a headscarf. I am not trying to do this with a stick but with design."[57] According to Karaduman, Tekbir has not received any loans from the state and has not benefited from any incentives because of its policy to avoid interest. Instead, the company has relied on informal business networks that he and his brothers have developed over the years with suppliers. Echoing the neoliberal mantra, he says he asks nothing of the state other than minimizing its interventions in the economy. He sees "free trade" as crucial to Tekbir's and the country's development, and taxes and tariffs on trade as artificial "barriers" that need to be lifted. According to Karaduman, Turkey's economic future lies in trade not with the E.U. but with its neighbors, including ones with non-Muslim populations like Russia, Bulgaria, and Greece. In Karaduman's words:

> Turkey's neighboring countries import 70-80 percent of their apparel. When customs barriers are lifted, Turkey with its proved status [as a global exporter of textiles and apparel] can easily dominate these markets [...] That's why [Tekbir's] priority is the lifting of customs barriers.[58]

Karaduman promotes this vision in his position as the CEO of Tekbir and the head of the textiles and apparel division of ASKON. As much as his ideas are in line with IMF-orchestrated policies, he is very critical of this organization which he sees as serving only U.S. interests and power. Yet while laying emphasis on building networks with Muslims nationally and transnationally, he is also not strictly discriminatory in terms of trade and production relations. Tekbir's recent hire of the German designer Heidi Beck is a case in point. This attitude is prevalent in other areas of the company as well. For example, Tekbir buys fabric from China and started to subcontract part of its headscarf and knit sweater production to Chinese companies in 2004. Cafer Karaduman of Tekbir states that the company has not shifted its production significantly to China (as other Turkish apparel

---

[57] Ben Barnier, "High Fashion in Turkey: A Headscarf Tycoon and a Lingerie King," *ABC News 2007* (http://i.abcnews.com/Business/story?id=3883012&page=1, accessed 16 June 2008).
[58] Mehmet Baydemir, "Gümrük duvarı tekstilimizin önündeki en büyük engel [Customs Barriers Are the Biggest Obstacle for Our Textiles]," *Milli Gazete* (8 February 2007, http://www.milligazete.com.tr/index.php?action=show&type=news&id=53943, accessed 16 June 2008).

companies have) because of the responsibility the Karaduman brothers feel towards their workers—a position that may shift in the future.[59]

In fact, Tekbir built a new, six-story building in one of the main textile and apparel districts of Istanbul (Mahmutbey) to house its garment factory and to bring all the departments of the company (design, cutting, sewing, quality control, accounting, management, marketing, etc.) under one roof. This building also includes a large wholesale showroom, recreation area for workers, and a *mesjid* for prayers. The factory is equipped with the latest technologies, increasing its production capacity significantly. Operating with only 60 percent of its capacity, as of December 2007, the factory produced 400,000 overcoats and 200,000 headscarves.[60] Tekbir's total sales in 2007 reached 39 million YTLs (approximately $30 million U.S.). Its growth is projected to continue into the future with the goals of having 50 stores and 2,500 workers in 2010 and 100 stores and 5,000 workers in 2015.[61]

Although the salesclerks and store managers of Tekbir are all headscarf-wearing women, perhaps ironically Karaduman's stated mission is not actualized among Tekbir's behind-the-scenes female workers, including some designers, cutters, sewers, and quality controllers, many of whom do not veil. The salesclerks, however, in their company-provided uniforms styled according to the latest trends, play a significant role in marketing Tekbir products. In addition to modeling veiling-fashion in the stores, they also provide personal assistance and advice to customers. Most of the sales clerks are young (between ages 18–25). Their performances (in terms of sales) are recorded on a whiteboard in the eating/resting area. The adjacent small *mesjid*—which spatially reflects the significance given to Islamic observance and would not be present in many other stores—provides space for fulfilling the religious duty of praying and, when not in use, also serves a storage space (for example, for decorative balloons in July 2004). Like the factory workers, salesclerks are paid the minimum wage determined by the state (about $322 U.S. in 2008). They work long hours with few breaks. Interviews with Karaduman and salesclerks in 2007 revealed that only a few are expected to stay and pursue this work as a career, even after becoming a store manager. Yet many underline the value of the women-only social net-

---

[59] Celil Çakır, "Cin misin, Çin misin? [What Comes Out of the Box of Neoliberal Economics? A Jinn or China?]" *Milli Gazete* (18 March 2007, http://www.milligazete.com.tr/?action=show&type=writersnews&id=11510, accessed 16 June 2008).

[60] D. Tezel, *Hadis Dairesinde küreselleşme [Globalization in the Hadith Department]*, 2008, http://www.tekbirgiyim.com.tr/content/view/35/34/lang,tr/, accessed 16 June 2008.

[61] Çakır, "Cin misin, Çin misin? [What Comes Out of the Box of Neoliberal Economics? A Jinn or China?]"

work they establish working at Tekbir stores and the relatively safe working environment.

As Tekbir continues to grow, it is also beginning new ventures in Islamic capitalism. In 2008, the company started to produce a men's line and opened its first men's clothing store in Istanbul. The company now has a Tekbir store card that gives many incentives (interest-free installments, discounts, etc.) to customers to spend their money at Tekbir. It is competing aggressively with a growing number of firms in the same industry, with frequent promotions and discounts, in addition to innovations in design and sale and ever more spectacular fashion shows. The company has also revised its position vis-à-vis some key traditional Islamic practices, for example stopping gender segregation among spectators at its fashion shows beginning in 2004.[62] Through its business practices and vision, as well as its controversial styles, Tekbir illustrates how contemporary Islamic entrepreneurs are operating within a neoliberal modality cast as Islamic—from its origins to ethical principles and ultimate goals. And as Islamic entrepreneurs formulate new forms of Islamic neoliberalism, they also reinterpret and transform Islamic values and practice to suit the imperatives of capitalism and the changing economic and cultural landscape, including the desires of the newly emergent devout middle class.

Gender, Subjectivity and Veiling-Fashion

> [Tesettür] makes a woman aware of her femininity, makes her feel her womanhood. (Cafer Karaduman of Tekbir[63])

> Women [in tesettür] like change. They like eye-catching models in their dress. They certainly do not want to purchase plain, simple clothes. They go for bright colors [...] Women in *tesettür* follow fashion trends very closely. Believe me sometimes they don't like the display combinations we make [in the store]; they have very different ideas in mind and they come up with beautiful combinations. (Ayşe, store manager, interview June 2004)

The producers and consumers of veiling-fashion participate in the construction of new Muslim subjectivities through the set of new meanings and practices enabled and promoted by this industry and its surrounding political and cultural debates. The proliferation of veiling-fashion and its diverse

---

[62] "Harem-selam karıştı [Women and Men Sat Together]," *Tercüman* (18 May 2004).
[63] Ceylan, "'Amacımız tesettürü sevdirmek' ['Our Goal Is to Make Tesettür Loved']," 1.

styles is embedded in the growth of consumer culture and the cultivation of subjectivities in increasingly commodified forms for the pious and the secular alike.[64] With its emphasis on the individual, even when part of an imagined national and transnational community of Muslims, veiling-fashion signals the emergence of a new female subject who navigates the multiple cross-currents of femininity, piety, modesty, sexuality, class, age, and urbanity. Veiling-fashion involves constructing anew not only ideas about femininity, but also of taste, social status, and distinction.[65] A new fashionable Muslim woman who is increasingly savvy about creating her own style, who wants to catch the eye, and who is often able and willing to pay the price has entered into the public imagination (see above quote). She is also the subject of much criticism and debate; the figure of the fashionably veiled women wearing brand names represents for Islamic critics the degeneration of Islamic values and the rise of an Islamic bourgeoisie, described as *Müslüman sosyete* ("Muslim high society"). For secular critics, the new veiled woman, no matter how much she does spend on her clothes, is not *really* fashionable or high society at all. This rejection of veiling-fashion's attempt at distinction is vividly illustrated by the press's endless critiques of the style *faux pas* of the Prime Minister's headscarf-wearing wife, Emine Erdoğan.[66]

Interviews with veiling-fashion salesclerks illustrate how Muslim women become subjects of piety, femininity, and consumption through veiling-fashion. For example, Ayşe (a pseudonym), the young female manager of a three-story store that sells veiling-fashion along with miniskirts, describes how veiled women's styles and sensibilities have changed in the two years since the store's opening:

> Just like women who are not dressed in *tesettür* follow fashion trends— fashion is always changing— women in *tesettür* lately began to act the same. We used to be able to satisfy them with a skirt-jacket combination. We cannot satisfy them with the same styles anymore. They want different and changing styles now. (June 2004)

She reflects back to the period in the early 1990s when she was a college student and the styles were much more limited and conservative in terms of available colors, patterns, and cuts. There has been a sea of change in the

---

[64] Navaro-Yashin, *Faces of the State: Secularism and Public Life in Turkey*.

[65] Saktanber, "'We Pray Like You Have Fun': New Islamic Youth in Turkey between Intellectualism and Popular Culture"; Secor, "The Veil and Urban Space in Istanbul: Women's Dress, Mobility and Islamic Knowledge"; White, "Islamic Chic."

[66] See, e.g., Mine Kırıkkanat, "Rüküş demokrasi [Schlumpy Democracy]," *Radikal* (30 June 2004, http://www.radikal.com.tr/haber.php?haberno=120826, accessed 16 June 2008).

industry since then and she, too, has abandoned her black, grey, and beige overcoats for more colorful and varied pants-tunic and skirt-jacket combinations. She further creates her own style using her sewing machine and is known among the salesclerks for her unique and tasteful creations. Because of the lack of interest in overcoats, especially during the summer, the store is considering closing down that department. Ayşe states matter-of-factly: "Our customers like modern clothes." She describes their customers as daring and bold, often surprising her and the salesclerks with their demands and choices. The salesclerks tell of intense negotiations and sometimes quarrels between daughters and mothers or between wives and husbands about the purchasing choices women make. Veiling-fashion consumers are as much, if not more, interested in self-stylization and are increasingly knowledgeable and tasteful about fashion, according to Ayşe. Further, she sees veiling-fashion as crucial to her subjectivity and to her positioning herself as an urban, educated, tasteful young woman who is Muslim and modern. She is aware of the negative attitude toward veiling in Turkey through first hand experience and is keen to counter this approach.

Yet Ayşe is very much aware of the criticism eye-catching veiling-fashion gets in Islamic circles (for example, in the pages of the daily *Milli Gazete*). She justifies her and her customers' choices, as well as the veiling-fashion industry more generally, by citing that it is not specified with what women's hair and body should be covered in Islam. There is only the injunction that a woman's hair and body should be covered in public spaces and in the company of non-related men. The lack of details about the exact clothing style in Islamic texts allow her and others flexibility in terms of interpretation as to with what to cover. But Islamist critics do not agree and are especially sensitive about the self-indulgence, wastefulness, and elitism they see in veiling-fashion and its consumers.[67] For them, these women represent the emergence of an "Muslim high society" or "the green[68] rich," terms that came into wide use at least since 2002, following the extravagant wedding party of the Islamist political leader Necmettin Erbakan's daughter at the international five-star Sheraton Hotel in Ankara. Veiling-fashion is taken as part of a consumerist lifestyle that puts this-worldly, hedonistic pleasures and concerns above everything else. Instead, these critics invoke solidarity and sharing with the poor and the disadvantaged in the transnational community of Muslims.

---

[67] Mehmet Şevket Eygi, "Müslüman Sosyete [Muslim High Society]," *Milli Gazete* (9 December 2005, http://www.milligazete.com.tr/index.php?action=show&type=writersnews&id=1928), accessed 16 June 2008).

[68] Green is generally considered the color of Islam and used to denote Islamic identity.

The secular media similarly criticizes consumers of veiling-fashion and depicts the new fashionable Muslim women as the symbols of the hypocrisy hidden under the mask of Islam by Islamic capitalists and politicians. The news stories about the Islamic high society focus mostly on women and their veiling-fashion, emphasizing their search for brand names and luxury items.[69] During the coverage of the 2008 Tekbir fashion show, a young woman in the audience attracted the attention of the media. The secular daily *Akşam* used the headline: "The white-Turk girl of the fashion show talked" along with "I read the Koran just as I put on make-up" (23 April 2008). Her name was Gül and she was presented as the synthesis of modernity and Islam with sarcasm. She was wearing bright yellow converses, jeans, a white tunic, and a very colorful headscarf tied on the side; it was noted that she had color contacts, tattooed eyebrows, make-up and fishnet stockings. The term "white-Turk" was coined a few years ago to emphasize the racialized and Europeanized elitism in Turkey; the use of this term to describe Gül underlined the emergence of a similar group of devout Muslims who are not only rich but also disinterested in and disconnected from the lives of "Others" in their pursuit of self-interest and privilege.

As women wear veiling-fashion, they inevitably enter a complex relationship with these ongoing debates about what it means to be a woman, to be Muslim and to be modern. Different social, political, and religious meanings are attached to different styles of veiling-fashion and their presentation.[70] In this way, the meanings of veiling-fashion travel across different sites and position their consumers and producers vis-à-vis moralist discourses about Islamism, gender roles, and consumerism.

Conclusion

By highlighting the ambivalences of veiling-fashion, both in practice and as it is produced as a political issue within national and transnational arenas, we aim to contribute to a nuanced understanding of emergent Islamic geographies. While Islam has been etched into discourses of security and geo-strategy in the context of the U.S. "War on Terror," in fact transnational Islamic networks encompass a wide range of movements for the spiritual

---

[69] Oya Doğan, "Müslüman sosyete nasıl yaşıyor? (How Does Muslim High Society Live?)" *Vatan* (26 September 2006, http://www.kenthaber.com/Arsiv/Haberler/2006/Eylul/26/Haber_1 68530.aspx, accessed 16 June 2008); Ahmet Hakan, "Dinsel maskaralık [Religious Ridicule]," *Hürriyet* (23 Nisan 2008, http://www.kenthaber.com/Arsiv/Haberler/2008/Nisan/23/Haber_ 373435.aspx, accessed 16 June 2008); "Yeşil zenginler nasıl yaşıyor? [How Do the Green Rich Live?]" *Tempo* (2008, http://www.tempodergisi.com.tr/yasam/15898/, accessed 16 June 2008).
[70] Navaro-Yashin, *Faces of the State: Secularism and Public Life in Turkey*; Secor, "Islamism, Democracy and the Political Production of the Headscarf Issue in Turkey."

and social Islamicization of society. Islamic business practices, financial networks, and the rise of Islamic consumption are prominent elements of this broader negotiation between Islamic ethics and the imperatives of neoliberal capitalism. Indeed, 'Islamic consumerism' may serve the vision of a global *umma* by cementing communal bonds between transnational Islamic actors at the same time as it creates and reveals differences among Muslims, especially those of class and gender.

Our discussion of veiling-fashion as a political, economic, and cultural phenomenon highlights the paradoxes and controversies that trouble the relationship between Islam and consumer capitalism. If consumption is considered constitutive of the neoliberal subject and her relationship to the state and society (the "consumer-citizen"[71]), it must be said that this version of subjectivity is very different from the one Islamist movements generally construct. Contemporary Islamism, especially its "moral capitalist" strand, emphasizes religious ethics and solidarity in the lives of Muslim subjects, and advocates moderation in consumption and the avoidance of extravagance and waste. Our discussion has shown some of the ambivalent ways these ideals play out on the ground through the Turkish veiling-fashion industry.

Finally, it seems that the bringing together of *veiling*, that erstwhile marker of piety and modesty, with the showy and ostentatiously wasteful cycles of *fashion* cannot but lead to controversy. While fashion is notoriously unmoored from meaning and judgment, the veil as Islamic practice is most definitely *supposed to mean something*. What veiling-fashion does is to reveal the sliding gap between the signifier (the veil) and its desired signified (Islamic womanhood). When the headlines cry, "From prayer to the catwalk," the very impossibility of fixing the veil becomes a spectacle itself. With fashion, the already multivalent veil becomes, in Baudrillard's conception, a free-floating signifier.

In its free play, the veil can become both the ultimate marker of Islam and a surface without clear referent. Consider Tekbir's mission: to increase the number of women who veil by making veiling attractive and fashionable. The allure of fashion and the attraction of its ever changing designs become vehicles for the spread of veiling among women, and this mass veiling is seen as a metonym for the Islamicization of society. But using fashion in this manner changes the practice of veiling and of Islam significantly. It becomes more difficult to identify what motivates a woman to wear veiling-fashion and it becomes impossible to identify *pure* intentions, be they religious, aesthetic, or social. In Baudrillard's terms, the immorality

---

[71] Nira Yuval-Davis, "Women, Citizenship and Difference," *Feminist Review* 57 (1997): 4–27.

of fashion is demonstrated in the emptying out of the meaning of one of the most potent symbols of Muslim femininity in the veiling-fashion industry. Yet as the controversies that we have analyzed here demonstrate, producers, consumers, and critics alike attempt to anchor veiling-fashion, attaching to it particular kinds of significance at the same time as it becomes part of the everyday, embodied practices of Muslim women. In the ongoing struggle to define what it means to be modern and Muslim today, women and the question of the veil remain at the very center of the storm.

Bibliography

Adaş, Emin Baki. "The Making of Entrepreneurial Islam and the Islamic Spirit of Capitalism." *Journal for Cultural Research* 10 (2006): 113–37.

Ahmed, Leila. *Women and Gender in Islam. Historical Roots of a Modern Debate.* New Haven: Yale University Press, 1992.

Akou, Heather Marie. "Building a New 'World Fashion': Islamic Dress in the Twenty-first Century." *Fashion Theory* 11 (2007): 403–422.

Aktaş, Cihan. *Mahremiyetin tükenişi [The End of Modesty].* İstanbul: Nehir, 1995.

———. *Tanzimattan günümüze kılık, kıyafet ve iktidar [Politics and Clothing since the Ottoman Constitutional Period].* İstanbul: Nehir, 1991.

Al-Hamarneh, Ala, and Christian Steiner. "Islamic Tourism: Rethinking the Strategies of Development in the Arab World after September 11." *Comparative Studies of South Asia, Africa and the Middle East* 24 (2004): 173–182.

Allievi, Stefano, and Jørgen Nielsen, eds. *Muslim Networks and Transnational Communities in and across Europe.* Leiden: Brill, 2003.

ASKON 2008. *Home page.* http://www.askon.org.tr/, accessed 6 June 2008.

———. *Movie: Haklı zenginlik [Sanctified Wealth].* http://www.askon.org. tr/mov.asp\#, accessed 6 June 2008.

Atasoy, Yıldız. "Explaining Local-Global Nexus: Muslim Politics in Turkey." In *Global Shaping and Its Alternatives*, edited by Yıldız Atasoy and William Carroll, 57–80. Aurora, Ontario: Kumarian Press, 2003.

Barnier, Ben. "High Fashion in Turkey: A Headscarf Tycoon and a Lingerie King." *ABC News 2007* (http://i.abcnews.com/Business/story?id= 3883012&page=1, accessed 16 June 2008).

Baudrillard, Jean. *Symbolic Exchange and Death.* London: Sage, 1993.

Baydemir, Mehmet. "Gümrük duvarı tekstilimizin önündeki en büyük engel [Customs Barriers Are the Biggest Obstacle for Our Textiles]." *Milli Gazete* (8 February 2007, http://www.milligazete.com.tr/index.php?action=show&type=news&id=53943, accessed 16 June 2008).

Begg, Bob, John Pickles, and Adrian Smith. "Cutting It: European Integration, Trade Regimes, and the Reconfiguration of East-Central European Apparel Production." *Environment and Planning A* 35 (2003): 2191–2207.

Bilici, Mücahit. "İslam'ın bronzlaşan yüzü: Caprice Hotel örnek olayı [The Suntanning Face of Islam: The Case of Caprice Hotel]." In *İslamın yeni kamusal yüzleri [The New Public Faces of Islam]*, edited by Nilüfer Göle, 216–236. Istanbul: Metis, 1999.

Brenner, Neil, and Nik Theodore. "Cities and the Geographies of Actually Existing Neoliberalism." *Antipode* 34 (2002): 349–379.

Buğra, Ayşe. "The place of the economy in Turkish Society." *The South Atlantic Quarterly* 102 (2003): 453–470.

Buğra, Ayşe. "Class, Culture and State: An Analysis of Interest Representation by Two Turkish Business Associations." *International Journal of Middle Eastern Studies* 30 (1998): 521–539.

Çakır, Celil. "Cin misin, Çin misin? [What Comes Out of the Box of Neoliberal Economics? A Jinn or China?]" *Milli Gazete* (18 March 2007, http://www.milligazete.com.tr/?action=show&type=writersnews&id=11510, accessed 16 June 2008).

Çiftçi, Halise. "Tesettür, moda ve defile [Veiling, Fashion and the Catwalk]." *Milli Gazete* (28 April 1993).

Ceylan, İsmail Fatih. "'Amacımız tesettürü sevdirmek' ['Our Goal Is to Make Tesettür Loved']." *Milli Gazete* (10 October 1992, http://www.milligazete.com.tr/index.php?action=show&type=news&id=53943, accessed 16 June 2008).

Crewe, Louise. "Geographies of Retailing and Consumption: Markets in Motion." *Progress in Human Geography* 27 (2003): 352–362.

Dean, Mitchell. *Govermentality: Power and Rule in Modern Society*. London: Sage, 1999.

Doğan, Oya. "Müslüman sosyete nasıl yaşıyor? (How Does Muslim High Society Live?)" *Vatan* (26 September 2006, http://www.kenthaber.com/Arsiv/Haberler/2006/Eylul/26/Haber_168530.aspx, accessed 16 June 2008).

"Dutch Government Backs Burqa Ban." *BBC News* (2006, http://news.bbc.co.uk/2/hi/europe/6159046.stm, accessed 16 June 2008).

Ehrkamp, Patricia, and Helga Leitner. "Transnationalism and Migrants' Imaginings of Citizenship." *Environment and Planning A* 38 (2006): 1615–1632.
El Guindi, Fatma. *Veil: Modesty, Privacy and Resistance*. Oxford: Berg, 1999.
Eygi, Mehmet Şevket. "Evlere senlik tesettür defilesi [An Odd Veiling-Fashion Show]." *Milli Gazete* (25 April 2008, http://www.milligazete.com.tr/index.php?action=show&type=writersnews&id=18157, accessed 16 June 2008).
———. "Müslüman Sosyete [Muslim High Society]." *Milli Gazete* (9 December 2005, http://www.milligazete.com.tr/index.php?action=show&type=writersnews&id=1928), accessed 16 June 2008).
Fanon, Franz. *A Dying Colonialism*. New York: Grove Press, 1967.
Ferguson, James, and Akhil Gupta. "Spatializing States: Towards an Ethnography of Neoliberal Governmentality." *American Ethnologist* 29 (2002): 981–1002.
Gill, Stephan. *Power and Resistance in the New World Order*. New York: Palgrave, 2003.
Gökarıksel, Banu. *Islams, Neoliberalism and Transnationalism: The Making of Subject-Citizens and Tesettür Fashions in Istanbul*. Paper presented at the Muslim Fashions/Fashionable Muslims Workshop, University of Amsterdam and the International Institute for the Study of Islam in the Modern World, Amsterdam, 15–16 April 2005.
Gökarıksel, Banu, and Katharyne Mitchell. "Veiling, Secularism and the Neoliberal Subject: National Narratives and Supranational Desires in Turkey and France." *Global Networks* 5 (2005): 147–165.
Gökarıksel, Banu, and Anna J. Secor. "New Transnational Geographies of Islamism, Capitalism and Subjectivity: The Veiling-Fashion Industry in Turkey." *Area* 41, no. 1 (2009): 6–18.
Göle, Nilüfer. *İslamın yeni kamusal yüzleri [The New Public Faces of Islam]*. Istanbul: Metis, 1999.
———. *The Forbidden Modern: Civilization and Veiling*. Ann Arbor: University of Michigan Press, 1996.
Gordon, Colin. "Governmental Rationality." In *The Foucault Effect: Studies in Governmentality*, edited by Graham Burchell, Colin Gordon, and Peter Miller, 1–52. Chicago: University of Chicago Press, 1991.
Gunster, Shane. *Capitalizing on Culture: Critical Theory for Cultural Studies*. Toronto: University of Toronto Press, 2004.
Hakan, Ahmet. "Dinsel maskaralık [Religious Ridicule]." *Hürriyet* (23 Nisan 2008, http://www.kenthaber.com/Arsiv/Haberler/2008/Nisan/23/Haber_373435.aspx, accessed 16 June 2008).

"Harem-selam karıştı [Women and Men Sat Together]." *Tercüman* (18 May 2004).
Harvey, David. *The New Imperialism*. Oxford: Oxford University Press, 2003.
Hausler, Ulf. "Muslim Dress-Codes in German State Schools." *European Journal of Migration and Law* 3 (2001): 457–74.
İlyasoğlu, Aynur. *Örtülü kimlik [Veiled Identity]*. Istanbul: Metis Kadın Araştırmaları Dizisi, 1994.
"Islamic Fashion Designer Sued for Islamic Name." *Turkish Daily News* (2008, http://www.turkishdailynews.com.tr/article.php?enewsid=1037 28, accessed 16 June 2008).
Jackson, Peter. "Commercial Cultures: Transcending the Cultural and Economic." *Progress in Human Geography* 26 (2002): 3–18.
Jackson, Peter, Phil Crang, and Claire Dwyer, eds. *Transnational Spaces*. London: Routledge, 2004.
Kahf, Mohja. *Western Representations of the Muslim Woman*. Austin: University of Texas Press, 1999.
Kandiyoti, Deniz, ed. *Women, Islam and the State*. Philadelphia: Temple University Press, 1991.
Karaosmanoğlu, Fatma. *Moda ve zihniyet [Fashion and Mentality]*. Istanbul: Iz, 2002.
Keyman, E. Fuat, and Ahmet İçduygu. "Globalization, Civil Society and Citizenship in Turkey: Actors, Boundaries and Discourses." *Citizenship Studies* 7 (2003): 219–34.
Kılıçbay, Barış, and Mutlu Binark. "Consumer Culture, Islam and the Politics of Lifestyle: Fashion for Veiling in Contemporary Turkey." *European Journal of Communication* 17 (2002): 495–511.
Kırıkkanat, Mine. "Rüküş demokrasi [Schlumpy Democracy]." *Radikal* (30 June 2004, http://www.radikal.com.tr/haber.php?haberno=120826, accessed 16 June 2008).
Larner, Wendy. "Neoliberalism?" 21 (2003): 509–512.
Lazreg, Marnia. *The Eloquence of Silence: Algerian Women in Question*. London: Routledge, 1994.
Mabro, Judy. *Veiled Half-Truths*. London: IB Tauris, 1996.
MacLeod, Arlene. *Accommodating Protest: Working Women, the New Veiling and Change in Cairo*. New York: Columbia University Press, 1991.
Mahmood, Saba. *Politics of Piety: The Islamic Revival and the Feminist Subject*. Princeton: Princeton University Press, 2005.
Mamdani, Mahmood. "Good Muslim, Bad Muslim: A Political Perspective on Culture and Terrorism." *American Anthropologist* (2002): 766–775.

Mandaville, Peter. *Transnational Muslim Politics*. London: Routledge, 2003.
Mansvelt, Julie. *Geographies of Consumption*. Thousand Oaks: Sage, 2005.
Maurer, Bill. "Anthropological and Accounting Knowledge in Islamic Banking and Finance: Rethinking Critical Accounts." *Journal of the Royal Anthropological Institute* 8 (2002): 645–667.
McRobbie, Angela. "Bridging the Gap: Feminism, Fashion and Consumption." *Feminist Review* 55 (1997): 73–89.
MÜSİAD. *Bülten [Bulletin]*. vol. 5, no. 24, 1997.
Nagel, Caroline, and Lynn Staeheli. "Citizenship, Identity and Transnational Migration: Arab Immigrants to the United States." *Space & Polity* 8 (2004): 3–23.
Navaro-Yashin, Yael. *Faces of the State: Secularism and Public Life in Turkey*. Princeton: Princeton University Press, 2002.
Neidik, Binnur, and Gary Gereffi. "Explaining Turkey's Emergence and Sustained Competitiveness as a Full-Package Supplier of Apparel." *Environment and Planning A* 38 (2006): 2285–2303.
Öniş, Ziya. "Neoliberal Globalization and the Democracy Paradox: The Turkish General Elections of 1999." *Journal of International Affairs* 54 (2000): 283–306.
Özyürek, Esra. *The Headscarf Knot in the Turkish Parliament*. Conference paper, Workshop on gendered bodies, transnational politics, American University in Cairo, 12–14 December 2003.
Peck, Jamie, and Adam Tickell. "Neoliberalizing Space." *Antipode* 34 (2002): 380–404.
Peet, Richard. *Unholy Trinity: The IMF, the World Bank and the WTO*. New York: Zed Books, 2003.
Pfeifer, Karen. "Islamic Business and Business as Usual: A Study of Firms in Egypt." *Development in Practice* 11 (2001): 20–33.
Pickles, John, et al. "Upgrading, Changing Competitive Pressures, and Diverse Practices in the East and Central European Apparel Industry." *Environment and Planning A* 38 (2006): 2305–2324.
Polhemus, Ted, and Lynn Proctor. *Fashion and Anti-Fashion*. London: Thames / Hudson, 1978.
Rose, Nikolas. *Powers of Freedom: Reframing Political Thought*. Cambridge: Cambridge University Press, 1999.
Saktanber, Ayşe. "'We Pray Like You Have Fun': New Islamic Youth in Turkey between Intellectualism and Popular Culture." In *Fragments of Culture: The Everyday of Modern Turkey*, edited by Deniz Kandiyoti and Ayşe Saktanber, 254–276. London: IB Tauris, 2002.

Samers, Michael. "Diaspora Unbound: Muslim Identity and the Erratic Regulation of Islam in France." *International Journal of Population Geography* 9 (2003): 351–364.
Sandıkçı, Özlem, and Güliz Ger. "Aesthetics, Ethics and Politics of the Turkish Headscarf." In *Clothing as Material Culture*, edited by Susanne Kuechler and Daniel Miller, 61–82. Oxford: Berg, 2005.
———. "Constructing and Representing the Islamic Consumer in Turkey." *Fashion Theory* 11 (2007): 189–210.
———. "Fundamental Fashions: The Cultural Politics of the Turban and the Levi's." *Advances in Consumer Research* 28 (2001): 146–50.
Secor, Anna. "Islamism, Democracy and the Political Production of the Headscarf Issue in Turkey." In *Geographies of Muslim Women: Gender, Religion and Space*, edited by Ghazi Falah and Caroline Nagel, 203–225. New York: Guilford Press, 2005.
———. "The Veil and Urban Space in Istanbul: Women's Dress, Mobility and Islamic Knowledge." *Gender, Place and Culture* 9 (2002): 5–22.
Shadid, W.A.R., and P.S. van Koningsveld. "Muslim Dress in Europe: Debates on the Headscarf." *Journal of Islamic Studies* 16 (2005): 35–61.
Silvey, Rachel. "Geographies of Gender and Migration: Spatializing Social Difference." *International Migration Review* 40 (2006): 64–68.
Şişman, Nazife. *Kamusal alanda başörtülüler: Fatma Karabıyık Karaosmanoğlu ile söyleşi*. Istanbul: Iz, 2001.
Soysal, Yasemin. *Limits of Citizenship: Migrants and Postnational Membership in Europe*. Chicago: University of Chicago Press, 1994.
Staeheli, Lynn, and Caroline Nagel. "Topographies of Home and Citizenship: Arab-American Activists in the United States." *Environment and Planning A* 38 (2006): 1599–1614.
Tezel, D. *Hadis Dairesinde küreselleşme [Globalization in the Hadith Department]*. 2008, http://www.tekbirgiyim.com.tr/content/view/35/34/lang,tr/, accessed 16 June 2008.
Tokatlı, Nebahat. "Globalization and the Changing Clothing Industry in Turkey." *Environment and Planning A* 35 (2003): 1877–1894.
Tuğal, Cihan. "Islamism in Turkey: Beyond Instrument and Meaning." *Economy and Society* 3 (2002): 85–111.
Türk, Eylem. "Tekbir'den üniversiteliye özel türban koleksiyonu [From Tekbir, a Special Collection for the University Student]." *Milliyet* (2 February 2008, http://www.milliyet.com.tr/2008/02/10/ekonomi/axeko03.html, accessed 16 June 2008).
Uddin, Syed. "Understanding the Framework of Business in Islam in an Era of Globalization: A Review." *Business Ethics: A European Review* 12 (2003): 23–32.

Veblen, Thorsten. *The Theory of Leisure Class. An Economic Study of Institutions.* New York: Mentor, 1953 [1899].
White, Jenny. "Islamic Chic." In *Istanbul between the Global and the Local,* edited by Çağlar Keyder, 77–91. Lanham: Rowman / Littlefield, 1999.
Wilson, Elizabeth. *Adorned in Dreams: Fashion and Modernity.* London: Virago, 1985.
Yavuz, M. Hakan. *Islamic Political Identity in Turkey.* Oxford: Oxford University Press, 2003.
Yeğenoğlu, Meyda. *Colonial Fantasies: Towards a Feminist Reading of Orientalism.* Cambridge: Cambridge University Press, 1998.
"Yeşil zenginler nasıl yaşıyor? [How Do the Green Rich Live?]" *Tempo* (2008, http://www.tempodergisi.com.tr/yasam/15898/, accessed 16 June 2008).
Yuval-Davis, Nira. "Women, Citizenship and Difference." *Feminist Review* 57 (1997): 4–27.
Yüzbaşıoğlu, Sevda. "Headscarfonomics: Wig Shops Wig Out." *Turkish Daily News* (5 February 2008, http://www.turkishdailynews.com.tr/article.php?enewsid=95492, accessed 16 June 2008).

CHAPTER THREE

THE SHOPPING MALL: THE ENCHANTED PART OF A DISENCHANTED CITY. THE CASE OF ANKAMALL, ANKARA

AKSU AKÇAOĞLU[1]

Introduction: Transformations in the Field of Consumption in Turkey

How many people in Istanbul are both a rich craftsman and a Muslim? Among the Jewish, Greek, and Armenian craftsmen of the city, I am the only one.[2]

This excerpt from Orhan Pamuk's first novel, *Cevdet Bey and His Sons*, captures the general perception of trade as almost a non-Muslim occupation in the beginning of the 20th century in the capital of Ottoman Turkey. Although patterns of conspicuous consumption were widespread, especially among Ottoman leisure class during the Tulip Age and after the first department stores opened in the 19th century, the values and practices of conspicuous consumption did not involve the majority of the population. The economic mentality of the majority during this period is embodied in the proverb *işten artmaz dişten artar* ("Money is made not by increasing earnings but by limiting consumption"[3]). Although this Muslim economic mentality, with its ascetic stance toward consumption, shares similarities with

---

[1] This paper is based on the author's master's thesis "The Mallification of Urban Life in Ankara: The Case of ANKAmall."
[2] Orhan Pamuk, *Cevdet Bey ve Oğulları* (İstanbul: İletişim Yayınları, 2007), 18.
[3] Suraiya Faroqhi, "Research on the History of Ottoman Consumption: A Preliminary Exploration of Sources and Models," in *Consumption Studies and the History of the Ottoman Empire*

Weber's Protestant Ethic,[4] it does not include the Protestant notion of achieving salvation by working hard. For Muslims in Ottoman Turkey the reference point for individual success was based on working for the state bureaucracy or military, the status of other lines of work, such as trade, was lower.

As Mardin argues, wealth was seen as a function of one's position in the political bureaucracy among the members of upper strata in the Ottoman society.[5] Since having a position in the political bureaucracy was the ultimate goal, regardless of the money it brings, the Ottoman wealth mentality lacked the spirit of capitalism, which sees making money as a purpose in itself. In addition, except for the elites of the period it is hard to run into the self-gratifying subject of the Romantic Ethic.[6] Even though it is not possible to identify the emergence of consumer society in the sense of capitalist and modern market society, as Frierson argues, we can see the creation of consumer culture in late Ottoman society. Blended with patriotism, the selective modernization, Westernization, and civility as the main dynamics of the consumer culture of that period maintain their fundamental role for the consumer culture of modern Turkey.

It can be argued that especially after the transition to a free-market economy in 1980, the previously flourishing consumer society became a "peculiar type of market society." Similar to the consumer society definition by Grazia,[7] as the Western capitalist system of exchange expanded in Turkey, the organization of institutions, resources, and values have been re-shaped around ever larger flows and accumulations of commodities. In addition, in the same period, "goods transformed from being static symbols around which hierarchies were ordered to being more directly constitutive of class, social status, and personal identity."[8] I argue that while the modern consumer society of Turkey rested on strong economic roots with the country's transition to free market economy, cultural changes during the Republican period paved the way for the rapid adoption of the values of consumer

---

1550–1922: An Introduction, ed. Donald Quataert (New York: State University of New York Press, 2000), 22.

[4] Max Weber, *Protestan Ahlakı ve Kapitalizmin Ruhu* (İstanbul: Ayraç Yayınları, 2003).

[5] Şerif Mardin, "Tanzimat'tan Sonra Aşırı Batılılaşma," in *Türk Modernleşmesi*, ed. M. Türköne and T. Önder (İstanbul: İletişim Yayınları, 1991), 24.

[6] Colin Campbell, *The Romantic Ethic and the Spirit of Modern Consumerism* (Oxford: Blackwell Publishers, 1987), 173-203.

[7] Cited from Elizabeth B. Frierson, "Cheap and Easy: The Creation of Consumer Culture in Late Ottoman Society," in *Consumption Studies and the History of the Ottoman Empire 1550–1922: An Introduction*, ed. Donald Quataert (New York: State University of New York Press, 2000), 243.

[8] Ibid., 243.

culture. Starting in 1950 and intensifying after 1980, the reference point for the Westernization of Turkey shifted from Europe to the United States. The European-centered Westernization rested on the philosophy of the Enlightenment, with the school as the spatial symbol. It promised success through education and looked to teachers as model citizens. In contrast, Turkey's American-centered Westernization rests on the values of the American Dream: it promises success in the economic sphere and holds up the entrepreneur as a model, with the shopping mall as one of the spatial symbols, especially in the late 1990s and 2000s. The ideal of the period was to transform Turkey into a small America. This ideal was embodied in the prime minister's slogan "each neighborhood will have a millionaire."

The Turkish-American Dream has never become a reality. Each neighborhood has not produced a millionaire, however shopping malls are now creating a miniature version of America in each neighborhood, as the media spreads the cultural values of this ideal to every segment of society. Therefore, the distance between being a Muslim and making money through trade, along with an ascetic approach toward consumption, disappeared as the motto of global consumerism "want more" replaced the motto of the traditional attitude against consumption *bir lokma bir hırka* ("one morsel one cardigan"). I argue that with the visible growth of the capitalist spirit in Turkey, the approach toward consumption has changed. In line with the argument of Bockock, the burdens of working conditions are now acceptable insofar as they provide the means to acquire the almost-holy commodities.[9] Therefore, visits to the shopping mall are now almost a daily pilgrimage[10] in modern Turkey and the shopping mall itself is becoming a Consumer Mecca.[11]

The Mallification of Urban Life in Ankara

Since the opening of the first shopping mall in Ankara in 1989, the number of malls in the city has mushroomed. As the number of malls increases from day to day; the city is now surrounded by new shopping malls. At the end of 2007, there were 24 malls in the city. What is even more important is that this number has doubled in the last two years.[12] The construction of shopping malls in Ankara is seen as one of the most profitable investments

---

[9] Robert Bocock, *Tüketim* (Ankara: Dost Kitabevi Yayınları, 1997), 56.

[10] George Ritzer, *Büyüsü Bozulmuş Dünyayı Büyülemek* (İstanbul: Ayrıntı Yayınları, 2000), 14.

[11] Mark Liecthy, *Suitably Modern: Making Middle-Class Culture in a New Consumer Culture* (Princeton: Princeton University Press, 2003), 88.

[12] "Ankara'da AVM Sayısı İkiye Katlandı," *Hürriyet* (www.hurriyet.com.tr/, accessed 24 April 2007).

for the holders of big capital in Turkey. That is one of the reasons why the number of the shopping malls and the accompanying changes in the social, economic, and cultural fabric of the city is expected to continue multiplying in Ankara.

For the last few years, we have been witnessing the emergence and formation of an increasingly mall-centered urban life in Ankara. The economy, culture, institutions, and social activities have all been shifting from the city center to the shopping malls. The end result of this process is a city under the roof of the shopping mall. Today the malls are one of the biggest business sectors in the city. ANKAmall includes 300 stores and approximately 3,000 employees. The total number of employees at all the shopping malls in the city is 36,000. Therefore, a shopping mall is like a central business district around which urban life takes shape. Cultural activities, such as going to the cinema, theater, or a concert, are part of going to a shopping mall. Social activities, such as meeting friends, sitting in cafes, and eating in restaurants, are also part of going to a shopping mall. Only by going to a shopping mall, can one have the possibility of doing everything in a city. The mall can be seen as an ant nest, the space where the population circulates endlessly.

In a very short period of time, shopping malls have become part of everyday life in Ankara. It is now possible to see shopping malls on the city maps and websites of the city. Moreover, the names of malls appear as station names and destination signs on the public transportation system. Furthermore, shopping malls dominate the social discourse of urban life. This shopping mall–based discourse is not restricted to the actual indoor space of the malls. The ads for the malls that appear on billboards, buses, and on the walls of houses are major components of this mall-based discourse, which is reproduced in countless daily conversations. Shopping malls are now an inseparable part of the urban life in Ankara.

Using the findings of an ethnographic study conducted at ANKAmall, the city's biggest shopping mall, I aim to explain the enchantment that the residents of Ankara have with their malls. Weber used the concept of enchantment as a peculiar aspect of the pre-modern societies. He argued that all the spheres of social life, as exemplified in capitalism and in the bureaucracy, were organized in the light of rationalization through the principles of control, efficiency, calculability, and predictability which disenchanted what was once an enchanted world..[13] Ritzer argues that rationalization of the means of consumption creates re-enchantment i.e, malls are transformed into magical spaces where new experiences can occur.[14] In the remaining

---

[13] George Ritzer, *Explorations in the Sociology of Consumption: Fast Food, Credit Cards, and Casinos* (London: Sage Publications, 2001), 23, 114.

[14] Ritzer, *Büyüsü Bozulmuş Dünyayı Büyülemek*.

sections, I articulate the new dynamics and resulting new experiences in the shopping malls of Ankara. First I discuss the emphasis on security and the juxtaposition of different activities in shopping malls that make them such centers of attraction. Then I explain the magic appeal that malls have to consumers with regard to their income, age, and gender.

Figure 3.1: An evening view of ANKAmall.

The Magical Dynamics of Shopping Malls

For the residents of Ankara, it is possible to draw the architectural typology of the shopping mall: the shopping mall is a huge three- or four-story building. The first two floors are full of clothing stores, and the upper floor consists of a food court, bookstore, and cinema. The huge size of the building and the vast parking area in front of the mall are its most distinctive features and also what differentiates a mall from other buildings in the city. Even if one has never been to a shopping mall, the architectural features of shopping malls are absorbed through the media. However, more than any particular architectural feature, the magical aspect of malls becomes apparent when you listen to how people describe them. A shopping mall is a magic box that compresses everything in one place. As a retired clerk says:

> Going to the shopping mall is similar to going to many places, such as restaurants, cafes, grocery stores, but at the same time it is different from all of these places. When you describe a restaurant you talk about the specific activities one can do in a restaurant. For example, you say that a restaurant is a place where you eat something. The difference of the shopping mall is that you cannot say any specific activity to do in the mall. You can do everything in the shopping mall. (65-year-old male in the middle-income group).

In the magical atmosphere of shopping malls, a new kind of social life comes into existence in which, as Helten and Fischer argue, security is one of the most alluring aspects.[15] The respondents emphasize that they walk around comfortably in the shopping malls without watching their pockets because of the low possibility of purse-snatching: Malls are described as the second-most-secure place in the city, after police stations. Trust-based social relations, however, do not spring from the character of social relations; they are rather the result of the security system. The technological control of the shopping malls seems to create trust in the social relations. Even though it seems paradoxical, the trust in the social life of the shopping malls is related to being watched and being controlled. The trust issue in the social relations of urban life, which Jane Jacobs addressed in her 1969 book,[16] seems to be solved in the shopping malls, because in malls, people are not as anonymous as they are in urban public spaces. Therefore, the description of mall visitors as "decent people" is related to spatial security technologies. Visitors to the mall are regarded as decent not only because they have relatively high social, economic, and cultural capital; even in the opposite condition, visitors are regarded as decent because it is thought that regardless of the degree of capital one has, the mall transforms people into decent people. Regardless of income, age, and gender variables, the secure atmosphere of the shopping mall and the decent appearance of visitors to the mall were emphasized by all respondents. While male respondents exemplify the decent character of the social relations at the shopping mall with the absence of the danger of purse-snatching, women appreciate that at the mall men seldom stare at women in a disturbing way.

---

[15] Frank Helten and Bernd Fischer, *Video Surveillance on Demand for Various Purposes? Berlin Shopping Malls as Socio-Technical Testbeds for CCTV*, RTD-Project, 5th Framework Programme for European Commision, 2003.

[16] Jane Jacobs *The Death and Life of Great American Cities* (New York: The Random House, 1969), chap. The Uses of Sidewalks: Safety.

> The shopping mall is one of the rare places in which you can walk around comfortably. If you go to Saman Pazarı, a traditional shopping district of the city, you have to pay attention to your wallet. But in the shopping mall you can attend to your wife and children more than your wallet. (45-year-old male in the low-income group).

> While walking around Kızılay I feel disturbed. All the men stare at me as if they will immediately attack. But the shopping mall is a modern space and the visitors behave decently. (34-year-old female in the upper-income group).

As the capital of Turkey, Ankara is seen as a bureaucratic city that is incapable of satisfying the expectations of the residents. Most of the respondents say that Ankara is a relatively new city, which lacks an entrenched culture and natural beauty. While talking about urban life, most of the people complain about the lack of alternatives in the city. Under such circumstances, the shopping malls are seen as an oasis in the middle of a desert. In defining city life in Ankara, Kızılay, Tunalı Hilmi Street, Bahçeli, and Ulus are given primary significance. However, although these districts of the city are the heart of urban life, their deteriorating conditions are the main focus of the residents' complaints about the city. These public spaces are seen under the invasion of the groups that are identified with crime. These places are no longer safe. Moreover, the traffic, noise, crowds, and dirtiness of these public spaces are also cited as factors that push people out. In addition, other non-social factors are helping to push people away from the old districts. Weather conditions and the time of the day can also restrict activities in public spaces. Walking around the city in hot and cold weather is seen as unhealthy, and being out late is considered dangerous. As a result, public spaces are to be avoided and the ties between these spaces and people are to be reduced to a purely functional level.

The address that most people escape to is a shopping mall. Going to a shopping mall is like walking around a city that has solved its problems. In the shopping malls, the activities of the urban public spaces are presented in a street-like atmosphere. The atmosphere in the mall is pure, free of danger and disturbance.[17] Malls have security guards at their gates, cameras in every corner, an orderly design and stainless cleanness to prevent any possible deviance. The absence of socially disadvantaged groups, such as beggars, prevents another possible distraction. Shopping malls are rationally planned

---

[17] Michael Southworth, "Reinventing Main Street: From Mall to Townscape Mall," *Journal of Urban Design* 10, no. 2 (2005): 154; Nancy Backes, "Reading the Shopping Mall City," *Journal of Popular Culture* 31, no. 3 (1997): 3.

to make visitors think only about shopping..[18] Even the weather and time are rationally controlled in the mall. The air-conditioned environment and the lighting system create a space that is not affected by the linear movement of time and nature..[19]

Shopping malls as an escape from the city are not wholeheartedly welcome. Residents of Ankara long for open-air activities. They live a paradox between the desire and practice of how to spend leisure time in the city. Most of the respondents say they prefer open-air activities, but they immediately add that they can rarely do that. The shopping malls in Ankara seem to create various questions in the minds of its residents. On one hand, while the new spaces of social change are visited more, on the other hand, the less visited spaces are romanticized. While people do enjoy the time they spend in the shopping malls, they often mention the good old days in the urban public places, such as the streets and squares.

Even as shopping malls are seen as part of Turkey's Westernization process and articulation with the global world, they are also approached with caution. This springs from a fear of over-consumption and of losing the traditional type of socialization that was established in the urban public spaces. Especially for the older generations who grew up in a protectionist economy, shopping malls signify excessive consumption. Since the economy of the country has so many problems, they see the investment in shopping malls as a waste. According to them, money should be invested in production to accelerate the economic development of the country. In this rationale, factories provide opportunities for employment and to increase savings, while shopping malls are seen as traps that waste the productive resources. Moreover, some respondents think negatively about the foreign shareholders of the shopping malls. They blame foreign shareholders for profiting from the local stores, hence draining the surplus created by domestic business.

These skeptical attitudes toward shopping malls do not, however, prevent people from visiting the malls. The general tendency is to identify the shopping mall with Westernization and modernization processes. The positive attitudes toward shopping malls originate in the everyday life experiences of individuals. Shopping malls are perceived as enchanted spaces in a disenchanted city. The huge size of the mall, the juxtaposition of a multitude of goods and activities, the extravagant design of space, the lightning system, and the endless variety of commodities are the major factors that mesmerize visitors. The image of walking around in a shopping mall is like being Alice in Wonderland.

---

[18] Mark Gottdiener, *Postmodern Göstergeler* (Ankara: İmge Kitabevi, 2005), 129.

[19] Ritzer, *Büyüsü Bozulmuş Dünyayı Büyülemek*, 220.

Twenty years ago, shopping malls would not have been familiar spaces to most of the residents of Ankara. Malls, therefore, are the new parts of the city. What's new about them is not only their abundance of commodities but also their style of presentation. Malls remove the strict boundaries between different activities and spaces; instead they juxtapose everything in an unfamiliar manner.[20] In the past, occupational specialization coincided with a designated space, such as a specialized store: butchers, green-grocers, tailors, bakers, manufacturers worked independently. Malls collect everything that plays a role in the economy of the city under one roof. This juxtaposition of unrelated activities and places makes the mall almost a magical place. Most respondents say they thought they were in a dream the first time they visited a shopping mall. To see garden tools and different kinds of bread sold in the same place was previously unimaginable. The extreme variety of commodities and services at the mall is another source of enchantment. This feature of the mall transforms it into a museum of the material culture of daily life in the city. People walk around the mall looking at the new commodities behind the store windows as if they are looking at objects protected under glass.

The main difference between museums and shopping malls is the inversion of what's worth seeing at the malls. The activities also have different meanings: the museum is identified with high culture, but visiting a mall, that is, "the museum of the new," is part of the everyday life of the city. A similar dynamic can be seen in the coincidence of luxury and ordinary in the shopping malls, hence amalgamating high culture and popular culture. Malls are extraordinary places, but they are quite an ordinary part of urban life. However, they transform daily life into a fable-like environment at the same time. As a young professional says, malls open doors to a dreamland that is experienced in ordinary life:

> Whenever I find myself at the entrance of ANKAmall, I feel as if I am entering an ultra-luxury hotel, as if I am at the Hilton. This place is like a huge palace, with its pleasant and bright luxury environment [that] you can easily reach by subway. (27-year-old female in the middle-income group).

---

[20] Eric Nelson, *The Mall of America: Reflections of a Virtual Community* (Minnesota: Galde Press, 1998), 31.

62   Chapter Three

Figure 3.2: A dinosaur display at ANKAmall.

21

The Fragmented Magic of the Shopping Mall

Other than these general features that transform the mall into an enchanted space, there are a number of reasons that make the mall a magical aspect of urban life. The magical aspects of the shopping mall change with regard to income group, gender, and age variables. For lower-income respondents who mainly live in the *gecekondu* (shantytown) areas of the city, going to the mall is a touristic journey. For them, visiting the shopping mall is not like loitering in the urban public spaces. It is a special activity that requires paying more attention to one's physical appearance. This attitude might be related to the purpose of going to the mall. For the lower-income groups, going to the shopping mall is a respectable leisure activity. For them, the mall is not so much related to shopping. Shopping in the mall is a dream that exceeds the family budget. Stimuli spreading from the stores create an atmosphere that is dominated by the shopping messages. This atmosphere creates double effects for lower-income groups: consciousness of incapability and daydreaming. The messages emanating from the stores call visitors to purchase the commodities that are exhibited behind the windows, as if these commodities magically contain the meaning of life. For the lower-income groups, however, loitering in the passages of the mall reminds them of their economic incapability. This reproduction of the consciousness of economic incapability is one of the reasons why lower-income groups rarely visit the mall. As a young worker explained, if he had more money he would visit the mall more frequently:

> Actually, I would like to visit the mall more. But when we come here as a family, I have to at least pay for the food, which is something I cannot afford. But if my salary were higher I would visit the mall more frequently. (28-year-old male in the low-income group).

On the other hand, the endless stimulus to shop in the mall engenders daydreaming. The unreplied shopping stimuli might be expected to create a blasé attitude in the visitors,[22] but it seems that these stimuli are not a source of disturbance, but rather a source of daydreaming. What is dreamed of in front of the store windows is a future of upward social mobility, having a better life by means of the offered commodities. Therefore, even as the shopping mall experience reproduces the disadvantaged position of the visitor in the economic structure, it also creates a hopeful future dream as an escape from the pains of reality. The way in which daydreaming in the shopping mall serves as compensation for relative deprivation can be seen in the following words of a young security guard:

> While shopping around, I start dreaming. You inevitably dream about what you don't have. I ask myself whether I can have them, and whether I can have a better future. (25-year-old male in the low-income group).

Going to the shopping mall was described above as a respectable leisure activity for the lower-income groups. The respectable attribute of the activity is related to sharing the same place with people from high culture. The relatively democratic aspect of the quasi-public space of the shopping malls creates a new meeting point for different groups in the city life. Following the establishment of the republic, the public space was identified with the elite culture in Turkey.[23] Participating in the public space required knowledge and interest in the cultures of modernity, such as theatre, dance, and opera. Inevitably it has segregated the groups spatially with high cultural

---

[22] Georg Simmel, "The Metropolis and Mental Life," in *Simmel on Culture*, ed. David Frisby and Mike Featherstone (London: Sage Publications, 1997), 174-187.
[23] Feyzan Erkip, "The Shopping Mall as an Emergent Public Space in Turkey," *Environment and Planning* 35 (2003): 1076.

capital and lower cultural capital by decreasing encounters with the others to the lowest degree.[24] The shopping mall seems to destroy this spatial segregation by gathering all kinds of different groups under its roof. The common reference point for this meeting is not citizenship, but being a consumer. As consumers, both income groups gather in the quasi-public space of the shopping mall. In this relatively more democratic structure of the quasi-public space of the shopping malls, in order to keep up with the luxury decoration and the middle-class majority of the visitors, the body of the poor is reshaped, aestheticized. Thus, the emphasis placed on physical appearance comes not only from going out of the home but also from the contact with people of high culture. The impact of going to the mall on the body of the poor can be seen in the following statement by a young worker:

> For me, going to the mall is like appearing on the TV screen. I sometimes see TV stars, singers in the mall. I may even run into the prime minister in the mall. Therefore I care for my physical appearance; at least, I don't come without wearing makeup. (28-year-old female in the low-income group).

Although the youth of *gecekondu* areas see malls as part of their social life in the city, the older generations equate going to the mall with a thriftless activity, i.e., a waste of money. For the youth of *gecekondu* areas, their parents are strangers to the shopping malls. When the older generations of *gecekondu* areas visit the malls, they are uncomfortable. The fear of not being able to keep up with the other visitors seems to create shyness, which is the main source of the uneasiness that older generations of lower-income visitors experience at the malls. Traces of this pressure can be found in the following quotes by respondents:

> There are differences between me and my parents in terms of our social lives. For example, my parents do not visit the shopping mall. They have rarely been to these places. They fear the security measures and the shopping mall environment. (23-year-old male in the low-income group).

> My father gets angry when I visit the shopping malls. He thinks that malls are not places for us: they are for wealthy people. Their styles of dressing and speaking and their tastes are different from us, according to my father. (34-year-old male in the low-income group).

While explaining the flexible structure of contemporary capitalism, Richard Sennett argues that innovations in information technology put the

---

[24] Erkip, "The Shopping Mall as an Emergent Public Space in Turkey," 1078.

older generations at a disadvantage in the services sector.[25] In a similar way, shopping malls as the center of global life styles are visited more by the youth who can more easily follow the rapid changes in life styles. In consumer capitalism, identities are fluid. Consumer capitalism is an alien culture to older generations who want to maintain a consistent identity. When they visit the malls their behavior is passive, as if they feel excluded, even though the gate guards let them enter. In the luxurious aesthetic of the shopping mall, they feel themselves restricted. This can be seen as passive social exclusion, since it is not directly implemented by the policy makers of the shopping malls. The unfamiliar environment of the shopping malls alienates the older generations of rural migrants. It should not be forgotten, however, that shopping malls are only one of the spaces in which passive social exclusion can be seen. Following Bourdieu,[26] it can be argued that passive social exclusion can be seen to drive one out of one's own habitus.

For lower-income youngsters, however, shopping malls provide new encounters with modernity. Spending most of their time at home, which is identified with tradition, young generations make a sharp distinction between their leisure time in the mall and their family life. Thus, for them, shopping malls are the places where they escape from the traditional to the modern. Shopping malls also offer an escape from the pressures of family and school. This feature of the shopping malls makes them the most appropriate place for permissive gender relations. Especially for males, the mall is a runway for an endless fashion show full of beautiful girls. Some young men visit shopping malls only because the mall is seen as a place for matchmaking:

> In my first days in Ankara, I visited ANKAmall with my friends only to see beautiful girls. (25-year-old male in the low-income group).

> One of my friends found a girl friend at the shopping mall. The girl was a salesperson in one of the stores. For a period of time, we had visited the shopping mall only to see that girl. After our third visit to the store they started dating. (23-year-old male in the low-income group).

Simmel claimed that the aesthetical sphere is distinct from the everyday life.[27] In the shopping malls, however, this separation is annihilated. What

---

[25] Richard Sennett, *Karakter Aşınması* (İstanbul: Ayrıntı Yayınları, 2002).
[26] Pierre Bourdieu, *Distinction: A Social Critique of the Judgment of Taste* (Cambridge: Harvard University Press, 1984).
[27] Mike Featherstone, *Postmodernizm ve Tüketim Kültürü* (İstanbul: Ayrıntı Yayınları, 1996), 168.

is aesthetic is not only observed but also experienced in everyday life. This is what makes the shopping malls spectacular places. In the malls, the aesthetic coincides with the ordinary. In general, the aesthetic appearance is identified with female. In the shopping malls, that is, in the aesthetic spaces of everyday life, both genders are expected to pay attention to their physical appearance, and they feel the need to look smart and beautiful. The aesthetic environment in the shopping malls affects the physical appearance of males as much as females:

> I prepare myself as carefully before going to the shopping mall as a woman who is going to a restaurant for dinner. That is, I comb my hair, and wear a nice suit. (32-year-old male in the low-income group).

For middle-aged, lower-income families, visiting the shopping mall is similar to a touristic journey. This activity is seen as the responsibility of the main breadwinner, that is, the male head of household. Men are responsible for taking their wife and children out for this activity. The opportunity for a family to get together by visiting the shopping mall is a rare occasion. Lower-income families generally prefer to spend their leisure time by gardening. For most first-generation migrants, a leisure activity is something that creates the possibility of reproducing rural life in the city. Spending a whole day at the shopping mall is seen as waste of time and money. They prefer Kızılay, the downtown area for shopping; they tend to go to the malls for other activities. In their minds, Kızılay is the place where one fulfills fundamental needs, whereas the mall is the place to fulfill desires. For the family activities of lower-income groups the mall is the place where one can enjoy life as an entertainment center.

For middle-income groups, shopping malls are an inseparable part of city life. They visit the malls more frequently than other groups. They have the strongest relationship with the mall. This relationship is more visible in the everyday life of young professionals. They visit the mall even for lunch. For the consumption activities that are central to their identities, shopping malls are seen as places for self-realization. The atmosphere in the shopping malls is not strange to them; they are as comfortable at the mall as they are in their private spaces. For them, the mall is just a more orderly form of a shopping street. Therefore, going to the mall does not require special care with their physical appearance. In addition to the security, luxury design, and the decent character of the visitors, the mall is described as a necessity of modern life. As is clear in the following words of a housewife, malls are seen as a modernization of the shopping space in the city:

When I first came to Ankara, there were department stores such as Sümerbank and 19 Mayıs stores, then YKM followed them. After the opening of Atakule, new shopping malls replaced all of them. (46-year-old female in the middle-income group).

The act of shopping seems to be a leisure activity at the malls. In other words, shopping and leisure seem to coincide. For middle-income groups it is impossible to differentiate between shopping for and shopping around activities. They say that even when they do not intend to shop, they generally leave the mall with shopping bags in their hands. The main difference between the experience of middle-income groups and lower-income groups at the mall is the capability of purchasing. Therefore, the visitors from middle-income groups are economically more active at the mall. They can respond to the stimuli emanating from the stores. Especially for women, responding to those stimuli is seen as an ability, because for them shopping is a thrift. Knowledge about when to shop, where to shop, with which credit card to shop is seen as a skill and a kind of thriftiness. This new understanding of thriftiness reflects a change in the mentality of middle-income groups. According to this new way of thinking, spending lots of money for a commodity might actually be a thrifty investment because the commodity is branded and high quality, which practically means that it can be used for a long time with its sign value.

Like lower-income groups, middle-income groups sometimes visit the mall as a family. However, for middle-income families, the mall does not have to be experienced as a unit. The members of middle-income families pursue their tastes at the mall individually. While the wife might see the mall as a place to joyfully spend the whole day, the middle-income husband sees the mall as a functional place that allows him to save time while completing his shopping list. For middle-income families with children, the mall is a place for both children and adults. The mall eliminates the spatial separation between activities for children and adults, since both kinds of activities exist at the mall. This juxtaposition of different activities is both time-saving and convenient: it allows the adults to shop while the children play.

Similar to the relation between the flaneur and passages, a new social type emerges from the strong relation between malls and the middle-income group. Traveling among sensations and taking passages as an existential home, the flaneur was a key figure in understanding the urban experience of the 19th century Paris.[28] Retired middle-income women take shopping mall visits as a goal, browsing the mall from store to store and traveling

---

[28] Keith Tester, "Introduction," in *The Flaneur*, ed. Keith Tester (London: Routledge, 1994), 17.

among sensations embody a new form of flaneur experience. This strong relation does not just spring from the fact that retired women have both time and money to spend at the malls. Rather, this strong relation lies in the transformation of passive post-retirement life into active at the malls. The process after retirement is generally described as home confinement in which women are almost destined to watch TV. The mall experience, however, makes an important inversion in the condition of the subject. The passive subject of the private domain turns into an active observer of the shopping mall. First of all, the mall experience makes her into a woman of the crowd, like the flaneur of the 19th century. Therefore, for retired women, escaping from the boring atmosphere of home means strolling in the crowd at the mall or having a seat and watching the crowd of strolling people. The malls enable retired women, who might otherwise lead a passive life, to be more active outside the home. In this escape from home, the shopping malls become an existential home for retired women:

> I feel happier when I visit the shopping mall. I feel that there is life in here. When I stay at home, however, I am alone. I do not like watching TV all the time. When I come here I feel myself linked to life. (61-year-old female in the middle-income group).

> When I visit the mall, I believe that I am happier and more peaceful. I believe that I find here the pleasure of life. I live the happiness in here. Actually, I don't do many things in here, but at least I am away from the boring atmosphere of the home. I find here the power of life. This power comes from shopping or the possibility of shopping. (67-year-old female in the middle-income group).

This strong relation with the shopping mall turns the quasi-public space of the mall into a private space. Social activities that were identified with the home, such as family and neighborhood gatherings, are now held at malls. A similar impact on social relations has been observed among housewives in relatively small Anatolian cities.[29] However, my research indicates that it is retired women whose social lives are most affected by malls. For example, the chores of preparing to entertain guests in the home are eliminated when the social gathering occurs at the mall. Therefore, what is presented to guests at a mall gathering is not homemade but mall-made:

---

[29] *Kayseri Park 2 ayda 650.000 ziyaretçi çekti*, www.referansgazetesi.com, accessed 10 August 2006.

> I have not seen my sisters for three months. Two days later, we will meet here for lunch, and then we will go to the cinema. Before leaving, we will chat by sitting in one of the cafes. (61-year-old female in the middle-income group).

For upper-income groups, malls are generally visited for shopping activities. Therefore, activities in the mall are need-centered. However, the term need is not used here in its biological meaning. In other words, desires are among the needs for upper-income groups; luxury and branded commodities are among their needs. Their thrift mentality is based on time. Therefore, the middle-income groups' motto "the best quality for the best price" is not valid for them. Their motto is rather "time is money." For them, the chore of browsing the stores and comparing prices takes too much time. They tend to make quick visits to their regular stores at the mall, and if they like something, they purchase it without hesitating. For upper-income groups, the mall is not such an enchanted place. The more their number increases, the more they are disenchanted. The longer the new malls are open, the clearer it is that the mall has a standardized structure. As a chief executive of a firm expresses the same architectural features, the same stores, the same cafes, and the same restaurants are the sources of standardization, that is, disenchantment:

> I have a friend from the U.S. who admires visiting malls. But it seems boring to me because it is hard to find individual differences among malls. All of them have the same stores. There is nothing distinct about the shopping malls. (45-year-old male in the upper-income group).

This similarity of the malls, however, changes when the visitor profile of each mall is taken into account. Although they generally accept the mall visitors as decent, they add that they are more comfortable with the visitors of suburban malls, such as the Bilkent Shopping Center. They seem displeased to see the strict borders disappear between themselves and the lower classes. They see this annihilation as a degeneration of culture. For them, the emergent culture in the malls is a fake culture. Thus, going to the mall is not a respectable experience that requires special preparation. Rather, for them, malls are a place where averse confrontations might be staged. As a high-level expert expresses, there is the possibility of conflict when you meet others at the mall:

> After my sister gave birth we went to the mall. Because we had a stroller, we wanted to use the elevator. But we had to have a quarrel to get in because the

people who can go up with moving stairs got in the elevator before us. Now, I also have children, but I fear to go to the mall because of the possibility of conflicts with the others. (34-year-old female in the upper-income group).

For upper-income groups, the shopping mall is not a place to have a good time by escaping the hubbub of the city. The mall itself is also to be escaped. For them, the destination for escape from the city has become fundamentally a suburb. The upper-income groups visit the malls more frequently. They just pop in to shop on their way home from work. The malls are a brief stop between home and work a place for meeting their needs, which are mixed with desires.

Conclusion

In less than 20 years, shopping malls have become part of urban life for almost all sections of the population in Ankara. This has to do with the unique aspects of shopping malls: the juxtaposition of different commodities, services, stores, and the annihilation of the borders between luxury and ordinary, between aesthetic and mundane. As such, the shopping malls have become enchanted places for the residents of Ankara. The shopping mall experience transforms urban everyday life into the spectacular for different segments of the population. However, the magic of the mall is not experienced equally. It appears that the higher the individual's income, the more disenchanted the shopping malls become. While the shopping mall experiences of low-income visitors are extraordinary, for high-income individuals, the malls are ordinary aspects of the urban life. It seems that the inequalities in the relations of production have an impact on how people experience the shopping mall. This study also shows that the transformations in the field of consumption can be better observed in relation to other fields. Therefore, the enchantment of the shopping malls can be seen as the product of intersections of different networks of social relations.

Bibliography

"Ankara'da AVM Sayısı İkiye Katlandı." *Hürriyet* (www.hurriyet.com.tr/, accessed 24 April 2007).
Backes, Nancy. "Reading the Shopping Mall City." *Journal of Popular Culture* 31, no. 3 (1997): 1–17.
Bocock, Robert. *Tüketim*. Ankara: Dost Kitabevi Yayınları, 1997.

Bourdieu, Pierre. *Distinction: A Social Critique of the Judgment of Taste*. Cambridge: Harvard University Press, 1984.
Campbell, Colin. *The Romantic Ethic and the Spirit of Modern Consumerism*. Oxford: Blackwell Publishers, 1987.
Erkip, Feyzan. "The Shopping Mall as an Emergent Public Space in Turkey." *Environment and Planning* 35 (2003): 1073–1093.
Faroqhi, Suraiya. "Research on the History of Ottoman Consumption: A Preliminary Exploration of Sources and Models." In *Consumption Studies and the History of the Ottoman Empire 1550–1922: An Introduction*, edited by Donald Quataert, 15–45. New York: State University of New York Press, 2000.
Featherstone, Mike. *Postmodernizm ve Tüketim Kültürü*. İstanbul: Ayrıntı Yayınları, 1996.
Frierson, Elizabeth B. "Cheap and Easy: The Creation of Consumer Culture in Late Ottoman Society." In *Consumption Studies and the History of the Ottoman Empire 1550–1922: An Introduction*, edited by Donald Quataert, 261–289. New York: State University of New York Press, 2000.
Gottdiener, Mark. *Postmodern Göstergeler*. Ankara: İmge Kitabevi, 2005.
Helten, Frank, and Bernd Fischer. *Video Surveillance on Demand for Various Purposes? Berlin Shopping Malls as Socio-Technical Testbeds for CCTV*. RTD-Project, 5th Framework Programme for European Commision, 2003.
Jacobs, Jane *The Death and Life of Great American Cities*, chap. The Uses of Sidewalks: Safety, 55–73. New York: The Random House, 1969.
Kayseri Park 2 ayda 650.000 ziyaretçi çekti. www.referansgazetesi.com, accessed 10 August 2006.
Liecthy, Mark. *Suitably Modern: Making Middle-Class Culture in a New Consumer Culture*. Princeton: Princeton University Press, 2003.
Mardin, Şerif. "Tanzimat'tan Sonra Aşırı Batılılaşma." In *Türk Modernleşmesi*, edited by M. Türköne and T. Önder, 21–81. İstanbul: İletişim Yayınları, 1991.
Nelson, Eric. *The Mall of America: Reflections of a Virtual Community*. Minnesota: Galde Press, 1998.
Pamuk, Orhan. *Cevdet Bey ve Oğulları*. İstanbul: İletişim Yayınları, 2007.
Ritzer, George. *Büyüsü Bozulmuş Dünyayı Büyülemek*. İstanbul: Ayrıntı Yayınları, 2000.
———. *Explorations in the Sociology of Consumption: Fast Food, Credit Cards, and Casinos*. London: Sage Publications, 2001.
Sennett, Richard. *Karakter Aşınması*. İstanbul: Ayrıntı Yayınları, 2002.

Simmel, Georg. "The Metropolis and Mental Life." In *Simmel on Culture*, edited by David Frisby and Mike Featherstone, 174–187. London: Sage Publications, 1997.

Southworth, Michael. "Reinventing Main Street: From Mall to Townscape Mall." *Journal of Urban Design* 10, no. 2 (2005): 151–170.

Tester, Keith. "Introduction." In *The Flaneur*, edited by Keith Tester, 1–22. London: Routledge, 1994.

Weber, Max. *Protestan Ahlakı ve Kapitalizmin Ruhu*. İstanbul: Ayraç Yayınları, 2003.

CHAPTER FOUR

BETWEEN EAST AND WEST: CONSUMER CULTURE AND IDENTITY NEGOTIATION IN CONTEMPORARY TURKEY

TANFER EMIN TUNÇ

A product of the postmodern world, the shopping mall is a socially-constructed *simulacrum*, a synthetic, technology-driven "copy for which there is no original, emptily duplicating itself to infinity ... [not] referr[ing] back to any standard measure or first instance, because it already contains all the information needed for its own replication."[1] Visit a mall in any major city across the globe and you will encounter clones of the same climate-controlled shops, fast-food restaurants, public facilities (courtyards, restrooms, parking lots), "exotic" foliage (palm trees and delicate flowers that could never survive outdoors), and architectural elements (steel beams, marble floors, and miles of glass and smoked mirrors). Yet, despite this seemingly aesthetic uniformity, as liminal, fluid, and anonymous microcities, shopping malls can be considered a significant locus of the postmodern culture wars. If, as Jon Goss contends, "you are what you buy," then malls become the ultimate planned fantasy spaces, or pseudo-communities, for the negotiation and performance of cultural identity.[2]

As a secular Muslim nation that eludes categorization—part of Europe and Asia, but somehow not comfortable with the socially constructed label "Eurasian"; bordered by the Mediterranean Sea, but somehow not "Mediterranean"; contiguous with the Middle East, but not "Middle Eastern"—Turkey, with its ever-increasing number of shopping malls, is currently engaging in its own identity negotiation. Occupying a liminal space between their

---

[1] Steven Shaviro, *Doom Patrols: A Theoretical Fiction About Postmodernism* (London: Serpent's Tail, 1997), 103; Jean Baudrillard, *Simulations* (New York: Semiotext(e), 1983), 11.
[2] J. Goss, "The Magic of the Mall," *Annals of the Association of American Geographers* 83, no. 1 (1993): 20.

Eastern heritage and the elusive/alluring "modernity" of the West, Turks have used material symbols, political strategies, and their agency as consumers to construct new globalized identities. Turkish shopping malls, with their focus on cosmopolitanism through consumption, have become a significant landscape for the refashioning of personal representations. Not only have the transactional/transnational terrains of malls allowed Turks to attribute individual meaning to their lives and lived environments, but they have also facilitated the construction of a new hybrid, interactive Turkish identity which equates "modernity" with the sophistication of mass consumption, globalization, and the commodification of national iconography.

Deconstructing the Mall: Theoretical and Methodological Framework

According to Foucault, there are two types of social spaces: utopias and heterotopias. "Utopias are sites with no real place ... They present society itself in a perfected form ... [and] are fundamentally unreal spaces." Heterotopias, on the other hand, are "real places that do exist ... [but] are countersites, a kind of effectively enacted utopia in which the real sites ... [of culture] are simultaneously represented, contested, and inverted."[3] Malls are both of these sites at once because they "appear to be everything that they are not. [They] contrive to be public, civic places even though [they] are private and run for profit. [Moreover, they] offer a place to commune and recreate, while seeking retail [revenues]. [The mall is thus] a representation of space masquerading as representational space; that is, a space conceptualized, scientifically planned, and realized through strict technical control, pretending to be a space imaginatively created by its inhabitants."[4] It is a landscape where the *utopia* of progress and the *dystopia* of alienation and domination have converged into a *heterotopic* countersite of postmodern iconography, which clearly complicates the extent to which politically meaningful identity negotiation can actually transpire within its walls.[5]

French Situationist theorist Guy Debord has addressed the problem of attempting to construct an "authentic" socio-political identity in an "inauthentic" space by contextualizing shopping malls within the "society of the spectacle."[6] According to Debord, the "society of the spectacle" is one in

---

[3] Michel Foucault, "Of Other Spaces," in *The Visual Culture Reader*, ed. Nicholas Mirzoeff (London: Routledge, 1999), 239.

[4] Goss, "The Magic of the Mall," 40.

[5] Steven Best and Douglas Kellner, *Debord and the Postmodern Turn: New Stages of the Spectacle*, http://www.gseis.ucla.edu/faculty/kellner/essays/debordpostmodernturn.pdf, accessed 21 May 2009, 4–5; Foucault, "Of Other Spaces," 239.

[6] Guy Debord, *Society of the Spectacle* (Oakland: AK Press, 2006).

which the state of *being* has been transformed into *having* (i.e., materialism) or merely "appearing to have." In this society, the authenticity of *being* has been replaced with a *representational, or semiotic, image* of life—one which is mediated not only through commodities—i.e., material objects—but also the technologies that sustain them. In the "spectacular" society, relations between material objects (symbols/images) have replaced human interaction, and passive recognition of the spectacle—i.e., through conspicuous consumption, and/or engaging with the technologies of the shopping venue—and the creation of alternate "situations," substitute for authentic social activity.[7]

The epistemological approach of socio-semiotics is particularly useful in analyzing "spectacular societies" such as malls because it prioritizes objects in their "everyday" environments—i.e., how they are used, and how they contribute to and/or shape their social systems—while simultaneously exposing the three layers of representation that connect objects and identity formation: the physical, mental, and the implied. Socio-semiotics considers what objects represent physically; what they signify psychologically, culturally, and politically; and what they connote, or suggest, subliminally.[8] This analytic framework is also significant because it allows for the negotiation of culture, and embraces the reality that that all knowledge is contextual, reflexive, and often the result of "lived" experiences.[9] That is, "meaning is constructed through a creative process in which the participant observer refers to the myths and metaphors of his or her own culture."[10] What emerges from this process is the redefinition of identity as a complex and contradictory set of terms operating on several simultaneous, intersecting levels: the local, the national and the global.

Consumer Culture in the Turkish Context

Enclosed shopping complexes are a relatively new addition to the Turkish landscape.[11] The first mall in Turkey's capital, Ankara, was Atakule,

---

[7] Best and Kellner, *Debord and the Postmodern Turn: New Stages of the Spectacle*, 12.

[8] Mark Gottdiener, *Postmodern Semiotics: Material Culture and the Forms of Postmodern Life* (London: Blackwell, 1995).

[9] Phillip Vannini, "Social Semiotics and Fieldwork: Method and Analytics," *Qualitative Inquiry* 13, no. 1 (2007): 119–121.

[10] Roberta Gilchrist, *Gender and Material Culture* (London: Routledge, 1994), 17.

[11] Parts of this chapter were taken from: Tanfer Emin Tunç, "Technologies of Consumption: The Social Semiotics of Turkish Shopping Malls," in *Material Culture and Technology in Everyday Life: Ethnographic Approaches*, ed. Phillip Vannini (New York: Peter Lang, 2009), 131–143. Used with permission.

which was built in 1989 and resembles the Seattle Space Needle in structure. Atakule was followed by Karum, a more traditional shopping center, which was completed in 1991.[12] Since the mid-1990s, malls have been built in rapid succession in Turkey. Currently, about half a dozen new shopping centers are under construction in Ankara alone, and many, such as the recently completed Forum, are vying to become not only the largest mall in Turkey, but also the largest mall in Europe.[13]

Others, such as Ankara's Armada, named after the Spanish fleet and shaped like a ship, and Istanbul's Kanyon, which resembles a canyon, have not pursued quantity of space, but rather quality of design. In fact, in 2004, the International Council of Shopping Centers (ICSC) voted Armada Europe's best new shopping mall under 35,000 square meters.[14] This award, which is prominently displayed in Armada's corporate office located in the adjacent office tower, is a constant reminder that even if "Europeanness" cannot be achieved through political negotiation, it can at least be acquired vicariously through the architecture of conspicuous consumption.

Despite Turkey's low per capita income compared to North America and Europe, Turks are becoming increasingly obsessed with the "malling" phenomenon. There are two driving forces behind this trend. The first is environmental; the second social. As Erkip has illustrated, the "contrived spaces of the shopping mall" contrast greatly with the "incivility of the [Turkish] city street."[15] This incivility is multilayered, and ranges from dangerously-cracked or missing sidewalks, to death-trap crosswalks, careless motorists, panhandlers, muggers, pushy pedestrians, and non-existent parking facilities. Malls offer "one-stop shopping": all "needs" can be acquired in the same location. Very little walking is required in the mall; instead, technologies, such as elevators and escalators, have replaced our feet.[16] Thus, with its "pristine," monitored environment, the mall provides an escape from the

---

[12] Feyzan Erkip, "The Rise of the Shopping Mall in Turkey," *Cities* 22, no. 2 (2005): 93.

[13] Cevahir, which is a 420,000 square meter mall located in Istanbul, contends that it is Europe's largest mall. However, this is contested by Cevahir's competitors, as an Internet search of "largest mall in Europe" reveals. One of the new players in the size wars—and certainly not the last—is London's Westfield Shopping Centre. Cf. Emil 2009 Pocock, *American Studies at Eastern Connecticut State University, Shopping Mall and Shopping Center Studies, World's Largest Shopping Malls*, http://nutmeg.easternct.edu/~pocock/MallsWorld.htm, accessed 21 May 2009.

[14] For more information, please see: http://www.icsc.org/srch/education/awards/EuroAward04F/edu_euro_awards.php (accessed May 21, 2009.)

[15] Erkip, "The Rise of the Shopping Mall in Turkey," 91.

[16] Mark Gottdiener, *New Forms of Consumption: Consumers, Culture, and Commodification* (Lanham, MD: Rowman / Littlefield, 2000), 276.

monotony of everyday life and the troubling quotidian realities of the Turkish city.

Over the past two decades, Turks have sought to recreate their personal and political identities through conspicuous consumption. The mall has become a key liminal space where, on a daily basis, Turkish identity and individuality are being performed, negotiated, hybridized, and repackaged as "European" modernity—a landscape where personal freedom has become equated with free enterprise and consumer choice. As Marianne Conroy has elucidated, "the shopping mall [has become the] premier site for the making of postmodern subjectivity—where boundaries between high and low culture are effaced, where commodities and consumer desire determine the organization of public space and the form of social exchange and, above all, where simulated experiences attenuate historical and temporal consciousness."[17] İsmail Acar's mural at Ankara's Cepa shopping mall, entitled *Büyük Türkiye Resmi* ("Big Picture of Turkey"), is a clear visual representation of the postmodern subjective negotiation that is currently under way in Turkey. A collage of traditionalism and modernity, this whirlwind of images includes not only *historical* scenes from Turkey's past (the Byzantine, Seljuk, and Ottoman Empires, and World War I), but also *temporal* cultural symbols such as the evil eye amulet, whirling dervishes, and Turkish tile patterns. The mural's "Western" symbolism—i.e., skyscrapers, airplanes, and alluring, sexualized, women—reminds consumers that their identity as "modern" Turks is comprised of both their nationalist past and their globalized future.

At Cepa and other malls around the country, personal identity has thus become equated with the commodification of national iconography and the sophistication of globalized mass consumption. The European Union flag—which is meant to symbolize Turkey's future as part of the global community—is commonly used as a semiotic marketing strategy to sell Turkish consumers the "prestigious"—and often useless—objects of a modern "refined" lifestyle: bagless vacuum cleaners, air purifiers, humidifiers, garbage compactors, waffle makers, and HDTV LCD televisions.[18] Even though many Turkish consumers realize that some of these products are unnecessary, they believe it is their prerogative as 21st century consumers to acquire these goods. The rationale is that the purchase of such consumer "fetish commodities" will automatically render Turkish consumers both "happy and healthy" and tastefully "in touch" with the culture of the outside world—in other

---

[17] Marianne Conroy, "Discount Dreams: Factory Outlet Malls, Consumption, and the Performance of Middle-Class Identity," *Social Text* 54 (1998): 63.

[18] Turkey has only recently begun to broadcast high definition programming, and the few channels that broadcast in HD can only be viewed through pricey satellite subscriptions.

78   Chapter Four

Figure 4.1: İsmail Acar's mural at Ankara's Cepa shopping mall, *Büyük Türkiye Resmi* ("Big Picture of Turkey")

words, ready for membership in the EU.[19] However, as Arjun Appadurai has noted, such material objects have not facilitated the construction of a global consumer identity, but have rather contributed to the formation of liminal "queer nationalities" based on internationally available goods which have no local meaning.[20] The reality is that many—especially working-class—Turks still do not know what waffles are, and/or do not have access to HD programming. Those Turkish consumers who are able to purchase, and use, such fetish commodities—i.e., members of the upwardly mobile middle-class—are thus automatically more cosmopolitan, more sophisticated, and more "global" than those who cannot.

One prominent material consumer object that has played a major role in the transformation of modern Turkish identity is the diamond solitaire engagement ring. Formerly a status symbol of the wealthy, the solitaire now, thanks to a massive media campaign by De Beers' Diamond Trading Company (DTC) and the 2006 song "Pırlanta" ("Diamond") by Turkish pop singer Nil Karaibrahimgil, has been embraced by the new emerging middle

[19] Henri Lefebvre, *The Social Production of Space* (London: Blackwell, 1991).
[20] Arjun Appadurai, *Modernity at Large: Cultural Dimensions of Globalization* (Minneapolis: University of Minnesota Press, 1996), 169–171.

class, and as a result, can be found in every mall jewelry shop. By responding to De Beers' world-renowned sales pitch *Pırlanta Sonsuza Kadar* ("A Diamond Is Forever"), Turkish women have become active participants in the formation of an urban consumer-based identity based on material symbols.[21] Traditionally, Turkish engagements were symbolically represented through the exchange of gold bands. However, since De Beers' marketing campaign began in the mid-1990s, the solitaire has become a marital prerequisite, as well as an expression of empowered individuality. The solitaire diamond ring not only defines middle-class Turkish women as "modern and liberated," but also characterizes their class position as being "above the masses." It functions as a material symbol of what C. Wright Mills termed "status panic," "wherein members of the new middle classes come increasingly to depend on the goods they consume to express their claims to social prestige and to enforce status distinctions leveled by income."[22]

For many members of the Turkish middle class, however, purchasing a diamond ring still remains a major financial investment—a proverbial "price" they have to pay for modernity. Since wages are low in Turkey—in January 2009, the salary for an entry-level "middle-class" government employee was set at around 1,200 Turkish Liras, or 550 Euros, a month—under normal circumstances, the average middle-class full-time employee would not be able to afford a diamond solitaire ring, which usually costs thousands of lira.[23] However, an artificial mechanism designed by vendors and credit card companies to "democratize consumption"—the *Taksit* system—has allowed them to indulge in material possessions previously limited to the wealthy. This payment installation plan (which can last anywhere from 6 to 24 months) facilitates both the acquisition of goods (sometimes luxury items, but mostly basic necessities like food and clothing), as well as the impersonation of class positions beyond actual income levels—i.e., social mobility, at least materialistically.

While buying on credit is nothing new in the West, what has to be kept in mind is that the prices of these goods are, due to heavy import taxes, usually double and sometimes even triple what they would cost in the United States or Europe. When coupled with low wages, "Keeping up with the [Global] Joneses" transforms from being an expression of personal identity into be-

---

[21] For more information on DTC's campaign in Turkey, see: http://arsiv.sabah.com.tr/2005/09/26/gny/gny104-20050926-200.html and http://hurarsiv.hurriyet.com.tr/goster/haber.aspx?id=4253716&yazarid=20 (accessed May 21, 2009).

[22] C. Wright Mills, *White Collar: The American Middle Classes* (New York: Oxford University Press, 1951), 74–75.

[23] For more information about government salaries, see: http://www.memurlar.net/haber/128521 (accessed May 21, 2009).

ing a perpetual cycle of "earn, spend, and accumulate debt." Despite the obvious mentality of consumption created by this system—as customers are reminded, "you can always pay in installments"—very few Turks complain, or seem to worry about the fact that they will be paying for products, such as perfume and cosmetics, long after they have been consumed. On the contrary, they perceive it to be a beneficial extension of the private enterprise system which increases—not decreases—their agency as consumers by facilitating the acquisition of previously inaccessible goods.

While the same phenomenon is clearly occurring in the United States but on a larger scale, the difference with the Turkish context is that Turkey, for the *first time in history*, has voluntarily become a nation of debtors. Until the 1990s, Turkey was a cash-based society—credit cards entered the market in 1988, about 40 years after the United States and Western Europe.[24] They did not become widespread, however, until about 10 years ago when restrictions on credit card issuance were eased. The response was a flood of purchases—and then of suicides—when credit card debts could not be paid. These suicides eventually subsided when laws were passed declaring that credit card debt could be inherited by spouses and children—i.e., the recipients of the deceased's estate. These same laws made filing personal bankruptcy to avoid payment almost impossible (a common loophole used in the United States to escape debt).[25] However, the new credit card laws did not put an end to the spending, which has become so irrational in some cases that a new reality show—Kanal Türk's "Krizdeyiz"—was developed to help guide offenders through their debt. Nevertheless, many Turks perceive credit cards and the *Taksit* system as their way of entering the world of global cosmopolitanism, albeit at potentially great personal cost, and are reluctant to critique the socio-economic incongruencies on which it rests. The ultimate message is that if one cannot achieve social-economic equality in the outside world, purchasing material goods offered at the mall can, at least temporarily, provide some semblance of egalitarianism and sophistication.

Semiotic Fetishism in the Turkish Mall

In consumer spaces such as malls, historic symbols are often idealized and repackaged: complex political events are replaced with stylized images, and pithy poetic quotes often substitute for meaningful introspection. As Jon Goss contends, music, art, and other forms of personal expression "become

---

[24] For a history of Turkey's first credit card, see: http://www.haberler.com/turkiye-nin-ilk-kredi-karti-15-yasinda-haberi/ (accessed May 21, 2009).

[25] Credit card laws have become a very hot topic on Turkish legal blogs. See, for example, http://www.hukuki.net/forum/showthread.php?t=20654 (accessed May 21, 2009).

fetishized in the retail setting because they are extracted from their 'natural' settings and 'dropped' into a space that is misaligned," oftentimes, with the intended messages of the creators.[26] One example of this was the Mevlana display at ANKAmall, which, at 300,000 square meters in total area, is competing with Forum for the distinction of being Ankara's "largest shopping mall." A hybrid of the words "Ankara" and "mall," ANKAmall is yet another monument to the cultural negotiation that is occurring in modern-day Turkey. Even its name, which was challenged in court by the Turkish Language Association (*Türk Dil Kurumu*) for not being "Turkish," has proven to be controversial.[27]

Figure 4.2: The Mevlana display at Antares, Ankara

The November 2007 display, with its stylized whirling dervishes and creative use of natural lighting, was designed to commemorate the 800th anniversary of the birth of Mevlana Rumi, a 13th Anatolian philosopher who wrote extensively about the emptiness of materialism, and the virtues of love, compassion, and humanity. The exhibit, which was meant to be a

---
[26] Goss, "The Magic of the Mall," 38.
[27] Hasan Aydemir and Pınar Acar, "ANKAmall ismi Türk Dil Kurumu'nu kızdırdı," *Zaman* (2006, http://www.zaman.com.tr/haber.do?haberno=292691&keyfield=414E4B416D616C6C, accessed 21 May 2009).

monument to Rumi's teachings and a social commentary on the nature of consumer identity in the age of globalization, became a sideshow spectacle. Rather than thinking introspectively about Rumi's ascetic message, shoppers snickered at the irony of a translucent multi-colored placard bearing Rumi's famous quote: *Ey altın sırmalarla süslü elbiseler giymeye, kemer takmaya alışmış kişi. Sonunda sana da dikişsiz elbiseyi giydirecekler'* ("Beware you who have grown accustomed to wearing clothing adorned with golden cords and belts! In the end, they will clothe you in a seamless shroud.") Mall visitors were amused and entertained by the display, but as observed rarely spent more than a few minutes interpreting the exhibit. Most continued to shop for the material articles critiqued by Rumi, and no visible effort was made—either by journalists or the laity—to examine the fundamental driving forces behind Turkish consumer culture, or the ways in which national and spiritual symbols are being negotiated and repackaged as markers of global sophistication—i.e., "Art, a mystified quality of high culture"—in the retail setting.[28]

The artwork and food courts found in Turkish malls are crucial in the assessment of identity formation in the retail setting because they serve as stages upon which the struggles between nationalism and internationalism are enacted. In order to be "all things to all people," Turkish food courts attempt to simulate a whole range of "international" culinary experiences that will appear non-threatening to their desired middle-class and foreign clientele.[29] In addition to the expected Turkish establishments, almost all food courts include a Burger King, McDonald's, Kentucky Fried Chicken, a generic Mexican restaurant, a Dominos or Pizza Hut, a Starbucks or Dunkin' Donuts, a baked potato stand, a deli-type sandwich vendor, and a salad bar. Because "foreign" fast food is usually double, and sometimes even triple, the cost of the local cuisine, eating KFC, or drinking a cappuccino from Starbucks—which costs just as much as a complete Turkish fast food meal—is not only part of the "modern" shopping and entertainment experience, but also a technique, or strategy, used by many Turks to distinguish class status through consumption.

Strolling through the mall with a Frappuccino in hand has become just as important as making purchases from Laura Ashley, Marks & Spencer's, or Sephora, because, as Jon Chase has elucidated, the symbolic value ascribed to prestige products often exceeds their material value. In other words, "the act of acquiring the product and the associations of the product's advertising and marketing [have] become ... more [significant] than the product

---

[28] Goss, "The Magic of the Mall," 38.
[29] Jonathan Sterne, "Sounds Like the Mall of America: Programmed Music and the Architectonics of Commercial Space," *Ethnomusicology* 41 (1997): 27.

Figure 4.3: Glimpse of a food court

itself."[30] Products emblazoned with English words are arguably the most potent consumer fetishes in Turkey because they "signal modernism and internationalism ... the *denotative* meaning attached to the words is often secondary. What is more important is an appreciation of the language's implicit, symbolic, [*connotative*] meaning."[31] In this context, consumer identity becomes an exercise in instant semiotic recognition: a Turkish shopper sporting clothing purchased from a high-end, foreign retailer—usually emblazoned with a distinctive monogram—is automatically assumed by onlookers to possess an "elite" socio-economic position.

As Jon Goss contends, nature is also an important factor in the negotiation of consumer identity in the built retail setting because it signifies the "final frontier" of the postmodern globalized world. The foliage (shrubs, topiaries, and plants), water (fountains, streams, and ponds), and specialized

---

[30] John Chase, "The Role of Consumerism in American Architecture," *Journal of Architectural Education* 44 (1991): 211-212.

[31] Dana Alden, Jan-Benedict Steenkamp, and Rajeev Batra, "Brand Positioning Through Advertising in Asia, North America, and Europe: The Role of Global Consumer Culture," *Journal of Marketing* 63 (1999): 77.

lighting (fiber optics, chandeliers, and skylights) of the mall not only create a mood of civilized adventure, adding excitement to the mechanized activity of shopping, but also substitute for exotic, cosmopolitan locales that are usually inaccessible to the average consumer.[32] In the Turkish built retail environment, architects and interior designers frequently manipulate "nature" and employ contrived exotic themes (such as the "nautical traveler" style) in an attempt to signify Western modernity and sophistication. Turkish malls can be shaped like boats (e.g., Armada), include maritime symbols (such as anchors, compasses, clouds, and sails), or be themed around escapist locales (e.g., Istanbul's Kanyon, with its sloping "canyon-esque" walls, or Ankara's Mina Sera, with its Italian Palazzo design). Thus, in Turkish malls, the "natural outdoors" is a *multipurpose* technique designed to attract shoppers, exoticize the mundane task of consumption, and redefine consumer identity.

Ankara's Panora, whose slogan is "Alişverişin Doğası" ("The Nature of Shopping"), is constructed around this semiotic strategy. Not only is the mall surrounded by lush gardens (which in Ankara's dry climate is truly a luxury), but it also houses two aquariums, complete with baby sharks. Moreover, Panora features a gigantic floor mosaic of 16th-century Ottoman admiral and cartographer Piri Reis' famous premodern world map, complete with wooden sailboats and an overhead illuminated glass dome, which, from the mall's exterior, resembles Epcot Center's "Golf Ball" structure. The use of such a theme not only suggests the possibility of traveling abroad and broadening one's horizons, at least vicariously, but also implies that those who consume the "lifestyle" signified by mall products will become instant members of the global network of modernity.[33] Thus, in the built retail setting, "artificial" nature functions as an appropriate strategy for the construction of an elusive, consumer-based, cosmopolitan identity. If Turks cannot assert themselves in the international arena politically, at least they can assert themselves materially in shopping malls by purchasing symbolic representations of worldly sophistication.

As this study has illustrated, consumption "serves not only to communicate one's self image to others, but also to reinforce it to oneself."[34] For fleeting moments in malls, Turkish consumers can construct substitute identities, and act out hidden parts of their egos by purchasing symbols repre-

---

[32] Goss, "The Magic of the Mall," 36.

[33] Most Turks never leave Turkey because only members of the upper-middle and upper classes can afford to travel abroad; a five-year passport, for example, costs approximately 250 Euros, which is, based on per capita income research conducted by the World Bank, the most expensive passport in the world. Cf. http://www.objektifhaber.com/yeni/objhab/default.aspx?id=2033033792 (accessed May 21, 2009).

[34] Kjell Arne Brekke and Richard B. Howarth, "The Social Contingency of Wants," *Land Economics* 76 (2000): 497.

senting their secret hopes and subconscious desires.[35] Standing between the ephemeral and concrete, the "mundane and exotic," the "local and global," and the East and the West, the Turkish mall has become the perfect space to perform cultural identity and construct personal representations, specifically because it is a place of "liminality ... a state between social stations, a transitional moment in which established rules and norms are temporarily suspended."[36] In Turkey, the mall is both a semiotic terrain used by retailers to market their goods, and a vehicle for the expression of modernity through the sophistication of mass consumption, globalization, and the commodification of national iconography. Not only have the transactional/transnational terrains of malls allowed Turks to attribute individual meaning to their lives and lived environments, but they have also facilitated the construction of a new hybrid, interactive Turkish identity which incorporates the old with the new, and reworks traditional elements to create personal representations through "cosmopolitan" enactments of consumption.

Bibliography

Alden, Dana, Jan-Benedict Steenkamp, and Rajeev Batra. "Brand Positioning Through Advertising in Asia, North America, and Europe: The Role of Global Consumer Culture." *Journal of Marketing* 63 (1999): 75–87.
Appadurai, Arjun. *Modernity at Large: Cultural Dimensions of Globalization*. Minneapolis: University of Minnesota Press, 1996.
Aydemir, Hasan, and Pınar Acar. "ANKAmall ismi Türk Dil Kurumu'nu kızdırdı." *Zaman* (2006, http://www.zaman.com.tr/haber.do?haberno= 292691&keyfield=414E4B416D616C6C, accessed 21 May 2009).
Baudrillard, Jean. *Simulations*. New York: Semiotext(e), 1983.
Best, Steven, and Douglas Kellner. *Debord and the Postmodern Turn: New Stages of the Spectacle*. http://www.gseis.ucla.edu/faculty/kellner/ essays/debordpostmodernturn.pdf, accessed 21 May 2009.
Brekke, Kjell Arne, and Richard B. Howarth. "The Social Contingency of Wants." *Land Economics* 76 (2000): 493–503.
Chase, John. "The Role of Consumerism in American Architecture." *Journal of Architectural Education* 44 (1991): 211–224.

---

[35] Chase, "The Role of Consumerism in American Architecture," 212.
[36] Goss, "The Magic of the Mall," 27.

Conroy, Marianne. "Discount Dreams: Factory Outlet Malls, Consumption, and the Performance of Middle-Class Identity." *Social Text* 54 (1998): 63–83.
Debord, Guy. *Society of the Spectacle*. Oakland: AK Press, 2006.
Erkip, Feyzan. "The Rise of the Shopping Mall in Turkey." *Cities* 22, no. 2 (2005): 89–108.
Foucault, Michel. "Of Other Spaces." In *The Visual Culture Reader*, edited by Nicholas Mirzoeff, 229–236. London: Routledge, 1999.
Gilchrist, Roberta. *Gender and Material Culture*. London: Routledge, 1994.
Goss, J. "The Magic of the Mall." *Annals of the Association of American Geographers* 83, no. 1 (1993): 18–47.
Gottdiener, Mark. *New Forms of Consumption: Consumers, Culture, and Commodification*. Lanham, MD: Rowman / Littlefield, 2000.
———. *Postmodern Semiotics: Material Culture and the Forms of Postmodern Life*. London: Blackwell, 1995.
Lefebvre, Henri. *The Social Production of Space*. London: Blackwell, 1991.
Mills, C. Wright. *White Collar: The American Middle Classes*. New York: Oxford University Press, 1951.
Pocock, Emil 2009. *American Studies at Eastern Connecticut State University, Shopping Mall and Shopping Center Studies, World's Largest Shopping Malls*. http://nutmeg.easternct.edu/~pocock/MallsWorld.htm, accessed 21 May 2009.
Shaviro, Steven. *Doom Patrols: A Theoretical Fiction About Postmodernism*. London: Serpent's Tail, 1997.
Sterne, Jonathan. "Sounds Like the Mall of America: Programmed Music and the Architectonics of Commercial Space." *Ethnomusicology* 41 (1997): 22–50.
Tunç, Tanfer Emin. "Technologies of Consumption: The Social Semiotics of Turkish Shopping Malls." In *Material Culture and Technology in Everyday Life: Ethnographic Approaches*, edited by Phillip Vannini, 131–143. New York: Peter Lang, 2009.
Vannini, Phillip. "Social Semiotics and Fieldwork: Method and Analytics." *Qualitative Inquiry* 13, no. 1 (2007): 113–140.

Part II

Facetted Consumer Identities: Politics and Strategies of Consumption

CHAPTER FIVE

CONSUMERS' MONARCHY: CITIZENSHIP, CONSUMPTION, AND MATERIAL POLITICS IN SAUDI ARABIA SINCE THE 1970S

RELLI SHECHTER[1]

How do we define citizenship in a non-democratic, theocratic, tribal, "rentier" monarchy that is also gender biased and family oriented? This form of citizenship most certainly does not consist of a universal conventional social contract or legal status securing individual freedoms, civil rights, and direct political participation in government. However, regardless of its inequities of freedom, citizenship occupies a crucial role in the life of Saudi citizens. Saudi citizenship is both a general organizing principle in a world made of nation states and a local construct that shapes Saudi political, socio-cultural, and economic realities.

In this chapter, I analyze the evolution and formation of citizenship in Saudi Arabia. I argue that the emergence of a Saudi mass consumer society shaped Saudi citizenship and its inherent social contract. The oil boom (approximately between 1974 and 1984) was largely responsible for the potentially revolutionary pace of these local transformations. Catch-up consumerism—the fast development of consumption levels based on earlier models in developed economies—however, did not entail the rapid sociocultural modernization (read Westernization) that is often associated with such change. Instead, a new world of commodities merged into a pre-existing socio-cultural/religious framework in a path-dependent process. A

---

[1] The author thanks Aviad Moreno and Asher Orkaby for their help in research and bringing this chapter to print. Research was supported by a grant from the Israel Science Foundation (grant no. 57/06).

particular Saudi nexus between local consumption and citizenship came to embody this new arrangement.

Recent developments in Consumption Studies have inspired the argument above. This field has expanded from the study of consumption as a market for identities and the politics of their creation, to the investigation of consumer politics as part of politics.[2] Scholars in the field show that different political economies produce different consumer societies. Furthermore, citizens and consumers, or citizen-consumers, act under similar ideologies and practices when shopping or participating in politics. It is this congruency in Saudi Arabia that I investigate in this chapter.

Saudi Arabia has been inscribed in both the local and international imagination as an authoritarian regime presiding over a conservative/traditional society, while maintaining a relatively open economy. Perhaps the most significant indication of the latter was Saudi integration into the world economy as an oil exporter and a large importer of goods and services. However, it was exactly this form of economic integration that facilitated the strict regulation of the local economy (and economic development) by local elites and by the state. Put differently, in Saudi Arabia the same principles that determined national policies also prescribed access to markets. The oil boom facilitated the spread of consumerism, free of the "democratization" associated with the political empowerment of participating in a free market. Consumerism was not simply a buffer or a ploy in which state largesse sponsored consumption of goods and services to keep political activism in check. Instead, in the Saudi consumers' monarchy material politics essentially replaced direct political participation with an alternative form of socio-political negotiations of things to come.

In this chapter, I develop three interrelated outlines of state, society, and economy in Saudi Arabia. First, in Saudi Arabia the role of the state in the economy increased rather than decreased, in contrast to other states developing mass consumption. In other parts of the world, catch-up consumerism was closely associated with neo-liberal economic reforms and a downsizing of the state. The empowered Saudi rentier/re-distributive state, in contrast, was responsible for the increase in both state and private demand. The Saudi regime was eager to maintain the existing political status quo that sustained its powerbase and legitimacy. In as such they also encouraged the integra-

---

[2] Lizabeth Cohen, *A Consumers' Republic: The Politics of Mass Consumption in Postwar America* (New York: Vintage Books, 2003); Martin Daunton and Matthew Hilton, *The Politics of Consumption: Material Culture and Citizenship in Europe and America* (Oxford: Berg, 2001); Kate Soper and Frank Trentmann, eds., *Citizenship and Consumption* (Houndmills et al.: Palgrave Macmillan, 2008).

tion of socio-political elites, including the religious establishment, into the rapidly developing state.

Second, local society, in opposition to other contemporary consumer societies, became more (rather than less) dependent on the state for both employment and consumption. The state initiated a process which facilitated the creation of a vast Saudi middle class through the allocation of goods and services and public-sector employment. This notion of middle class was associated with local consumerism. In a society where the presence of non-Saudis dominated so much of the public sphere, to consume like a Saudi was a clear mark of social distinction in Bourdieu's sense.[3] This dependence on the state broke the connection between being middle class and this strata's role in open political activism.

Hertog termed "segmented clientelism," a situation in which family, tribe, and religious affiliation have a significant impact on uneven allocation of state resources.[4] In a similar manner, preferential citizenship, as opposed to universal citizenship, determined consumption levels of public and private goods. New legalism and access to state allocation, both based on neo-patriarchal order, infused this new concept (citizenship) with existing socio-political practice. In other words, neo-patriarchy re-enforced male dominance over women and youth, in order to counter the challenges that state allocation and new consumption patterns raised for traditional familial and social practices. The family, rather than the individual, remained the basic unit of citizenship and consumption, regardless of the change taking place.

Third, religiosity, religious practice, and religious discourse continued to be central to the Saudi way of life throughout the transition. Moreover, religion helped to negotiate consumerism into the Saudi socio-cultural fabric through religion-based material politics. The religious influence on politics opened a venue for public debates about the meaning of the economic transformation and its desirability, in a society where more participatory political exchange was not allowed. Religion also provided new legal tools to examine, verify, and adapt novel consumption patterns and commodities to daily use.

My purpose in this chapter is both integrative and interpretative. It integrates available research on the Saudi state, society, and religion/culture into a new explanatory effort, one that emphasizes the nexus between mass

---

[3] Pierre Bourdieu, *Distinction: A Social Critique of the Judgment of Taste* (Cambridge: Harvard University Press, 1984).

[4] Steffen Hertog, "Segmented Clientelism: The Political Economy of Saudi Economic Reform Efforts," in *Saudi Arabia in the Balance: Political Economy, Society, Foreign Affairs*, ed. Paul Aarts and Gerd Nonneman (London: Hurst & Company, 2005), 111–143.

consumption and local citizenship. Moreover, the chapter carries a relatively narrow understanding of Saudi socio-politics as "regime survival," to a wider interpretation of society and state path-dependent development during and following the oil boom.

State and Consumerism

Modern consumerism is associated with past and present regional expansions of free markets during the two eras of globalization.[5] Through liberal (later neo-liberal) reforms, markets became less determined by state regulation and intervention, and more open to exchange beyond state borders. Free markets, in turn, allowed the flow of new goods and services into developing localities, creating opportunities for (unequal) improvement in the material quality of life. Modern consumerism may also be contrasted with the earlier centralities of economic nationalism, socialism (Arab Socialism in the Middle East), and communism—ideologies that supported state involvement in the economy. While state centered ideologies represented calls for frugality and often individual sacrifice of material comforts for the sake of the collective, modern consumerism embodies the right of an individual or family to fulfill its respective needs. Consumerism exemplifies the reward of independent economic activity and individual success.

In Saudi Arabia, modern consumerism did not conform to the narrative above. The state never officially espoused a central role in the economy, but called for free market economic development. Paradoxically mass consumption developed during a period when the state and its involvement in the economy grew exponentially, the result of new oil riches that filled state coffers. In contrast to other developing countries, therefore, local consumerism became more dependent on state resources than on individual economic activity. Throughout much of the developing world, national citizenship was losing its appeal because the state was increasingly unable to supply material benefits to its citizens. In contrast, Saudi Arabia's ability to meet the financial demands of the social welfare state strengthened the nexus between consumption and citizenship in this country.

To what extent does the enhanced nexus between citizenship and consumption (expressed in the notion of a consumers' monarchy) explain local politics? Research on the Saudi state and politics is dominated by two approaches. Based on historical analysis, the first approach emphasized

---

[5] The first era of modern globalization started during the 19th century and ended with the First World War. The second era of modern globalization began with the oil boom of the 1970s and is still with us today.

the gradual transition of Saudi Arabia from a chieftaincy to a monarchical state.[6] According to this narrative, the significant effects of the oil boom should be read in the context of a broader story of how the Saudis came to dominate the peninsula, and establish and control their new state. Emphasizing the importance of taking *all* contextual factors into account, Vitalis recently added a missing piece to the narrative by stressing the colonial role in shaping "America's Kingdom."[7]

A second framework, preferred on the whole by political scientists, is a rentier-state model.[8] Here, state ownership of oil resources enabled state independence of local economy. Such independence allowed ruling elites to maintain the loyalty of their constituencies and their political power. The model emphasizes a comparative perspective through which the Saudi state is explained in relation to other rentier-states. Recently, amendments to the model came from scholars who rightly argued that it does not account for the politics of decision making, segmented clientelism, or the political complexity of client-patron relations in determining redistribution.[9]

The two narratives may initially seem mutually exclusive. The first focuses on process and political continuity, while the second emphasizes structural change emanating from a drastic increase in oil revenues. However, a synthesis of the two frameworks better explains the nature of the oil boom transition and the consumers' monarchy that took its final shape during this period. In Saudi Arabia, the development of state and private consumerism was very much path-dependent because history shaped existing socio-cultural institutions and political practices. The oil-boom era was *a path-dependent revolution* rather than a *revolutionary path-break*. Indeed, the magnitude of the change and the rapid pace at which it took place made the transformation that much more dependent on the past.

Under the extraordinary conditions brought by in-pouring revenues, it was easier—both socially and politically—to employ and reinforce earlier arrangements than to risk across-the-board transition. To put it in Pierson's terms, we may associate the oil-boom era with an "increasing returns" pro-

---

[6] Joseph Kostiner, *The Making of Saudi Arabia, 1916–1936: From Chieftaincy to Monarchical State* (New York: Oxford University Press, 1993).

[7] Robert Vitalis, *America's Kingdom: Mythmaking on the Saudi Oil Frontier* (Stanford: Stanford University Press, 2007).

[8] Kiren Aziz Chaudhry, *The Price of Wealth: Economies and Institutions in the Middle East* (Ithaca and London: Cornell University Press, 1997); Giacomo Luciani, "Allocation vs. Production States: A Theoretical Framework," in *The Arab State*, ed. Giacomo Luciani (London: Routledge, 1990), 65–84.

[9] See Gwen Okruhlik, "Rentier Wealth, Unruly Law, and the Rise of Opposition: The Political Economy of Oil States," *Comparative Politics* 31, no. 3 (1999): 295–315; Hertog, "Segmented Clientelism: The Political Economy of Saudi Economic Reform Efforts," respectively.

cess, in which it benefitted most players to rely on the existing Saudi cosmology and way of doing things to steer the evolving structure of the state and local consumer society through a "safe" course.[10] Oil revenues ensured a more controlled state guided transition. Significant change was taking place in the economy, but one, which contrary to what we may expect, enhanced existing social and political arrangements.

The synthesis of these two approaches helps to further explain preferential citizenship in a recently enriched consumers' monarchy. Far from being equal and universal, such citizenship represented an entitlement to consume based on neo-traditional conventions. Saudi citizenship was associated with a receiving subject, a citizen-consumer provided by state allocation. However, adequate state redistribution, in terms of both quantity and quality (its socio-religious acceptance), became the obligation of good government, and a yardstick by which to judge the conduct of local rulers.

Citizens-Consumers

The following section details how Saudi state and society enforced existing social hierarchies despite rapid economic transition. This separation of the socio-political and economic realms presumably conflicted wisdoms of Marxists and others about the intricate relationship between the two. Indeed, contemporary social scientists, accounting for the emergence of a new middle class in Saudi Arabia, suggested that the discrepancy between this new class and older socio-political patterns could soon challenge existing socio-political arrangements.[11] My argument here is that tying consumption to preferential citizenship reduced the impact of this new middle class. Moreover, preferential citizenship determined private consumption in an economic transformation where commodities and labor were mostly imported and therefore independent of local production. The disassociation of production and consumption combined with the state centrality in the Saudi economy joined the new middle class to the current political structure.

During the oil boom, Saudi Arabia experienced exponential growth of a new middle class, which associated its "middle classness" (social identity) with new sensibilities of propriety and consumption. Urbanization, supported by state investments in infrastructure, public housing, and subsidies for private construction was at the core of this process. New homes,

---

[10] Paul Pierson, "Increasing Returns, Path Dependence, and the Study of Politics," *The American Political Science Review* 94, no. 2 (2000): 251–267.

[11] William Rugh, "Emergence of a New Middle Class in Saudi Arabia," *Middle East Journal* 27, no. 1 (1973): 9–22; Mark Heller and Nadav Safran, *The New Middle Class and Regime Stability in Saudi Arabia*, vol. 3 (Cambridge, 1985).

household items, and cars became a mainstay of this local consumerism. Inequality and poverty remained a constant in Saudi Arabia. Nevertheless, the development of a large middle class, its place in economy and politics, and the debate over its identity and lifestyle became central to Saudi society.

It is not surprising to scholars in the field of Consumption Studies that ownership and consumption were significant in formulating an emerging middle class. However, such demand-side middle classness was uniquely pronounced in Saudi Arabia because the supply-side sector, where middle class identities were long formulated, was largely occupied by imported labor. Indeed, working for the state, the main employer of this class, became a form of social welfare or service rather than a simple workplace. State requirements did not strictly determine employment, and labor-market equilibrium only partially dictated compensation rates. The entitlement to be employed by the state and well compensated increased the dependence of the middle class on the state and further enforced the consumer-citizen tie. Saudi citizenship allowed relative enrichment thus allowing for the formation of a middle class.

Subsidized employment of Saudis by the state succeeded because expatriate labor occupied crucial positions in state service and the private sector's main working force. Expatriates were a highly significant force in construction, further facilitating imports, local industry, distribution, and retailing. They even provided hired help for home chores thus commercializing household work (the private as opposed to the public sphere where economy traditionally took place). More so, an agent (*kafīl*) system and mediation (*wasṭa*) practices allowed Saudi citizens to collect rent from migrant labor, foreign enterprises and the state.[12] Most important, the *kafīl* and *wasṭa* mechanisms facilitated the elaboration of older forms of social patronage in a rapidly expanding economic environment. Impossible boundaries between Saudi and non-Saudi citizens (no expatriate could get citizenship) secured the above settings. Segregated social environments outside the workplace maintained this engineered social hierarchy.

While citizenship directed the quick transformation of supply by allowing Saudis dominion over non-Saudis, neo-patriarchy enhanced social continuity over change when mass consumerism emerged. Neo-patriarchy meant the re-establishment of the family as the basic unit of this society and polity,

---

[12] The *kafīl* system legally required the Saudi ownership of firms registered in Saudi Arabia, and employment of Saudis by non-local enterprises engaged in business with the Saudi state. *Wasṭa* was an unofficial mediation amongst businessmen and especially between entrepreneurs and the state. For an extended discussion of such business practices in what he termed "*ʿaṣabiyya* capitalism," see Daryl Champion, *The Paradoxical Kingdom: Saudi Arabia and the Momentum of Reform* (New York: Columbia University Press, 2003), ch. 3.

reaffirmation of existing social hierarchies, and unequal power relations based on the preeminence of the adult male. To use the notion of increasing returns again, the state—together with leading communal players—stemmed potential, rapid social transition by re-enforcing an existing social order. Neo-patriarchy stood at the core of family, rather than individual citizenship and allowed prevailing social norms to legally govern changing social and economic modes.

Access to new state and market resources presented a potential social threat to the preservation of an older status quo based on family, tribe and clientele arrangements. It meant a potential real and symbolic empowerment of the new middle class, particularly women, as citizens and consumers. Women were emphatically made to withdraw from public life and unmediated access to public and private goods and services, in an effort to curtail female empowerment. They were instead confined to their roles at home as mothers and home-keepers. This same system, however, also confined men to traditional socio-political hierarchies. While still mediating the rights and duties of their families, men were themselves subject to strict political control.

Female participation in social life was both contingent and mediated by the family[13] and the same was true for women's participation in the economy as consumers. Zirinski illustrated this point through a study of advertisements in *Sayyidati* ("My Lady"). The magazine, despite its title and by its own admission, is a family publication. Men are omnipresent in ads and "[E]ven when he is not visible in the ad, the man is always standing guard, overseeing the woman's action. Women are always covered, always concealed by something—a veil, a partition, a wall, or a mask of makeup."[14] Women also were banned from mixed gender working environments, thus preventing their full participation in the labor-market. Their opportunity for economic independence through direct involvement in manufacturing, and especially services, was placed out of reach.

Arguably, the best example of female-constrained citizenship and participation in the economy and society was the ban on driving for all Saudi women, which forbade women free use of the most-efficient transportation vehicle in the country.[15] The ban enforced the dependent status of

---

[13] Soraya Altorki, "The Concept and Practice of Citizenship in Saudi Arabia," in *Gender and Citizenship in the Middle East*, ed. Joseph Saud (Syracuse: Syracuse University Press, 2000), 215–236.

[14] Roni Zirinski, *Ad hoc Arabism: Advertising, Culture and Technology in Saudi Arabia* (New York: P. Lang, 2005), 130.

[15] Eleanor Abdella Doumato, "Women and the Stability of Saudi Arabia," *Middle East Report* 171 (1991): 34–37.

women and their indirect access to state resources, including the juridical system. Furthermore, driving and ownership of cars was highly symbolic: cars constituted the quintessential modern/Western consumer product and were therefore perceived as a threat to a traditional way of life, or, conversely, its reaffirmation. It was also expensive and visible enough to be highly significant in a process of consumption-based stratification. The female driving ban neutralized the revolutionary aspects of this new commodity and consumption pattern, especially considering the public nature of this action.

Doumato's discussion of the perception of the idealized Islamic woman and its role in local politics explains the important symbolic aspect of female invisibility outside the home. "Women separation ... is enforced because it can be."[16] Official female dependency status was one of the more salient social-turned-legal and political features of Saudi neo-patriarchy. "When adopted as a moral cause by the monarchy ... the public invisibility of women becomes a visible sign of the monarch's piety." These restrictions allowed the more conservative segments in society to have a big impact on public life. It also enabled the government to score easy points by reinforcing the paternal form that guided local governance, thereby enhancing its legitimacy during a period of rapid change.

Neo-patriarchy prevented a potentially revolutionary youth culture from emerging in Saudi Arabia. Although Saudi society was becoming younger and younger, the elder generation continued to dominate the young. The enforcement of a traditional system of socio-cultural control made the emergence of an alternative youth consumer culture increasingly unlikely. A family-oriented approach to state and market ensured continued dominance. The existing social, economic, and political connections and patronage kept young Saudis under the thumbs of their elders.

Material Politics

Neo-patriarchy across society and state translated into an authoritarian regime with little open and active participatory politics.[17] In such an environment, parallel, material politics helped the negotiation of the "morality of

---

[16] Eleanor Abdella Doumato, "Gender, Monarchy, and National Identity in Saudi Arabia," *British Journal of Middle Eastern Studies* 19, no. 1 (1992): 45.
[17] Another explanation for the near absence of participatory politics in "rentier" states is that when the state owns sufficient economic resources it has little need to negotiate their use. The principle of "no taxation, no representation" was highly significant in excluding citizens from direct participation in political decision-making. See Luciani, "Allocation vs. Production States: A Theoretical Framework."

spending" and its permissibility that shaped public and private affairs and social control.[18] A public discourse on "we are what we consume," often put in religious terms, represented Saudi idealism and criticism of sociopolitical conduct against various manifestations of conspicuous consumption.[19] Moreover, in the Saudi consumer monarchy, religious—rather than civic—virtue stood at the core of citizenship. It therefore served as a rubric through which to evaluate the conduct of both the rulers and the ruled.

Let me further explain the term material politics as it is related to Saudi society. Material politics represented discourse and discipline in the adaptation of modernity to local society. This modernity was significantly expressed in the deluge of novel goods and services that created a yet unknown local world of commodities, and therefore a significant thrust in local politics on how to guide it. Conventional wisdom in research, however, hardly treated it as such. Rather, scholars mostly argued that with contemporary cooptation of the religious establishment to the state, the ᶜulamaʾ regulated and depoliticized the adaptation of such modernity leaving "real" politics to those in power. The negotiation and means of controlling materialism expressed in quotidian personal, gender, family, and communal life—i.e., material politics—were not considered the realm of politics. Scholarship, like the official Saudi stand, treated them simply as disconnected social and religious affairs.

Since my point here may seem controversial, let me cite, at length, Madawi Al-Rasheed, a significant authority in the field:

> Although Saudi ᶜulama appear to enjoy more power, financial resources, prestige and privileges than their counterparts elsewhere in the Muslim world, it must be emphasized that the modern state has pushed them towards a ceremonial role. This does not rule out influence and control: unlike their counterparts in other Arab countries, Wahhabi scholars have considerable control over the social sphere. However, like other religious scholars in the Arab world, Wahhabis lost control over policy and politics to royalty and state bu-

---

[18] The term "morality of spending" is adapted from Daniel Horowitz, *The Morality of Spending: Attitudes toward the Consumer Society in America, 1875–1940* (Baltimore: Johns Hopkins University Press, 1985).

[19] Above, and elsewhere in this section, "material politics" closely dialogs with the Hanbali-expanded principle of "commending right and forbidding wrong" (*al-amr bi-l-maᶜrūf wa-l-nahy ᶜan al-munkar*). On the history of this principle in Islamic thought and practice, including in Saudi Arabia, see Michael Cook, *Commanding Right and Forbidding Wrong in Islamic Thought* (Cambridge: Cambridge University Press, 2000). I thank Nimrod Hurvitz for bringing this to my attention.

reaucrats and technocrats—the political sphere is beyond Wahhabi control.[20]

It is exactly this seeming detachment of the social and ceremonial from the political that I want to contest here.

The separation between material and real politics is surprising for at least two reasons. To disentangle the social from the political sphere in such a manner seems outdated after Foucault who taught us that these spheres are tightly connected through various forms of power relations and governmentality.[21] Moreover, such separation stands in opposition to the basic tenant of Islam as a religion of shari^{c}a. Regulation of every aspect of daily life is at the center of Islamic belief, and, as I will argue below, of being a Saudi. It is hard to see how an extensive transformation of material life would not interact with an existing political structure. The question is more in the ways that such an interaction was taking place.

Material politics were based on two pillars—neo-patriarchy and neo-religiosity. As we saw above, neo-patriarchy preserved a male-dominated family metaphor across society and politics. Neo-religiosity, the institutionalization of Islamic principles through state mechanisms, especially the bureaucracy and the legal system, controlled unwanted influence from the market. The most notable neo-religious expression of domination was over the national morality of spending. The regulation and discipline of Saudi private and public consumerism determined the proper conduct in the purchase and use of things.

Local purchase and use of commodities and services were sanctioned as long as they withstood certain moral/religious junctures. The religious establishment, however, greatly facilitated state-led material modernization by developing a legitimizing mechanism (siyāsa shar^{c}iyya[22]), and a new, conditional permissibility to consume modern goods and services ranging from electronic appliances to Islamic banking. Consumption was tolerable from a religious perspective after negative aspect of innovation (bid^{c}a) were removed, allowing the introduction of "Faust without the Devil"[23] to Saudi

---

[20] Madawi Al-Rasheed, *Contesting the Saudi State: Islamic Voices from a New Generation* (Cambridge: Cambridge University Press, 2007), 4.

[21] For the term "governmentality" see Graham Burchell, Colin Gordon, and Peter Miller, eds., *The Foucault Effect: Studies in Governmentality* (London: Harvester Wheatsheaf, 1991).

[22] Muhammad Al-Atawneh, "Religion and State in Contemporary Middle East: The Case of Saudi Arabia," *Journal of Islamic State Practices in International Law* 2, no. 2 (2006): 28–45.

[23] Sharif Elmusa, "Faust without the Devil? The Interplay of Technology and Culture in Saudi Arabia," *Middle East Journal* 51, no. 3 (1997): 345–357.

life. Neo-religiosity, like neo-patriarchy stood for top-to-bottom moral and practical guidelines in an era of rapid economic transitions.

To better understand material politics within the context of the Saudi state, we should examine its relationship to local citizenship. Revising the Turner model of citizenship is a good starting point. Turner's model of citizenship placed "civic virtue," or the culture and values of a civil society, at the core the citizenship model.[24] He suggested that citizenship was closely connected with national identity and community, yet was also associated with the legal definition of citizenship and state allocation of coveted resources. This model fits nicely in the case of Saudi citizenship, with one important difference; it is religious rather than civic virtue at the center. The culture and values of a society closely associated with a community of believers, shape citizen entitlement to resource allocation and delineate proper consumption behavior (see Figure 5.1[25]).

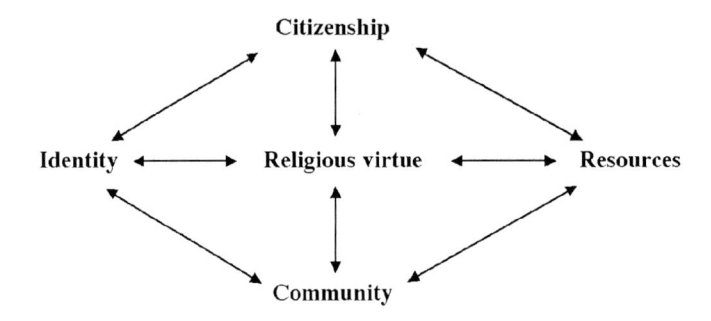

Figure 5.1: A model of Saudi citizenship

In the revised model of citizenship, top-down material politics translated religious virtue into daily life. The religious establishment exercised their authority over this material politics through the issuance of fatwas, the legal system, and the direct supervision of the morality police (*muṭawwaʾūn*).

Material politics, however, was a two-way street in which alternative religious virtue(s) could challenge those in authority. In other words, the local moral guidelines of spending could be rewritten by the opposition and

---

[24] Bryan S. Turner, "Islam, Civil Society, and Citizenship: Reflections on the Sociology of Citizenship and Islamic Studies," in *Citizenship and the State in the Middle East: Approaches and Application*, ed. Nils A. Buthenschon Uri Davis and Manuel Hassassian (Syracuse: Syracuse University Press, 2000), 28–48.

[25] Revised from ibid., 37, figure 2.1.

turned against those in power who had breached its normative code. This subversion also served arguments against the wrongful conduct by rulers as having caused the perceived social decay and crumbling social solidarity. By contesting existing religious virtue and the citizenship it implied, such arguments allowed a venue for "negative" inclusion into the nation and a form of citizen-consumer participation in local material politics.[26]

The recent history of Saudi Arabia gives ample example of such opposition and negative inclusion. The 1979 occupation of the Great Mosque in Mecca by the Juhayman al-ᶜUtaybi group and the almost simultaneous uprising of Shiites in the eastern province were about negotiating material modernity, rejecting it altogether in the first example and rejecting its unequal allocation in the second. More contemporary trends in Saudi Islamism, from the exclusionist to the reformist movement (the ṣaḥwīs) further challenge the state by criticizing dominant yet flawed religious virtue through the employment of material politics.

Material politics were also present, though seldom discussed, in the form of qualified resistance and quest for change through the market. These included a closer adoption by female, male, and youth of imported commodities and lifestyles beyond that sanctioned by religious orthodoxy and often in defiance of patriarchical authority. One outstanding example for this was the women driving incident discussed above. We also have some evidence of youth seeking spaces of mitigated parental control in commercial venues, private leisure resorts, and abroad. For youth, electronic gadgets from videotapes to the internet and mobile phones of today allows easier access to uncensored content and new public arenas to engage in more open association, especially across gender lines.[27] Without over-stating such actions, they exemplify how daily-life is negotiated via consumption.

Conclusion

Stearns[28] and others—Starrett for Egypt; Cohen for the U.S.—rightly pointed out that the emergence of mass consumer societies often coincided with

---

[26] I develop the notion of negative citizenship/participation based on Okruhlik, "Rentier Wealth, Unruly Law, and the Rise of Opposition: The Political Economy of Oil States," and Lisa Wedeen, "Seeing like a Citizen, Acting like a State: Exemplary Events in Unified Yemen," *Comparative Studies in Society and History* 45, no. 4 (2003): 680–713.

[27] Lisa Wynn, *Pyramids & Nightclubs* (Austin: University of Texas Press, 2007); Mai Yamani, *Changed Identities: The Challenge of the New Generation in Saudi Arabia* (London: The Royal Institute of International Affairs, 2000).

[28] Peter Stearns, *Consumerism in World History: The Global Transformation of Desire* (London: Routledge, 2001).

the intensification of religion.[29] Religious belief and practice mitigated the rapid socio-cultural transformation mounting, at times, an opposition to inequality and discontent rising from this rapid change. Saudi Arabia was somewhat of an exception to this rule because religion was omnipresent in its society and state when mass consumption spread. In Saudi Arabia, intensification of religion was more closely dependent on an existing path and manifested in rapid institution-building and religious-legal expansion.

For scholars in the field of Consumption Studies, the Saudi consumers' monarchy stands as a reminder of non-linearity, or at least a possible exception, in the creation of mass consumer societies worldwide. In other words, catch-up consumerism was not linked with the swift socio-cultural transitions of the modernization-theory type that are sometimes found in the literature. Neo-conservatism, a confluence of neo-religiosity and neo-patriarchy, enhanced by new oil riches, shaped local consumer society. Saudi consumerism became embedded in an existing socio-political and cultural system because of increasing returns in adapting to past structure during an era of rapid economic change. Put differently, it was easier for leading coalitions within state and society to depend on existing conventions than to develop new ones in adjusting to novel material life.

A new middle class emerged, primarily through state economic development programs. Their Saudi citizenship served as an entry ticket to a new world of commodities. Citizen-consumer status was family based and associated with male domination over female and youth. Men were also stratified based on segmented clientalism, which meant male preferential access to state resources determined by tribe, ethnicity, and religious orientation. Citizen-consumer discipline was based on strict religious virtue, the core of Saudi identity and citizenship. Religious virtue, however, could be conversely used to serve Islamic-based state opposition. Furthermore, material politics was as an important although indirect venue through which Saudi citizen-consumers participated in politics, often in the form of negative action (or reaction) to unequal allocation or perceived immorality in spending. Nevertheless, in Saudi Arabia we find a stifling stability enhanced by a personal desire to consume.

---

[29] Cf. Stearns, *Consumerism in World History: The Global Transformation of Desire*; Gregory Starrett, "The Political Economy of Religious Commodities in Cairo," *American Anthropologist* 97, no. 1 (1995): 51–68; Cohen, *A Consumers' Republic: The Politics of Mass Consumption in Postwar America*.

Bibliography

Al-Atawneh, Muhammad. "Religion and State in Contemporary Middle East: The Case of Saudi Arabia." *Journal of Islamic State Practices in International Law* 2, no. 2 (2006): 28–45.

Al-Rasheed, Madawi. *Contesting the Saudi State: Islamic Voices from a New Generation*. Cambridge: Cambridge University Press, 2007.

Altorki, Soraya. "The Concept and Practice of Citizenship in Saudi Arabia." In *Gender and Citizenship in the Middle East*, edited by Joseph Saud, 215–236. Syracuse: Syracuse University Press, 2000.

Bourdieu, Pierre. *Distinction: A Social Critique of the Judgment of Taste*. Cambridge: Harvard University Press, 1984.

Burchell, Graham, Colin Gordon, and Peter Miller, eds. *The Foucault Effect: Studies in Governmentality*. London: Harvester Wheatsheaf, 1991.

Champion, Daryl. *The Paradoxical Kingdom: Saudi Arabia and the Momentum of Reform*. New York: Columbia University Press, 2003.

Chaudhry, Kiren Aziz. *The Price of Wealth: Economies and Institutions in the Middle East*. Ithaca and London: Cornell University Press, 1997.

Cohen, Lizabeth. *A Consumers' Republic: The Politics of Mass Consumption in Postwar America*. New York: Vintage Books, 2003.

Cook, Michael. *Commanding Right and Forbidding Wrong in Islamic Thought*. Cambridge: Cambridge University Press, 2000.

Daunton, Martin, and Matthew Hilton. *The Politics of Consumption: Material Culture and Citizenship in Europe and America*. Oxford: Berg, 2001.

Doumato, Eleanor Abdella. "Gender, Monarchy, and National Identity in Saudi Arabia." *British Journal of Middle Eastern Studies* 19, no. 1 (1992): 31–47.

———. "Women and the Stability of Saudi Arabia." *Middle East Report* 171 (1991): 34–37.

Elmusa, Sharif. "Faust without the Devil? The Interplay of Technology and Culture in Saudi Arabia." *Middle East Journal* 51, no. 3 (1997): 345–357.

Heller, Mark, and Nadav Safran. *The New Middle Class and Regime Stability in Saudi Arabia*. Vol. 3. Cambridge, 1985.

Hertog, Steffen. "Segmented Clientelism: The Political Economy of Saudi Economic Reform Efforts." In *Saudi Arabia in the Balance: Political Economy, Society, Foreign Affairs*, edited by Paul Aarts and Gerd Nonneman, 111–143. London: Hurst & Company, 2005.

Horowitz, Daniel. *The Morality of Spending: Attitudes toward the Consumer Society in America, 1875–1940*. Baltimore: Johns Hopkins University Press, 1985.

Kostiner, Joseph. *The Making of Saudi Arabia, 1916–1936: From Chieftaincy to Monarchical State*. New York: Oxford University Press, 1993.

Luciani, Giacomo. "Allocation vs. Production States: A Theoretical Framework." In *The Arab State*, edited by Giacomo Luciani, 65–84. London: Routledge, 1990.

Okruhlik, Gwen. "Rentier Wealth, Unruly Law, and the Rise of Opposition: The Political Economy of Oil States." *Comparative Politics* 31, no. 3 (1999): 295–315.

Pierson, Paul. "Increasing Returns, Path Dependence, and the Study of Politics." *The American Political Science Review* 94, no. 2 (2000): 251–267.

Rugh, William. "Emergence of a New Middle Class in Saudi Arabia." *Middle East Journal* 27, no. 1 (1973): 9–22.

Soper, Kate, and Frank Trentmann, eds. *Citizenship and Consumption*. Houndmills et al.: Palgrave Macmillan, 2008.

Starrett, Gregory. "The Political Economy of Religious Commodities in Cairo." *American Anthropologist* 97, no. 1 (1995): 51–68.

Stearns, Peter. *Consumerism in World History: The Global Transformation of Desire*. London: Routledge, 2001.

Turner, Bryan S. "Islam, Civil Society, and Citizenship: Reflections on the Sociology of Citizenship and Islamic Studies." In *Citizenship and the State in the Middle East: Approaches and Application*, edited by Nils A. Buthenschon Uri Davis and Manuel Hassassian, 28–48. Syracuse: Syracuse University Press, 2000.

Vitalis, Robert. *America's Kingdom: Mythmaking on the Saudi Oil Frontier*. Stanford: Stanford University Press, 2007.

Wedeen, Lisa. "Seeing like a Citizen, Acting like a State: Exemplary Events in Unified Yemen." *Comparative Studies in Society and History* 45, no. 4 (2003): 680–713.

Wynn, Lisa. *Pyramids & Nightclubs*. Austin: University of Texas Press, 2007.

Yamani, Mai. *Changed Identities: The Challenge of the New Generation in Saudi Arabia*. London: The Royal Institute of International Affairs, 2000.

Zirinski, Roni. *Ad hoc Arabism: Advertising, Culture and Technology in Saudi Arabia*. New York: P. Lang, 2005.

CHAPTER SIX

THE COLA TURKA CONTROVERSY: CONSUMING COLA AS A TURKISH MUSLIM

DILEK KAYA MUTLU

In July 2003, the Turkish food and beverage group Ülker, which is known for its Islamic leanings, launched Cola Turka as a local competitor to Coca-Cola and Pepsi. In accordance with an advertising phenomenon of the time that attempted to sell "Turkish authenticity,"[1] Cola Turka was introduced to the public in a series of humorous television commercials that conveyed the message that as Coca-Cola Americanizes, Cola Turka "Turkifies" those who drink it—even Americans. With American comedians David Brown and Chevy Chase in the leading roles, the commercials presented a funny utopia in which Americans in New York become Turkish after sipping Cola Turka—they adopt Turkish customs such as holding beads, growing a moustache, sending a shopping basket down a skyscraper, cooking *biber dolması* (stuffed green peppers), kissing the hands of elders, pouring water after a departing car so it has a safe trip, and singing a Turkish marching song. These traditional motifs suggest that Cola Turka was not simply intended to "Turkify" its consumers but to make them *alaturka* (from the Italian *alla turca*, meaning "Turkish style"), a concept apparent in the brand name. As opposed to *alafranga* (*alla franca*, i.e., European) mode and behavior, being *alaturka* has long signified, especially for the West and Westernist Turks, being backward, uncivilized, and against change and progress.[2] Cola Turka

---

[1] Yael Navaro-Yashin, "The Market for Identities: Secularism, Islamism, Commodities," in *Fragments of Culture: The Everyday of Modern Turkey*, ed. Deniz Kandiyoti Saktanber and Ayşe (London: I. B. Tauris, 2002), 230.
[2] Nilüfer Göle, *The Forbidden Modern: Civilization and Veiling* (Ann Arbor: University of Michigan Press, 1996), 15.

commercials not only saved the term *alaturka* from its negative connotations but transformed it into the symbol of a "lost" national essence. Targeting the supposedly "Americanized" Turkish consumers of American cola brands, Ülker invited them to return to their fundamental nature by drinking Cola Turka. By promoting an *alaturka* version of Turkishness, Cola Turka also presented a soft critique of Westernization.

Cola Turka seemed to capitalize on the growing anti-American sentiment in Turkey, following the U.S. invasion of Iraq. Moreover, it was launched during the time when Turkish soldiers in northern Iraq were arrested by U.S. troops, deported with hands cuffed and heads hooded, and imprisoned and interrogated for 60 hours. The incident, called the "Hood Event," was viewed in Turkey as an insult to the Turkish Army and the nation,[3] and was interpreted as revenge for the vote by the Turkish Parliament that denied the U.S. request to use Turkish territory to invade Iraq.[4] The Hood Event was not the first crisis in the history of U.S.–Turkish relations, but it was registered in the Turkish national memory as "the most humiliating event" between the two NATO allies.[5] It was argued that Cola Turka helped relieve Turkish anger toward the United States and repair Turkey's damaged national pride.[6]

Ülker officials and their advertising team, however, rejected the notion that they were inciting anti-Americanism. "This is not Turkish propaganda, but rather positive nationalism," which is not based on hatred and antagonism, said Serdar Erener, one of the makers of the television commercials.[7] Indeed, perhaps, as one columnist argued, Cola Turka's promotional discourse was "not political but fantastic" because it was more motivated by "conquering" America, rather than "cursing" it.[8] Yet even if Cola Turka was

---

[3] Turan Yavuz, *Çuvallayan ittifak* (Ankara: Destek Yayınları, 2006), 215–223.

[4] Ertuğrul Özkök, "Domuzlar körfezi fiyaskosu gibi," *Hürriyet* (7 July 2003): 23; Mehmet Yılmaz, "PKK kartı yine masada," *Aksiyon*, no. 449 (14 July 2003): 40–46 [41–42].

[5] Ufuk Şanlı, "Süleymaniye baskınının şifreleri," *Aksiyon*, no. 604 (3 July 2006): 48–49 [49].

[6] Resul Tosun, "Amerika'dan hırsımızı Cola Turka ile çıkartıyoruz," *Yeni Şafak* (9 July 2003): 15; Yılmaz Yıldız, "Ülker'in 'Cola Turka'sı Türkler'i Türkleştiriyor," *Yeni Şafak* (11 July 2003): 7.

[7] As cited in Ruhi Sanyer, "Aslında Amerikalıymış," *Radikal* (21 March 2004): 15; Mevlüt Tezel, "Chevy Chase gibi Hollywood starının oynatılmasını Plato Filmciliğe borçluyuz," *Hürriyet* (13 July 2003): 6. See Derya Özkan and Robert J. Foster, "Consumer Citizenship, Nationalism, and Neoliberal Globalization in Turkey: The Advertising Launch of Cola Turka," *Advertising & Society Review* 6, no. 3 (2005), for a discussion of Cola Turka's marketing strategy, described as "positive nationalism."

[8] Tayfun Atay, "Cola'nı imanla iç," *Milliyet* (28 April 2004), http://www.milliyet.com.tr/2004/04/28/sanat/san09.html, accessed 10 June 2008).

not seriously anti-American, it was so timely that it became a phenomenon when it was initially released.[9]

Although Cola Turka can be seen as part of a growing trend (i.e., Zam Zam Cola in Iran, Mecca Cola in France, and Qibla Cola in Britain), it differs from other Islamic cola brands with its emphasis on being Turkish rather than on being Islamic. In addition to the absence of any religious word in its brand name, the initial TV commercials commodified the traditional Turkish way of life more than they commodified Islam.[10] Moreover, although Ülker is one of the major representatives of "green capital"—i.e., Islamic capital—in Turkey, unlike other Islamic cola brands, it did not launch Cola Turka as a political statement against the exploitation of Muslims. For instance, Tawfik Mathlouthi, the Tunisian French businessman who launched Mecca Cola in 2002 with the slogan "Don't drink stupid, drink committed," explained the motivation behind that beverage to a reporter: "[It is all about combating] America's imperialism and Zionism by providing a substitute for American goods and increasing the blockade of countries boycotting American goods."[11]

Although a soft criticism of Americanization was apparent in the initial television commercials, Cola Turka was not launched with such a political and missionary statement. Nor did it invite its consumers to be politically committed. Company officials even rejected media accusations that they were promoting nationalism.[12] A company official stated, "We have nothing to do with nationalism and politics. We are entrepreneurs and we are doing our job."[13]

---

[9] Arguably, Cola Turka would not have the same social impact if it were launched today. Although the use of local images and motifs has continued, the direct emphasis on Turkishness has gradually disappeared from Cola Turka commercials. For instance, the commercial that aired throughout the summer in 2008 emphasizes more joy and entertainment (like Coca-Cola advertisements), than Turkishness.

[10] In one of the early television commercials that aired during Ramadan, David Brown is shown fasting and waiting for the azan to break his fast and drink Cola Turka. Pretending to be a pious Muslim, he says to Turks who are impatient to break their fasts, "No azan, no iftar" ("No breaking of the Ramadan fast before the call for prayer"). However, Ramadan is a special period in Turkey during which almost all food and drink commercials give way to religious motifs.

[11] As cited in Uri Ram, "Liquid Identities: Mecca Cola versus Coca-Cola," *European Journal of Cultural Studies* 10, no. 4 (2007): 467.

[12] Fatma K. Barbarosoğlu, "'Cola Turka' içmek ya da 'ala turka' olmanın pozitif milliyetçiliğe katkısı," *Yeni Şafak* (11 July 2003): 18; Kürşat Bumin, "'Cola Turka' iç, 'pozitif milliyetçilik' safına geç," *Yeni Şafak* (12 July 2003): 5; Ali Bulaç, "Cola Turka," *Zaman* (2 August 2003): 13; Yurtsan Atakan, "Kola Turka vadisi," *Hürriyet Kelebek* (8 February 2006): 3.

[13] Cited in "Light Cola Turka geliyor," *Yeni Şafak* (22 October 2003): 8.

Although Cola Turka was not discursively constructed as an anti–U.S. "boycott cola" or as an Islamic alternative to American cola brands, it was welcomed by some Islamist circles in Turkey, who rejected Coca-Cola and Pepsi on the basis that they were not permissible by Islam or that they were "anti-Muslim" and "supportive of Israel."[14] A Cola Turka debate between some Islamists soon followed: Was it truly authentic, or simply a sign of the "cola-ization" of Muslim lifestyles? Was its Turkishness enough to make it permissible or suitable for consumption by Muslims?

In this paper, I explore Cola Turka in relation to the processes of identity formation and negotiation in Turkey. In an attempt to explain the exceptionality of Cola Turka compared with other Islamic cola brands, I begin with an overview of "Turkish Islamic exceptionalism"—that is, the interpenetration of Islam and secularism in Turkey, which distinguishes it from Arab Islam.[15] I then examine Cola Turka's reception by some Islamist circles in Turkey, based on opinion pieces in Islamist newspapers and in forums on Islamist websites. Finally, I attempt to show that Cola Turka is only one case among many that underlines the changing consumption patterns of Islamic/Islamist circles in Turkey and implies an Islamization of modernity.

Turkey between Islam and Secularism

Turkey is a predominantly Muslim but officially secular country. The invisibility of a pro-Muslim discourse in Cola Turka's initial promotion must be partially related to the secular radicalism in Turkey that was institutionalized during the early Republican era. With the establishment of the Turkish Republic in 1923, Turkey entered a fast process of modernization/Westernization. As Şerif Mardin points out, "the Turkish Revolution was primarily a revolution of values,"[16] in that it attempted to change not just the social structure but the symbolic system of the society, namely, the culture, within which Islam played a fundamental role.[17] Viewing modernization and Westernization as inseparable and inevitable, the founders of the Republic, led by Mustafa Kemal (Atatürk) and the modernizing elites saw

---

[14] The media also reported that the Iranian Embassy in Ankara, which refused to serve Coca-Cola at the embassy's official invitations, began to serve Cola Turka in 2005; cf. Bahadır Selim Dilek, "Patates, telaffuz sorunu ve Irak'taki kontrol noktaları," *Birgün* (20 July 2005, http://www.tumgazeteler.com/?a=893356, accessed 20 July 2005).

[15] Şerif Mardin, "Turkish Islamic Exceptionalism Yesterday and Today: Continuity, Rupture and Reconstruction in Operational Codes," *Turkish Studies* 6, no. 2 (2005): 148.

[16] Şerif A. Mardin, "Ideology and Religion in the Turkish Revolution," *International Journal of Middle East Studies* 2, no. 3 (1971): 209.

[17] Ibid., 202.

Islam as "a marker of oriental identity" and believed that "in order to westernize they had to de-Islamize—that is, they had to remove the influence of Islam from their societies."[18]

Assuming secularism as one of its founding principles, the Republican government undertook many reforms that distanced the country from its Islamic and Eastern past and from traditions characterized by "backwardness" and religiosity, in order to bring it closer to contemporary Western societies. Reforms included the abolition of the Caliphate; the abolition of the religious courts; the proscription of the fez and its substitution with the Western hat; the dissolution of the dervish orders and brotherhoods; the adoption of the Western calendar and the Latin alphabet; the adoption of civil, commercial, and penal codes based on European models; the abolition of traditional religious schools and the establishment of a secular system of education; and the abolition of the clause in the constitution that mentioned Islam as the religion of the Turkish state. The Kemalists attempted to modernize/Westernize not just the public sphere but also the private sphere, by discoursing on "matters from the clothing of its citizens to the music they were to listen to, from the type of leisure activity they would be engaged in to the type of family relations they would have."[19]

As part of the project of creating a new Turkish identity rather than a Muslim identity, the Kemalists also rooted Turks to a past that predated Islam. School textbooks of the 1930s described Turks as the "Turano-Aryans—blond, blue-eyed ancestors of the current 'Aryan' race in northern Europe"—and portrayed Islam as an "Arab, not a universal, religion which corrupted and stifled the secular genius of the Turkish people."[20] While the new state proclaimed itself a secular republic, Turkish officials were well aware that Islam, which had provided both the governing and living principles in the country for centuries, could not be removed immediately from everyday life. Therefore, rather than excluding Islam altogether, the state attempted to incorporate religion within its political system and discourse. Besides putting religion under state watch,[21] Kemalists discursively con-

---

[18] Bobby S. Sayyid, *A Fundamental Fear: Eurocentrism and the Emergence of Islamism* (London and New York: Zed Books Ltd., 1997), 69.

[19] Alev Çınar, *Modernity, Islam, and Secularism in Turkey: Bodies, Places, and Time* (Minneapolis and London: University of Minnesota Press, 2005), 15.

[20] Sam Kaplan, "'Religious Nationalism': A Textbook Case from Turkey," *Comparative Studies of South Asia, Africa and the Middle East* 25, no. 3 (2005): 670.

[21] As is often noted, Kemalist secularism differed from the Western models of secularism. Rather than fully separating religion and state affairs, the Republican government put religion under the direct monitoring of the state by means of establishing the Directorate of Religious Affairs in 1924. Cf. Paul Dumont, "Islam as a Factor of Change and Revival in Modern Turkey," in *Turkic Culture: Continuity and Change*, ed. Sabri M. Akural (Indiana University

structed a version of Islam that would implant their new ideas and ideals. For instance, religion textbooks stressed that Islam was compatible with a secular worldview, even positing the prophet Mohammad as a promoter of modernity and secularism.[22] Such textbooks also included prescriptions suggesting that the primary duty of a Muslim was to be a model modern citizen.[23]

Until the 1980s, the state, especially the military, had perceived unofficial Islam as a rival source of legitimacy and a threat to the modern secular legacy of the Turkish Republic. The 1980s, which began with a military coup, marked a shift in this perception. In an attempt to stop the ideological division between the Right and the Left, social chaos, and political violence in the streets, the generals sought to "reinvent a more politically docile Turkish youth"[24] by mobilizing religion/Islam as an antidote to ideological division, especially to communism.[25] They drew on an intellectual movement called Turkish-Islamic synthesis, which advocates "greater integration of Islamic values in the nation's political culture."[26] After a three-year military administration with the new civil government led by Prime Minister Turgut Özal, Turkey entered a new era characterized by economic, social, and cultural liberalization. Özal also saw Islam as a unifying element in society. Moreover, as Kevin Robins remarks, he sought to achieve "real" social change, "a change from below," by engaging all sections of society,

---

Press, 1987), 2; Hakkı Taş and Meral Uğur, "Roads 'Drawn' to Modernity: Religion and Secularism in Contemporary Turkey," *PS: Political Science and Politics* 40, no. 2 (2007): 311; Nilüfer Göle, "Modernist kamusal alan ve İslami ahlak," in *İslam'ın yeni kamusal yüzleri*, ed. Nilüfer Göle (Istanbul: Metis, 2000), 22.

[22] A passage in a religious textbook from the late 1920s reads: "If [the Prophet] had lived in our day there is no doubt that he would have commended Boy Scouting and modern games like football, volleyball, tennis and hiking, and he even would have played himself. He would have made his people wear hats, which is a civilized and healthful covering . . . The Prophet ate and drank with good manners and behaved absolutely like a civilized man" (as cited in Kaplan, "'Religious Nationalism': A Textbook Case from Turkey," 672).

[23] Paul Dumont remarks, "a Muslim truly worthy of that name had to love his country, pay his taxes regularly, respect the laws of the Republic, submit to the progressive guidance of the State officials, do his utmost to learn modern techniques, apply scrupulously the principles of good hygiene, consult a doctor in case of illness to avoid being the cause of epidemics, and work energetically for the development of the country." Cf. Dumont, "Islam as a Factor of Change and Revival in Modern Turkey," 3.

[24] Kaplan, "'Religious Nationalism': A Textbook Case from Turkey," 666.

[25] Ayşe Kadıoğlu, "The Paradox of Turkish Nationalism and the Construction of Official Identity," *Middle Eastern Studies* 32, no. 2 (1996): 190; Kevin Robins, "Interrupting Identities: Turkey / Europe," in *Questions of Cultural Identity*, ed. Stuart Hall and Paul Du Gay (London: Sage Publications, 1996), 71.

[26] Kaplan, "'Religious Nationalism': A Textbook Case from Turkey," 666.

including Islamic circles, in the modernization process.[27] To this end, he encouraged greater participation of Islamic capital and of Islamic circles in the economy and in the public sphere. All these changes paved the way for the revitalization of Islam in Turkey during the 1980s and 1990s.

As Ayşe Saktanber remarked, if the early Republican era was characterized by a "modernization from above," the post-1980 period could be characterized as an "Islamization from below."[28] A phenomenal emigration from rural areas to the cities marked, in Robins' words, "the return of the repressed": "the arrival in the cities of an Ottoman-Islamic culture" together with the Anatolian people.[29] This arrival was accompanied by the growing visibility of Islamic identities (i.e., veiled women) and practices in urban public life. These culminated in the 1990s with the rise of the Islamist Refah (Welfare) Party (RP) and Islamism as a new political ideology, which adopted "East-oriented Ottoman-Islamic nationalism as its constitutive base"[30] and searched for "alternative Islamic life politics and new social order."[31] The RP's supporters celebrated the victory of the party in the 1994 municipal elections with the slogan "The Other Turkey Is Coming to Power."[32] Indeed, in 1995, the RP became a coalition government, and in 1996, the party's leader, Necmettin Erbakan became prime minister.

Yet the RP did not last long. In 1997, Erbakan was forced by the military to resign, and the party was closed. This was a "postmodern intervention" according to the Turkish press. Like the Demokrat (Democrat) Party of the 1950s, the RP's liberal policy toward religion and religious groups was anxiously perceived by the military and secular circles as undermining the modern secular legacy of the Republic.[33] More recently, the Islamist Adalet ve Kalkınma (Justice and Development) Party (AKP), which has been in power since 2002, has been the target of massive public demonstrations on the same grounds. Eventually, the AKP was taken to the Constitutional Court where it was fined, although not closed down.

The Turkish state has been so inflexible about the principle of secularism that it even rejects the interpretation of a moderate Islamic country or

---

[27] Robins, "Interrupting Identities: Turkey / Europe," 73–74.
[28] Ayşe Saktanber, "'We Pray Like You Have Fun': New Islamic Youth in Turkey between Intellectualism and Popular Culture," in *Fragments of Culture: The Everyday of Modern Turkey*, ed. Deniz Kandiyoti and Ayşe Saktanber (London: IB Tauris, 2002), 255.
[29] Robins, "Interrupting Identities: Turkey / Europe," 75.
[30] Çınar, *Modernity, Islam, and Secularism in Turkey: Bodies, Places, and Time*, 9.
[31] Saktanber, "'We Pray Like You Have Fun': New Islamic Youth in Turkey between Intellectualism and Popular Culture," 257.
[32] Çınar, *Modernity, Islam, and Secularism in Turkey: Bodies, Places, and Time*, 19.
[33] Kaplan, "'Religious Nationalism': A Textbook Case from Turkey," 665–666; Dumont, "Islam as a Factor of Change and Revival in Modern Turkey," 4.

a model of how Islam and democracy can successfully coexist—an image promoted by the United States within the framework of its foreign policy in the Middle East. For instance, in 2004, when Colin Powell referred to Turkey as an "Islamic Republic," he became the target of Turkish officials, who reminded American officials that Turkey was a secular democracy in which religion was a private affair.[34]

Cola Turka and Islamists

Ülker's avoidance of a pro-Muslim discourse and its emphasis on Turkishness more than Islam in the promotion of Cola Turka is understandable within the context described above.[35] Yet perhaps Ülker did not need to make explicit that its beverage was pro-Muslim, since there was already a significant Islamic and secular public who perceived it as such. Ülker was among the Islamic companies that proliferated, beginning in the 1990s. During this period, a growing Islamic capital began to compete in many sectors of the economy by producing a variety of "Islamic" goods, from food to clothing, and by creating a prolific consumption market for "believers."[36] In an attempt to compete with their secular counterparts, Islamic companies introduced their goods not as being Islamic but as being moral and permissible from an Islamic standpoint.[37] For instance, Ülker claimed that its biscuits contained no lard, which put the rival biscuit company Eti at a disadvantage in the eyes of religiously oriented consumers.[38] This approach resembles a "guerilla tactic," a "clever trick" of the "weak" to resist the system from

---

[34] Aylin Güney, "Anti-Americanism in Turkey: Past and Present," *Middle Eastern Studies* 44, no. 3 (2008): 484.

[35] It should also be kept in mind that Ülker commissioned a secular advertising agency to create the commercials for Cola Turka. An interview with Serdar Erener, director of that advertising agency, revealed that the agency was much more active in formulating the Cola Turka brand and its advertising concept than were the Ülker officials. Cf. Tezel, "Chevy Chase gibi Hollywood starının oynatılmasını Plato Filmciliğe borçluyuz."

[36] Yael Navaro-Yashin, *Faces of the State: Secularism and Public Life in Turkey* (Princeton: Princeton University Press, 2002), 224; Özlem Sandıkçı and Güliz Ger, "Constructing and Representing the Islamic Consumer in Turkey," *Fashion Theory* 11 (2007): 194.

[37] Moreover, Ayşe Öncü, who has examined commercials on Muslim television channels, points out that Islamic companies attempted to give their goods legitimacy and approval in the eyes of their Islamic consumers, by framing their goods with keywords such as *huzur* ("peace and quiet") and *bereket* ("abundance of yield, fertility"), which have Islamic connotations. She argues, "When framed in the language of *huzur* and *bereket*, consumption practices which might be considered hedonistic, and hence a deviation from Islamic ideals, acquire legitimacy and acceptance." Cf. Ayşe Öncü, "The Banal and the Subversive: Politics of Language on Turkish Television," *European Journal of Cultural Studies* 3, no. 3 (1995): 311–313.

[38] Navaro-Yashin, "The Market for Identities: Secularism, Islamism, Commodities," 223–224.

within.[39] Today, a large number of pious Muslims habitually consume Ülker products because of the company's Islamic identity, and some pro-secular Turks refuse to consume them for the same reason. Arguably, by emphasizing Cola Turka's Turkishness more than its Muslimness, Ülker, as usual, attempted to expand its market beyond its loyal, religiously oriented consumers.

Cola Turka became a milestone in the cola wars in Turkey, where a billion liters of cola are consumed per year.[40] Only two weeks after Cola Turka came on the market, Coca-Cola and Pepsi, which controlled 90 percent of the cola market as the first and second brands, respectively, lowered their prices by 12.5 percent and gave a higher margin of profit to distributors.[41] In six months, Cola Turka had the same market share as Pepsi (15 percent). By 2005, it rose to the second rank, after Coca-Cola, with a 20 percent market share.[42] It is reported that Cola Turka entered 63 of every 100 houses.[43] Although, in the beginning, Cola Turka was welcomed by consumers from almost every circle, it was particularly supported by some Islamic/Islamist circles for the long run. Below, I explore Cola Turka's reception by some Islamists in Turkey, based on opinion pieces in Islamist newspapers (i.e., *Zaman*, *Yeni Şafak*, and *Vakit*) and in forums on some Islamist websites (i.e., imamhatip.com, imamhatiplim.com, kartalimamhatip.com, ihlforum.net, islamforum.net, and ezan.vakti.com).

Hüseyin Öztürk from *Vakit*, a radical Islamist daily, was the only opinion writer who affirmed Cola Turka without any reservations, mainly because it represented national capital.[44] He and others ended their cola (Coca-

---

[39] Michel de Certeau, *The Practice of Everyday Life* (Berkeley: University of California Press, 1984).

[40] Osman İridağ, "Gazozuna savaş," *Aksiyon*, no. 449 (14 July 2003): 20–22 [22].

[41] "Cola Turka yok satınca Coca Cola fiyat indirdi," *Yeni Şafak* (19 July 2003): 8.

[42] "Cola Turka, pazarı yüzde 25 büyüttü," *Zaman* (9 February 2005): 10; "Cola'ya 'Turka gazı'," *Yeni Şafak* (24 February 2005): 9; "Cola Turka zirveye oynuyor," *Akşam* (24 February 2005): 10.

[43] "Cola Turka ve Golf, Ülkeri zirveye taşıdı," *Yeni Şafak* (5 September 2005): 7.

[44] Interestingly, another defense of Cola Turka came in 2006 from İlhan Selçuk, one of the most prominent adherents of Kemalist secularism in Turkey, from *Cumhuriyet*. When Ülker was condemned to a 35 million YTL-penalty on the grounds that it exceeded the state-endorsed quota for the use of starch-based sugar in the manufacturing of Cola Turka, Selçuk criticized the Islamist AKP government for not protecting national interests and for supporting the monopoly of American cola brands in Turkey. Selçuk argued that the penalty proved AKP's hypocrisy and showed that it was so dependent on the United States that it did not hesitate to hit even the Islamic capital. Cf. İlhan Selçuk, "Gazoz oyunu," *Cumhuriyet* (3 August 2006): 2; İlhan Selçuk, "Bir gazozluk müslümanlık," *Cumhuriyet* (5 August 2006): 2. Selçuk's support for Cola Turka prompted reactions from other secular columnists who were disappointed to see one of the most loyal defenders of Kemalism and secularism in Turkey support Cola Turka and Ülker, which was known for its Islamist leanings and support for Islamist groups. Cf. Vahap

Cola and Pepsi) boycott with Cola Turka. Noting that Muslim countries were betraying themselves by consuming 60 percent of the world market of Coca-Cola, Pepsi, and American cigarettes, he argued that Ülker provided an "extremely important service" and that Cola Turka was a "proud stance against American drinks."[45] Rejecting Cola Turka's claimed authenticity, many opinion writers in the Islamist press, however, perceived it as an imitation of Coca-Cola and a case of the "cola-ization" of Muslim lifestyles.

Ali Bulaç, a prominent Islamist intellectual writing for *Zaman,* saw Cola Turka as a case in point of the "Turkish tendency of imitating and consuming a given culture without contributing to it anything original and authentic." Commenting that Coca-Cola was the only genuine cola, and that all the others, be it Mecca Cola or Cola Turka, were just copies, Bulaç argued, "it does not matter whether it is Mecca Cola or Cola Turka; in the end everybody drinks cola." Pointing to the richness of Turkish cuisine in terms of non-alcoholic beverages and fruit juices, he remarked that if one of these could be developed and marketed to the world then it would be an authentic production as well as a national response and contribution to the process of globalization.[46] Cola Turka was debated in *Yeni Şafak,* a liberal-Islamist daily affiliated with the AKP, along similar lines, but in a harsher manner. It was argued that Cola Turka made cola attractive even to those who used to reject it.[47] Remarking that Cola Turka "hoodwinked" people by "localizing the international instead of internationalizing the local," Fadime Özkan wrote:

> I neither like the taste nor the name of cola no matter what you put in front of it, including "Mecca" [...] I strongly reject all colas, primarily Coca-Cola which is supportive of American terrorism and which is the unique symbol of capitalism and imperialism. Instead, I humbly suggest everyone to drink *ayran* [a drink made of yogurt and water], *şerbet* [sweetened fruit juice] and *hoşaf* [compote].[48]

Munyar, "Ülker'in Cola Turka'sına İlhan Selçuk'tan destek," *Hürriyet* (4 August 2006): 10; Ahmet Kekeç, "Aferin İlhan Selçuk," *Star* (19 August 2006): 2.

[45] Hüseyin Öztürk, "Cola Turka ve Ülker," *Vakit* (13 July 2003): 15.

[46] Bulaç, "Cola Turka," 13.

[47] Kürşat Bumin, "Ha gayret, aman ülkede eline 'cola' bulaşmamış kimse kalmasın," *Yeni Şafak* (19 July 2003): 5; Fehmi Koru, "Bu bir tavla yazısı değildir," *Yeni Şafak* (21 September 2003): 12.

[48] Özkan and Foster, "Consumer Citizenship, Nationalism, and Neoliberal Globalization in Turkey: The Advertising Launch of Cola Turka," 18. Similar comments were made in the secular press. Gündüz Vassaf, from the liberal daily *Radikal,* suggested that Coca-Cola, Cola Turka, and Mecca Cola were all the same "muddy water" that was presented to consumers

Similarly, Özlem Albayrak thought that more than being an authentic local alternative to Coca-Cola, Cola Turka just added to Coca-Cola's worldwide hegemony.[49] Yet she argued, "nevertheless one should prefer Cola Turka so that children in other countries do not die, so that less money is allocated to guns that threaten humanity."[50]

These opinion pieces suggest that although the authenticity of Cola Turka is highly debatable, it can still function as a serious alternative to Coca-Cola simply because it is not American and because Muslims manufacture it, and therefore, it does not represent the United States and its military imperialism in the Middle East. This idea is strongly supported by the forums on Cola Turka on some Islamist websites whose members appear to be young Islamists. Although many of the Islamist youth who participate in these forums like cola as a refreshing drink and even find it "irresistible," they refrain from drinking it either because they believe it is forbidden by Islam or, more importantly, because of the allegations that it is anti-Muslim. Believing that Coca-Cola contains alcohol and Pepsi contains pork, some argue that Islam forbids both. Even if Islam does not forbid cola, others argue, it falls into the category of *israf* (waste), since it is not useful or essential to human survival. However, the strongest reason for rejecting, even boycotting, Coca-Cola and Pepsi is the belief that they are "anti-Muslim" and "supportive of Israel."

No other commercial product in Turkey has been so identified with and boycotted to protest against American foreign policies. This was not the first time that Coca-Cola was boycotted in Turkey. Soon after its introduction to Turkey in 1964 by a prominent Turkish entrepreneur,[51] Coca-Cola was

---

with different symbols. Cf. Gündüz Vassaf, "Hilal, haç ve sonrası," *Radikal* (1 August 2004): 19.

[49] Indeed, Cola Turka never had an impact on the market share of Coca-Cola. Stating that they were not unhappy with Cola Turka, a Coca-Cola company official in Turkey noted that "people try cola for the first time and buy it. We always prefer competition because it expands consumership" (as cited in "Pazardaki rekabet Coca-Cola'ya yaradı," *Akşam* (2 March 2004): 9). By 2006, Cola Turka had increased the cola market in Turkey by 50 percent; cf. "Ülker: Kolada Pepsi'yi yakaladık," *Sabah* (12 September 2006): 12.

[50] Özlem Albayrak, "Türkiye'de bir 'drink'," *Yeni Şafak* (10 July 2003): 19.

[51] Until the 1960s, Coca-Cola was only available to the U.S. military at U.S. military bases in Turkey. It could also be found at bazaars for smuggled goods. Kadir Has, a prominent Turkish entrepreneur, who introduced Coca-Cola to Turkey in 1964, encountered this soft drink at such a bazaar in Adana, near the U.S. military base in İncirlik. In his memoir, he explains that he used to get Coca-Cola, which he "loved too much," from the bazaars and from his visits to Beirut. He used to stock the soda at his house. During his first visit to the United States in 1950, Has saw Coca-Cola everywhere and thought about bringing it to Turkey. Although his friends told him this was impossible, he began to work on this issue when he returned to Turkey. In 1964, with the help of his friend Behçet Türkmen, then director of the Turkish National Intelligence Agency (MIT), he got permission from Turkish authorities to manufacture

the target of leftist youth, who associated it with American imperialism.[52] Today, it has become mainly the target of Islamist youth, who perceive it as a symbol of American imperialism and "cruelty" in the Middle East. "I do not drink Coca-Cola because it symbolizes American and Zionist imperialism," writes a forum member on imamhatip.com.[53] Referencing a CNN report that the Coca-Cola Company will donate its profits to the Israeli Navy (which is actually a Turkish variation of a rumor circulating via e-mail, especially in the Middle East),[54] or interpreting fake Coca-Cola web advertisements (that are offensive to Muslims) as actual advertisements of the company, many forum members invite all Muslims to boycott Coca-Cola with statements such as "we fire another bullet over Palestine each time we buy a Coca-

---

Coca-Cola in Turkey and established the 1,916th factory of Coca-Cola, in Bakırköy, Istanbul. This was followed by an interesting promotion campaign called "hidden treasure." Newspaper advertisements reported that prizes—such as refrigerators, radios, records, and lots of free Coca-Cola—valued then at 400,000 Turkish liras could be won inside the caps of Coca-Cola bottles. These advertisements juxtaposed Coca-Cola with Turkish food, such as *kebab* and *döner*, and stated, "Everything goes better with Coca-Cola." Has states, "Yes, Turkish people loved Coca-Cola. Especially the youth liked this American soft drink very much. People were drinking and drinking; our factory was unable to meet the demand. We made a lot of money out of Coca-Cola in a short period of time." Cf. Kadir Has, *Vatan borcu ödüyorum* (Istanbul: Kadir Has Vakfı Yayınları, 2002), 180–186.

[52] The first call to boycott cola came from the socialist periodical *Yön*, which claimed that Coca-Cola was a poison that caused immense harm to human health. Quoting from *Fact*, an American magazine, about the physical harm ranging from tooth decay to mutated offspring, *Yön* complained that many dollars were wasted to harm public health. It also criticized the Turkish government and businessmen for allowing the "invasion," "colonization," and "exploitation" of Turkey by the "Cola empire." Cf. "Coca-Cola zehirdir, içmeyiniz," *Yön*, no. 119 (9 July 1965): 7. Coca-Cola was also boycotted in universities. For example, students at the Istanbul Technical University attempted to prohibit Coca-Cola sales in the student canteen. Company officials tried to convince the students to stop by saying that they would guarantee that an automobile prize would be inside one of the lids of Coca-Cola sold in the canteen if the students allowed the sales. Kudret Emiroğlu, *Gündelik hayatımızın tarihi* (Ankara: Dost, 2002), 362.

[53] fashizan, *Meselenin özü*, Message posted to http://www.imamhatip.com/kamusalalan/cocacolacola-turkazemzem-cola-ulkernestlevs-uzerine-t2187.15.html, 20 October 2004.

[54] In other versions of the rumor, the source of the report is given as NBC. In the Turkish version of the report, NBC is replaced by CNN, probably because the former is not as widely known in Turkey. The Coca-Cola Company attempts to refute some Middle Eastern anti-Coca-Cola claims on its website in a special section entitled "Middle East Rumors." The company site also denies the rumor that it contributes profits to Israel. Cf. Coca-Cola Company, *Rumor: Anti-Muslim messages appear in graphics (No Mohammed, No Mecca)*, http://www.thecocacolacompany.com/contactus/myths_rumors/middle_east_subliminal.html, accessed 12 August 2008; Coca-Cola Company, *Statement on NBC rumor*, http://www.thecoca-colacompany.com/contactus/myths_rumors/middle_east_nbc.html, accessed 12 August 2008.

Cola"[55] and "we kill our Muslim brothers with our own hands by buying Coca-Cola."[56] A forum member on ihlforum.net even compares the dark color of Coca-Cola to the blood of Palestinian children.[57]

Sometimes all Jewish and non-Muslim goods are imagined as "bullets to Muslims." Some even sincerely believe the legend that an anti-Muslim message, which reads *Lā Makka, Lā Muḥammad* ("No Mecca, No Mohammed") in Arabic, is hidden in the mirror image of the Coca-Cola trademark.[58] It is also believed that the word "Pepsi" is the abbreviation of the statement "**Pay Every Penny to Save Israel**." For some, boycotting Coca-Cola is a Muslim duty so important that they walk through the streets in missionary gangs to warn those who appear to be drinking Coca-Cola.

Claiming that the money spent on Coca-Cola and other non-Muslim goods goes to *kafirler* (unbelievers, infidels), forum members invite each other to support Muslims, including Palestinians, by consuming Muslim brands, such as Cola Turka. For them, consuming Cola Turka as opposed to Coca-Cola is so important that they will spend hours looking for a Cola Turka to buy. A forum member on imamhatip.com writes:

> It is a pity that you have to go to at least five groceries to buy one Cola Turka. You need to go to big supermarkets to buy it; otherwise you cannot find it. Two days ago we walked through all Esentepe, but unfortunately we could not find any Cola Turka. In the end, we sat down on a corner to rest. I could not stand, I got up and shouted in the middle of the street: "These people are *gavur* [infidels]; everywhere is Coca-Cola but no Cola Turka. Everywhere is their [infidels'] goods, foods and drinks; we cannot find national goods so that we can buy."[59]

Apparently, this Islamist youth perceives Cola Turka as a Muslim substitute for Coca-Cola not simply because it is local but because it is manufac-

---

[55] Cita, *Ynt: Coca-Cola/Cola Turka/Zemzem Cola-Ülker/Nestle/..vs.üzerine*, Message posted to http://www.imamhatip.com/kamusalalan/coca-colacola-turkazemzem-cola-ulkernestlevs-uzerine-t2187.30.html, 3 June 2007.

[56] Ebrar, *Message posted to http://ezanvakti.com/cola-harammi, 13 August 2007*.

[57] hayrunnisa, *Coca cola zıkkımlanmak*, Message posted to http://www.ihlforum.net/coca-cola-zikkimlanmak-t-5156.html, 21 May 2008.

[58] In 2000, upon the request of the Coca-Cola Company, the Grand Mufti of Al-Azhar, Egypt, had the trademark examined by a group of researchers and concluded: "The trademark does not injure the true Islamic religion directly or indirectly." Cf. Coca-Cola Company, *Rumor: Anti-Muslim messages appear in graphics (No Mohammed, No Mecca)*.

[59] Spark, *Ynt:Son sınıflar buyurun kardeşlerde gelebilir*, Message posted to http://www.imamhatip.com/kamusalalan/son-siniflar-buyurun,kardeslerde-gelebilir-t16870.0.html, 3 March 2006.

tured by Ülker. A forum member on imamhatip.com notes, "Ülker is owned by pious Muslims. Moreover, they provide huge monetary helps to Islamist organizations and students."[60] Mecca Cola had publicized that "10 percent of the profits are dedicated to charities operating in Palestinian territories and that another 10 percent are passed to international peace-oriented nongovernmental organizations based in Europe."[61] The perception of Ülker as an Islamist company supporting Islamist circles, underlines the idea that Cola Turka did not need an explicitly pro-Muslim promotional campaign, as did Mecca Cola.

The comments in the forums suggest that the perception of Cola Turka by Islamists is not independent of their perception of Coca-Cola. For them, Cola Turka, as a product manufactured by an Islamist company, symbolizes the opposite of everything that Coca-Cola symbolizes. Coca-Cola was perceived to be so anti-Muslim that it was enough for these Islamist consumers that Cola Turka was not Coca-Cola. Moreover, no other local cola had expressed this sentiment as thoroughly as Cola Turka, whose commercials cleverly emphasized that it was not American.

Cola-Turka is not Turkey's first local Cola. In fact, the first cola brand in Turkey was a local brand, Nur Cola, manufactured by Uludağ in 1955.[62] Soon after Coca-Cola was introduced to the country in the 1960s, several local cola brands emerged, such as Mr. Kola, Katibim Kola, and Klüp Kola.[63] From the 1980s to the 2000s, several local cola brands were launched by Turkish companies under both Turkish and foreign names: Bixi Cola, İxir Cola, Kristal Cola, Uludağ Cola. A dozen more local colas were sold only in some small towns (i.e., Chat Cola, Efe Cola, Can Cola, Beylik Cola, Huzur Cola, Fizzy Cola, and Zafer Cola).[64] None of these, including Kristal Cola, which was introduced in 1996 by the Islamist İhlas group as a "decaf Cola" and as "Turkey's Cola,"[65] was as popular as Cola Turka. A simple reason might be the better taste of Cola Turka, which, the manufacturers claim, is a taste between Coca-Cola and Pepsi.[66] The most powerful reason, however, must be that Cola Turka was the first and only local cola brand that explicitly declared at the right time that it was an "authentic" local alternative to

---

[60] fashizan, *Meselenin özü*.
[61] Ram, "Liquid Identities: Mecca Cola versus Coca-Cola," 468.
[62] "Efsane Gazoz Uludağ, kola pazarında," *Ntvmsnbc* (8 April 2003, http://www.ntvmsnbc.com/news/209726.asp, accessed 30 June 2008).
[63] "Coca-Cola zehirdir, içmeyiniz," 7.
[64] İridağ, "Gazozuna savaş," 21.
[65] Ibid., 21.
[66] "Ülker'e çok cazip bir teklif gelmişti, satsaydık başka ne iş yapabilirdik ki," *Zaman* (28 June 2007, http://www.zaman.com.tr/haber.do?haberno=557024, accessed 30 June 2008).

American cola brands, especially to Coca-Cola. Cola Turka so firmly established its public image as non-American that even the news that the cola concentrate in Cola Turka was imported from the American RC Cola Company,[67] did not significantly affect its popularity. Perhaps Cola Turka was not authentic enough, but it was still a good local alternative to Coca-Cola.

Departing from the argument that in the global era, commodification heterogenizes symbolically yet homogenizes structurally, Uri Ram argues that despite a symbolic "Mecca-ization," Mecca Cola still indicates a structural "Cola-ization" of world cultures..[68] He points out that "Mecca Cola achieves the opposite of what it declares it does: it dispenses the Muslim idiom into the vessels of American commodified culture. While 'Mecca' wins symbolically, 'Cola' wins structurally."[69] As suggested by Cola Turka's reception by the majority of the opinion writers in the Islamist press, a similar argument would also apply to Cola Turka.

In an age in which people express their identities not only by what they consume but also by what they do not, consuming Mecca Cola or Cola Turka—as opposed to Coca-Cola—might convey a stronger political message than it would if they never consumed any cola. After the emergence of Cola Turka, some Islamist circles passed from the category of non-consumers of cola to non-consumers of Coca-Cola. The latter shift, I argue, embodies a more active, even militant Muslim identity than the former. While Islamists' rejection of cola all together would help the West and the secular circles in Turkey to Otherize them as "traditionalists" or "reactionaries," both Cola Turka's reappropriation of cola and the Islamists' appropriation of Cola Turka as a means of resistance to American economic and military imperialism suggests that Muslim identity might be a lot more complex, clever, and challenging than the West and the secular circles assumed—and not simply traditional or reactionary.

An Islamic Mode of Modernization and Consumption

Cola Turka is not a unique case of transformation in the consumption habits of Islamist circles in Turkey, which has continued since the 1980s. Owing mainly to the new liberal economic order established by the Özal government and the application of a free market economy open to foreign investment and trade, Turkey witnessed throughout the 1980s and 1990s the expansion of a rich consumer culture, stimulated by such novelties as su-

---

[67] Sanyer, "Aslında Amerikalıymış," 15.
[68] Ram, "Liquid Identities: Mecca Cola versus Coca-Cola," 466.
[69] Ibid., 480.

permarkets, shopping centers, fast-food chains, entertainment centers, and summer resorts. As, for the urban middle and upper classes, consumption became a means to refashion identities, a serious transformation appeared not only in secular but also in Islamic urban lifestyles.

Until the 1990s, Islamism in Turkey was considered a mode of thought and a way of life that contrasted modernity. In the secular view, it was often looked down on as being "backward, uncivilized, fundamentalist, incompetent, and lacking taste and culture."[70] This view was seriously challenged during the administration of the RP. While the leader of the RP and Prime Minister Necmettin Erbakan, who appeared in the media in fashionable suits with Versace ties, created an "image of modern and competent Islamist statesmanship,"[71] Tekbir Giyim, one of the leading companies of Islamic attire in Turkey, held fashion shows in which top models displayed dresses and headscarves that not only complied with Islamic dress code but also were as elegant and stylish as secular attire sold in expensive stores. While Tekbir Giyim was harshly criticized by Islamist circles and intellectuals for "degenerating Islam" and commodifying the headscarf and the veil, which had been "an item of identity and political struggle,"[72] an Islamic mode of modernization and consumption had been infusing every facet of Islamic everyday life.

Umut Azak remarks that in the 1990s, rather than representing themselves in reaction to modernity, Islamist circles in Turkey attempted to add an "Islamic essence" to everything associated with "being modern."[73] The emergence of Islamic radio stations[74] and television channels,[75] the expansion of Islamic serials, movies, music ("green pop"), and romance novels ("green

---

[70] Çınar, *Modernity, Islam, and Secularism in Turkey: Bodies, Places, and Time*, 88.

[71] Ibid., 88.

[72] Cf. Çınar, *Modernity, Islam, and Secularism in Turkey: Bodies, Places, and Time*, 89; Navaro-Yashin, "The Market for Identities: Secularism, Islamism, Commodities," 242–243. In May 2008, İlhami Güler, a professor of theology, and Süleyman Bayraktar, the editor of *İslamiyat* journal, sued Tekbir Giyim and requested the annulment of the company's brand name on the grounds that the term *tekbir*, which commonly refers to the saying "Allah u Akbar (Allah is the greatest)," was a religious symbol, and, therefore, according to the law, could not be used as a brand name. Owner Mustafa Karaduman defended the company by arguing that *tekbir* simply meant "unique," and, therefore, was not a religious value or symbol. Cf. "'Tekbir dini bir sembol değil'," *Akşam* (2008 July 2008, http://www.aksam.com.tr/haber.asp?a=124902,3&tarih=28.07.2008, accessed 18 August 2008). For details, see chapter 2 of this volume.

[73] Umut Azak, "İslami radyolar ve türbanlı spikerler," in *İslam'ın yeni kamusal yüzleri*, ed. Nilüfer Göle (Istanbul: Metis, 2000), 97.

[74] See ibid. for a discussion of Islamic radio stations.

[75] See Öncü, "The Banal and the Subversive: Politics of Language on Turkish Television" for a discussion of Islamic TV channels.

serials"); and the establishment of private schools and hospitals, parks and gardens, tea and coffee houses, and cafeterias catering to religiously oriented customers[76] were signs of the development in the 1990s of an Islamic everyday culture. Currently, one can even find Islamic chat and wedding sites on the internet (i.e., gonuldensevenler.com, zevac.merihnet.com and islamievlilik.com), which help pious men and women find a pious mate to marry. The 1990s also witnessed the rise of an "Islamic bourgeoisie" or "Islamic high society," which was, in Özlem Sandıkçı and Güliz Ger's words, "conservative in values but avant-garde in consumption practices."[77]

Shopping in the United States and Europe, consuming luxurious foreign brand-name goods, appearing in lavish cafes and restaurants, and holding expensive weddings at grand hotels were among the signs of belonging to this class.[78] To these, one could add the expansion of summer resorts that attempted to meet the "holiday need" of upper-class pious Muslims, such as the five-star Caprice Hotel (currently Caprice Thermal Palace), where alcoholic beverages are not served, men and women use separate swimming pools and beaches, and people dine at an open buffet restaurant under the hadith (a saying by the Prophet Mohammed), "eat and drink, but do not waste."[79] These examples not only suggest that Islamism was not against modernity per se but also that it was as "equally capable as secularism of producing an alternative high modernism."[80]

---

[76] Saktanber, "'We Pray Like You Have Fun': New Islamic Youth in Turkey between Intellectualism and Popular Culture," 262–267; Azak, "İslami radyolar ve türbanlı spikerler," 97.

[77] Sandıkçı and Ger, "Constructing and Representing the Islamic Consumer in Turkey," 192.

[78] A newspaper described the consumption habits of this class as follows: "Men get dressed from Emenegildo Zegna and Nina Ricci. Women's turbans are from Longchamp and Dior, their overcoats from Escada, shoes and purses from Gucci and Dior, and jewelry from Gilan. Veiled women smoke *nargile* [water pipe] in luxurious cafes, get in 4x4s, break their fasts in hotels, and they go to brunches. They shop in New York, Paris, and London and come back with jam-packed suitcases." Cf. Eylem Türk, "Müslüman burjuvazi," *Milliyet Business* (5 October 2003): 1, 8–9 [1]. The current Prime Minister, Recep Tayyip Erdoğan, and his family are also mentioned as being the representatives of this Muslim bourgeois class: "They seem to reject the West, but they are strongly committed to the West. They send their children to the West, mostly to the U.S. for education. Their brides give birth in the U.S. so that their children will be U.S. citizens by birth. They say, 'waste is not permissible by religion,' but they use Swedish handmade wristwatches, American clothes exclusively made for them, Italian shoes which are worth diamonds, Versace ties, and Louis Vuitton purses. Women of this new class, buy their turbans from Paris and their underwear from London. Their children drive the latest and the most expensive cars." Cf. Uğur Cilasun, "AKP iktidarına sınıfsal bir bakış," *Radikal* (18 March 2008, http://www.radikal.com.tr/ek_haber.php?ek=r2&haberno=8117, accessed 10 June 2008).

[79] Mücahit Bilici, "İslam'ın bronzlaşan yüzü: Caprice Hotel örnek olayı," in *İslam'ın yeni kamusal yüzleri*, ed. Nilüfer Göle (Istanbul: Metis, 2000), 216–236.

[80] Çınar, *Modernity, Islam, and Secularism in Turkey: Bodies, Places, and Time*, 90.

Today, while Islamist political parties continue to interpellate their religious supporters via a discourse of exclusion and victimization, and some Islamist intellectuals continue to incite moral panic around the "commodification," "profanation," or "degeneration" of Islam, Islamist everyday practices suggest that Islamic identities insist on actively participating in modern everyday life and benefiting from current material culture as much as secular identities do. As the Caprice Hotel advertisements read, "You also deserve holiday,"[81] or as Cola Turka suggests to Islamists that they also deserve drinking cola, today, Islamic identities appear to be no longer conservative and modest in their consumption demands, but assertive in their "right" to a modern, prosperous life. This right might seem to contradict such tenets of Islam as avoidance of waste, modesty, asceticism, and abstention from worldly pleasures and might give the impression that Islam is conquered and "contaminated" by Western individualism and modernism.[82] Yet these changing Islamic everyday practices could also be approached as "creative adaptations,"[83] as a critical site where Islamic identities meet, negotiate, and appropriate modernity in their own fashion. Moreover, although many Islamists appreciate modernity as technology and material abundance, several studies[84] show that they discursively distinguish themselves from Western/secular modernism by despising and rejecting a "blind emulation" of "hedonistic" Western/secular lifestyles through a spirituality and morality that is still derived from or imagined through Islam.[85] Arguably, as the sec-

---

[81] See, for example, *Yeni Şafak*, 5 July 2003, 11.

[82] Navaro-Yashin questions Islamists' claim to authenticity by pointing out their "inauthentic" consumption habits. Referring especially to the growing consumption of foreign brand-name goods among Islamists, he remarks that in their attempt to refashion themselves as modern subjects, "Islamists have drawn more inspiration from secularists and from the West than they have from the Islamic and Ottoman past." Navaro-Yashin, "The Market for Identities: Secularism, Islamism, Commodities," 248.

[83] Dilip Parameshwar Gaonkar, "On Alternative Modernities," *Public Culture* 11, no. 1 (1999): 1–18.

[84] Göle, *The Forbidden Modern: Civilization and Veiling*; Azak, "İslami radyolar ve türbanlı spikerler"; Saktanber, "'We Pray Like You Have Fun': New Islamic Youth in Turkey between Intellectualism and Popular Culture."

[85] For instance, Göle points to the discrepancy between young veiled women's claims for personality and their disavowal of femininity. Cf. Göle, *The Forbidden Modern: Civilization and Veiling*, 127–130. Saktanber refers to Islamist girls who perceive themselves as being on the "true path," which means avoiding self-indulgence while still participating in modern everyday life. She describes this "true path" as follows: "This path was not contaminated by the blind emulation of Western lifestyles; they rejected the seductive idleness of an irreligious life marked by personal indulgence, listening to meaningless Western music, watching illusory and also risqué movies, dancing in night clubs, and flirting on the street corners or in silly Western-style pubs and cafes. Instead, they preferred to spend time enhancing their knowledge of religion, science and social matters, helping those in need of both moral and material sup-

ular discourse has been homogenizing and Otherizing Islamists, Islamists have also been homogenizing and Otherizing "Westernized" secular lives. As modernity has been transforming Islamists, Islamists have been claiming that they are transforming modernity.[86] Not being against modernity per se, but against its supposed Western/secular definition, and distinguishing between modernization and Westernization, Islamists have been attempting to "indigenize" and Islamize modernity.[87] By being not prohibitive but selective, they have been struggling tactically to resist the secular system without leaving it.

Bibliography

Albayrak, Özlem. "Türkiye'de bir 'drink'." *Yeni Şafak* (10 July 2003): 19.
Atakan, Yurtsan. "Kola Turka vadisi." *Hürriyet Kelebek* (8 February 2006): 3.
Atay, Tayfun. "Cola'nı imanla iç." *Milliyet* (28 April 2004, http://www.milliyet.com.tr/2004/04/28/sanat/san09.html, accessed 10 June 2008).
Azak, Umut. "İslami radyolar ve türbanlı spikerler." In *İslam'ın yeni kamusal yüzleri*, edited by Nilüfer Göle, 93–109. Istanbul: Metis, 2000.
Barbarosoğlu, Fatma K. "'Cola Turka' içmek ya da 'ala turka' olmanın pozitif milliyetçiliğe katkısı." *Yeni Şafak* (11 July 2003): 18.
Bilici, Mücahit. "İslam'ın bronzlaşan yüzü: Caprice Hotel örnek olayı." In *İslam'ın yeni kamusal yüzleri*, edited by Nilüfer Göle, 216–236. Istanbul: Metis, 2000.
Bulaç, Ali. "Cola Turka." *Zaman* (2 August 2003): 13.

---

port who had lost their enthusiasm for leading a proper, honest life as a result of the unbearable pressures of a pitiless, chaotic and unjust social system [. . .] They are also consumers of 'secular' popular culture. However, they were quite careful, in making the effort to criticize, to distinguish themselves from, the habitual consumers of those products." Cf. Saktanber, "'We Pray Like You Have Fun': New Islamic Youth in Turkey between Intellectualism and Popular Culture," 259–260. Azak makes a similar remark in her discussion of the young religious female anchors employed by Islamic radio stations. Cf. Azak, "İslami radyolar ve türbanlı spikerler," 99–100.

[86] A *haşema* (the name given to swimsuits that comply with the Islamic dress code) advertisement, which uses the slogan "the changing face of swimsuit," tells a lot about the way Islamists see their participation in modernity. While *haşema* could also be posited as an expression of the changing face of Islam, the advertisement claims that it is not Islam that is changing but the modernity embodied in the modern swimsuit. See *Yeni Şafak*, 12 July 2003, 2.

[87] See Nilüfer Göle, "Global Expectations, Local Experiences: Non-Western Modernities," in *Through a Glass, Darkly: Blurred Images of Cultural Tradition and Modernity over Distance and Time*, ed. Wil Arts (Leiden, Boston and Köln: Brill, 2000), 41, for a discussion of the concept "indigenization of modernity."

Bumin, Kürşat. "'Cola Turka' iç, 'pozitif milliyetçilik' safına geç." *Yeni Şafak* (12 July 2003): 5.

———. "Ha gayret, aman ülkede eline 'cola' bulaşmamış kimse kalmasın." *Yeni Şafak* (19 July 2003): 5.

Certeau, Michel de. *The Practice of Everyday Life*. Berkeley: University of California Press, 1984.

Cilasun, Uğur. "AKP iktidarına sınıfsal bir bakış." *Radikal* (18 March 2008, http://www.radikal.com.tr/ek_haber.php?ek=r2&haberno=8117, accessed 10 June 2008).

Çınar, Alev. *Modernity, Islam, and Secularism in Turkey: Bodies, Places, and Time*. Minneapolis and London: University of Minnesota Press, 2005.

Cita. *Ynt: Coca-Cola/Cola Turka/Zemzem Cola-Ülker/Nestle/..vs.üzerine*. Message posted to http://www.imamhatip.com/kamusalalan/cocacola-turkazemzem-cola-ulkernestlevs-uzerine-t2187.30.html, 3 June 2007.

Coca-Cola Company. *Rumor: Anti-Muslim messages appear in graphics (No Mohammed, No Mecca)*. http://www.thecoca-colacompany.com/contactus/myths_rumors/middle_east_subliminal.html, accessed 12 August 2008.

———. *Statement on NBC rumor*. http://www.thecoca-colacompany.com/contactus/myths_rumors/middle_east_nbc.html, accessed 12 August 2008.

"Coca-Cola zehirdir, içmeyiniz." *Yön*, no. 119 (9 July 1965): 7.

"Cola Turka, pazarı yüzde 25 büyüttü." *Zaman* (9 February 2005): 10.

"Cola Turka ve Golf, Ülkeri zirveye taşıdı." *Yeni Şafak* (5 September 2005): 7.

"Cola Turka yok satınca Coca Cola fiyat indirdi." *Yeni Şafak* (19 July 2003): 8.

"Cola Turka zirveye oynuyor." *Akşam* (24 February 2005): 10.

"Cola'ya 'Turka gazı'." *Yeni Şafak* (24 February 2005): 9.

Dilek, Bahadır Selim. "Patates, telaffuz sorunu ve Irak'taki kontrol noktaları." *Birgün* (20 July 2005, http://www.tumgazeteler.com/?a=893356, accessed 20 July 2005).

Dumont, Paul. "Islam as a Factor of Change and Revival in Modern Turkey." In *Turkic Culture: Continuity and Change*, edited by Sabri M. Akural, 1–15. Indiana University Press, 1987.

Ebrar. *Message posted to http://ezanvakti.com/cola-harammi, 13 August 2007*.

"Efsane Gazoz Uludağ, kola pazarında." *Ntvmsnbc* (8 April 2003, http://www.ntvmsnbc.com/news/209726.asp, accessed 30 June 2008).

Emiroğlu, Kudret. *Gündelik hayatımızın tarihi*. Ankara: Dost, 2002.
fashizan. *Meselenin özü*. Message posted to http://www.imamhatip.com/kamusalalan/coca-colacola-turkazemzem-cola-ulkernestlevs-uzerine-t2187.15.html, 20 October 2004.
Gaonkar, Dilip Parameshwar. "On Alternative Modernities." *Public Culture* 11, no. 1 (1999): 1–18.
Göle, Nilüfer. "Global Expectations, Local Experiences: Non-Western Modernities." In *Through a Glass, Darkly: Blurred Images of Cultural Tradition and Modernity over Distance and Time*, edited by Wil Arts, 40–55. Leiden, Boston and Köln: Brill, 2000.
———. "Modernist kamusal alan ve İslami ahlak." In *İslam'ın yeni kamusal yüzleri*, edited by Nilüfer Göle, 19–40. Istanbul: Metis, 2000.
———. *The Forbidden Modern: Civilization and Veiling*. Ann Arbor: University of Michigan Press, 1996.
Güney, Aylin. "Anti-Americanism in Turkey: Past and Present." *Middle Eastern Studies* 44, no. 3 (2008): 471–487.
Has, Kadir. *Vatan borcu ödüyorum*. Istanbul: Kadir Has Vakfı Yayınları, 2002.
hayrunnisa. *Coca cola zıkkımlanmak*. Message posted to http://www.ihlforum.net/coca-cola-zikkimlanmak-t-5156.html, 21 May 2008.
İridağ, Osman. "Gazozuna savaş." *Aksiyon*, no. 449 (14 July 2003): 20–22.
Kadıoğlu, Ayşe. "The Paradox of Turkish Nationalism and the Construction of Official Identity." *Middle Eastern Studies* 32, no. 2 (1996): 177–193.
Kaplan, Sam. "'Religious Nationalism': A Textbook Case from Turkey." *Comparative Studies of South Asia, Africa and the Middle East* 25, no. 3 (2005): 665–676.
Kekeç, Ahmet. "Aferin İlhan Selçuk." *Star* (19 August 2006): 2.
Koru, Fehmi. "Bu bir tavla yazısı değildir." *Yeni Şafak* (21 September 2003): 12.
"Light Cola Turka geliyor." *Yeni Şafak* (22 October 2003): 8.
Mardin, Şerif. "Turkish Islamic Exceptionalism Yesterday and Today: Continuity, Rupture and Reconstruction in Operational Codes." *Turkish Studies* 6, no. 2 (2005): 145–165.
Mardin, Şerif A. "Ideology and Religion in the Turkish Revolution." *International Journal of Middle East Studies* 2, no. 3 (1971): 197–211.
Munyar, Vahap. "Ülker'in Cola Turka'sına İlhan Selçuk'tan destek." *Hürriyet* (4 August 2006): 10.
Navaro-Yashin, Yael. *Faces of the State: Secularism and Public Life in Turkey*. Princeton: Princeton University Press, 2002.
———. "The Market for Identities: Secularism, Islamism, Commodities." In *Fragments of Culture: The Everyday of Modern Turkey*, edited by

Deniz Kandiyoti Saktanber and Ayşe, 221–253. London: I. B. Tauris, 2002.
Öncü, Ayşe. "The Banal and the Subversive: Politics of Language on Turkish Television." *European Journal of Cultural Studies* 3, no. 3 (1995): 296–318.
Özkan, Derya, and Robert J. Foster. "Consumer Citizenship, Nationalism, and Neoliberal Globalization in Turkey: The Advertising Launch of Cola Turka." *Advertising & Society Review* 6, no. 3 (2005).
Özkök, Ertuğrul. "Domuzlar körfezi fiyaskosu gibi." *Hürriyet* (7 July 2003): 23.
Öztürk, Hüseyin. "Cola Turka ve Ülker." *Vakit* (13 July 2003): 15.
"Pazardaki rekabet Coca-Cola'ya yaradı." *Akşam* (2 March 2004): 9.
Ram, Uri. "Liquid Identities: Mecca Cola versus Coca-Cola." *European Journal of Cultural Studies* 10, no. 4 (2007): 465–484.
Robins, Kevin. "Interrupting Identities: Turkey / Europe." In *Questions of Cultural Identity*, edited by Stuart Hall and Paul Du Gay, 61–86. London: Sage Publications, 1996.
Saktanber, Ayşe. "'We Pray Like You Have Fun': New Islamic Youth in Turkey between Intellectualism and Popular Culture." In *Fragments of Culture: The Everyday of Modern Turkey*, edited by Deniz Kandiyoti and Ayşe Saktanber, 254–276. London: IB Tauris, 2002.
Sandıkçı, Özlem, and Güliz Ger. "Constructing and Representing the Islamic Consumer in Turkey." *Fashion Theory* 11 (2007): 189–210.
Şanlı, Ufuk. "Süleymaniye baskınının şifreleri." *Aksiyon*, no. 604 (3 July 2006): 48–49.
Sanyer, Ruhi. "Aslında Amerikalıymış." *Radikal* (21 March 2004): 15.
Sayyid, Bobby S. *A Fundamental Fear: Eurocentrism and the Emergence of Islamism*. London and New York: Zed Books Ltd., 1997.
Selçuk, İlhan. "Bir gazozluk müslümanlık." *Cumhuriyet* (5 August 2006): 2.
———. "Gazoz oyunu." *Cumhuriyet* (3 August 2006): 2.
Spark. *Ynt:Son sınıflar buyurun kardeşlerde gelebilir*. Message posted to http://www.imamhatip.com/kamusalalan/son-siniflar-buyurun, kardeslerde-gelebilir-t16870.0.html, 3 March 2006.
Taş, Hakkı, and Meral Uğur. "Roads 'Drawn' to Modernity: Religion and Secularism in Contemporary Turkey." *PS: Political Science and Politics* 40, no. 2 (2007): 311–314.
"'Tekbir dini bir sembol değil'." *Akşam* (2008 July 2008, http://www.aksam.com.tr/haber.asp?a=124902,3&tarihi=28.07.2008, accessed 18 August 2008).

Tezel, Mevlüt. "Chevy Chase gibi Hollywood starının oynatılmasını Plato Filmciliğe borçluyuz." *Hürriyet* (13 July 2003): 6.

Tosun, Resul. "Amerika'dan hırsımızı Cola Turka ile çıkartıyoruz." *Yeni Şafak* (9 July 2003): 15.

Türk, Eylem. "Müslüman burjuvazi." *Milliyet Business* (5 October 2003): 1, 8–9.

"Ülker: Kolada Pepsi'yi yakaladık." *Sabah* (12 September 2006): 12.

"Ülker'e çok cazip bir teklif gelmişti, satsaydık başka ne iş yapabilirdik ki." *Zaman* (28 June 2007, http://www.zaman.com.tr/haber.do?haberno= 557024, accessed 30 June 2008).

Vassaf, Gündüz. "Hilal, haç ve sonrası." *Radikal* (1 August 2004): 19.

Yavuz, Turan. *Çuvallayan ittifak*. Ankara: Destek Yayınları, 2006.

Yıldız, Yılmaz. "Ülker'in 'Cola Turka'sı Türkler'i Türkleştiriyor." *Yeni Şafak* (11 July 2003): 7.

Yılmaz, Mehmet. "PKK kartı yine masada." *Aksiyon*, no. 449 (14 July 2003): 40–46.

CHAPTER SEVEN

CONSUMPTION IN YEMEN: CONTINUITY AND CHANGE

ULRIKE STOHRER

Yemen has been part of a global consumption and trade network since antiquity. Yemenites have engaged in long-distance trading that connects Northern Arabia, the Mediterranean, East Africa, India, and Southeast Asia since the days of the Incense Road. Rather than being just a transmitter of goods, Yemen and its culture have been strongly shaped by diverse influences from abroad.

Due to this history, different regions in Yemen are connected with different parts of the world. For instance, the eastern region Wadi Hadhramawt and the southern coast are oriented toward the Arab Gulf, India, and Southeast Asia. The western coast (Tihama), on the other hand, has strong ties to East Africa. Some parts of Yemen have been temporarily occupied by the Ottomans or Europeans, which also brought cultural influences with them. Now Yemenites from all regions of the country migrate to the capital Sanaa (located in the central highlands) and make these cross-cultural influences come together in one place. The emigration of Yemenites looking for work in Europe and the United States further widens this process. Finally, the mass media (e.g., American video clips and Indian Bollywood films) are also having an effect on fashion and lifestyle and sparking a demand for new goods. Yemenites, however, do not see themselves as being situated at the margins of the globalized world, but rather as living at the crossroads, where goods from the East and the West meet. They do not feel that they are being passively inundated with new commodities, but act self-confidently by selecting actively from both sides what in their eyes fits in with their own culture.

This chapter examines the appropriation of imported goods—i.e., clothing—in a process of "Yemenization" that preserves in the view of Yemenite consumers the continuity and integrity of their cultural identity during a time of rapid social and economic change. A deeper historical look reveals that even goods that Yemenites now see as originally Yemenite were actually imported decades ago. As time passed, those goods went through a process of appropriation, adaptation, and traditionalization until they came to be considered "authentic Yemenite."

My analysis focuses on the consumption behavior of the new middle class in the capital Sanaa. Most members of this part of the urban population stem from the tribal rural areas of the central highlands of Yemen and have been migrating to the city since the 1970s. I will begin my analysis by outlining the traditional tribal values and attitudes with respect to consumption and the market. Then I will describe recent developments in the market system in Yemen and in the consumption behavior of the middle class in Sanaa. Finally I will present examples of clothing that has strong connotations of "tradition" (*turāth*) and "authenticity" (*aṣāla*) in Yemen, and look at the ways in which these clothes are currently being altered or replaced by new goods from abroad, without losing their authenticity as "Yemenite clothing."

Traditional Tribal Values Concerning Consumption and the Market

The tribal population of the highlands in Yemen consists of farmers and craftsmen. Traditionally there were only weekly markets in the highlands of Yemen. Markets are located at the borders of two or more tribal territories and in towns. The marketplace has a special juridical status (*hijra*) that guarantees its neutrality and inviolability.

A central value of the tribal society is the economic and moral autonomy of its members. Tribesmen regard the relationship between seller and buyer as unequal and as contradicting the tribal social model constructed around the concept of equality and reciprocity. In accordance with this ideology, traditionally tribesmen did not engage in trading and selling. They sold their agricultural products (grain, fruits) through a broker (*dallāl*) of non-tribal descent (*dawshān*, pl. *dawāshīn*) to avoid direct contact with tribal customers. In the highlands of Yemen the term *bayyāʿ* (trader or vendor) is often used as a synonym for people of non-tribal descent.[1] The non-tribal "people of the market" (*ahl al-sūq*) are of low social status. As a result of these concepts, tribesmen see the market (*sūq*) as a place of dishonor. Though the market is a public space where social affairs are negotiated, a tribesman is required to go directly to the shop or trader whose goods or services he needs. He should leave the market as soon as he has finished his

---

[1] Paul Dresch, *Tribes, Government and History in Yemen* (Oxford: Clarendon Press, 1989), 120–121; 152, n. 5.

shopping. Wandering through the market without a specific destination or hanging around on the street without a purpose is seen as immoral for both men and women. In Yemen, social life usually takes place inside residential buildings.

Recent Developments in the Consumer Landscape in Yemen

Since the revolution of 1962, tribesmen in the highlands of Yemen have modified both their consumption behavior and their values regarding commercial activities. The Yemen Arab Republic opened itself rapidly to the global market. Starting in the 1970s, the emigration of thousands of Yemenite workers to the United States, Europe, the Arab Gulf States, and Saudi Arabia and the remittances these workers have sent back to their families have strengthened the cash economy in Yemen. Increasing wealth has brought a demand for new goods, which have been imported in massive amounts. The unification of north and south Yemen in 1990 also helped develop the market because the formerly socialist south was now open to the global market.

This market development ended abruptly in 1991. Because Yemen was on the side of Saddam Hussein during the first Iraqi war, Saudi Arabia repatriated 800,000 Yemenite migrant workers. As a consequence, the number of unemployed in Yemen increased and the economy has been weakened. The tribal concept of autarchy has also changed considerably during the recent decades. Because autarchy is no longer maintainable, tribesmen have found new ways of earning money, and some restrictive tribal values have been modified in such a way that many tribesmen no longer consider it shameful to buy and sell at the market. Thus they have been able to become entrepreneurs or to take on work in the newly developing service sector, which has enabled them to become upwardly mobile and wealthy. They express their new wealth through consumption.

In recent years commercial centers in Sanaa have shifted from the old *sūq* to several new quarters in the expanding city. Increasingly, the *sūq* is the center for wholesale clothing sales. Retail clothing sales now occur at the margins of the *sūq* (Bab al-Sabah, Bab Shu^{c}ub, Bab al-Qasr) and outside the old city—for example, on Haddah Street, Jamal Street, or Hayil Street. The areas near the old *sūq* are frequented by lower-income customers. Middle- and upper-class customers shop on Jamal and Haddah streets. These changes have also affected how the textile trade displays its commodities in the shops of Sanaa. Twenty years ago, textile shops were plain and unadorned. Commodities were presented in a stockroom. There were many undistinguishable shops selling the same kind of commodities side by side on the same street.

Figure 7.1: A woman wearing the *sitāra* in a shop for fabrics in Sanaa, 1989

In the past few years this has begun to change. Shops selling different commodities are now located side by side. A few warehouses and shopping centers have opened with a conglomerate of different shops spread over several floors. Increasingly, shops in Sanaa have colorful advertising signs. Electric lighting and fantasy names, often in English or French—such as "Happiness" or "La Reine"—attract customers and help distinguish one shop from another. Recently, glass display windows and mannequins have begun to appear. This process has spread so rapidly across the city that some streets now look like a "forest of signs." In short, commodities are now displayed much more aesthetically than they were just a few years ago.

Figure 7.2: Shops in Sanaa now have colorful advertising signs.

Gender-Specific Consumption Behavior in the Middle Class of Sanaa

There is a considerable difference in the shopping behavior of men and women of the middle class in Sanaa. Men tend to see shopping as a duty, rather than as an event or a way to pass the time. Daily shopping for the needs of the household is the duty of men. Men shop in the morning on the way to their business, or at noon on the way home. They buy clothing for themselves when they need it. They buy their long, preferably white, garment (*zanna*) and the jacket (*jāket*) from professional specialized male tailors that sew these items on demand. Usually a man buys from the shop of an owner whom he personally knows and trusts.

Women do not go out to purchase the daily needs of the household. They let the male members of the household or children bring these items home. Yet, women of the Sanaani middle class sometimes do go shopping by themselves: not only when they need something for themselves, but also for pleasure or as a way to pass the time. The appropriate time for shopping is in the afternoon, the time when social gatherings take place in Yemen. At this time, men as well as women, go out separately to meet friends, relatives, or business partners in their houses. Women also use this time for shopping. They usually go shopping in a small group of two to five or six female friends or relatives. Women are seldom alone when they shop, and decisions about what to buy are discussed within the group. Women often wander first from shop to shop, comparing items, quality, and price, before ultimately making their purchase at a shop where they already know the owner. There is also an important interaction between female customers and male traders and tailors as they discuss the quality of fabrics as well as the pattern, cut, size, workmanship, and price of garments. Many traders in the textile sector are of non-tribal descent, or come from Taizz and the southern regions of Yemen, which are not affiliated with a tribe. The women therefore talk and interact more freely with these tradesmen than they would with men of their own tribal status.

Clothing is an important element of representation in formal and informal social gatherings for both men and women. Talking about the style, quality, and cost of clothing, and where they bought it, is an important topic of conversation among women at these occasions. Men also talk about clothing and prices and exchange the addresses of shops, but in contrast to women men tend to do this only when they need to buy something, not as a general topic of conversation.

Women have altered their consumption behavior significantly in the last 20 years, whereas men still seem to adhere much more to traditional values and practices regarding consumption. As a result, shops that cater to female customers have changed their appearance more rapidly than shops with male customers. Some streets in Sanaa, such as Jamal Street, have become centers for female shopping. In keeping with these new shopping practices, individual shops and shopping streets have altered their appearance. Snack bars, juice bars, and ambulant sellers of sandwiches and cold soft drinks now appear in the main shopping areas of the city.

One side effect of the new shopping behavior of women is that some young men now like to pass the time on the well-known streets in Sanaa where women shop. The men do not buy anything; they are just hanging around "watching women." Although both men and women criticize this practice as immoral ($^c ayb$), it does give young people the opportunity to have some contact in public with the opposite sex and to discreetly exchange telephone numbers as they pass by.

The Significance of Imported Clothing for Yemenite Identity

In Sanaa and in the highlands of Yemen, men wear a coat (*jāket, kūt*) over a long robe-like garment (*zanna*), a dagger (*janbiyyah*) in an embroidered belt, and a large variety of headgear (*sumāṭa, shāl*, etc.).[2] European style jackets were introduced in Yemen at the beginning of the 20th century, and are now produced in Yemen by specialized tailors. Today it is characteristic for Yemenites to wear a jacket over the *zanna* and the dagger *janbiyya*, thus distinguishing themselves from men of other Arab countries who might wear a long garment (*dishdasha, jalabiyya* or similar) and a dagger but no jacket. Additionally they wear a long, white cotton cloth with bright red, yellow, green, and black stripes (*liḥfa*) over the left shoulder, which can also be used as a sack. The *liḥfa* was traditionally woven in the Tihama (coast of the Red Sea); today it is imported from India.[3] A large cashmere shawl imported from Pakistan can also substitute for the *liḥfa*. The same is true for the many kinds of the headgear called *sumāṭa*, which are now imported from Syria, Pakistan, and India.

In the coastal areas of Yemen, men wear a *sarong* imported from Indonesia (called *fūṭa* in Yemen) combined with a European shirt or T-shirt.

Women's clothing in Yemen consists of many kinds of dresses that are worn daily or at festive occasions, such as *zanna, dhirᶜa, jalabiyya*, or *fustān*.[4] The women in the highlands consider the *zanna*, a knee-length dress with a tight bodice and a wide plissé skirt, being "the" Yemenite female dress, although it was actually introduced by the Ottomans at the beginning of the 20th century. Women in Sanaa usually buy only the fabric, not the whole dress. They sew their dresses at home, according to their own patterns and styles. Therefore there is much creativity and individuality in the styles of women's dresses.[5] They use all kinds of fabrics from cotton to velvet, brocade, taffeta, and silk, which are imported from India, especially the very popular *sari*-clothes. Women also use men's *fūṭa*'s or *sumāṭa*'s as fabrics for their own dresses. Almost all dresses that women wear in Yemen are adorned by their wearers with sequins, embroidery, and other appliqués.

---

[2] For a detailed overview on men's clothing in Yemen see Ulrike Stohrer, *Barᶜa. Rituelle Performance, Identität und Kulturpolitik im Jemen* (Berlin: Klaus Schwarz Verlag, 2009), 35–41.

[3] Martha Mundy, "Sanᶜāʾ Dress 1920–1975," in *Sanᶜāʾ, an Arabian Islamic City*, ed. Robert B. Sergeant and Ronald Lewcock (London: World of Islam Festival Trust, 1983), 533.

[4] For details see Ulrike Stohrer, "Gegenwärtige Modetrends in Sana," in *Töchter des Jemen*, ed. Museum für Völkerkunde, Ausstellungskatalog Museum für Völkerkunde zu Leipzig (Leipzig, 2005), 15–21.

[5] Ibid.

Figure 7.3: A "typical" Yemenite couple. The woman is wearing a *sharshaf*.

As a result of this aesthetic preference, there are many shops selling notions on the main shopping streets.

The women wear all kinds of dresses (*zanna, dhirᶜa, jalabiyya*) in combination with wide cotton leggings (*sirwāl*), which were traditionally produced in Yemen, but are now often imported from Pakistan or replaced by tight-fitting synthetic leggings from China. Jeans trousers are also worn under dresses. Women also combine their traditional dresses with European garments, such as blouses or cardigans. European-style long and short skirts, together with jeans, are also popular.

Traditionally shoes were not elements of representation at formal gatherings. Men and women wear sandals or slippers, which they take off when they enter a house or room. Since the mid-1990s, the women of the upper-middle class of Sanaa have increasingly held their wedding celebrations in rented suites (*qāᶜa*), instead of in their own homes. It has become the custom in these rooms not to remove one's shoes at the door. Thus, shoes have become an important element of representation for women. They now have

Figure 7.4: New shop for fabrics in Sanaa 2006

to buy fashionable shoes, such as high-heeled sandals, exclusively for such occasions. As a result, shops in Sanaa that sell women's shoes have altered their appearance significantly, and they now present their commodities in a more "Western" style.

The clothing that women in the Middle East wear in public is often studied with a focus on Islamic morality. In Yemen the population is almost exclusively Muslim, with great regional, denominational, and cultural differences; consequently public garments have a strong association with class, region, and nationality. Although most of the "Islamic" garments worn in Yemen today were introduced from abroad, these garments can also have a national connotation as traditional Yemenite clothing.

The traditional blue and red dyed cotton wrap *sitāra* of the women of Sanaa is seen as a typical Yemenite cloth, though it is now only worn by women of lower status. Yet this typical Yemenite wrap was introduced to Yemen from India in the 1940s.[6] To this day, it is produced in India exclusively for export to Yemen, and its patterns and colors have remained unchanged over the years.

The black *sharshaf* is the outdoor garment preferred by Sanaani women of the upper and middle class. It was introduced by the Ottomans at the be-

---
[6] Mundy, "Sanᶜāʾ Dress 1920–1975," 535, n. 9.

Figure 7.5: Shop for Western-style clothing in Sanaa 2008

ginning of the 20th century,[7] and before the revolution of 1962, the *sharshaf* was a garment of the upper class. With the revolution it became a symbol of democracy, and is now worn all over the country. Many Yemenites now see the *sharshaf* as an original Yemenite piece of clothing. During the past four years, the *sharshaf* has gone out of fashion in Sanaa, whereas in the same time it has largely replaced the local black velvet outdoor garment in the Wadi Hadramawt.

In Sanaa, the *sharshaf* has been widely replaced by a long coat *baltō* (from French *paletôt*), which was first imported from Syria in the 1990s.[8] Today, specialized male tailors sew the *baltō* in Yemen. While the *sharshaf* has not changed in shape over the years, the *baltō* is a very fashionable garment that changes its cut and trimmings nearly every month, and with increasing rapidity.[9]

This short overview of "Yemenite dress" shows that essential items of clothing that now constitute the regional and national identity of Yemenites, have never been, or are no longer, produced in Yemen. Nevertheless these

---

[7] Mundy, "San^{c}ā$^{\circ}$ Dress 1920–1975," 539; 539–540, n.85.

[8] Annelies Moors, "Islam and Fashion on the Streets of San^{c}a, Yemen," *Ethnofoor* 16, no. 2 (2003): 50.

[9] For details see Stohrer, "Gegenwärtige Modetrends in Sana."

Figure 7.6: New shoe shop in Sanaa, 2008

items have not lost their "aura" as "authentic and original" (*aṣlī*) Yemenite clothing.

A common way of appropriation is to incorporate imported goods into the local culture by renaming them. In Yemen, some newly introduced garments that replace traditional ones with the same function, adopt the name of the replaced item, like the cashmere shawl, which in Yemen is called *liḥfa*, or the sarong, which is called *fūṭa* in Yemen. However, it is interesting that in Yemen imported goods do not necessarily lose their names after they have been adopted as uniquely "Yemenite," even if the name is an indicator of origin. This is remarkable particularly for the *sharshaf* and *baltō*.

Yemenites do not adopt an entire costume from abroad. They usually select some elements of foreign clothing and combine them with traditional Yemenite elements, according to a given purpose or situation. In doing so, women are more playful and creative than men. Women actively shape fashions by altering the garments physically and combining different elements to create a new form. Women even alter ready-made manufactured garments, for example, by cutting the sleeves or adding appliquées. Men seem to be more passive about fashions that are created outside Yemen.

European fashions arrive in Yemen six months before they get to Europe because in Yemen the clothes are imported directly from the production centers in East Asia. Therefore the style of how to wear European garments does not necessarily come from TV, since TV films arrive after the goods are already available in shops and being worn by Yemenites. People create their own specific "Yemenite" dress style by the way they drape and combine garments of different origin. Several Yemenites told me that Europeans are "poor" (*masākīn*) because they can only wear European fashions, whereas Yemenites can choose from all over the world, taking from here and there what best fits in their own culture (*al-munāsib*).

Clothing, consumption, and fashion are also means of distinction between social classes in Sanaa. The middle class of Sanaa has fewer moral scruples concerning consumerism and fashion than the old urban elite (*sāda*). The old Zaidi elite of Sanaa claims descent from the Prophet Muhammad and defines its identity in terms of piety and Islamic scholarship. They distinguish themselves from newcomers by rejecting consumerism, and espouse instead a certain asceticism.[10] In contrast, the middle class has abandoned its previous disregard for consumerism and commerce and now displays its new wealth with pride. Controversies about the "right" Islam (*al-islām al-ṣaḥīḥ*) now occur between these two social classes. The middle class sees the upper class as arrogant and hypocritical. They consider upper-class moral values and concepts of Islam to be exaggerated (*mutakabbir*), whereas they see themselves as keeping the right measure and balance (*al-mīzān*).

Tribal values are not expressed in Islamic terms. People of tribal origin see themselves as proper Muslims, but do not emphasize piety. They do not care about Islamist publications or slogans condemning fashion and consumerism (for examples see Moors 2003). They say, "This is not Islam but politics" (*mish islām—siyāsa*). Therefore, among women of this class the decision to buy, for example, a new *baltō* is much more a question of fashion than morality. Recently, Islamists introduced a new headscarf, which covers the head and upper torso of the bearer. The Islamists call it "Islamic headscarf" (*ḥijāb islāmī*)[11] and define it as the only appropriate outdoor-garment for pious women. Women of tribal origin, however, contradict this attempt. They simply call this item the "Egyptian headscarf" (*ḥijāb miṣrī*), because it is being imported from Egypt, and treat it as just one new fashion style among others.

---

[10] Gabriele vom Bruck, "The Imagined 'Consumer Democracy' and Elite (Re-)Production in Yemen," *Journal of the Royal Anthropological Institute* n.s. 11 (2005): 255–275.

[11] Moors, "Islam and Fashion on the Streets of Sanʿa, Yemen," 48.

The debate on Islam in Yemen is also a matter of nationalism. The Islamist movement in Yemen is led by Saudi Arabia, and therefore Wahhabite (Sunnite). The majority of the population in the highlands of Yemen, however, is Zaidite (Shiite). Many Yemenites suspect Saudi Arabia of influencing Yemen through religion, in order to extend its political power over the entire Arabian Peninsula. Thus, when Yemenites reject some goods or practices defined as "Islamic," they may have nationalist, rather than religious, reasons for this.

Conclusion

Is there a Yemenite consumer? I do not think so. Although most Yemenites consider some goods to be Yemenite, consumption behavior in Yemen differs widely according to social class, gender, region, and denomination. Rather than defining what a Muslim, Arab, or Yemenite customer is, this chapter has focused on the dynamic complexity of consumerism in an Islamic society. In my opinion this leads to further considerations and questions about the study of consumerism and fashion in the Middle East.

Most academic literature on clothing and dress in the Middle East focuses on moral debates and fundamentalist views about the "right" way to dress. Generally, research so far concentrates on women and on outdoor dress, especially the veil.[12] Almost nothing has been written on the clothing worn every day inside the house and outside the house under the veil.[13] Many scholars also construct a dichotomy between "Islam" and "fashion," which they see as mutually contradictory.[14] In other regions of the world, such as Africa, recent research focuses on the dynamic and creative aspects of clothing and consumerism.[15] In contrast, until recently research on clothing in the Middle East has, in my opinion, focused too strongly on Islam and morality, thereby neglecting the various strategies consumers employ

---

[12] Karen Tranberg Hansen, "The World in Dress: Anthropological Perspectives on Clothing, Fashion and Culture," *Annual Review of Anthropology* 33 (2004): 382–383; Moors, "Islam and Fashion on the Streets of Sanʿa, Yemen."

[13] For Yemen, there is only Mundy, "Sanʿāʾ Dress 1920–1975"; Stohrer, "Gegenwärtige Modetrends in Sana."

[14] Anne Meneley, "Fashions and Fundamentalisms in Fin-de-Siècle Yemen: Chador Barbie and Islamic Socks," *Cultural Anthropology* 22, no. 2 (2007): 214–243 For a discussion, see also Moors, "Islam and Fashion on the Streets of Sanʿa, Yemen," 51–53.

[15] Hansen, "The World in Dress: Anthropological Perspectives on Clothing, Fashion and Culture," 374–377; Ilsemargret Luttmann, *Mode in Afrika: Mode als Mittel der Selbstinszenierung und Ausdruck der Moderne*, Ausstellungskatalog Museum für Völkerkunde (Hamburg: Museum für Völkerkunde, 2005); Margaret Maynard, *Dress and Globalization* (Manchester: Manchester University Press, 2004).

for adapting clothing and making it appropriate in different contexts. "Traditional" dress is often thought of as "timeless" and unchangeable, while fashion is seen as an entirely European and "modern" phenomenon. Thus changes over time within tradition are seldom studied. Men's clothing and its moral aspects is equally neglected.

I propose a wider anthropological approach that simultaneously looks at both men's and women's clothing and at the specific ways they deal with consumption. Furthermore, I would like to emphasize the practical aspects of everyday and festive dress behavior. Strategies of conformity to norms and subversion of norms (and also the creation of norms) are dependent on the context in which social values in general are negotiated, like informal social gatherings or festivities and rituals. The cultural heterogeneity of Yemen provides a rich field for studying consumption, identity, and morality on several levels within an entirely Muslim society that has historically been confronted with a "global" market and the adaptation of foreign goods to its own culture. Yemenites are well prepared by history and tradition to retain their own stable identity, even as they confront new and foreign influences on their culture.

Bibliography

Bruck, Gabriele vom. "The Imagined 'Consumer Democracy' and Elite (Re-)Production in Yemen." *Journal of the Royal Anthropological Institute* n.s. 11 (2005): 255–275.

Dresch, Paul. *Tribes, Government and History in Yemen*. Oxford: Clarendon Press, 1989.

Hansen, Karen Tranberg. "The World in Dress: Anthropological Perspectives on Clothing, Fashion and Culture." *Annual Review of Anthropology* 33 (2004): 369–392.

Luttmann, Ilsemargret. *Mode in Afrika: Mode als Mittel der Selbstinszenierung und Ausdruck der Moderne*. Ausstellungskatalog Museum für Völkerkunde. Hamburg: Museum für Völkerkunde, 2005.

Maynard, Margaret. *Dress and Globalization*. Manchester: Manchester University Press, 2004.

Meneley, Anne. "Fashions and Fundamentalisms in Fin-de-Siècle Yemen: Chador Barbie and Islamic Socks." *Cultural Anthropology* 22, no. 2 (2007): 214–243.

Moors, Annelies. "Islam and Fashion on the Streets of San^{c}a, Yemen." *Ethnofoor* 16, no. 2 (2003): 41–56.

Mundy, Martha. "San‍ᶜā' Dress 1920–1975." In San‍ᶜā', an Arabian Islamic City, edited by Robert B. Sergeant and Ronald Lewcock, 529–541. London: World of Islam Festival Trust, 1983.

Stohrer, Ulrike. *Barᶜa. Rituelle Performance, Identität und Kulturpolitik im Jemen*. Berlin: Klaus Schwarz Verlag, 2009.

———. "Gegenwärtige Modetrends in Sana." In *Töchter des Jemen*, edited by Museum für Völkerkunde, 15–21. Ausstellungskatalog Museum für Völkerkunde zu Leipzig. Leipzig, 2005.

CHAPTER EIGHT

(UN-)ISLAMIC CONSUMERS? THE CASE OF POLISH TATARS

KATARZYNA GÓRAK-SOSNOWSKA AND MICHAŁ ŁYSZCZARZ

Although Islamic products targeting Muslim consumers are becoming popular, or at least known, in many EU countries, Islamic products seem to be non-existent among Polish autochthonous Muslims—the Tatars. Consumption plays an important role in Tatar identity formation—the selection of goods is, however, a mixture of Tatar and Polish, with some influxes of Islamic mainstream goods. Still Tatars are more likely to enjoy Oriental (in the case of Poland, it is mostly Middle Eastern) popular culture, which has become trendy in Poland, rather than Muslim consumer products, which do not seem to belong to their world.

This article explores Tatar consumption patterns and attitudes toward so-called Muslim products. In order to make the analysis broad and to portray the realities of the Podlasie region, where most of the Tatar settlements are, a wide definition of Muslim consumer products was adopted, including some products that are not really Muslim and others that do not fit into popular culture. This article will illustrate not only the scarcity of Muslim products in Poland but also the particular approach that the Tatars have developed, in which the real distinction is between Tatar and Arab goods, rather than between Islamic and Polish (or Western) goods.

This research is based on semi-structured interviews with 11 Tatars. The sample includes the most appropriate and representative segments of the Tatar community. The respondents are predominantly male (8 males, 3 females) and live in the Podlasie region, in Eastern Poland (6 in Białystok, which is the main city in the region; others live in small villages and the towns of Sokółka [1] and Kruszyniany [2]). Two respondents live in Bydgoszcz, a city in north-central Poland with a relatively active Muslim community. The sample includes respondents from most age groups: the oldest respondent is almost 60, the next oldest is 50, and three are around 40. The other six respondents are in their 20s. The predominance of younger respondents in the sample is due to the scope of the research—i.e., young people seem to be the most evident consumers of popular culture. The respondents differ with respect to their education: 2 have a basic education; 4 completed secondary school; 5 are graduates of institutions of higher education. The sample also includes representatives of religious institutions and a local folklore group. All interviews were conducted in June 2008.

Muslims in Poland

Unlike many EU countries with large Muslim populations, the Muslim population in Poland is very small and is estimated at 25,000 to 35,000, or less than 0.1 percent of the Polish population. One could therefore assume that Muslims in Poland have a very short history and are a homogenous group, but neither of these assumptions are true. In fact, the Muslim population in Poland is very diverse, and the immigrant and autochthonous Muslim communities have to negotiate their roles and positions within the Muslim community.

Tatars are the autochthonous Muslim population in Poland, with a presence that dates back to the Mongol invasions in the 14th century. In the succeeding centuries they became fully integrated in the mainstream society, and their Islam was "Slavicized" in terms of their religious observance.[1] One example is the Five Pillars of Islam: Tatars mostly pray only during the Friday afternoon prayer because performing the five daily salat (prayers) would not be possible in a non-Muslim environment. This is also the reason for their selective fasting—abstaining from consuming coffee, alcohol, and cigarettes—during Ramadan. Zakat is not institutionalized (however there are facultative alms called *sadoga* [ar. *ṣadaqa*]), and hajj is the privilege of only a few, due to the financial burden of such travel.[2] What's more, religion is limited to the private sphere, which is the single, most significant element that differentiates Tatars from other Poles. The estimated number of Tatars in Poland is 3,000 to 5,000.

---

[1] Andrzej Drozd, "Współczesne oblicza kultury Tatarów Rzeczypospolitej," in *Zagadnienia współczesnego islamu*, ed. Adnan Abbas (Poznań: UAM, 2003), 41–60; Marek M. Dziekan, "Tradycje ludowe i folklor Tatarów polsko-litewskich," in *Piśmiennictwo i muhiry Tatarów polsko-litewskich, Res Publica Multiethnica*, ed. Andrzej Drozd, Marek Dziekan, and Tadeusz Majda (Warsaw, 2000); Marek M. Dziekan, "Historia i tradycje polskiego islamu," in *Muzułmanie w Europie*, ed. Anna Parzymies (Warsaw: Dialog, 2005), 199–228.

[2] Michał Łyszczarz and Karol Marek, "Rola islamu i obrzędowości religijnej w tradycjach Tatarów," in *Arabowie—islam—świat*, ed. Marek Dziekan and Izabela Kończak (Łódź: Ibidem, 2007), 632–634.

Beginning in the 1970s, the ethnic and national structure of Polish Muslims began to change rapidly, as immigrants outnumbered the Tatars and brought their new "Oriental" type of Islam.[3] The first Muslim immigrants came to Poland from other socialist countries in the 1970s in order to study. Those who decided to settle in Poland and start a family now belong to the middle- and upper-middle class and are well integrated in Polish society. The early 1990s brought economic immigrants to Poland, most of whom have been making their living working in small shops, kebab bars, or as hired labor. Another significant immigrant category is refugees—of which about 90 percent (about 5,000) came from Chechnya. The number of converts is estimated to be less than a thousand.

The new, emerging Islamic presence in Poland and the fact that immigrants outnumber the autochthonous Muslim population has resulted in tension between the two groups. In 1925 the *Muzułmański Związek Religijny* (MZR or Muslim Religious Union) was established as a Tatar-oriented Muslim organization. One of the most visible results of the tension occurred in 2001 when a second Muslim religious community was established, and then officially registered in 2004 as the *Liga Muzułmańska w RP* (LM or Muslim League in Poland). Creating a new Sunni Muslim organization with similar statutes, aims, and activities challenged the legacy of the Tatar MZR. Most of the LM's members were immigrants and converts who did not feel fulfilled by the Tatar Islam or were not able to join the MZR due to the requirement of Polish citizenship. These tensions are also evident in the attitudes of Tatars toward Muslim products.

Muslim Consumer Culture: Poland and Wider Europe

The last few years have brought a significant number of so-called "Muslim products" to the market. Some of them fit into the so-called "Cool Islam" category—a way of both promoting Islam to young Muslims in the West and reaching mainstream society. This includes Muslim music (mostly rap), Muslim streetwear, and Muslim fast food and soft drinks.[4] Other products—for instance, the *burqini* or Islamic banking—seem to be aimed primarily at enhancing the participation of Muslims in society. These products combine Islam with modernity—they offer a way to maintain one's religious identity even as they provide an opportunity (tailored to Muslim needs) to participate in the global culture.

---

[3] Paweł Kubicki, "Muzułmanie w Polsce," *Studia i prace Kolegium Ekonomiczno-Społecznego* 12 (2007): 60–80.

[4] Amel Boubekeur, "Cool and Competitive. Muslim Culture in the West," *ISIM Review* 16 (2005): 12.

148 Chapter Eight

Figure 8.1: Polish Tatars during a prayer at the Muslim cemetery in Warsaw

According to Akbar Ahmed, such products are a clear symptom of local cultures adjusting to globalization processes, since "imitation is the sincerest form of flattery."[5] Some researchers perceive these products as signs of the Americanization of the Orient, which is occurring from the back door. One must bear in mind that the most popular Muslim Colas (Mecca Cola and Qibla Cola) and the Fulla doll all visually resemble their American prototypes—so in some way they cling to the already established and well-known brands. Although these Muslim products seem to fit into a Western lifestyle and culture, it is the ethical—and sometimes the political—part that differs.

Before 1989 one could hardly even speak about consumer culture in Poland. The social structure was egalitarian and determined by forced industrialization, while consumer choices were limited to what was available in the shops. The Round Table Agreement not only transformed the system but also introduced a new economic model, which was driven by market

---

[5] Catherine Donaldson-Evans, "Muslim-Themed Products Mimic Icons in American Popular Culture," *FOX News* (11 October 2006, http://www.foxnews.com/story/0,2933,219864,00.html).

forces rather than a central plan. After almost 20 years of transformation there are certainly patterns that signify the Europeanization of consumption patterns, however Polish consumption styles are still not on the European level. Increasingly, Polish consumers tend to shop in malls, and the internet is becoming a more and more popular tool for communication, banking, and shopping. Polish people also seem to "live 99 lives" which means increased mobility, lack of free time, and multitasking.[6] Young people are most susceptible to global trends in terms of pop culture,[7] and also egonomics—expressing oneself and determiniation to stress one's uniqueness.[8] In 2000 the income distribution of Polish households (even the rich ones) was still much lower than the income distribution in other EU states, however it is believed that convergence will occur.[9]

The absence of consumer patterns similar to those in Western Europe might explain the absence of an emerging Muslim consumer culture. However, the most significant factor seems to be the marginal role and number of Muslims in Poland. This leads to what could be called "the invention of the Orient," rather than the introduction of Muslim products. The cultures of Muslim people are reflected in businesses such as Oriental-style fastfood chains (e.g., Sphinx), bars offering water pipes, and clubs with bellydancing and Arab pop music. All of these are, however, secular, and most of its producers and consumers are native Poles. These places are not designed by immigrants and for immigrants so they feel "like home"; they are designed to look like an "Oriental place" to a Polish layman. A brand-new Orient is being invented this way. An Orient that does not exist in reality—an Orient with no Orientals. Particularly in middle-size cities it implies sometimes rather odd combinations of "Orient" and Orient representations—e.g., playing Arab pop with visualizations showing Qurʾanic calligraphy, a bellydancer performing the dance with a cabaret-like stick, or a pub called Mecca [sic!]. In the biggest Polish conurbations (Warsaw, Kraków), the Oriental market is much more professional. Among some circles of Polish youth it has become trendy to go to such clubs, listen to Tarkan or Amr Diab, smoke *shīsha*, and even take a belly-dancing workshop. There, many of them find

---

[6] Mateusz Jaworowski and PawełPola ński, *Trendy społeczne i konsumenckie w Polsce u progu Unii Europejskiej*, Paper presented at the 5th all-Poland Congress of Market and Opinion Researchers, Warsaw 21–22 October 2004, p.27, 8–12.

[7] *Marketing News*, http://www.marketing-news.pl, 26 July 2007.

[8] Jaworowski and Polański, *Trendy społeczne i konsumenckie w Polsce u progu Unii Europejskiej*, 17.

[9] Agata Niemczyk, "Wzory konsumpcji gospodarstw domowych w Polsce i w wybranych krajach Unii Europejskiej," *Zeszyty Naukowe Akademii Ekonomicznej w Krakowie, Kraków* 716 (2006): 21–22.

an alternative to the MTV pop culture—regardless of whether it is a Polish or a Western alternative.[10]

Muslim consumer culture as such is not known by mainstream Poles, and it appears only occasionally in the form of tidbits in the newspapers. Few Muslim products are ever mentioned. Islamic banking and finance are usually presented in magazines that target management and finance professionals. There are also several scholarly articles that tackle this issue; most of these articles were written by economists with little exposure to Islamic culture or religion. Another set of publications—in the form of short news, marketing articles, or blog entries—tackles the issue of Muslim Colas and, separately, Fullas. Some articles present the soft drink and the doll with a marketing-oriented approach, while others' point of view is characterised by irritation and apprehension in the face of an "Islamist threat." Other Muslim products, such as Muslim rap or clothing (both streetwear and the *burqini*), are far less present in the Polish public.

Introducing the most well known Muslim products to a wider audience, at least in newspaper headlines, could be a good sign, albeit in the case of the Polish media the introduction often lacks a deeper background and is presented as a Muslim whim or response to global products. Without any cultural context, the products might be perceived in terms of a clash of civilizations rather than as glocalization.[11] Another possible danger is the lack of any other articles about consumption patterns in Muslim societies, as well as among Muslim communities in the West. This in turn might lead to a generalization of Muslim products as representing the whole world of Islam. Adding the fact that Muslims tend to be perceived as religious, this can be easily translated into cultural (or rather religious) determinism. Muslims are put in one category with monks, rather than ordinary humans, while the economic, political, and social realities of Islamic countries tend to be explained only in terms of religious factors.[12] These two issues make it easy to believe that all Muslims keep their savings in Islamic banks, drink only Mecca or Qibla Cola, and buy their daughters only Fulla dolls—because they perceive the alternatives as rotten/Western/incompatible with Islamic law.

---

[10] Katarzyna Górak-Sosnowska, "Organizacje muzułmańskie w Polsce," in *Instytucje religijne i religijność w krajach Unii Europejskiej*, ed. Elżbieta Firlit (Warsaw: SGH, forthcoming).

[11] The term "glocalization" described the adjustment of global trends to local needs.

[12] Katarzyna Górak-Sosnowska, "Jak uczyć o świecie islamu?" *Ateneum Kapłańskie* 151, no. 2 (2008): 258–266.

Muslim Products in Poland

A presentation of the consumption patterns among Polish Tatars should be preceded by a short explanation of the boundaries of the "Muslimness" of the products that were inquired about in the interviews. There are basically three sorts of products that will be labeled as "Muslim," even though only one of them truly fits into Muslim consumer culture, if understood narrowly:

1. Products that originate in Muslim countries are associated with the so-called "Orient," but the products themselves are not linked to religion. However, they fit into the consumer culture mainstream;

2. Products of religious significance that are not sufficiently commercial to be attributed to the concept of Muslim consumer culture;

3. Products that easily fit into the concept of Muslim consumer culture due to their religious link and consumer nature.

Products		Religious	
		Yes	No
Consumer	Yes	Fulla, Islamic banking, Mecca Cola, Muslim rap	kebab, *shīsha*, Arafat scarf, Arab pop, and raï music
	No	halal food, *muhirs*, hijab	—

Table 8.1: Muslim consumer products matrix

Limiting the scope of interest to only the last category might have resulted in a rather scanty outcome, with most of the speakers stating that they do not know, or have never heard about such products—as these products simply do not exist in their environment (or even in the whole country). On the other hand, including the other two categories in the research makes it possible to gasp the full panopy of Tatar attitudes and opinions about so-called "Muslim" products—and Arab products in particular.

Non-Religious Consumer Products

The most popular product from this category is the kebab, which has been widely adopted in Polish society and is similar to other ethnic fast foods. Tatar attitudes toward the kebab do not differ from the attitudes of Polish mainstream consumers, but still one can see some other elements showing through, such as the relation of the kebab to Tatar tradition, to Arabs, and to religious rules.

The role of tradition is so deeply rooted in Tatar culture that even mass consumer products cannot downgrade it. Some of the respondents connect kebab with *pierekaczewnik*[13]—the most typical Tatar dish—pointing to the uniqueness of the latter. They are proud of their heritage, and cuisine is one of its elements.

> Kebabs are good, but I prefer our cuisine. Maybe because *pierekaczewniks* are once in a blue moon, they have some unique value. It is not a kebab that everyone can buy around the corner. [W9]

> Anyway our Tatar *pierekaczewnik* is better than all the kebabs! [W6]

Associating kebabs with Arab culture, which is widespread in Poland, does not seem to pose a problem. Tatars like this kind of fast food, regardless of its Middle Eastern origin:

> Frankly speaking I am not really interested in Arab-Islamic culture; I do not really care about it. This culture is predominantly kebabs that are available in the city. [W9]

> I like Arab cuisine, and that's it. The same way I like Mexican or Italian cuisine. It is insignificant to me where it comes from. It is important that it is tasty and healthy. [W4]

> I like kebabs because I guess that everyone likes them. That they are Arab is not important in this case, because if they were Chinese, I would also like them. I can see many positives in spreading kebabs—people become more open, they learn about another culture. If they like kebabs, they will also like the Arabs more. [W5]

For many Tatars it is important that kebabs do not contain pork for religious dietary reasons. Even though one could dwell on whether it really corresponds to halal principles, the majority of interviewees said that this is good enough for them.

---

[13] *Pierekaczewnik* is a traditional Tatar pie stuffed with layers of filling (beef, mutton, cheese, apples etc.). The pie is shaped in a roll, with both its sides stuck together. As the preparation is toilsome, it is only served on special occasions.

I like kebab—it is good and has no pork. It is not important to me where it comes from. [W11]

Another product of Middle Eastern provenance that can be attributed to consumer culture in Poland is the *arafatka*—a kerchief ‡ la Yasser Arafat, the icon of the Palestinian national independence movement. The *arafatka* has been popular in Poland since the early 1990s as a symbol of support for Palestinian struggle. Today the *arafatka* is treated as a trendy element of dress among some young people, but not many attach a symbolic meaning to it. Instead, they simply treat it as a scarf. Similar attitudes are apparent among the Tatars:

> I used to wear an *arafatka* when I was 17, and then it was a symbol of political support for Palestine. Now as you can see, I don't wear it anymore. *Arafatka* grew stale. Teens in gymnasium use them as a scarf and treat it like an ordinary part of their dress. Some years ago the same thing happened to the images of Che Guevara. Then too hardly anyone knew what lies behind it. [W4]

> I don't wear *arafatka*, but someone might like it. For some other person it might be a way of manifesting his support for Palestine. It is a very individual matter. [W11]

Shīsha is barely used—mostly because it is unobtainable for most of the respondents. Smoking a water pipe is as much a novelty for the Tatars as it is for other Polish citizens. However, due to links with the Orient, Tatars seem to be more exposed to *shīsha*. In Poland, the water pipe is known and smoked predominantly by urban youth who fancy Oriental culture.

> I don't have a water pipe at home. It is not possible to get one in Białystok; one has to go specially to Warsaw to buy one. Sometimes I smoke one with Arab friends, however it happens rarely, because I don't have much free time. Smoking with Arabs is pretty unique, they can sit and talk for several hours. I envy them because it must be quite a stress reliever. [W1]

> I have some water pipes; I got them from Tatars from Bashkiria. It is very trendy over there. I think this is a Turkish custom, anyway I don't really associate it with Arabs. [W6]

Tatar consumption patterns do not seem to differ significantly from the Polish mainstream with respect to products that originate in the Middle East, have no religious connotation, and have became a visible element of popular culture. Tatars tend to perceive these products just as they would any other popular consumer products—regardless of their origin or meaning. At the same time, especially in the case of products that are less available (e.g., *shīsha* and to some extent *arafatka*), Tatars seem to be more aware of the existence and peculiarity of these products—probably because the products have had a bigger exposure and also because Tatars have had contact with the Muslim population of immigrant origin.

Non-Consumer Muslim Products

Several products have religious significance, but their use is limited to particular social groups in the Tatar population. Some products are of Tatar origin, while the use of others is dictated by religious rules.

As mentioned, long centuries of co-existence with the Polish Catholic majority has created a particular model of Tatar religiousness, with religion being limited to only the private sphere—unlike citizens of many Islamic countries. It seems to be a natural reaction in the assimilation process. Tatar religious practice is manifested within the family and on various holidays. Two of the most important are Kurban Bajram (Arab. $^c\bar{\imath}d$ al-$ad\d{h}\bar{a}$) and Ramazan Bajram (Arab. $^c\bar{\imath}d$ al-$fi\d{t}r$), which gives Tatars a chance to meet one other, pray together, and spend some time in the mosque.

This model of religiousness does not, however, exclude all elements of religious symbolism from daily life. Some religious symbols have great significance for Tatars. One of them is the Arabic language—which although hardly known—is very venerated. Most of the Tatars—especially the older generation—have very limited knowledge of Arabic, not even sufficient for the liturgy. Arabic has never been widely used among Tatars. Moreover, in the 18th century, Tatars switched to Polish as their mother tongue. An important exception to this linguistic assimilation was the religious literature of Tatars, which was written in Polish but in the Arabic alphabet adjusted to Slavic languages. This might be explained by the notion of $i^cj\bar{a}z$ al-$qur^{\circ}\bar{a}n$ (the Inimitability of the Qur°an). Writing religious scriptures with Arabic letters (even though in the Polish language) was a way of showing respect for the Arab script and strengthened their religious character.[14]

Interestingly, admiration for the Arabic language grew stronger under socialism, when any contact with the Arabic language was limited for political reasons. Some Tatars used to collect labels in Arabic, which they cut from

---

[14] Marek M. Dziekan, "Einige Bemerkungen über die islamische Literatur der polnisch-litauischen Tataren," in *Studies in Arabic and Islam. Proceedings of the 19th Congress, Union Europeennee der Arabisants et Islamisants, Halle 1998*, ed. Stefan Leder (Paris: Sterling, 2002), 185–191.

imported products, mostly sweets. Often they were used as religious ornaments, as it was not easy to get oneself a real *muhir*.[15] Sometimes the *muhirs* were hung upside down, simultaneously indicating both a lack of knowledge of written Arabic and a deep admiration for the language. *Muhirs* are still important products for many Tatars:

> Since I can remember, I used to have a *muhir* in my room. It used to be very difficult to get one, now there are no problems anymore, as many are brought from Arab countries. That they are ugly and kind of plastic is another issue. Nor are the pictures sold at church fairs beautiful. Good that there are *muhirs* at all. One shall not complain, they are cheap, such industrial, mass work. One can get an Arab *muhir* even for free, I got one myself in religion class as a reward for my progress in reading the Qurʾan. Now everyone can have a *muhir*—nice ones that you can get from abroad [...]. It's not like it used to be when it was a treasure. [W1]

> There was always a demand for devotional items. Tatars value Arab *muhirs* a lot; also Qurʾans are needed. The reason is that no one produces such items in Poland. World War II caused a loss of many precious items of religious worship, and those weathered were usually left behind the Eastern border. After the war the Tatar community got dispersed, there was no one who could turn back to the tradition of producing *muhirs* [...]. Not until the 1980s was there a revival. When people started to travel to Turkey for trade, then they always brought back some small Islamic souvenirs. [W8]

Another product from this category is halal food. Also in this case one can notice the degree of assimilation, as the Tatars understand halal in a very broad context as "no pork." The "more orthodox" concept of halal is relatively new. Some Tatars are starting to define their diet according to the halal rules, mostly younger, religious ones, who took part in religion classes offered by Arab teachers. Otherwise halal is perceived as a recommendation, rather than an order.

> I don't eat halal as we don't have any. Religion prohibits eating pork and carrion, and I abide it [...]. In fact we never had any halal, even this word is rather new. Arabs came in the early 1990s and then people started to talk about it. [W5]

---

[15] *Muhir* is a word of Turkish origin (a $m_h h_r r$ is a seal) meaning a framed piece of fabric with Qurʾanic inscriptions, a kind of Islamic devotional item.

> I don't use halal because one can't buy it anywhere, and my husband has no heart to slaughter a pet. So I cook meat from a shop, only without pork. [F6]

> Halal is not really known among the Tatars, there is no such tradition. Once in the countryside people bred animals for their own use and only cared that it was not pork. However, we became more open to the world as Arabs came, and halal became a necessity. Maybe not necessary for Tatars themselves because changing dietary habits is not easy and quick, but for the image of MZR as a Muslim organization. [W8]

At the same time some interviewees point to the high dietary quality of halal food:

> If halal food was available in shops, I would buy it, as it is always a guarantee that the meat is clean and healthy. [W5]

> It is important for me that halal meat is clean and healthy. [W10]

The last product from this category is hijab, but its use is very limited among Polish Tatars—and actually always was. Some older women wear a headscarf, but this might be attributed to the fact that they live in the countryside—some older Catholic women from small villages also wear a headscarf. One of the interviewees comments aptly:

> The case of hijab is an interesting one. The older women accept it, as it's a traditional element of religious life; they pray in hijab in the mosque or at the cemetery. That it is often tied wrongly, so it doesn't cover all the hair, is in this case a detail that Tatars overlook. Younger people have a different attitude. Most of them reject hijab completely. For them hijab is an example of the village bigotry of the Sokółka Tatars, or of the zeal of the Arab immigrants. [W8]

Use and popularity of these products reflect individual religiousness and the far-reaching assimilation of the Polish Tatars. Adjusting to local conditions while simultaneously maintaining some elements of religious symbolism has resulted in understanding some of the practices and rites in a new way. In this way the Tatar difference is twofold: they differ from the Polish mainstream by their religion, and they differ from mainstream Islam with some rites and the role of religion in the public sphere.

Muslim Consumer Products

Keeping these two categories in mind, one can take a closer look at the Tatar approach to Muslim consumer products known in Western Europe. Most striking is the lack of these products in the Tatar environment. One has to be really interested in the subject to even know about such products, otherwise many respondents were unaware of their existence.

> I have never heard about Mecca Cola. Probably I would buy it, especially as the earnings go for a noble cause. Definitely I would like to taste it. [W2]

> I don't know Mecca Cola, never tried it. Certainly, if I would come across it, I would taste it to see if it's good. [W11]

> Barbie doll in hijab? Eeee, that is quite excessive. Do they want to indoctrinate children from an early age, or what? [W11]

> The way Islamic banks are working is cool [...] but I don't think that something like that will be established. In Polish realities it is not possible; the media would make a fuss right away. [W5]

> It's the first time that I hear about Mecca Cola or this Barbie doll in hijab. I don't need it to live on. I treat it as something humorous, novelties from far away. [W6]

Tatars treat the new products ambiguously. Some of them express interest, while others approach the products with humor or treat them as a sort of whim. The respondents are aware that such products will not turn up in Poland, but also they do not seem to desire any of them. From this perspective, the interviewees show a great deal of indifference, maybe even resistance, toward such novelties:

> [...] moreover, Tatars are quite conservative, all novelties meet with the resistance of the older generation of our community, for whom tradition is the indicator of taste and even norms of conduct. The younger generation is more open, which might be attributed to their age, dispositions, and the conditions in which they were brought up. [W8]

> We are very attached to our tradition. In every home there has to be a *muhir* and a prayer rug, or an Arabic souvenir. This is what the Tatars have always known, this is important for them. But Arab consumer culture is not known at all. I guess, because it is not needed over here. Tatars have their tradition

and customs, and what one can buy in Polish shops is sufficient. This is such a passive attitude—it is cool what was always present, and that's it. One can see it especially among the elders—they accept Islamic symbolism, but have no interest in what the world follows; there is no will to get to know Arab culture. [W2]

An interesting point in this regard is the generation gap. One could also sense the generation gap in the two other categories, but in this case it seems to be most noticeable. Even if it makes the younger generation of Tatars better recipients of Muslim consumer culture, it still does not mean that many of them would follow this path.

Attitudes Influencing Tatar Consumption Patterns

The categories of Muslim products presented above not only provide information about the attitudes of Tatar consumers toward these products, but also provide significant background data, which sheds light on relations between the Middle Eastern (mostly Arab) immigrant population and the autochthons (Tatars). Religion seems to be the only link between these two communities, while the scope of differences is overwhelming. The crux of mutual animosities seems to be the struggle for primacy in Polish Islam. The Tatars wish to maintain the status quo, which according to the Law of 1936 allows MZR to represent Muslims in Poland, even though immigrant Muslims outnumber them threefold. Another issue is the "clash of Islams"—as both communities understand religious practice differently.[16] Many Tatar respondents felt the need to refer to the Arab population and Arab culture when talking about Muslim consumer culture. They clearly distinguished between the religion of Islam and Arab culture:

> The distance between religion and culture is very clear. [W8]

> For me religion is tradition and inner experience. Arabs have a completely different attitude, for them religion is the whole life, regardless of what they would be doing at the moment. For me it is zealotry. [W3]

> For me religion is one issue, and culture—another [...]. I don't need that culture, I draw from it only what I like. I try to differentiate clearly what is religion and what is culture. [W4]

---

[16] Górak-Sosnowska, "Organizacje muzułmańskie w Polsce."

For me, Islam is important and not Arab culture. Arab culture had an impact on Islam; that is clear. But Arabs themselves don't differentiate what is their own culture and what is the tradition of Prophet Muhammad. It is important what Muhammad did, not that he was an Arab. [W10]

I am Muslim and Tatar, that's why Arab culture, music, or art is not as important for me as the religion. [W2]

Figure 8.2: Mufti Tomasz Miśkiewicz, the leader of the Polish Tatars community, and Halina Szahidewicz, chairwoman of the Muslim Religious Union in Białystok

Some of the respondents point to a great divide between Arabs and Tatars that hinders mutual contact and understanding. The categorization of "us" and "them" seems to be very strong:

> I am not fond of Arab-Islamic culture, because I associate it with religion classes led by Arabs. That wasn't a nice experience; that's why often I didn't take part. Arabs imposed on us their interpretation of religion, they told us what is allowed and what's not. Instead of teaching us prayers, we crammed Arabic alphabet, but we will never use it [...]. Arabs didn't understand at all that we live in Poland, that it is the 21st century. They are from another

world. I am Muslim, my ancestors were Muslim, but I keep away from Arabs, because they don't understand us. [W3]

[...] but it's the culture that divides us. We don't understand Arabs and they—us, Tatars. [W10]

More than once, I've heard from different people coming here that eating non-halal food is a sin. I kept answering that we have been living here for 600 years and survived without halal, and still are Muslim. Besides, the Arabs who started families and have lived here for a dozen years or so, begin to see it themselves. The old zeal fades, they notice that in the long run the life here is completely different than one in the Arab countries or in the West, where many Muslims live. [W6]

Contact with the Arabs has also strengthened the Tatars' own ethnic and religious identity. Ethnicity and religion had always been the factors that differentiated the Tatars from the rest of society, but now the emphasis was different. Before the immigrant Muslim population became more numerous, what was Tatar was equated with what was Muslim, since there were hardly any non-Tatar Muslims in Poland—and besides Tatars had very limited contact with them.[17] Increased Muslim immigration brought not only division between religion and ethnicity but it also revived the Tatar tradition, which needed to be built up and reinforced. At the same time the Tatars remained proud of their own heritage.

We have been living in Poland for 600 years, so Polish culture is for us the most important one. This influence has been so strong that apart from religion—you know, mosques, cemeteries, and some family mementos—and these dishes of ours, nothing actually remains from the ancestors' heritage. We missed this folklore [...], so we've decided to establish a folk group. "Buńczuk" is sort of our Orient, because we learned Crimean dances from Lewiza that we then rounded out with our own sequences based on Turkish and Tatar music [...]. Tatars treat this folklore as if it is their own, because it resembles the old culture. It stirs some sort of sentiment for what used to be in the old days, for our roots. It is cultivated to such an extent that no one would agree to include any Arab elements in the repertoire, because it doesn't have a lot in common with us. [W9]

---

[17] Tatars could have referred, e.g., to a Sudanese Muslim as a "Sudanese Tatar," thus equating religious and ethnic identity. Cf. Bogusław Zagórskis vivid description in his lecture during a teacher training *W kręgu kultury islamu*, organized by the Polish National Commission for UNESCO in Warsaw, 25–26 April 2008.)

I accept Oriental culture; I like its colors and exoticism, but in my life I am traditional. One has to know what's going on in the world, and try out some novelties, but one also has to remember about our heritage. [W6]

I definitely prefer Tatar culture, because it's mine. As I take a look in the past I can see Muhammad—the founder of my religion on one side and Genghis Khan on the other, because my ancestors had Mongol roots. [W5]

Another factor influencing Tatar attitudes toward Muslim products is the lack of them. It refers not only to the consumer products, which are hardly known and treated as novelties from far away, but even more popular products. Oriental culture becomes trendy among some youth groups in Poland, but as Tatars inhabit mostly rural areas, they have limited access to consumer culture—regardless of whether it is Oriental or Western. In geographic terms, Podlasie—the main Tatar center—is a distant area, far from a big metropolis or natural hubs of consumer culture.

I really regret that I have to travel to Warsaw in order to buy anything. If I am on Wiertnicza St. [in the Islamic center of MZR] I buy halva, desserts, and cured meat for storing [...] I buy my clothes in Warsaw. There are some Oriental shops [...] Many things I also bring from abroad [...] There is no halal in Białystok, only in Warsaw. Possibly one can buy meat in Suwałki, but only in big, retail quantities' [W2]

Here in Białystok [...] there are no products like Mecca Cola, and there probably won't be any for a long time, because there is no interest. Actually it would be hard to have any interest, since no one knows about it. Well, I've just heard about this Mecca Cola. Here it is hard to buy cardamom, let alone Mecca Cola! [W1]

Lastly, it is interesting to note that some attitude patterns among Tatars and some Western Muslim consumers are similar. For instance, some of the people interviewed related Arab/Muslim products to American ones, and they also expressed their opinions on the United States. One must keep in mind that some of the Muslim products take an ethical stance or advocate for a particular idea: the popular Muslim Colas, in particular, tend to arouse anti-American sentiments.[18] Some of the Tatar respondents expressed an

---

[18] See, e.g., Katarzyna Górak-Sosnowska, "Między religią, polityką a komercją. Muzułmańskie cole jako produkty etyczne," *Marketing i rynek* 3 (2008): 25–31; Jon Henley and Jeevan Vasagar, "Think Muslim, drink Muslim, says new rival to Coke," *The Guardian* (8 January 2003, http://www.guardian.co.uk/media/2003/jan/08/marketingandpr.internationalnews); Michael Mönninger, "Mit den Waffen des Gegners," *Die Zeit*, no. 14 (23 April 2003,

unfavorable attitude toward the United States, however it is hard to know whether the disfavor is directed at U.S. politics or culture. The criticism of the United States is rational, infrequent, and far from being outraged:

> I strongly support such products [kebab], and that I also don't like Americans is another issue. I am very happy that Poles have swung from hamburgers to kebab. [W7]

> As you can see, I'm wearing American trousers, I don't have any qualms about it. They have been produced in the United States, so what? They are comfortable and nice. That's it. This is what counts for me. I might dislike the USA, but I won't boycott their trousers, because that would make me paranoid. [W11]

As mentioned, references to the United States occurred rarely, and due to the small size of the sample selection, the results cannot be generalized. Yet according to a representative Poland-wide opinion poll, year after year the United States are among the most-favored nations, scoring from 64 percent positives in 1997 to 44 percent positives in 2007 on the attitude scale—similar to some of the most-favored Western European nations.[19]

Conclusion

As Muslims, Tatars should have become a natural target for Muslim consumer products in Poland. However, long centuries of assimilation have made the Tatar consumption patterns similar to the Polish patterns. Muslim consumer products are perceived as exotic novelties from far away, with no link to the real lives of Polish Tatars. Islamic mainstream products are treated suspiciously and adopted selectively, because they might pose a challenge to the fragile Tatar culture. What Tatars seem to enjoy are non-religious consumer products, originating in the Middle East. However, in this way they follow the general fashion for the Orient. All that separates the Tatars from mainstream society is a greater access to Muslim products, due to their relations with the immigrant Muslim population and socialization.

At the same time, the interactions with immigrants, contact with novelties, and the greater availability of Middle Eastern and Islamic products is

---

http://www.zeit.de/2003/14/Mecca_Cola_14); Michael Theodoulou, "Muslim wage war on US cola giants," *The Australian* (12 October 2002): 12–13.

[19] *Sympatia i niechęć do innych narodów*, CBOS, BS/144/2007, September 2007, Warsaw, p. 22.

forcing the Tatars to redefine their ethnic and religious identity. The elders stick to their traditions and show a greater degree of conservatism, which is common in the rural areas where the main Tatar settlements are. The younger generation is much more open-minded and experiments with different factors—the Polish mainstream, ethnic Tatar, mainstream Islamic, and popular Oriental. These changes are recent and quite intense and are further stimulated by the media discourse on Islam in Europe, so it is hard to predict which identity component will be most prevalent. It seems likely that the small Tatar population will become even more fragmented, and that their local customs will, in all likelihood, be slowly eradicated.

Bibliography

Boubekeur, Amel. "Cool and Competitive. Muslim Culture in the West." *ISIM Review* 16 (2005): 12–13.
Donaldson-Evans, Catherine. "Muslim-Themed Products Mimic Icons in American Popular Culture." *FOX News* (11 October 2006, http://www.foxnews.com/story/0,2933,219864,00.html).
Drozd, Andrzej. "Współczesne oblicza kultury Tatarów Rzeczypospolitej." In *Zagadnienia współczesnego islamu*, edited by Adnan Abbas, 41–60. Poznań: UAM, 2003.
Dziekan, Marek M. "Einige Bemerkungen über die islamische Literatur der polnisch-litauischen Tataren." In *Studies in Arabic and Islam. Proceedings of the 19th Congress, Union Europeennee der Arabisants et Islamisants, Halle 1998*, edited by Stefan Leder, 185–191. Paris: Sterling, 2002.
———. "Historia i tradycje polskiego islamu." In *Muzułmanie w Europie*, edited by Anna Parzymies, 199–228. Warsaw: Dialog, 2005.
———. "Tradycje ludowe i folklor Tatarów polsko-litewskich." In *Piśmiennictwo i muhiry Tatarów polsko-litewskich, Res Publica Multiethnica*, edited by Andrzej Drozd, Marek Dziekan, and Tadeusz Majda. Warsaw, 2000.
Górak-Sosnowska, Katarzyna. "Jak uczyć o świecie islamu?" *Ateneum Kapłańskie* 151, no. 2 (2008): 258–266.
———. "Między religią, polityką a komercją. Muzułmańskie cole jako produkty etyczne." *Marketing i rynek* 3 (2008): 25–31.
———. "Organizacje muzułmańskie w Polsce." In *Instytucje religijne i religijność w krajach Unii Europejskiej*, edited by Elżbieta Firlit. Warsaw: SGH, forthcoming.

Henley, Jon, and Jeevan Vasagar. "Think Muslim, drink Muslim, says new rival to Coke." *The Guardian* (8 January 2003, http://www.guardian.co.uk/media/2003/jan/08/marketingandpr.internationalnews).

Jaworowski, Mateusz, and PawełPola ński. *Trendy społeczne i konsumenckie w Polsce u progu Unii Europejskiej*. Paper presented at the 5th all-Poland Congress of Market and Opinion Researchers, Warsaw 21–22 October 2004, p.27.

Kubicki, Paweł. "Muzułmanie w Polsce." *Studia i prace Kolegium Ekonomiczno-Społecznego* 12 (2007): 60–80.

Łyszczarz, Michał, and Karol Marek. "Rola islamu i obrzędowości religijnej w tradycjach Tatarów." Chap. 629–642 in *Arabowie—islam—świat*, edited by Marek Dziekan and Izabela Kończak.Ł ódź: Ibidem, 2007.

Marketing News. http://www.marketing-news.pl, 26 July 2007.

Mönninger, Michael. "Mit den Waffen des Gegners." *Die Zeit*, no. 14 (23 April 2003, http://www.zeit.de/2003/14/Mecca_Cola_14).

Niemczyk, Agata. "Wzory konsumpcji gospodarstw domowych w Polsce i w wybranych krajach Unii Europejskiej." *Zeszyty Naukowe Akademii Ekonomicznej w Krakowie, Kraków* 716 (2006): 5–23.

Sympatia i niechęć do innych narodów. CBOS, BS/144/2007, September 2007, Warsaw, p. 22.

Theodoulou, Michael. "Muslim wage war on US cola giants." *The Australian* (12 October 2002): 12–13.

CHAPTER NINE

MARKETING THE ALEVI MUSICAL REVIVAL

AYHAN EROL

Defining the Alevis

There probably is no best way to define the Alevis since they are large and diverse communities. To some it is important to stress Alevism as a tradition within Islam. Others more easily conceive of Alevism as a conglomeration of groups that do not necessarily define themselves as religious but as the basis for the formulation of various alternative lifestyles.[1] In other words, some people describe Alevism as the original, true essence of Islam or the most authentic expression of Turkish Anatolian Islam, while others define it as a heterodox sect within Islam or a mixture of the best elements of Islam, Christianity, Manichaeism, Shamanism, and 20th century Humanism. Basically Alevi is an umbrella term for a large number of different heterodox communities, whose beliefs and ritual practices differ significantly. Thus, both insider[2] and outsider[3] perspectives stress the heterodox or syncretic feature of Alevism as a tradition within Islam.

---

[1] Karin Vorhoff, "Academic and Journalistic Publications on the Alevi and Bektashi of Turkey," in *Alevi Identity*, ed. Elizabeth Özdalga Tord Olson and Catharine Raundvere (Istanbul: Swedish Research Institute, 1998), 23.

[2] Ahmet Y. Ocak, *Alevi ve Bektaşi İnançlarının İslam Öncesi Temelleri* (Istanbul: İletişim Yay, 2003), 55; Reha Çamuroğlu, "Alevi Revivalism in Turkey," in *Alevi Identity*, ed. Tord Olson, Elizabeth Özdalga, and Catharine Raundvere (Istanbul: Swedish Research Institute, 1998), 25; Faruk Bilici, "The Function of Alevi-Bektashi Theology in Modern Turkey," in *Alevi Identity*, ed. Elizabeth Özdalga Tord Olson and Catharina Raundvere (Istanbul: Swedish Research Institute, 1998), 53.

[3] Martin Van Bruinessen, "Kurds, Turks and the Alevi Revival in Turkey," *Middle East Report* 26, no. 3 (1996): 8; David Shankland, "Anthropology and Ethnicity: The Place of Ethnography in the New Alevi Movement," in *Alevi Identity*, ed. Elizabeth Özdalga Tord Olson and Catharine Raundvere (Istanbul: Swedish Research Institute., 1998), 171; Irene Melikoff, "Bek-

Determining how many Alevis live in Turkey today is practically impossible because they have had a long experience of needing to conceal their identity. In the past two decades, however, there has been an unprecedented rise in their political exposure. Although it is impossible to do more than estimate, it can be reasonably argued that Alevis are not a minor group. They represent at the very least between 5 to 10 million adherents and more probably 15 to 20 million, which means they constitute between 10 to 25 percent of the Turkish population, which is 73 million.

Anatolian Alevis are ethnically mixed communities. They have allegiance to the Twelve Imams, who are patrilineal descendants of the Prophet Muhammad's cousin and son-in-law Imam Ali, but they are certainly not a part of Iranian Shi^{c}i Islam.[4] Culturally, Alevism is linked to the Muslim world. However, it represents an Islam that has distanced itself from everything that represents Muslim orthodoxy, even with Shi^{c}i Islam. One of the most obvious differences between the Shi^{c}i Islam of Iran and the Shia^{c}a-related Alevis of Turkmenistan, Azerbaijan, and Turkey is their attitude toward music.[5] It would be a big mistake to consider Alevis as Shia^{c}a Muslims. Alevism is a kind of religious syncretism or semi-syncretistic religious belief based on ancient Turkish beliefs that still have some elements of animism and shamanism in them and which, at some point in their history, have integrated ideas borrowed from Shi^{c}i Islam. It can be argued that the Anatolian Alevism is a third way, rather than a development along the path of Sunni Islam or Shi^{c}i Islam.[6] In practice, however, any claim to be a true form of Alevism will be empirically incorrect, simply because Alevism has taken very complex forms as it has adapted to new conditions over the centuries.

Alevi Belief and Culture

In contrast to the superficial formalism of Sunni orthodoxy, Alevi belief is based on the mystical ability to perceive the hidden spiritual order. According to Alevis, the Qur'an should be interpreted esoterically, inwardly, and mystically. For them, there are much deeper spiritual truths in the Qur'an

---

tashi/Kızılbaş: Historical Bipartition and Its Consequences," in *Alevi Identity*, ed. Elizabeth Özdalga Tord Olson and Catharina Raundvere (Istanbul: Swedish Research Institute, 1998), 6.

[4] Ayhan Erol, "Change and Continuity in Alevi Musical Identity," in *The Human World and Musical Diversity*, ed. Rosemary Statelova et al., Bulgarian Musicology Studies (Sofia: Institute of Art Studies, 2008), 109.

[5] Gloria L. Clarke, "Mysticism and Music," *Folklor/Edebiyat* 21, no. 1 (2000): 66.

[6] Ayhan Erol, "Reconstructing Cultural Identity in Diaspora: Musical Practices of Toronto Alevi Community," in *Music from Turkey in Diaspora*, ed. Ursula Hemetek and Hande Sağlam (Wien: Institut für Volksmusikforschung und Ethnomusikologie, 2008), 151.

than the strict rules and regulations that appear on the literal surface. However, many Alevis do not read the Qur'an or the other holy books, nor do they base their daily beliefs and practices on them. Since Alevism is an oral culture, there are a significant number of unwritten Alevi teachings and legends credited to Imam Ali, Hacı Bektas Veli, and other saints. Alevis believe that to be Alevi is encapsulated in the saying *Eline, diline, beline sahip ol* ["Be master of your hands, tongue and loins"]. Glosses on this vary, but the most frequent is "Do not take what is not yours, do not lie, and do not make love outside marriage!" The phrase is well-known within mystical Islam, where it is called *edep*: the Alevi are unique in that they have made it part of the very core of their concept of religious fulfillment.[7]

Throughout history Alevis have been discredited and persecuted by the Sunni orthodoxy, and they have been marginalized since the 16th century. Within this religiously marginalized and closed social structure they formed their own rules, and thus drew apart from the direction of the central authorities. In this process, the religious and social authority within the community has been held by "holy men" (*dede*) who belong to a hereditary priestly caste. It is the *cem* ritual that appears as the most significant phenomenon in this process. The *cem* ceremony officiated by the *dede* is a ritual of intense communal significance for Alevis.[8] The *cem* rituals could be conceived of as secret gatherings of the Alevi communities who cannot express themselves and their identity within the framework of the prevailing social order and who want to live outside that order. The *cem* rituals often involve other kinds of latent functions. Both men and women worship together at the *cem*; so for the Alevi masses, the *cem* functions as a mechanism for delivering justice, education, ordering social relations, and solving the spiritual problems of the society. Until the 1990s, the Alevi traditionally did not allow non-Alevis access to their rituals, nor did they provide detailed accounts of their ceremonies, procedures, and doctrines. This is no longer the case. Since the 1990s, Alevism is no longer secretive; in the cities they now hold their rituals in the *Cemevis* (literally the *cem* houses), and the diaspora community holds rituals publicly in their culture centers.

The Alevi Musical Tradition

Having central significance in the *cem* rituals, songs (*deyiş* and *nefes*) and dances (*semah*) simultaneously are perceived in the rituals as an expression

---
[7] Shankland, "Anthropology and Ethnicity: The Place of Ethnography in the New Alevi Movement," 19.
[8] Erol, "Reconstructing Cultural Identity in Diaspora: Musical Practices of Toronto Alevi Community," 152.

of faith. The religious repertory is usually based on subjects that relate to the Prophet Muhammad, Imam Ali, Imam Hüseyin, and others. These songs have followed the Turkish Sufi tradition since the 13th century. However, the musical practices of Alevis are not restricted to the intimate domain of religious practice: many texts are secular and romantic and sociopolitical.

The Republic of Turkey was founded in 1923 as a modern nation state. During the foundation era, the state collected many rural songs from Anatolia as a result of its desire to identify the national characteristics of the "invented culture." Thus the songs and *semah* tunes belonging to Alevis—like the songs of other communities with various ethnic, religious, regional, and local origins—were classified by the state as Turkish folk music. Thus, one could argue that until 1990 Alevi music was very much determined by the state-endorsed canons of music and the media policy of the state. Although Alevi musicians began to appear in the music industry in the 1960s, they were recognized nationally as folk musicians, not as Alevi musicians.

From the beginning until the 1960s, Alevi musicians gave the secular policy of the state strong ideological support through their poetry and music, and thus helped to bolster national identity and ensure the support of the masses. For example, Alevi minstrels and musicians—such as Aşık Veysel, Aşık Ali İzzet, and Hasan Hüseyin—were popularized through performances at cultural centers known as *Halk Evleri* ("People Houses"). They also appeared at festivals and concerts and on state radio programs and made recordings for Columbia, Odeon, and RCA Victor.[9] The support of the Alevi poet-minstrels for the musical polity of the state could be seen as a reflection of the transition of Alevis from a secular community to becoming a part of the modern nation. However, during the period of right/left polarization in the 1970s, the repertoire of some Alevi musicians was increasingly politicized and appropriated by leftist revolutionaries because their themes spoke to contemporary struggles. In accordance with the avowed secularism of the state, the Turkish Radio and Television Corporation (TRT), the state-run broadcast media, imposed some limitations on the amount of Alevi music it played. Nonetheless some elite professional musicians associated with the TRT did promote the Alevi religious repertory—including *semah* melodies and *deyiş* and *nefes* tunes—on air.

In spite of these precedents, Alevi music occupied a marginal place in commercial recordings until the Alevi musical revival in the late 1980s and the early 1990s. It was during that period that Alevis became an integral

---

[9] Irene Markoff, "Alevi Identity and Expressive Culture," in *The Garland Encyclopedia of World Music*, ed. Virginia Danielson, Scott Marcus, and Dwight F. Reynold, vol. 6 (London and NewYork: Roudledge, 2002), 796.

part of consumer society, and they began to rediscover their religious and cultural heritage.

Consuming the Alevi Musical Revival

The Alevi musical revival is a coming together, a convergence of various circumstances and personal motivations centering on the fascination and emulation of a tradition that has become culturally and historically distant from its rituals. In fact, the music revival is an integral part of the Alevi revival generally. The Alevi used to live in remote mountain villages with closed economies. However, due to mass migration to the cities in the 1960s and the 1980s, and the mobility of today's Turkish population, Alevis now live in almost all provinces of the country. Thus they are now clearly very much a part of consumer society. What I want to discuss here is whether identifiable modes of consumption have emerged from the Alevi musical revival. Before I examine some of ways in which the Alevi musical revival has accommodated itself to consumer culture, I would like to make a few introductory remarks on the concept of consumer culture.

To use the term "consumer culture" is to emphasize that the world of consumer goods and its principles of structuration are central to the understanding of contemporary society. Featherstone, in this context, identifies three main types of theories of consumer culture: the first analyses consumerism as a stage of capitalist development; the second is more of a sociological concern about how people delineate their class and status, and how they distinguish themselves via their consuming habits; and the third is concerned with the creativity of consumer practices and how this leads to the aesthetic and emotional pleasure of consumption.[10]

As far as Alevi consumers are concerned, it could be argued that this study should concentrate on the second theory, since it is concerned with how Alevis delineate their ethnicity and status, and how they distinguish themselves via their consumption habits. However, the consumer's habits are not fixed immutable processes like cultural identities. So, the consumer's identity must be viewed as a process of ongoing construction. The need of urban Alevi people for cultural representation might be answered by "traditional" Alevi music. However, the musical tastes and choices of the Alevi are not static. In other words, if Alevis are interested in traditional music that does not preclude that they might also like popular music, or vice versa. Moreover, there is a "mutual fit,' an "elective affinity," between the recent "popular" products of the revivalist and the demands of the Alevi audience.

---

[10] Mike Featherstone, *Consumer Culture & Postmodernism* (London: Sage, 1998), 15–27.

This study will not overlook the importance of the third theory, which is concerned with the emotional pleasures of consumption—the dreams and desires induced by particular shopping environments and the imagery of consumption.

Some social scientists maintain that ethnicity has a strong influence on consumption decisions. However, they argue that any evaluation of the influence of ethnicity over consumption must be framed within a wider understanding of the operation of other categories of social identity, such as class, age, gender, economic status, and so on. Taking a broad approach, these studies suggest that it is not sufficient to focus on a single aspect of identity. They argue that "the relationship between consumption and identity should not be reduced to the level of individual 'lifestyle choice' but related to wider structures of social interaction, especially concerned with gender relations and the family, with generational differences and competing constructions of race, place and nation."[11] These approaches are, of course, based on a dynamic identity concept that also sheds light on the relationship between shopping and identity. Identity a mobile configuration continuously formed and transformed in the different forms through which we are represented in the various social systems surrounding us. Admittedly, temporary identities can only be conjured up through differentiation from the past: "today" derives its meaning by cutting itself off from "yesterday." The never-ending process of identification can go on, undisturbed by the vexing thought that identity is one thing it is conspicuously unable to purvey.[12]

At this stage, I will first describe the various levels of the Alevi musical revival that I have been able to discern and their associated modes of consumption: then I will outline the complex relationships that exist between these patterns. Listening to music is an integral and consistent part of everyday life. But before the advent of electronic media, it was only possible to listen to music at live performances in locations such as private homes, concert halls, opera houses, wedding halls, festival arenas, ritual settings, and so on. These live performances, which once formed the backbone of social interaction, still serve an important entertainment and social role. In industrialized societies where music is important commercially, however, people now mostly satisfy their musical needs through the mass media. Mass-media dissemination of music introduces fundamental changes in traditional patterns of musical production, consumption, and meaning.[13] With

---

[11] Jane Hamlett et al., "Ethnicity and Consumption: South Asian Food Shopping Patterns in Britain, 1947–75," *Journal of Consumer Culture* 8, no. 1 (2008): 93.
[12] Zygmunt Bauman, "Consuming Life," *Journal of Consumer Culture* 1, no. 1 (2001): 24.
[13] Peter Manuel, *Cassette Culture: Popular Music and Technology in North India* (Chicago: University of Chicago Press, 2003), 7.

the introduction of records, tapes, and compact discs, music has become a commodity and consequently an opportunity for profit making. As a quotation by Lewis highlights, music is an important way to let other people know who we are or who we would like to be, and what group we belong to or would like to belong to.[14] In other words the use of music "can be a badge of identity—a means of showing others (and ourselves) to what cultural group or groups we belong to" and as such, music fulfils a social need.[15] Mary Douglas argues: "[...] to the consumers themselves, consumption is less like a pleasure for its own sake and more like a pleasurable fulfillment of social duties."[16] Thus, it is important to note that consumption is not simply a matter of "personal preference" but is, in part, socially constructed.

Modes of Consumption

Embedded in the *cem*, traditionally, the songs have been ontologically separated from the ceremonies together with the development of the recording industry and the state-run mass media in the 1950s. However, the emergence of Alevi music as a representative means of Alevi cultural identity occurred with the beginning of commercial mass media and the development of the music industry in the 1990s. In other words, this religiously specific and contextually embedded musical tradition became an omnipresent product through the production and dissemination of its recordings. Although the most powerful agents in the process of gaining visibility for the Alevi musical revival have been the recording industry and mass media, in fact, there exists a complex pattern of modes of consumption in relation to the Alevi musical revival. These include buying recorded music, viewing TV and music videos, listening to the radio, and downloading music from the internet. Add to these various non-profit and/or commercial levels of involvement that cater to the revivalist market, such as of concert-going, "clubbing" (*Türkü bars*), festival promotions, sales of musical instruments and supplies, music education, and pedagogical publications.

Transnational Alevi organizations, especially in European countries such as Germany, France, Austria, the Netherlands, and Belgium, have increased the awareness of belonging to a wider and supranational Alevi community. Thus it is important to say that revivalist communities are sometimes non-territorial, with their membership spanning local and national boundaries.

---

[14] Avi Shankar, "Lost in Music? Subjective Personal Introspection and Popular Music Consumption," *Qualitative Market Research: An International Journal* 3, no. 1 (2000): 31.
[15] Pete Nuttall, "Thank You for the Music? The Role and Significance of Music for Adolescents," *Young Consumers* 9, no. 2 (2008): 104.
[16] Mary Douglas (1982) in Featherstone, *Consumer Culture & Postmodernism*, 119.

In order to create a sense of Alevi community, recorded music (which has become an omnipresent product, such as a cassettes, records, or CDs) helps to bring Alevi people separated by geographical space together. Moreover, today it becomes quite easily to access them through commercial digital (i.e, online) music services or non-commercial file-sharing services via the internet. However, the purchase of recorded music as a product is still an important cultural behavior, and consumption in its most general sense is therefore an intensely performative and creative fact.

Here we might usefully introduce the concept of cultural capital that has been developed by Pierre Bourdieu and others. This concept points the way in which parallel to economic capital (which is immediately calculable, exchangeable, and realizable) there also exist modes of power and processes of accumulation based upon culture in which the value of the latter, the fact that culture can be capital, is often hidden and unrecognized. Bourdieu points to three forms of cultural capital: It can exist in the embodied state (a style of presentation, mode of speech, beauty, etc), objectified state (cultural goods such as pictures, books, machines, buildings, etc.) and in the institutionalized state (such as educational qualifications).[17] It is the objectified state that is of particular interest with respect to buying the recorded Alevi music. The consumption of music is not a passive activity. Acquiring any form of recorded Alevi music serves as an objectified state of cultural capital. Moreover, the semiotic relevance of this music as cultural consumption goods is not only substantial in relation to outsiders, but also within the Alevi consumers: putting the more "commercial" recordings of Kıvıcık Ali or Arzu on the CD player is quite different from having recordings by the "avant garde" Adil Arslan on the music archive.

The new technologies of communication facilitate distinctively modern senses of religious and political identity that, rooted in specific local context, are also systematized on a translocal horizon opened by new forms of communication.[18] The media industry not only perpetuates revivalist doctrine and practices, but it is a valuable adjunct to organizations for the formation and maintenance of a tight-knit society based on a shared interest and consumption patterns.[19] Regarding the structural conditions, it is not surprising that the Alevi revival expressed itself very much through the ex-

---

[17] Cited from Featherstone, *Consumer Culture & Postmodernism*, 106.

[18] Dale F. Eickelman and Jon W. Anderson, "Redefining Muslim Publics," in *New Media in the Muslim World*, ed. Dale F. Eickelman and Jon W. Anderson (Bloomington: Indiana University Press, 2003), 5.

[19] Tamara Livingston, "Music Revivals: Towards a General Theory," *Ethnomusicology* 43, no. 1 (1999): 79.

tensive use of modern media.[20] Several radio stations and TV channels with an unmistakable Alevi stance were started during the 1990s.[21] In addition, today there are so many websites dedicated to the Alevi identity and community. The recorded music at the same time serves as the content focus for another medium. In other words the recorded Alevi music or live performances of Alevi musicians are also offered for public consumption on radio or television.

Unlike the recordings, live musical performances of concerts, festivals and competitions bring Alevi people together physically. These events are crucial to the Alevis because they meet each other face-to-face to share repertoire and playing techniques, to discuss the strengths and weaknesses of artists within the tradition, to actively learn and experience the revivalist ethos and aesthetic code at work, and to socialize with other "insiders." Moreover, these kinds of musical events provide a range of shared symbols that communicate a sense of an Alevi community to participants. It is therefore possible to say that listening to recorded music or going to a concert enables Alevis who are not able to take part in the actual rituals to continue to identify with their cultural heritage. Basically, it is also possible to say that the concerts, which bring Alevi people together physically, are indeed a ritual. When we review the conceptual content of the term "ritual," in fact, we can see that the concept of rituals is often erroneously interpreted as only behavior of religious or mystical significance. Religious rituals are of course an important type of ritual, but its definition is not restricted to religious ceremonies.

The term ritual refers to a type of expressive, symbolic activity constructed of multiple behaviors that occur in a fixed, episodic sequence, and that tend to be repeated over time. Ritual behavior is dramatically scripted and acted out and is performed with formality, seriousness, and inner intensity.[22] Concerts, aside from being an important mode of consumption within the Alevi musical revival, are a form of ritual for both performers and their audiences. Small sees symphony orchestra concerts as celebrating the power-holding class in our society.[23] In a similar fashion, "rock" concerts celebrate youth. It's not purely youth as a demographic group that's

---

[20] Vorhoff, "Academic and Journalistic Publications on the Alevi and Bektashi of Turkey," 34.
[21] M. Hakan Yavuz, "Media Identities for Alevis and Kurds in Turkey," in *New Media in the Muslim World*, ed. Dale F. Eickelman and Jon W. Anderson (Bloomington: Indiana University Press, 2003), 184.
[22] David Luna and Susan Forquer, "An Integrative Framework for Cross-Cultural Consumer Behavior," *International Marketing Review* 18, no. 1 (2001): 51.
[23] Christopher Small, "Social Character of Music: Performance as Ritual," in *Lost in Music: Culture, Style and Musical Events*, ed. Avron L. White (London: Routledge, 1987), 8.

being celebrated, but rather the idea of "youth."[24] In a similar way, the concerts performed by Alevi musicians celebrate Alevi ethnicity. Therefore it is important to see concerts performed by Alevi musicians, especially prominent revivalists, in the context of a growing awareness of Alevism that unites the Alevis.

The Alevi musical revival must be seen as not just activity by some prominent Alevi musicians but as a "contextual aggregate" that enjoys widespread support and participation at the local level of music making. A Türkü bar, a place where live music is essential, is a good example to consider this issue. It is clearly a revivalist phenomenon that can be confined to particular spaces or tied to particular performances. It is also clearly a meeting point for the production and consumption of Turkish folk music, especially Alevi music. The term *Türkü* refers to any piece of Turkish folk music, it also indicates its anonymity. Türkü bars are a kind of pub, a "space" constructed around Turkish folk music, including Alevi tunes. Türkü bars, one of the most important aspects of the revival, began to emerge in the 1990s. Although not all of the consumers at these venues are Alevis, the vast majority of the regular visitors are young Alevis.

I conducted a case study of Türkü bars in the city of Izmir in Turkey in 2005. One thing that struck me was the ethnicity of both musicians and the owners of the Türkü bars: many of them were Alevis, just like the vast majority of the customers. For many of the young Alevis I interviewed, Türkü bars provide an acceptable place to socialize—and spend time and money—as opposed to *pavyon* (casino), *kahvehane* (cafe), or *birahane* (pub). Musicians performing in Türkü bars were first introduced to Alevi music in the mid-1990s, when an innovative Alevi repertory suddenly re-entered the music industry. This early repertoire of the revival not only stimulated the interest of the urban Alevi communities who interpreted it as legitimizing their identitiy, but it also stimulated the emergence of amateur-turned-professional Alevi musicians. In other words, Türkü bars created a new market. Moreover, there is a symbiotic relationship between the repertory performed by the young musicians in such places and the recordings released by prominent Alevi musicians. This promotes and increases the exchange and distribution of music commodities and products. In other words these live performance venues also serve as the socio-economic hub of the revival, providing a space where musicians and new musical styles and the revivalist repertory can interact and where the revival is made more visible, physical, and real.

---

[24] Roy Shuker, *Understanding Popular Music* (London: Routledge, 2001), 205.

The *bağlama* also has a significant place in both Turkish musical life and in the modes of consumption of the Alevi musical revival. The *bağlama*, the general name of the long-necked lute, also called *saz*, was originally referred to as the *kopuz* in the 14th-century book of Dede Korkut, and was found in various forms throughout the Turkic world. In its various lengths and sizes, ranging from *Meydan* and *Divan*, through *Tanbura* and *Bağlama* to *Cura*, the *Bağlama* family forms the core of the Turkish folk music ensembles "invented" by the state in the 1940s. It is therefore recognized as an icon of Turkish folk music. However, this cannot be compared to the importance of *bağlama* in the Alevi belief and culture. For the Alevis, the *bağlama* has become a powerful symbol of their group identity and their creed. It is also a material representing Imam Ali and the tenets of his faith: the resonator is said to represent his body, the neck his sword *Zülfikar*, the 12 strings (and sometimes frets) the 12 Shi'i imams, and the lower course of strings, the Prophet Muhammad.[25] One of the most important examples of the Alevi mystical rhetoric surrounding the playing of the *bağlama* is that some view this musical instrument as a *Telli Kuran* (the stringed Qurʾan).

Until the end of the 1980s, the *bağlama* was looked down upon as a rural music. Since then, it has largely become a legitimate instrument in Turkish musical life through the Alevi musical revival. There is no official data about how many *bağlamas* are manufactured in Turkey. According to some estimates, between 1 million and 2 million *bağlamas* are produced there every year. However, it could be reasonably argued that 1.5 million *bağlamas* are manufactured in Turkey a year, since many of the *bağlama* players and makers I interviewed in Izmir quoted that number.

Although it is important to buy a *bağlama* from a master craftsman, it is now a widely popular and cheap instrument that is mass-produced in the big cities of Turkey. Prices in 2008 ranged from less than 50 TL (25 euros) to around 500 TL (250 euros). It goes without saying that the explosion in sales of the *bağlama* in the last two decades demonstrates that in terms of the revival the most important form of consumption is the purchase of a *bağlama*. However non-Alevis also buy *bağlamas* and take classes in the *bağlama*, because those who are interested in folk music consider the *bağlama* the most logical and representative instrument of Turkish folk music. At this point, the most important question must probably be about learning the *bağlama*.

In all Turkish cities today, the *cemevis* provide free training in a number of skills—in particular, playing the *bağlama* and teaching *semah* (ritual dance). The *cemevis*, offering classes in *semah* and *bağlama*, stress the contribution they make to maintaining the music and dance of the Alevis, providing Alevi

---

[25] Markoff, "Alevi Identity and Expressive Culture," 798.

society with able players and representing Alevi culture.[26] These courses are mostly attended by younger Alevis, ranging from children of primary school age to young adults in their late 20s. The *bağlama* and *semah* courses provided by the Alevi associations—such as the *cemevi, dernek* (association), *vakıf* (foundation) and *kültür merkezi* (cultural center)—are generally noncommercial activities of the Alevi musical revival, even though the *bağlama* teachers and *semah* trainers are paid by the associations. However the pedagogical components of the revival are not restricted to non-profit organizations. The role of private *bağlama* education is crucial in terms of modes of consumption in the context of the Alevi musical revival. Although the educational system of the *bağlama* began to shift from the apprenticeship model to a formal system of education through private associations in the 1960s and the State Conservatories of Turkish Music in the 1970s, a high degree of enthusiasm for learning the *bağlama* is based on the climate of the revival. Many of the private teaching centers in large cities, known as *dershane*, are run by prominent Alevi *bağlama* players. Young musicians and amateurs are educated in the *dershane* run by revivalist musicians. They are based on a semi-formal system of education. Notation is an essential part of the curriculum in all the *dershane*. Thus, the Alevi musical revival has a strong pedagogical component that passes on the tradition in a modernized manner.

In addition to these traits, Martin Stokes's outsider observations on the owners might be useful here: Extra income is earned from the *dershane*, but the considerations that lead musicians to open a *dershane* may vary and may embody several strategies. These include enabling the owner to participate in wider social networks, providing employment for musician friends and instrument makers, and supplying the owner with a source of material, along with technical, and moral support for their other professional activities as musicians.[27] Such relationships comprise a formal and informal economy of the revival. It is obvious that the attempts to create a cohesive sense of identity through modes of consumption that can be associated with the Alevi music revival have succeeded. To see how this is done, it is necessary to shift the focus from the ways in which the Alevi music is consumed to the ways in which it is performed and marketed.

---

[26] Erol, "Reconstructing Cultural Identity in Diaspora: Musical Practices of Toronto Alevi Community," 156.
[27] Martin Stokes, *Arabesk Debate: Music and Musicians in Modern Turkey* (Oxford: Oxford University Press, 1992), 43.

Marketing the Alevi Musical Revival

Marketing may be defined as a set of human activities directed at facilitating and consummating exchanges. Jamal argues that marketing plays an important role in facilitating the co-existence of a variety of modes of consumption and of a sense of being in the contemporary marketplace.[28] As far as the music industry is concerned, it has centered on the marketing of genre styles and stars, which have come to function in a similar manner to brand names, "serving to order demand and stabilize sales patterns."[29] Although the inevitable partnership between Alevi musicians, in particular prominent revivalists, and the culture industry has transformed their repertoire and ultimately the musicians into a popular culture phenomenon, it would certainly be incorrect to see them as nothing more than a pale imitation of popular music stars. In any case, none of the Alevi musicians calls himself a popular music artist, and the audience never perceives them as pop singers, despite their use of conventional norms of popular music in their performances. Yet this does not decrease the importance of prominent Alevi musicians in terms of the Alevi and non-Alevi audiences. Thus it would certainly be more correct to refer to them as the leader revivalists or the "core revivalists," because of their significance role within the revival.

As Livingston has argued, one of the most important features of music revivals is the central role played by a few individuals known as the "core revivalists."[30] Although core revivalists almost always come from the ranks of the middle class—as scholars, professional or amateur musicians, dilettantes, and those involved with the music industry—in the case of the Alevi musical revival, core revivalists are professional Alevi musicians. Those who have benefitted the most from the revival, in fact, are the Alevi musicians themselves. From the perspective of contemporary marketing strategies the philosophy of marketing needs to be owned by everyone within the organization. Concern and responsibility for marketing must permeate all areas of the enterprise. It is therefore possible to say that as the "core producers" musicians have responsibility for marketing. The public success and longevity of musical revivals certainly depends in part on the strength and vitality of the revival industries. The authenticity debates are viewed by the industry as getting in the way of marketability. Owing to the creativity involved in the construction of an authenticity discourse and practice by the core revivalists, this section concentrates on the strategies of the

---

[28] Ahmad Jamal, "Marketing in a Multicultural World: The Interplay of Marketing, Ethnicity and Consumption," *European Journal of Marketing* 17, no. 11–12 (2003): 1609.
[29] Shuker, *Understanding Popular Music*, 45.
[30] Livingston, "Music Revivals: Towards a General Theory," 70.

core revivalists that focus on not only identifying customer needs but also satisfying them (short-term) and anticipating them in the future (long-term retention).

Alevi musicians often performed Turkish folk music—i.e., songs of different ethnicities—in order to maximize their popularity and respectability in the eyes of the Turkish people. As far as I'm concerned, this is one of the most important marketing strategies of Alevi musicians. The musicians associated with the Alevi musical tradition in Turkey negotiate their professional identities in terms of the authenticity of Turkish folk music. Thus, they participate in the construction of the folk music myth as long as it suits their commercial interests, but have recourse to a variety of strategies to negotiate their musical identities in their community. Based on their marketing plan Alevi musicians try to determine who their audiences are, and to decide whether their audiences can be segmented either vertically or horizontally. On one hand, they define their performances as folk music to make sense of their experience in the music industry and to attract to a wider audience, on the other hand they construct categories within folk music by considering themselves as the representatives of "real" Alevi music.

Marketing the Alevi musical revival is essentially about marshalling the resources of Alevi musical culture so that they meet the changing needs of the customer. The revivalists searching for the roots of Alevi music dug up old recordings and tried to revive pieces of music that may not have been played for decades. The field recordings collected from Anatolia allowed the revivalists to determine authentic performance styles. They became known for their musical involvement based on playing the *bağlama* and singing traditional Alevi tunes. However, while the early revivalists were very intolerant of any change introduced by young musicians, they have always pursued innovations. The balance between individual innovation and adherence to the stylistic norms of tradition were reconstructed by the revivalists themselves. As an innovator, Ali Ekber Çiçek (1935–2006) was perhaps one of the best-known Alevi musicians and masters of the *divan bağlama*. It might be argued that his famous song *Haydar*, a complex and dramatic creation composed for voice and *bağlama* in 1965, largely of his own inspiration, was the first piece from the Alevi musical revival to achieve mass popularity.

The re-emergence of Alevi music based on *bağlama* playing in the music industry, around the 1980s, was closely associated with three or four *bağlama* players; Arif Sağ, Musa Eroğlu, Yavuz Top, and Muhlis Akarsu. Thus, the origins of the movement in the mid-1980s should be credited to a series of commercial cassettes, labeled *muhabbet*, released by these revivalists. They employed traditional instrumentation in their *muhabbet* releases, which consisted only of *bağlamas*, and retained a certain classicism in their use of the *bağlama* and their improvised flavor and avoidance of Western harmony and instruments. The repertory, including religious songs and an innovative style they popularized, can be seen in a commercialized and free continuation of their limited performances on TRT. Through their activities, including live performances, they succeeded in transforming the practice of traditional Alevi music on the *bağlama* from an isolated activity of a few individuals into a popular form of *zikir* (ar. *dhikr*, "remembrance") in cultured urban Alevi society.[31] These cassettes became widely popular amongst Alevis, particularly among amateur Alevi and non-Alevi musicians. "Consumers of different ethnic backgrounds, at the same time, also have the opportunity to interact with one another and to shop around and make their consumption choices as per their interactions and experiences with marketers of different ethnic backgrounds."[32]

The revivals partake of the discourse of modernity even as they set themselves in opposition to certain manifestations of modernity.[33] The most important musical orientation of the core revivalist in the late 1980s was the polyphonization of monophonic Alevi music as a myth of modernity. Some of the core revivalists who were ideologically bound to the idea of universalism tended to determine the universalist characteristics of Alevi music. Seeing the pursuance of local musical differences as a separation from universal ideals, they considered the polyphonization of monophonic Alevi musical tradition as the best way to go. For instance, Yavuz Top, a core revivalist, an instructor, has argued "tribal" musical elements should be subordinated to the universalism. Since the ideology of Third World socialism involves the project of Westernization from above, it has strong parallels to Kemalism.[34] In this respect, the universalist ideology of Enlightenment is a common value for both the Kemalist political elite and Alevi musicians who consider themselves as modernists and socialists or leftists. There is, therefore, a strong relationship between the Kemalist music reform and the polyphonization of monophonic Alevi melodies by the core revivalists.[35] Striking examples of this kind of instrumental polyphony are the album *Western-Eastern Divan: the Semahs for Saz and Orchestra*, released in 1987, by Adil Arslan, a *bağlama* player living in Germany; and the album *Concerto for Bağlama*, composed by Arif Sağ in the mid-1990s. However these poly-

---

[31] Erol, "Change and Continuity in Alevi Musical Identity," 112.
[32] Jamal, "Marketing in a Multicultural World: The Interplay of Marketing, Ethnicity and Consumption," 1599.
[33] Livingston, "Music Revivals: Towards a General Theory," 81.
[34] Çamuroğlu, "Alevi Revivalism in Turkey," 80.
[35] Erol, "Change and Continuity in Alevi Musical Identity," 116.

phonic recordings have not attracted significant amounts of attention, among either Alevis or non-Alevi audience. It is possible to consider these recordings as a temporal avant garde attempt by the core revivalists. It is also possible to say that these musicians became more aware of the power of the popular music market in the 1990s. In either case it is necessary to mention that these recordings did not appeal to audiences and did not achieve wide sales. They have not composed such polyphonic works since the middle of the 1990s. The bundling of monophonic Alevi melodies and some components of Western polyphony as popular arrangements was another common practice until the late 1980s. Yavuz Top, with his arrangement, *Otme Bülbül Ötme* and Arif Sağ with the song *İnsan Olmaya Geldim* provided two rich examples of this kind of popular arrangement.

The polyphonization of monophonic Alevi melodies is based on the rationality of modernism as an ideology. However, the rationality of consumer society is built on the irrationality of its individualized actors.[36] The core revivalists noticed that their attempts came up against the irrationality of tastes because the musical choices of the Alevis people are not just a matter of rationality. As Jamal has argued, the interdependence between consumption and ethnicity are moments in the ongoing construction of personal and social identity.[37] Having already claimed that the Alevi musical tradition was diluted by some popular music singers, the revivalists less than 10 years later had to face a revivalist community that asked them to perform again in a style that was not their first choice from the start.[38] In the beginining of the 1990s, the modernizing elements of Western polyphonization accepted by the revivalists as "progress" were absorbed into the vocabulary of the revived Alevi music associated with popular music styles.

According to Jamal, for some, mass marketing is a thing of the past and one needs to respond to consumer differences with differentiation and segmentation strategies. Thus a characteristic feature of a multicultural marketplace is the positioning of the marketers and consumers of different ethnic backgrounds into multiple and traversing cultural spheres.[39] The core revivalists responded to consumer differences with these strategies. Alevi musicians adapted pre-existing popular styles to the tastes and demands of the new urban Alevis, whereas they did not also marginalize the music market because it comprises such a small proportion of the total population and

---

[36] Bauman, "Consuming Life," 17.
[37] Jamal, "Marketing in a Multicultural World: The Interplay of Marketing, Ethnicity and Consumption," 1602.
[38] Erol, "Change and Continuity in Alevi Musical Identity," 116.
[39] Jamal, "Marketing in a Multicultural World: The Interplay of Marketing, Ethnicity and Consumption," 1599.

therefore was not worth investing the resources to target. Since Turkish listeners often prefer indigenous music in the local style and melodies of their own region, the albums of the revived Alevi music are made up of a mixed repertoire. In other words, the revivalists soon learned that there was an album concept that could be sold to all Turkish audiences. One of the earliest examples of this concept is the album *Biz insanlar*, released by Arif Sağ in the early 1990s. The album incudes a variety of Alevi religious and non-religious genres, political protest songs, and Turkish folk songs appealing to all Turkish listeners.[40] Having used new sounds, such as sampled and electronic drums, synthesized bass and computer-generated string glissandi in the album *Biz İnsanlar*, Arif Sağ has successfully combined Turkish folk music with the mainstream popular music styles. The other core revivalists, such as Musa Eroğlu, Yavuz Top, and Sabahat Akkiraz, have performed a similar content and sonic design in their albums since the 1990s.

By the late 1990s, however, Alevi music had evolved into a popular form that, despite retaining many musical figures from its roots, sounded increasingly Western. It might be argued that there has probably been a decrease in the diversity of performance styles. At the same time, there has been an increase in the variety of musical experiments and forms that young musicians perform. Clifford Geertz has stated in his *Interpretation of Cultures* that the desire once aroused in a population to become a recognized and respected people in the world, with their own rights, cannot be quenched.[41] Initially, some young aspiring musicians who dream of national fame tried to copy the styles of the core revivalists. However, young Alevi musicians soon began to develop in their own directions. By the 2000s, some young Alevi musicians, such as Arzu, Ayşegül, Kıvırcık Ali, and Güler Duman, used *bağlama* with electric instruments, strong percussion, and sometimes string orchestras in their albums, so that songs that might belong to the Arabesk, which is one of the two main streams of Turkish popular music, conformed closely to the popular music aesthetic. These albums were an "intensifying fusion" of popular music components and Alevi musical experience. Even Sabahat Akkiraz, as a well-known revivalist Alevi singer, joined in this tendency in a different way. Her recent recordings, combining Alevi melodies with electronic music and jazz, epitomize the different styles. Needless to say, the future will show us how the Alevi musical revival develops. However, it is obvious that the interaction between traditional Alevi music and popular music depends on the reproducibility of the perceptions of Alevi musicians and their audiences themselves. Thus, it also needs to be recog-

---

[40] Erol, "Change and Continuity in Alevi Musical Identity," 115.

[41] Clifford Geertz, *The Interpretation of Cultures: Selected Essays* (New York: Basic Books, 1973), 237.

nized that how well mainstream popular music components are used in the traditional Alevi music varies according to the individual dispositions and marketing strategies of Alevi musicians.

Conclusion

In the beginning of this article, I tried to explain that both production and consumption are not to be regarded as fixed, immutable processes but must be viewed as engaged in a dialectic. If cultural appropriation is defined as processes by which meanings are transformed within specific hierarchical structures of power, it could be argued that cultural consumption could be explained as processes by which meanings are transformed within the self.[42] Orthodox psychology defined "need" as a state of tension that would eventually disperse and wither away once the need has been gratified. The "need" that sets the members of consumer society in motion is, on the contrary, the need to keep the tension alive and, if anything, it is stronger with every step.[43] This argument can be read in the context of change and continuity in Alevi music: the need which sets the Alevi consumer in motion is the need to keep the tension alive between "traditional" Alevi music and popular music styles. Under conditions of de-monopolization of the "real" or "authentic" Alevi music, the revivalists have relinquished their commitment to *traditionalism* and *avant-gardism* and have adopted an increasingly open attitude towards *consumerism* by popularizing Alevi music and making it more accessible to wider audiences.

For Alevi musicians, I would argue that the revival has provided them with a language in which their professional activities can be legitimately represented in a commercial market. They have still been trying to survive in a highly competitive market. Alevi musicians who use popular music styles and techniques in their performance and recordings believe that the introduction of Western instrumentation, harmony, and technology in Alevi music has never distanced this music from its traditional ethos. Thus, the revivalist considers the popular music components of this music as a symbol of musical progress. In this case, the notion of progress as a myth of modernity plays a part in defining the revived Alevi music and its authenticity. This discourse of authenticity not only serves as the legitimization of the practice but also as an important marketing strategy.

---

[42] Michel A. Possamai, "Cultural Consumption of History and Popular Culture in Alternative Spiritualities," *Journal of Consumer Culture* 2, no. 2 (2002): 204.
[43] Bauman, "Consuming Life," 13.

Bibliography

Bauman, Zygmunt. "Consuming Life." *Journal of Consumer Culture* 1, no. 1 (2001): 9–29.
Bilici, Faruk. "The Function of Alevi-Bektashi Theology in Modern Turkey." In *Alevi Identity*, edited by Elizabeth Özdalga Tord Olson and Catharina Raundvere, 51–63. Istanbul: Swedish Research Institute, 1998.
Çamuroğlu, Reha. "Alevi Revivalism in Turkey." In *Alevi Identity*, edited by Tord Olson, Elizabeth Özdalga, and Catharine Raundvere, 79–85. Istanbul: Swedish Research Institute, 1998.
Clarke, Gloria L. "Mysticism and Music." *Folklor/Edebiyat* 21, no. 1 (2000): 59–74.
Eickelman, Dale F., and Jon W. Anderson. "Redefining Muslim Publics." In *New Media in the Muslim World*, edited by Dale F. Eickelman and Jon W. Anderson, 1–19. Bloomington: Indiana University Press, 2003.
Erol, Ayhan. "Change and Continuity in Alevi Musical Identity." In *The Human World and Musical Diversity*, edited by Rosemary Statelova et al., 109–117. Bulgarian Musicology Studies. Sofia: Institute of Art Studies, 2008.
———. "Reconstructing Cultural Identity in Diaspora: Musical Practices of Toronto Alevi Community." In *Music from Turkey in Diaspora*, edited by Ursula Hemetek and Hande Sağlam, 151–161. Wien: Institut für Volksmusikforschung und Ethnomusikologie, 2008.
Featherstone, Mike. *Consumer Culture & Postmodernism*. London: Sage, 1998.
Geertz, Clifford. *The Interpretation of Cultures: Selected Essays*. New York: Basic Books, 1973.
Hamlett, Jane, et al. "Ethnicity and Consumption: South Asian Food Shopping Patterns in Britain, 1947–75." *Journal of Consumer Culture* 8, no. 1 (2008): 91–116.
Jamal, Ahmad. "Marketing in a Multicultural World: The Interplay of Marketing, Ethnicity and Consumption." *European Journal of Marketing* 17, no. 11–12 (2003): 1599–1620.
Livingston, Tamara. "Music Revivals: Towards a General Theory." *Ethnomusicology* 43, no. 1 (1999): 66–86.
Luna, David, and Susan Forquer. "An Integrative Framework for Cross-Cultural Consumer Behavior." *International Marketing Review* 18, no. 1 (2001): 45–69.
Manuel, Peter. *Cassette Culture: Popular Music and Technology in North India*. Chicago: University of Chicago Press, 2003.

Markoff, Irene. "Alevi Identity and Expressive Culture." In *The Garland Encyclopedia of World Music*, edited by Virginia Danielson, Scott Marcus, and Dwight F. Reynold, 793–800. Vol. 6. London and NewYork: Roudledge, 2002.

Melikoff, Irene. "Bektashi/Kızılbaş: Historical Bipartition and Its Consequences." In *Alevi Identity*, edited by Elizabeth Özdalga Tord Olson and Catharina Raundvere, 1–9. Istanbul: Swedish Research Institute, 1998.

Nuttall, Pete. "Thank You for the Music? The Role and Significance of Music for Adolescents." *Young Consumers* 9, no. 2 (2008): 104–111.

Ocak, Ahmet Y. *Alevi ve Bektaşi İnançlarının İslam Öncesi Temelleri*. Istanbul: İletişim Yay, 2003.

Possamai, Michel A. "Cultural Consumption of History and Popular Culture in Alternative Spiritualities." *Journal of Consumer Culture* 2, no. 2 (2002): 197–218.

Shankar, Avi. "Lost in Music? Subjective Personal Introspection and Popular Music Consumption." *Qualitative Market Research: An International Journal* 3, no. 1 (2000): 27–37.

Shankland, David. "Anthropology and Ethnicity: The Place of Ethnography in the New Alevi Movement." In *Alevi Identity*, edited by Elizabeth Özdalga Tord Olson and Catharine Raundvere, 15–22. Istanbul: Swedish Research Institute., 1998.

Shuker, Roy. *Understanding Popular Music*. London: Routledge, 2001.

Small, Christopher. "Social Character of Music: Performance as Ritual." In *Lost in Music: Culture, Style and Musical Events*, edited by Avron L. White, 7–21. London: Routledge, 1987.

Stokes, Martin. *Arabesk Debate: Music and Musicians in Modern Turkey*. Oxford: Oxford University Press, 1992.

Van Bruinessen, Martin. "Kurds, Turks and the Alevi Revival in Turkey." *Middle East Report* 26, no. 3 (1996): 7–10.

Vorhoff, Karin. "Academic and Journalistic Publications on the Alevi and Bektashi of Turkey." In *Alevi Identity*, edited by Elizabeth Özdalga Tord Olson and Catharine Raundvere, 23–50. Istanbul: Swedish Research Institute, 1998.

Yavuz, M. Hakan. "Media Identities for Alevis and Kurds in Turkey." In *New Media in the Muslim World*, edited by Dale F. Eickelman and Jon W. Anderson, 180–199. Bloomington: Indiana University Press, 2003.

Part III

Islamic Products, Islamic Brands, and Muslim Target Groups

CHAPTER TEN

BARBIE, RAZANNE, FULLA: A TALE OF CULTURE, GLOBALIZATION, CONSUMERISM, AND ISLAM

PETRA KUPPINGER[1]

When Fulla arrived at our house in fall 2004, she had already traveled halfway around the globe. Originating in China, she had stopped at a retail outlet in the United Arab Emirates. From there she took the long postal trip to the U.S. Midwest. Fulla is a pretty young woman wearing the black abaya (cloak and headscarf) worn by Emirati women. Under her headcover, Fulla has long black hair with red highlights. She wears high heels and a long, tight, colorful skirt, which is barely visible under her abaya. She wears bright red lipstick. Fulla is a Barbie-type doll, yet it is important to know that she is not a Barbie. Razanne, a similar doll wearing an ankle-length skirt, long-sleeve blouse, and white hijab joined our multi-ethnic doll family in summer 2005. Razanne has the body of a pre-pubescent girl and wears no makeup. She was ordered from an Islamic online distributor and shipped from Baltimore, U.S., where she had traveled from a Chinese production site.

What makes Razanne and Fulla interesting and analytically fascinating is their status as, for lack of a better term, Barbie-like non-Barbies. As such, they have been creating niches for themselves in the globalized consumer marketplace and the universe of commercialized children's culture. Fulla and Razanne are indirect descendants of the Western popular culture queen Barbie, yet they reject central elements of "Barbieness," and thus position themselves in opposition to aspects of Barbie's cultural universe. While Fulla and Razanne feed on the Barbie-craze, they deny similarities in culture

---

[1] I want to thank Johanna Pink for organizing a great conference in Berlin and for getting this volume together. Thanks go to Tamima and Tala for being the joy of my life and for sharing their dolls with me.

and lifestyle with her. These newer dolls are situated on an ambivalent cultural fault-line, yet in their own ways they bridge that very line. Razanne and Fulla symbolize an intricately interwoven 21st century global economy and culture. Examining their cultural identities and economic contexts, some questions emerge: Do they represent an ingenious victory of global capitalism by successfully marketing culturally appropriate products in specific market niches? Are they indicators of a growing ethno-capitalism? Do they represent the commercial exploitation of religious and cultural sentiments? And, slightly differently, but equally important, what sorts of reactions—if any—have these dolls triggered?

The existences of Razanne and Fulla are analytically complex. They are more than toys. Conceived in a time when ethnic and religious stereotyping and enemy imagery guide dominant Western politics and views of Muslims, the dolls, their reception, and the debates about them are embedded in larger contexts of political, cultural, and religious conflict. Analyzing debates about the dolls, their marketing and cultural contexts, it is evident that voices and opinions feed on political, cultural, and economic discussions situated on the complex stage of globalized encounters and entanglements, where ill-defined dichotomies of East/West, multifaceted struggles of definitions of Islam, and the vast diversity of globalized Muslim and non-Muslim worlds contend with one another.

In this paper, I argue that Razanne and Fulla are examples of a new profitable, culturally sensitive consumerism. They produce profits in cultural niches that did not previously exist or were not considered profitable. Simultaneously, they symbolize a new, vaguely defined Muslim popular and consumer culture. The dolls are products of an emerging profitable consumer industry that seeks to identify "Muslim" needs and supply them with appropriate products. As more new products are designed, aspects of what it means to be "Muslim" are tied to the consumption of such specific identity-constructing products. Of course, not all Muslims (or members of any ethnic or religious group) are easily drawn into processes of identity construction via consumption. However, consumer dynamics are an important aspect of wide-ranging debates about identities and the construction and everyday maintenance of those identities. Fulla and Razanne, moreover, created small political and cultural platforms on which different cultural actors debate the phenomena of the dolls and their cultural, religious, and political contexts and meanings. An examination of such seemingly irrelevant platforms reveals how tense and rife with misunderstandings these encounters are. Reactions to the dolls cover a wide spectrum from passionate support to ironic belittlement, ridicule, and politically motivated rejection and fear. Some observers even identify the dolls as politically dangerous.

In order to analytically situate Fulla and Razanne, I will first examine debates about globalization, global consumer cultures, and ethnically or culturally marked consumerism. I will then examine toy manufacturing and marketing as a global multi-billion dollar consumer industry. I discuss the production, marketing, and cultural significance of Barbie since she is the undisputed prototype that inspired her Muslim sister dolls. Subsequently I illustrate aspects of the reception and controversies around Barbie in parts of the Muslim world. Then I explore Razanne and Fulla, their dynamics of production and marketing and cultural contexts. Moreover, I examine the reception of the dolls in different contexts, and how they reflect larger political encounters and controversies. Finally I introduce Fulah (different spelling!) and other "cheap" copies of Razanne and Fulla that have appeared in Middle Eastern popular markets. I will end on a note about Fulla as a possibly potent political danger.

Talking about the dolls and their cultural contexts, it is important to stress that dichotomies such as East/West or Muslim/non-Muslim are not very helpful. Discussing their designs and economic contexts I obviously do not assume there is anything "Muslim" or "Western"; indeed such categories are limiting. Who are Muslims, and who are Westerners? Who are Western Muslims? Who are Muslim Westerners? The simplistic use of such concepts is of little analytical use. Not all Westerners like Barbie, and not all Muslims like Fulla. Muslims love Barbie, and Westerners or Christians might appreciate the modesty of Razanne. Not all Arabs or Middle Easterners are Muslims, just as not all Westerners are Christian. When I occasionally use blanket terms such as "Muslim" or "Western," I do with a clear understanding that they are problematic and analytically flawed since they do not represent the complex current reality of layered and complex identities that combine and exclude a wide variety of elements. What I attempt to show are the dynamics of a vast cultural field where notions of Islam, Christianity, capitalism, consumerism—and places such as the Arab Middle East, Europe, and the United States—all play important roles, but none of them acts as a distinct and well-bounded unit. Neither are their inhabitants or adherents seen as acting in unison. Indeed my assumption is that each entity or concept is under debate and includes opposing views and groups, and is constantly in flux.

Globalization, Ethnic Consumerism and Muslim Consumerism

Globalization, far from being a homogenizing force, has in recent years accommodated considerable instances of localization. TV channels in the United States and Europe catering to the specific linguistic and cultural needs of immigrants are only one of the most important examples of such localization. In an era that is marked by ethnic and religious consciousness, revival and conflict, it is not surprising to see that economic forces are quick to discover and exploit new ethnic markets and niches. This is particularly true in the United States. Reading marketing manuals and analyses,[2] one detects an immense optimism about the future success of ethnic marketing. These manuals provide population projections for the United States and describe the amazing potential of its ethnic markets. They project that soon more than half of the U.S. population will be of African-American, Latino, or Asian descent.[3] These experts insist that to just dub commercials in Spanish or Hindu will not do the job. Instead one needs to speak "culture," and speak it correctly, to enter the hearts, minds, and—most importantly—the wallets of different ethnic groups.

Looking through such manuals one is struck by the almost complete absence of Muslims. Pires and Stanton[4] include a very brief chapter on the growing economic impact and potential of second-generation upwardly mobile European Muslims (Yummie: for Young Upwardly Mobile Muslim), yet they give no advice about how to tap this market. Muslims fall between ethnic lines, as they come from many different countries. Nonetheless, by their sheer numbers (estimates speak of 8 million in the United States[5] and 12 million in Europe[6]) they would seem to be an attractive group for keen marketers, considering also the presence of sizable middle and upper-middle class contingents among expatriate Muslims in the United States.[7] This is not to speak of the vast Muslim populations in Africa and Asia. While there are obvious religious and cultural differences among Muslims, there are nonetheless overarching themes and needs that can be identified as vaguely Muslim (nothing is purely Latino or Jewish either). Ethnic marketing is a

---

[2] Elena Del Valle, ed., *Hispanic Marketing and Public Relations* (Boca Raton: Poyeen Publishing, 2005); Alfred Schreiber, *Multicultural Marketing. Selling to the New America* (Lincolnwood IL: NTC Business Books, 2001); Guilherme Dias Pires and John Stanton, *Ethnic Marketing* (Florence KY: Cengage Learning Business Press, 2005); Marilyn Halter, *Shopping for Identity. The Marketing of Ethnicity* (New York: Schocken Books, 2000).

[3] See, e.g., Francisco J. Valle and Judy M. Mandel, *How to Win the Hispanic Gold Rush* (New York: iUniverse, 2003).

[4] Pires and Stanton, *Ethnic Marketing*.

[5] Kari Huus, "Quest for the Muslim Market Niche," *MSNBC* (3 October 2003, http://msnbc.msn.com/id/3130288/print/1/displaymode/1098/, accessed 5 September 2005).

[6] Pires and Stanton, *Ethnic Marketing*, 263.

[7] Huus, "Quest for the Muslim Market Niche"; Asra Nomani, "Hijab Chic. How Retailers Are Marketing to Fashion-Conscious Muslim Women," *Washingtonpost/Newsweek Interactive Co./slate.com* (2005, http://www.slate.com/toolbar.aspx?action=print&id=2129906.Accessed2 9.4.20062005.http://www.slate.com/toolbar.aspx?action=print&id=2129906, accessed 29 April 2006).

tricky issue. As Arlene Davila discussed regarding the context of Latino culture and the marketing industry in the United States,[8] being a focus or target of this industry is for the most part less than desirable, as trends and ideas from within the community are marketed to the mainstream, while mainstream products in turn are pushed on minority communities by advertisement campaigns, which are designed to be culturally appropriate.

As U.S. consumer industries cash in on ethnic waves and holidays, mine ethnic communities for various products, ideas, and trends, and in return, use an odd mix of anthropology and marketing expertise to lure these same communities into buying mainstream goods and services, it is curious to see that Muslim communities have only tangentially been mined or addressed in this marketing circus. Does this reflect the diverse nature of the Muslim community, or the mainstream's ignorance of Muslims? For instance Hallmark—the expert and inventor of holidays, celebrations, and festivities—offers only three, decidedly lame, $^{c}\bar{I}d$ (Muslim feast) cards. Similarly, while kosher foods are standard products in food industries, halal markings have yet to appear on a larger scale. The U.S. Postal Services launched its first $^{c}\bar{I}d$ stamp two or three years ago, but it never penetrated the mainstream consciousness. When I asked for the stamp at my local rural post office, the clerk said, "Oh you mean the Christmas stamp?" because the stamp was issued in the late fall and included golden calligraphy. This relative lack of mainstream responsiveness has fostered the recent emergence of companies that offer "Muslim" products.

Dozens of companies market Islamic clothing via the internet. They cater to South Asian, Arab, or Western fashion preferences with a long list of products and a wide range of prices. Larger companies, like Shukr and Jelbab, conduct very active internet marketing. If you register with the site, you get monthly (or even weekly) updates and sales offers, with wording that, apart from a few Muslim phrases and greetings, differs only slightly from mainstream marketing. Both companies provide excellent products with fast and efficient service. An order placed with Jelbab arrived within days and was shipped straight from Amman to the United States.

New products also include a growing number of financial services. Looking through the pages of *Islamic Horizons*, a publication of the Islamic Society of North American, or other diasporic Muslim publications (e.g., *Islamica*), one encounters ads for Islamic investment funds—for instance the Dow Jones Islamic Fund,[9] the Amana Mutual Funds Trust Income,[10] and

---

[8] Arlene Davila, *Latinos Inc. The Marketing and Making of a People* (Berkeley: The University of California Press, 2001).
[9] *Islamic Horizons* July/August 2005:3.
[10] *Islamic Horizons* July/August 2005:4.

the Guidance Financial Groups, which offers "Home Financing the Sharia Way."[11] The Amana Funds are a product line of the British mainstream HSBC bank, which offers the funds as a "Sharia compliant alternative." Their services include the Amanah bank account for daily transactions, including all the "functionality you would expect from a leading current account: checkbook and Amanah debit card, standing order and direct-debit facilities, statements and cash withdrawals," and Amanah Home Finance, which "is based on the diminishing Musharakah mode of financing and helps you buy your residential property without compromising your beliefs."[12]

The last 10 years have witnessed an unprecedented growth in Islam-based commercial companies that market to a diverse global clientele, in particular diasporic groups in the United States and Europe. Investment funds, inspirational literature, educational books, toys and films for children, clothes, greeting cards for holidays, upscale glossy magazines, and cool urban gear for youth can be purchased in a few stores, but more importantly from myriad websites. These products are designed, redesigned, and marketed to match the specific needs, values, ideas, and pocketbooks of different Muslim consumers. Some products are Islamized for better sales in the Muslim world, while others are made in Europe or the United States by Muslim and other companies to serve diasporic Muslims. Some items are shipped from the Muslim world to be marketed to the diaspora.

Children's Consumer Culture

Since the 1980s, children's consumer cultures in the United States and other Western countries, and increasingly among post-colonial elites and middle classes, have grown dramatically.[13] As recently as the 1950s, the "kids' market was an industrial backwater."[14] Starting in the 1970s and gaining unprecedented momentum in the 1980s, larger family budgets, intense social competition expressed via material goods, and most importantly the

---

[11] *Islamic Horizons* March/April 2005:35.

[12] Ibid. See also Mariem Qamaruzzaman, "Lease of Faith," *Islamic Horizons* (March/April 2006): 48–49.

[13] Daniel Thomas Cook, *The Commodification of Childhood: Personhood, the Children's Wear Industry and the Rise of the Child-Consumer 1917–1962* (Durham NC: Duke University Press, 2004); Susan Linn, *Consuming Kids. The Hostile Takeover of Childhood* (New York: The New Press, 2004); Alissa Quart, *Branded. The Buying and Selling of Teenagers* (New York: Basis Books, 2004); Juliet Schor, *Born to Buy* (New York: Scribner, 2004); Shirley Steinberg and Joe Kincheloe, *Kinderculture: The Corporate Construction of Childhood* (Boulder: Westview Press, 2004).

[14] Schor, *Born to Buy*, 40.

direct access of companies via the media to children's rooms and hearts have triggered a veritable children's consumer revolution. Simultaneously in the United States, regulations on advertising to children were loosened or eliminated, which led to more aggressive targeting of ever-younger children (even in public schools).[15] Children who in the preceding decades had been (lamely) targeted by way of their mothers were now directly addressed and encouraged to circumvent their parents' wishes and guidelines. Schor aptly noted that "the new norm is that kids and marketers join forces to convince adults to spend money."[16] A powerful manufacturing and marketing crusade was unleashed, which invaded every aspect and stage of childhood with an incredible momentum, aiming to supply children with "appropriate" products. Today, marketing companies target the youngest to create brand recognition, brand loyalty, and to inculcate notions of "cool."

Figure 10.1: The multicultural doll family

Based on sophisticated psychological studies, marketing companies thrive on a combination of children's genuine curiosity and their desire to be "cool"

---
[15] Linn, *Consuming Kids. The Hostile Takeover of Childhood*; Schor, *Born to Buy*.
[16] Schor, *Born to Buy*, 16.

(however vaguely defined),[17] and the sense of guilt that busy parents have with respect to their children. Even the youngest are not spared these marketing efforts. Targeting infants (Baby Einstein) and toddlers (Teletubbies), industries have discovered that children are an endless source of profit.[18] Children's toys, entertainment, clothes, and food are marketed under the pretext of ensuring children's happiness, physical well-being, and intellectual development. Trying to build brand loyalties at a very young age, companies that sell children's products are particularly eager to introduce items that necessitate the purchase of endless related items. "Brand extension"[19] is the name of the game, and Barbie is one of its veterans.[20] It is not enough to own a Barbie: she needs clothes, a car, a house, furniture, a swimming pool, a sister, friends, and more. In addition, the Barbie owner needs to "Barbie-ize" her own existence with Barbie backpacks, clothes, dishes, and movies. Based on children's tireless ability to want and nag, the industry perpetually keeps ahead of its customers by offering more new products. Two marketing research companies published a 1998 study entitled "The Nag Factor," which identified nagging as a key element in purchases of children's products; children have considerable influence on family decisions about fast food, entertainment, and of course, toys.[21] One marketing newsletter celebrated these insights by announcing "The Old Nagging Game Can Pay Off for Marketers."[22] The industry celebrated the study and thus increased children's consumerist nagging.

Through successful global marketing (e.g., MTV, Nickelodeon, internet), brand recognition, brand loyalty, and brand extension have reached middle- and upper-class children all over the globe.[23] Barbie, Spiderman, and other toys have long since joined wealthier households in India, Egypt, Mexico, and Indonesia. Two Barbies are sold every single second somewhere in the world.[24] No child with a cable or internet connection can escape the child consumerism of which Barbie is just one representative. Using refined psychological tools and cutting-edge technologies, companies produce more and more new toys to capture children's attention and desires. The recent battle between Barbie and her Bratz-doll competitors illustrates how fiercely

---

[17] Schor, *Born to Buy*, 47.
[18] Linn, *Consuming Kids. The Hostile Takeover of Childhood*, 41.
[19] Schor, *Born to Buy*, 26.
[20] Quart, *Branded. The Buying and Selling of Teenagers*.
[21] Linn, *Consuming Kids. The Hostile Takeover of Childhood*, 33–34.
[22] Quoted in ibid., 34.
[23] The spread of a children's consumer culture has followed the broader patterns of neo-liberal economic politics and globalization at large.
[24] Schor, *Born to Buy*, 22.

companies fight for market shares.[25] For the current context, Barbie is fundamental to an understanding of Fulla and Razanne because she was *the* prerequisite for their appearance.

Barbie

Barbie is to the world of toys what McDonald's is to fast food and Coca-Cola is to soft drinks. They are icons of their kind and beyond that have become symbols of global capitalism.[26] Despite her subsequent success, Barbie's birth was less than perfect. Ruth and Elliott Handler, the owners of a toy company named "Mattel,"[27] took a vacation in the mid-1950s in Europe. On that trip they encountered the doll "Lilli," who was an adult (men's) toy, modeled after a cartoon figure in the German tabloid *Bild*. Appearing in cartoons that were daring for their time, Lilli was after men largely for financial gain; bourgeois decorum was not one of her qualities.[28] Ruth Handler was intrigued by the doll and the way it prompted her daughter Barbara (Barbie's namesake) and her friends to play out how they would be as adult women. Upon her return to the United States, Handler set out to design and produce a Lilli equivalent. Engineers told her that this was technically too complicated. Barbie's conception then spanned another continent, as Handler sent one of her top engineers, Jack Ryan, to Japan to inquire about production there. Ryan was successful. The first Barbies were produced partly industrially, partly manually (faces were hand painted) in Japan. Barbie was introduced to the public in 1959 at the American Toy Fair in New York City.[29]

Barbie was an instant success. New outfits were designed for her, and they sold with equal success. In addition to being conceptualized much differently from previous toys, Barbie was also a pioneer of new marketing techniques. Mattel hired the successful and controversial psychologist Ernest Dichter, who was involved in what was called motivational research. Dichter's revolutionary method of marketing research centered on

---

[25] Dorothy Pomeranz, "The Barbie Bust," *Forbes* (3 March 2005, http://www.forbes.com/business/forbes/2005/0328/064a.html, accessed 5 September 2005).
[26] Yona Zeldis McDonough, *The Barbie Chronicles. A Living Doll Turns Forty* (New York: Touchstone Books, 1999).
[27] M.G. Lord, *Forever Barbie. The Unauthorized Biography of a Real Doll* (New York: Avon Books, 1995), 20.
[28] Ibid., 25.
[29] Ibid., 24.

the (Freudian) unconscious as an eager receptor and activator of desires.[30] David Bennett summarizes Dichter's marketing breakthrough:

> Dichter's own insight into commodity fetishism came in the form of his groundbreaking "concept of the 'personality' or 'image' of a product"—a notion now banally familiar but one that was as novel to American business in the 1930s as the whole philosophy of branding that would soon be built on it.[31]

Barbie was an early example of a product with a distinct character. She did not encourage girls to free play; instead Barbie came with a story, character, tastes, and preferences. Barbie wanted to be Barbie, and that meant to accumulate more Barbie products. Barbie was the object of TV advertising campaigns that were increasingly aimed at young consumers instead of their mothers. Barbie modeled a new lifestyle, which was an alternative to household labor and child-rearing. In addition to being sexy and consumption-oriented, Barbie personified a new female type: she had a job as a stewardess or nurse, and she was on the move and self-sufficient.

Barbie was more than a toy. She was at the forefront of the construction of a dramatically new consumerism. Her unique design and marketing created her as "an object of female childhood desire that was a prototype of the compulsive spender and guiltless consumer driven by desublimated sexual desire."[32] Indeed, Barbie was paramount to ushering in an era where "the girl-as-fancy-free consumer" became a central economic and cultural player.[33] Barbie soon owned more clothes, shoes, and accessories than she could possibly wear, and never felt guilty about it. On the contrary, there were always reasons for buying more. Barbie lacked only one thing: a companion. Mattel was hesitant. "Consumer demand, however, overcame Mattel's reluctance to make a male doll, and in 1961 it brought out Ken."[34] In his more than 40 years of existence, Ken (named after Handler's son) has never amounted to more than a dull sidekick of the flamboyant Barbie, who

---

[30] Lord, *Forever Barbie. The Unauthorized Biography of a Real Doll*, 36; David Bennett, "Getting the Id to Go Shopping: Psychoanalysis, Advertising, Barbie Dolls, and the Invention of the Consumer Unconscious," *Public Culture* 17, no. 1 (2005): 4.

[31] Bennett, "Getting the Id to Go Shopping: Psychoanalysis, Advertising, Barbie Dolls, and the Invention of the Consumer Unconscious," 10.

[32] Ibid., 15.

[33] Ibid., 14.

[34] Lord, *Forever Barbie. The Unauthorized Biography of a Real Doll*, 48.

has remained "forever independent, subservient to no one."[35] With Barbie's success, Mattel expanded and acquired doll companies overseas.[36]

While social unrest marked the United States in late 1960s, Barbie happily pursued her careers and indulged her excessive consumption habits, seemingly oblivious to the world around her. In 1969 Barbie was somewhat regrounded in a vague social reality. She received two African-American friends: Christie and Julia.[37] Mattel had realized that there was a need (and source of profit) for African-American friends for Barbie. Soon Christie and Julia got a male companion, Jamal, who in an interesting twist, carried an African-American Muslim name.[38] Jamal's fate was the same as Ken's: he remained insignificant.

The 1970s were probably Barbie's most troubled decade. In 1971 the National Organization of Women (NOW) launched a formal assault on Barbie "when its New York chapter issued a press release condemning ten companies for sexist advertising."[39] Mattel was one of them. The 1970s were marked by tension between the new feminist movement and Barbie. Barbie, the career women of the 1960s, was at a loss for a response or new identity, and lingered on throughout the decade. In addition Mattel and the Handlers were caught up in a financial scandal. Ultimately, Mattel and Barbie survived and received a boost in 1980 when President Reagan took office. Popular and political sentiments changed, as M.G. Lord so aptly phrased it: "Debt was good; greed was good; Barbie was good."[40] Reagan created a climate in which career/consumer Barbie could climb to unprecedented heights of popularity and profitability. Indeed, Barbie *was* the new woman of the 1980s and, even more so, the 1990s.

As noted above, the Reagan years witnessed a rapid deregulation of the children's consumer and marketing field, which allowed Mattel to directly reach ever larger numbers of girls. Barbie experienced an amazing revival based on this shift in zeitgeist and the hard work of new female managers who took charge of Barbie's fate, most prominently Jill Barad.[41] Barad and some of her female colleagues personified essential Barbie characteristics as they were independent, successful, beautiful, and invested in consumer culture. They had a feel for the "inner being" of Barbie and refined Barbie's appearance, activities, and marketing strategies. Barbie was refashioned in a

---
[35] Ibid., 51.
[36] Ibid., 59.
[37] Ibid., 62.
[38] Ibid., 81.
[39] Ibid., 89.
[40] Ibid., 105.
[41] Ibid., 108.

1984 campaign that dwelt on her contribution to female empowerment with the slogan "We Girls Can Do Everything."[42] Barbie was "positioned *as* a career woman *by* career women who knew what it took to achieve in the business world."[43]

And, once again Barbie was situated in a multi-ethnic context. In the 1980s the U.S. market was ready for not just black companions for Barbie but the first Black Barbie. Styled by Kitty Black Perkins, an African-American designer, Black Barbie was launched in 1980. Hispanic Barbie followed but was seriously flawed because she did not represent the reality of Hispanic women in the United States. Wearing a peasant blouse, two-tiered skirt, and mantilla, she looked "like a refugee from an amateur production of *Carmen*; she even had a rose pinned to her neck."[44] Nonetheless, Black and Hispanic Barbies represented a new understanding of the toy market, and a recognition of new market niches. As indicated in the catalogue text for Hispanic Barbie: "Little Hispanic girls can now play with their very own Barbie."[45]

Besides issuing African-American and Latino dolls, Mattel now recognized the potential of diversity and "ethnic" companies as entry points into market niches. After the Watts riots, Mattel "helped set up Shindana Toys—[...] a black run—South Central Los Angele-sbased company that manufactured multicultural playthings before they were trendy" in 1968.[46] Among other products, Shindana produced Malaika and Career Girl Wanda, two Barbie-type dolls.[47] Shindana folded in the early 1980s.[48] Nonetheless Shindana was instrumental in the emergence of an ethnic market that was eagerly taken up by new companies.

Barbie in the Middle East and Muslim World

The new children's consumer culture is spreading rapidly around the globe by way of satellite TV, internet, and elite global travel. Barbie, Spiderman

---

[42] Lord, *Forever Barbie. The Unauthorized Biography of a Real Doll*, 115.
[43] Emphasis in the original; ibid., 117.
[44] Ibid., 108.
[45] ibid., 108. Already in the 1960s Mattel had issued Japanese Barbies in Japan. When the first series was not very successful for various cultural reasons, Mattel was quick to respond and refashioned the doll accordingly; Marco Tosa, *Barbie. Four Decades of Fashion, Fantasy and Fun* (New York: Harry N. Abrams, Inc., Publishers, 1998), 143. On other international/ethnic Barbies, see ibid., 135, and Janine Fennick, *The Collectible Barbie Doll* (Philadelphia: Courage Books, 1999), 105.
[46] Lord, *Forever Barbie. The Unauthorized Biography of a Real Doll*, 160.
[47] Ibid., 162.
[48] Ibid., 170.

and Co. are beaming into wealthier households and children's rooms, especially in globalizing post-colonial metropolises. The expansion of consumer culture designed and implemented as part of neo-liberal economic policies is facilitated by the rapid spread of malls, megastores, and other sites of conspicuous consumption. For the past 10 to 15 years, glitzy shopping malls have been mushrooming in the Middle East.[49] Dubai has taken the lead in building ever-larger, more glamorous malls, with an endless variety of additional features and entertainments. Regional trendsetters are copied in Cairo or Amman. In the process urban spaces and cultures are dramatically remade.[50] The number of retail outlets constantly increases, and along with it the sales of multinational companies.

Yet even before the explosive growth of upscale consumerism in the 1990s, Barbie had resided in select Middle Eastern households for decades. She was not, however, a mass phenomena: her pricetag kept her out of most households. With the growth of upper/middle-class incomes, the number of families who can afford Barbie, and other expensive toys, has increased. The Middle East and the Muslim world, which consist of very young populations and continue to have higher birthrates than Europe, Japan, and the United States, are a toy sellers' paradise. One observer noted that the Middle East has more toy outlets relative to its population than any other region in the world. This vibrant toy market is said to be worth about $1 billion per year.[51] By the end of the 20th century, the vast majority of these toys were imported from East Asia, Europe, and the United States.[52] Global companies recognize the enormous potential of this market and vie for shares in this niche.

One runner in this race is, of course, Barbie. The doll was and is actively marketed and promoted in the Middle East (e.g., Dubai Toy Fairs in

---

[49] Mona Abaza, "Shopping Malls, Consumer Culture and the Reshaping of Pubic Space in Egypt," *Theory, Culture and Society* 18, no. 5 (2001): 97–122.

[50] Abaza, "Shopping Malls, Consumer Culture and the Reshaping of Pubic Space in Egypt"; Mona Abaza, "Brave New Mall," *Al-Ahram Weekly* (16–22 September 2004); Petra Kuppinger, "Exclusive Greenery: New Gated Communities in Cairo," *City and Society* 16, no. 2 (2004): 35–61; Petra Kuppinger, "Pyramids and Alleys: Global Dynamics and Local Strategies in Giza," in *Cairo Cosmopolitan: Urban Structure, Spaces and Identities in the New Middle East*, ed. Diane Singerman and Paul Amar (Cairo: American University in Cairo Press, 2006), 313–344; Timothy Mitchell, "Dreamland. The Neoliberalism of Your Desires," *Middle East Report*, no. 210 (1999): 28–33.

[51] Paul Martin, "Religious Police Take After Barbie," *The Washington Times* (2 January 2004, http://washintongtime.com/world/20040102\bibrangedash112738\bibrangedash9433r.htm, accessed 5 September 2005).

[52] Mona Eltahawy, "Barbie Faces Rival for Arab Affections," *The Guardian* (8 June 1999, http://www.guardian.couk/interantional/story/o,,292295,00.html, accessed 26 August 2005).

2003 and 2005[53]). For example, in April of 2005, the Lamcy Plaza Mall in Dubai hosted a "three-day Barbie wonderland for girls in the age groups of 4 to 11 years."[54] An announcement stated that the event will include a "special fashion show" where little girls "will walk down the ramp created at the atrium of Lamcy Plaza." Simultaneously, "Barbie will be seated on her beautifully created throne and will crown three lucky winners [...] as 'Barbie Princess.' The winners will receive fabulous prizes from Mattel and all 100 participants will get goody bags from Barbie for their efforts." Barbie Wonderland is designed to "bring cheer to the entire family whilst fulfilling the wishes of those little girls who have always dreamt of being Barbie."[55] Cairo's gigantic Stars Mall boosts an entire Barbie and Disney store. Divided by an invisible border, the left half of the store is all pink (Barbie), while the right half is blue (Disney).

Barbie's existence in the Middle East is not all pink and easy. On the contrary, she is viewed with suspicion by many. Saudi-Arabian authorities have taken offense at Barbie for years. Barbie repeatedly came under attack as authorities were pondering the question of whether human-shape toys were appropriate according to Islam. Several bans have been issued against her, the first one in 1994.[56] In fall 2003, after Barbie had already been an outlaw for several years, Saudi-Arabia banned imports of all female dolls, and shopkeepers had to purge their stocks within three months.[57] More than other dolls, Barbie had been deemed "offensive to the conservative Saudi interpretation of Islam." Authorities had taken offense with her "revealing clothes and shameful postures."[58] In January 2004, one observer reported that "stick-wielding Saudi religious police" raided toy and gift stores in the Kingdom, seizing among other things the remaining Barbies. Nonetheless,

---

[53] See Tdc.trade.com, *New Cars and Hand-Made Stars at Middle Eastern Toy Jamboreee*, Report from Toy Fair 2003, Dubai, 29 May 2003, http://tdctrade.com/imn/03052905/tradefairs006.htm, accessed 5 September 2005; *Show News*, Toy Fair 2005, http:\\www.toyfairdubai.com, accessed 5 September 2005.
[54] "Lamcy Plaza to Host Barbie Wonderland," *Strategiy.com* (19 April 2005, http://www.strategiy.com/inews.asp?id=20050419155902, accessed 17 August 2005).
[55] Ibid.
[56] Lord, *Forever Barbie. The Unauthorized Biography of a Real Doll*, IIX.
[57] "Saudi Ban in Female Doll Imports," *Guardian Newspapers* (18 December 2003, http://buzzle.com/editorials/text12\bibrangedash18\bibrangedash2003\bibrangedash48740.asp, accessed 5 September 2005); "Barbie—or Jezebel?" *St. Petersburg Times* (11 September 2003, http://www.sptimes.com/2003/09/11/Worldandnation/Barbieor_Jezebel.shtml, accessed 7 September 2005); "Saudi Police Say Barbie Doll a Threat to Morality," *CNN* (10 September 2003, http://cnn.com/2003/WORLD/meast/09/10/saudibarbie.ap/index.html, accessed 10 September 2003).
[58] "Saudi Police Say Barbie Doll a Threat to Morality."

Barbie is still available on the Saudi black market.[59] The Kuwaiti religious scholar Khalid al-Mathkoor also advocated banning Barbie, yet it was never instituted in Kuwait.[60] Unease over Barbie's cultural appropriateness is not limited to religious scholars. Popular sentiments reflect similar opinions. In addition, many parents resent Barbie's pricetag.[61] Barbie simply never fit smoothly into many Middle Eastern households. Dr. Abla Ibrahim, an official of the Arab League, summarized these vague sentiments: "Barbie wears a bikini and drinks champagne," yet those things are not part of the everyday lives of most girls in the region.[62] From this cultural unease emerged the idea to create a more appropriately Arab doll that would not throw girls in the midst of global cultural tensions. This doll should not have a boyfriend, drink alcohol, or wear revealing clothes. Ibrahim asked: "What is wrong with having an Arab doll?"[63]

Studies conducted by the Arab League resulted in the birth of Laila. Conceived in the final years of the 20th century, she was to be a "representative Arab girl."[64] Her name was chosen to accommodate both Muslim and Christian girls. In contrast to the super-sexed adult Barbie, Laila was envisioned to be a pre-pubescent girl, "somewhere between 10 and 12 years in age, with big black eyes, long lashes, pink cheeks, full lips and wavy black hair." Laila's closet would contain modest Western-style clothing and "folkloristic dress from Egypt, Syria, Palestinian areas, North African and the Persian Gulf region."[65] In hindsight it is interesting to note that the idea of Laila was a (late) expression of Arab nationalism, shortly before the ill-defined polarization between the West and Islam became a dominant political factor. Laila is an almost nostalgic (pan-Arab) idea of the last millennium that no longer captures the needs and controversies of the 21st century. She was never mass-manufactured.

---

[59] Martin, "Religious Police Take After Barbie."
[60] Donna Abu-Nasr, "Kuwait Debates U.S.-Islamic Life," *Dailynews.yahoo.com* (29 Nov 2001, http://dailynews.yahoo.com/h/ap/20011129/wl/islamic_dilemmas_1.html, accessed 7 September 2005); Eltahawy, "Barbie Faces Rival for Arab Affections"; Gillian Rice and Mohammed Al-Mossawi, "The Implications of Islam for Advertising Messages: The Middle Eastern Context," *Journal of Euromarketing* 11, no. 3 (2002): http://www.haworthpressinc.com/store/product.asp?sku=J037.
[61] Douglas Jehl, "It's Barbie vs. Laila and Sara in Mideast Culture War," *New York Times* (2 June 1999): A4.
[62] Ibid.
[63] Eltahawy, "Barbie Faces Rival for Arab Affections."
[64] Jehl, "It's Barbie vs. Laila and Sara in Mideast Culture War."
[65] Ibid.

In the late 1990s, Iranian authorities were similarly uneasy with Barbie. Majid Qaderi, head of the Creative Toys Division at the Institute for the Intellectual Development of Children and Young Adults in the Islamic Republic noted that "Barbie is a symbol of American culture, it invites early maturity in girls, and it is not only harmful to Asian children but to American children as well."[66] Qaderi pointed to the "Barbie syndrome, one that is infecting everyone around the world," as a "dangerous threat" to a society. Qaderi's institute created two dolls, Sara and Dara, to counter Barbie's influence. Based on a series of popular stories, these siblings are now successfully marketed in Iran, competing with Barbie and her cheaper copies.[67]

The Stage Is Ready

These voices and concerns illustrate that the scope of views on Barbie is vast. Some oppose all dolls as being un-Islamic because they are humanlike depictions. Others oppose Barbie as an icon of U.S. culture, and there are the vast numbers who cannot afford Barbie or simply do not care. Finally there are those who attend the Barbie Fair in Dubai or frequent the Barbie store at the Stars Center in Cairo. Some parents in the region have become wary of Barbie's presence in their children's rooms and worlds.

In a highly competitive global market, companies closely monitor markets. Thus the unease of some Arab parents did not escape notice by keen observers of consumer habits. The logical response was to create a product that responded to this niche: the Muslim non-Barbie that is a Barbie lookalike. Simultaneously, debates in marketing circles clearly pointed in the direction of culturally sensitive product design and marketing. Rice and Al-Mossawi noted that culturally appropriate marketing has been successful in some Muslim contexts. They quote a 1994 study that "concluded that enhanced knowledge of religious difference in consumer decision-making should have significant impact on the effectiveness of global marketing strategies."[68] Rice and Al-Mossawi suggest that "religious terminology may be used in advertisements to reassure consumers of the Islamic integrity of products and services."[69] The product and the niche with eager consumers existed, the market was staked out and expanding, someone just had to design the product. A company in the Muslim diaspora acted first.

---

[66] Ali Mafi, "Sara and Dara Are Here!" *TehranAvenue.com* (April 2002, http://tehranavenue.com/print.php?IN=en&id=212, accessed 7 September 2005).
[67] Ibid.
[68] Rice and Al-Mossawi, "The Implications of Islam for Advertising Messages: The Middle Eastern Context," 2.
[69] Ibid., 7.

Razanne

In 1996, Ammar Saadeh and his wife Noor started Noorart, a Michigan-based company that sells Muslim toys.[70] Dedicated to a sound Muslim education, Noorart started with children's songs (Noor Saadeh was an opera singer before her conversion to Islam). Soon the company added educational toys. Noorart also distributes Islamic and Arabic curricula to Islamic schools in North America. In 1999 the prototype for Razanne was released. While Razanne is a response to the Barbie craze, Razanne is very different from Barbie. The doll has the body of a pre-pubescent girl. She wears long-sleeve dresses and a headscarf. Razanne does not wear lipstick, and she comes in three skin colors ("Pakistani India Olive heritage, African-American Black heritage, White Caucasian heritage"[71]). Although the doll has the typical bended foot for high heels, she comes with flat loafers and white long socks/stockings.[72] Here is what Noor Saadeh says about the birth of Razanne:

> For Noorart, the concept of Razanne is based on an ideal and mission. The ideal is that any item that speaks for or represents women should focus on the entire person and not just her physical features. Our mission in developing Razanne, was to offer Muslim girls a toy, often used for role modeling, that promoted Islamic self-esteem and self-worth that the Muslim female garb provides.
>   We saw our Muslim "daughters" receiving Barbie Dolls as gifts for the Islamic holidays. This struck a chord in us that we were offering toys that led them in a completely different direction than their upbringing would. The concentration on the latest fashion and make-up styles hardly set the stage for how these girls would be encouraged to dress as they matured. Certainly Barbie did not look like "mom" with her long covering clothes and scarves!
>   My husband and I decided to design a prototype doll to test the market. We first offered Razanne in a simple dishdasha (long dress) and white scarf. The dresses were of royal blue, emerald green and the ever popular pink! We also offered 3 ethnicities: Caucasian, Asian and African. How many years would it be before Barbie offered more than the initial blond, blue-eyed

---

[70] I am very grateful to Noor Saadeh who took the time to answer my questions about Razanne in an e-mail interview/questionnaire. Considerable parts of the following paragraphs are based on her detailed response to my questions.

[71] Noorart.com, *Who We Are!* 2003, http://noorart.com/whoweare.shtml, accessed 9 September 2005.

[72] This causes some problems because her shoes keep falling off her feet.

doll?! We focused globally immediately! This expression [sic] of Islam's global appeal.[73]

Razanne is a student or teacher. Her hijab testifies to her participation in public life. There is a Praying Razanne who wears a modest prayer dress and scarf, and "In and Out Razanne" who is "dressed in smart but covering long dress with additional brightly colored, short sleeved and short skirted dress for home wear."[74] There is a Community Service Razanne who volunteers at a hospital, Muslim Scout Razanne, and Islamic Ritual Razanne (performing the Hajj/pilgrimage). Noorart also introduced coloring books with a Razanne "storyline that featured Razanne throughout a typical day, using all her fashions."[75] The dolls sell between $9 and $25. The company also offers a Razanne Scout Cheers CD, Razanne $^c\bar{I}d$ Card (holiday greeting card). Next to be released will be Dr. Razanne. Saadeh notes about Razanne:

> Many Muslims talked about designing a doll like this and many parents promised their daughters to make head scarves for their Barbie Dolls but I believe we were the first to truly set the stage for an Islamic alternative to Barbie. Iran had a boy and girl doll but these did not mimic the fashion maven, Barbie. We never spoke negatively of Barbie. We only wanted to provide an alternative for our girls, closer to the image of mom and other Muslim women.[76]

Designed and distributed in the United States, Razanne is aimed at the Muslim community in North America, and to a lesser extent Europe and elsewhere. Noorart's website includes notes from Christian customers who applaud the modesty of the doll.[77]

Razanne: Marketing

Razanne was launched in the United States in the late 1990s. She is promoted as an educational toy that "builds Muslim identity and self-esteem; provides Islamic role model; promotes Islamic behavior; shapes interactive play" (Razanne: The Muslim Doll 2005). The text on the box of the 2005 Play Day Razanne notes that she "builds character. It's what's inside that

---

[73] Noor Saadeh, *Private Communication*, E-mail: 3 October 2005.
[74] Noorart.com, *Who We Are!*
[75] Ibid.
[76] Saadeh, *Private Communication*.
[77] Noorart.com, *Who We Are!*

Figure 10.2: Razanne

counts!" And, that "unlike other toys that promote only fashion and beauty, *Razanne* Dolls help girls focus on building character and inner worth. Every girl needs a role model. Make hers *Razanne!*" Razanne advances an image of a confident modern Muslim girl characterized by modesty, piety, and dedication to education. By 2005, Razanne had firmly established herself in the U.S. market, where she is sold either in Muslim/Middle Eastern/South Asian book and food stores, or most importantly via the internet (e.g., SoundVision.com, OnlineIslamicStore.com, halalplaza.com). Observers have noted that Noorart sells about 30,000 dolls annually (Costanzo 2004). Globally, Razanne is marketed in Canada (SoundvisonCanada.com), Australia (iqra4kids.com.au), Singapore, and Malaysia (ilhamfcpages.com). About their product philosophy Noor Saadeh remarks:

> Because Noorart has additional focuses, Razanne unfortunately does not receive the time she deserves. Marketing has largely been done simply by the fact that Razanne attracts attention. 9/11 was very good for Razanne, as were sensational comments made about Barbie by the governments of Saudi Arabia and Iran.[78]

---
[78] Saadeh, *Private Communication.*

Indeed, I have never seen a Razanne ad. Saadeh describes the forces and dynamics that I analyzed above as contributing to their success. She adds that

> Razanne has received quite a lot of recognition and applause from non-Muslims as well, who wrote us long and grateful letters, supporting our mission and adding that they wished they had something more tangible and dignifying to offer their daughters.[79]

Razanne positions herself as a Muslim first, and part of an ethnic group second. Razanne's white/Arab and African-American personae wear modest dress, based on Western fashions. Razanne's South Asian sister wears a colorful *shalwar qamīz*, complete with a scarf. Saadeh sees Razanne's special role as making precisely this kind of pan-Islamic, and to a minor extent, anti-glitzy fashion statement.

> Razanne represents all Muslim women, not just one region. We'd like to think she stands for all women at all times and offers little girls more to grow on than just fashion and fluff. I doubt that we will ever reach the popularity of Barbie and not even Fulla, whose appeal seems designed to reach the masses by offering an Arabic version of Barbie.[80]

Although Razanne is a commercial product, she comes with a mission: she speaks for Islam, wants to educate, and challenges current Western beauty and fashion standards. While aiming at commercial success, Razanne and similar products are also part of a larger quest to formulate new (Western-based) Muslim communities, cultures, and identities.

Fulla

Having followed the details of Barbie's story, it is not surprising that a culturally appropriate sister of Barbie would emerge and capture diverse Arab/Muslim markets, in particular at this historical moment when neoliberal global economies boost the ranks of the upper middle classes. In 2003, Fulla appeared in the Middle East accompanied by a massive marketing blitz. Like Barbie, but unlike Razanne, Fulla has the body of an adult woman. She has dark brown eyes and long black hair, sometimes with red highlights. She wears bright red lipstick and high heels.

---

[79] Saadeh, *Private Communication*.
[80] Ibid.

Despite Fulla's grand stage entry, her origins and birth remain shrouded in mystery.[81] Most news reports about Fulla in the U.S. press can be traced back to two reports written by Susan Taylor Martin, a correspondent at the *St. Petersburg Times* in Florida whose short articles[82] were reprinted in several papers and appeared on numerous websites. In January 2004, Martin first spotted Fulla at Toyland in Kuwait's huge Marina Mall. Martin noted that Fulla cost about $19, and her outfits sold for $6. Produced by a company named New Boy, Martin was puzzled about the doll's background and origins; New Boy, she noted, did not even have a website.[83] In May 2005, Martin solved the puzzle of Fulla's origins. She had been conceived in Syria, and in just 18 months became the "hottest selling doll in the Middle East."[84] The Fulla craze gained momentum and New Boy now offered a "Singing Fulla and a Walking Fulla, pushing a luggage cart with suitcases to hold the dozens of seasonal outfits that crowd her closet. Fulla has two new friends, Yasmeen and Nada, and will soon be joined by a little brother and sister."[85] There also is Prayer Fulla, all in white and complete with a *subḥa* (prayer beads). The product note in the box of Singing Fulla presents other Fullas in elegant evening gowns (with transparent sleeves). There are also three Fullas with different color pastel *jilbāb*s (overcoats) and white hijabs.

Fulla: Marketing

Launched in 2003 with a marketing blitz, as Noor Saadeh observed "with top of the line marketing, packaging and presentation,"[86] Fulla became an instant success. Brand extension and immediate proliferation of accessories and additional products followed. At the Dubai Toy Fair in May 2005, the Show News announced that New Boy will offer "exciting extensions to the enormously successful 'Fulla'." The newsletter further noted that the "vast

---

[81] I contacted Fawaz Abidin, the Fulla Brand Manager at New Boy. He agreed to answer my questions. In the end, however, he never sent me his answers. See Fawaz Abidin, *Private Communication*, E-mail: 11 September 2005; 3 October 2005; 7 October 2005.

[82] Susan Taylor Martin, "Coverup Girl," *St. Petersburg Times* (12 January 2004, http://www.sptime.com/2004/01/12/Floridian/Coverup_girl.shtml, accessed 26 August 2005); Susan Taylor Martin, "Call It the Fulla Phenomenon," *Chicago Tribune* (25 May 2005); Susan Taylor Martin, "The Doll That Has Everything—Almost," *St. Petersburg Times* (15 May 2005, http://www.sptimes.com/2005/05/15/Floridian/The_doll_that_has_eve.shtml, accessed 26 August 2005).

[83] NewBoy does have a website which indicates that it has existed since 2003 or 2004. See http://www.new-boy.com/.

[84] Martin, "The Doll That Has Everything—Almost."

[85] Ibid.

[86] Saadeh, *Private Communication*.

Figure 10.3: Singing Fulla and Outdoor Fulla

majority of their products [New Boy] will be supported by heavyweight TV advertising and with distribution centres throughout the Middle East."[87] Tarek Mohammed, chief salesperson at Cairo's Toys R Us, commented on Fulla's success: "Fulla sells better because she is closer to our Arab values—she never reveals a leg or an arm."[88]

Fulla's triumph is illustrated in an article about parents' financial pains in the back-to-school season in Qatar. Mohammed Salem notes that putting children back to school comes with considerable expenses for bags, stationary and other items, as parents are increasingly forced by their consumption-savvy offspring to purchase "chic school bags."[89] Salem adds that children take their consumer wisdom from popular TV stations that air foreign and Arab shows. He observes that "young boys would not like to be seen with-

---

[87] *Show News*.
[88] "Barbie Loses Out to Veiled Rival," *BBC News* (12 Jan 2006, http://www.bbc.co.uk/go/pr/ fr/\bibrangedash/2/hi/middle_east/4605334.stm, accessed 13 January 2006).
[89] Mohammed Ahmed Salem, "Stores Cashing in on Back-to-School Fever," *The Peninsula* (29 August 2005, http://thepeninsulaqata.com/Display_news.asp?section=Local_news& subsection=, accessed 7 September 2005).

out an Incredibles or Fantastic-4 bag, girls demand those of Fulla [...] or Power Puff Girls among others."[90]

Fulla's design, marketing, and brand extension almost duplicate that of her shunned competitor, Barbie. Even the logo, gently curved letters, moving slightly upward, and the five-leaved flower that follows the name resemble the Barbie logo. "Fulla Pink," so similar to Barbie pink is, like Barbie pink, trademarked. Fulla duplicates Barbie in many design and marketing aspects, except Fulla covers her elbows and knees and does not have a male companion.

Fulla's and Razanne's marketing differ. While Fulla is a well-calculated product that responds to a specific demand and is designed to create demand for more products, Razanne remains on the margins of glitzy marketing. Noor Saadeh explains:

> Unlike Fulla, which hit the market with top of line marketing, packaging and presentation, Razanne continues to be a work in progress. Future ideals hope to see Razanne with a more realistic figure (we have already reduced the bust line on our model), more competitive packaging, yet still remaining true to our original concept of promoting character and modesty. Razanne is a concept and has never been about commercialization. Marketing for us is a way to get Razanne into the hands of our girls, to act as an Ambassador of Islam and to make a statement about the real value of women in society.[91]

Fulla, with her multiplying clothes (the product note of Singing Fulla depicts more than a dozen different outfits), teaches girls Fulla's consumption habits. In contrast to Razanne with her limited wardrobe and low-key marketing, Fulla thrives in the glitzy environment of upscale malls and global media.

Fulla Observed

Cairo, Ramadan 2005: I am on the trail of Fulla. My first stop is a toy store in the upscale neighborhood of Zamalek. I am greeted by Fulla backpacks and Fulla disposable cameras in the shop window. In the doll department, there is Barbie (LE 120)[92] next to her streetwise recent competitors, the Bratz dolls (LE 392!). Third in line is Fulla (LE 59 to 119). There are abaya Fullas and numerous "indoor fashion" dolls with tight and glittery outfits

---
[90] Ibid.
[91] Saadeh, *Private Communication*.
[92] LE 1 equals 17 cents; LE 6 roughly equals $1.

that reflect Western fashion trends, except that the dolls' knees and elbows are covered. Propped up against a shelf stands an enormous box of the "Star Party," a Fulla product that promises party fun with a microphone and tape recorder (LE 399).

A few days later I visit a popular favorite, the Arkadia Mall. On a quiet Ramadan afternoon, I enter Toys R Us. Fulla has a considerable presence here: Fulla goggles, fins, float belts, air mattresses, backpacks, pencils, erasers, "Jewelry Mirror" (with jewel box), the Star Party (only LE 199 here), jump ropes, Frisbees, net ball, catch ball, ping pong, badminton, slippers, cyber hopper, and aqua socks are on display. Fulla herself takes up a long shelf at the center of the store. Classic abaya Fulla stands next to a two-pack of abaya and indoor fashion Fulla, and other indoor Fullas. The latter outnumber the abaya Fullas by about 8:1. There is Fulla in her evening dress and Prayer Fulla.

A few days later I venture to the CityStars Mall in Medinet Nasr. Located in the enormous CityStars complex that includes hotels, offices, and residences, this mall is a gigantic multi-story facility. In the midst of splendid architecture (pink "pharaonic" columns that stand six floors tall, beautifully crafted lit ceilings, slanted glass roofs on the peripheral areas, a giant waterfall at ground level, and large live palm trees) are hundreds of local, regional, and global stores; several enormous food courts with impressive assortments of local and global foods; and an indoor entertainment center with children's rides. The mall has several thematic subsections. I head to the children's section.

At the toy retailer Kams, one is greeted by a life-size cardboard abaya Fulla who stands in front of a display of outdoor toys for Fulla. There are ball games, a Fulla hula hoop, and a beauty party set with mirror and beads (LE 249.90). Opposite Fulla is a shelf with war action figures from "The Valiant," also distributed by New Boy. The Fulla shelf has a selection of dolls similar to Toys R Us. There are tens of other dolls, numerous Barbies and Barbie imitations, with names such as Steffi, Sindy, Susie, Bessie, and Lelia, who range in price from LE 19.90 to 95. An oversize Bratz doll (two feet tall) awaits an owner for LE 1149.90.

The Next Generation: Fulah and Fulona

Within a few years of their birth, Fulla and Razanne's fates took another predictable turn. A Chinese manufacturer, by way of Utmaster Import & Export Co., Ltd., in Zhejiang, is offering a "Fulah" copy. Utmaster advertises Fulah: "The muslim [sic] doll is no more than a doll for muslim world girls [sic]. Our doll is the copy of razanne [sic]."[93] Producers of the new doll aim their product at both the Fulla and Razanne markets: they call their doll Fulah but state that she is a copy of Razanne. Yifeng Imp.& Exp. Trading Co., Ltd., operating out of Shantou City in China, offers under the category "Doll (4 Arabian Dresses)" four similar (nameless) dolls with different veiled outfits.[94] Susan Martin reports about another "inevitable knock-off" called Fulona in Syria.[95] New Boy quickly reacted and published a warning in a Jordanian newspaper stating that "it is forbidden to use the New Boy trademark on any counterfeit products" (IP Pro 2005). While the real Fulla sells at JD 7 in Jordan, fakes start at JD 3.[96] Yacoub Al Kilani, the branch manager of New Boy in Jordan complained that "around 90 if not 100 percent of 'New Boy' products have been copied and distributed in the Jordanian market." Subsequently, New Boy announced a more affordable version called Fulla Style.[97] The fake-Fulla craze also plagues the Gulf. Sohail Rana at Toys R Us in Qatar notes that there are various Fulla imitations on the market.[98]

Fulah Observed

Cairo, another night in Ramadan 2005: If I am going to find Fulah in Cairo, I assumed it would be in a market like the Ataba/Sharia El Muski area. At 8 p.m. I am walking in the midst of a dense after-*ifṭār* (fast-breaking) crowd of shoppers, westward on Sharia El Muski toward Midan Ataba. About two weeks before the end of Ramadan, with the upcoming feast and gift-giving, El Muski is at its busiest. Clothes, shoes, household items, a few bulk food items, and toys are the main merchandise of the western part of the street (the east end caters to tourists). The further west I walk, the more squeezed

---

[93] Ltd Utmaster Import & Export Co., 2005, http://alibaba.com/catalog/111008636Muslim_ Dolls.html, accessed 26 August 2005. On a different page Utmaster Imp. & Exp. Co., Ltd identifies itself as "I am a specialized muslim [sic] products dealer." They list items such as "electronic tasbee / quran reciter / glass ornaments with the Holy Qur'an words / ... mosque statues" and others as part of their program; see Ltd. Utmaster Import & Export Co., *Offer Muslim Toys and Muslim Ornaments*, 25 August 2005, www.alibaba.com/manufacturer/12425 002/Offer_Muslim_Toys_Muslim_Orna..com, accessed 9 September 2005. They also market a "Makkah Bag," prayer rugs, and hijabs.
[94] *Yifeng Imp. & Exp. Trading Co., Ltd.*, 2005, http://yifengtrading.en.alibaba.com/product/0/ 50268590/Doll__4_Arabia_dresses/sho..., accessed 26 August 2005.
[95] Martin, "The Doll That Has Everything—Almost."
[96] 1 JD equals $1.41 (January 2006). Cf. ibid.
[97] The article adds that the New Boy trademark (despite its Syrian headquarters) is registered in the United Arab Emirates, from where Fulla is distributed to other countries, including Saudi-Arabia and Jordan (IP Pro 2005). See ibid.
[98] Salem, "Stores Cashing in on Back-to-School Fever."

Figure 10.4: Fulah

I get between my fellow shoppers, wares on display, pushcarts, bicycles, scooters, itinerant vendors, and the rare car. Many shops here sell wholesale and retail, supplying smaller merchants or vendors. Occasionally one can see a woman with a dozen balls or dolls in large plastic bags, or other large bags with undisclosed wares which they will sell at a small profit in their neighborhoods.

By the side of the way stand huge boxes and displays of all sorts of items, including cheap toys. One of the larger toy stores has massive boxes full of toys at its entrance. Here is where I first encounter Eliana, a Barbie-look alike. Slightly smaller than Barbie, Eliana wears a miniskirt and shoulder free shirt. Her hair is bright blond. She sells for LE 1.50. Eliana looks as if her average lifespan—in one piece, that is—cannot be much longer than a week. Next to Eliana are boxes with cars, drums, animals, and the obligatory Ramadan lanterns of similar quality and price range. A little further down the street, high up on a shelf inside a store, I finally find her: Fulah. Her price tag is LE 90. At that price (that of the "real" Fulla) one wonders whether the store owners themselves believe they are selling the real thing? A few minutes later, I find Fulah again a few stores further down. This time she costs LE 15. I happily buy two (one with a black abaya and one with a white abaya). Both have bright blond hair and wear bright red lipstick.

Razanne and Fulla: Debating Religion and Culture

Debates about Razanne and Fulla illustrate that they are more than toys. The dolls have prompted applause, ridicule, and rejection from individuals and groups. From the pages of the Italian newspaper *La Repubblica* to Muslim discussion sites in Indonesia, Fulla and Razanne have invited comments from friends and foes alike.[99] I will analyze some of the reactions found in newspaper articles, websites, online discussions, and blogs. First, there are debates in some Muslim circles about the appropriateness of dolls in general. More prominent are arguments in religious Muslim contexts that point to the positive role that dolls in hijabs can play in the socialization of girls. Then there are those voices that simply applaud Razanne and Fulla's cultural "victory." Finally, there is the broad spectrum of non-Muslim responses that range from surprise or genuine curiosity to bewilderment, ridicule, and hostility. While none of these voices represents any fixed group or constituency, they illustrate aspects of the debate.

Since Islam does not encourage the depiction of humans, the question of whether to allow children to play with dolls precedes the question of the appropriateness of Razanne and Fulla in some religious circles. In an exchange on the *New Muslim Message Board*, one participant, Jihadia, noted:

> I think dolls that look like humans isn't [sic] allowed my parents didnt [sic] allow me to have them (when I was little) they used to say u will have to put a Ruh [soul, spirit; PK] in them on judgement [sic] day but toys that look like animals they must be allowed.[100]

Jihadia posted her note in response to an inquiry about whether the Muslim ban on images extended to toys, which was prompted by Fulla's appearance in Saudi-Arabia.[101] Another contributor ("Insanity") added that "my Sheikh let his grand daughters [sic] play with faceless dolls."[102] One

---

[99] Alessandra Vitali, "Velo, pudore e un piccolo Corano e Razanne, la Barbie musulmana," *La Repubblica* (31 October 2003, http://www.repubblica.it/2003/j/sezioni/esteri/Barbie,usul/barbiemusul/barbiemusul.html, accessed 9 September 2005); swaramuslim.com 2005. I am grateful to Louise Medrano for translating the Italian article for me.
[100] 8 December 2003.
[101] Hussein, 7 December 2003.
[102] 12 December 2003.

214   Chapter Ten

day later, Aaminah posted a message by Mufti Muhammad ibn Adam al-Kawthari, an expert from the United Kingdom:

> Therefore, if the dolls are fully structured, meaning they have the head with the eyes, ears, mouth, etc..., then it will be impermissible to acquire them, give them as a gift or for small children to play with.
>
> However, if the dolls do not have a head, meaning they do not have eyes, ears, nose or mouth which make them incomplete, then it will be permissible to make them and give them to small children. [...] The hadith which indicated that Sayyidatuna Aisha (Allah be pleased with her) used to play with dolls, recorded by Iman Abu Dawood and others, does not signify the permissibility of the present day dolls.[103]

Mufti Muhammad further elaborates on why the case of ᶜAʾisha's (a wife of the Prophet Mohammed) doll was not comparable to today's dolls. Yumna from Kentucky reinforced the Mufti's words stating that a South African religious scholar had similarly commented on Aisha's doll.[104] Subsequently, Um Ibrahim Isa asks:

> So what do we do about the razanne [sic] dolls? The muslim dolls that are like the Barbie dolls but in a halal kind of way, they come in niqab, jelbab, hijab and all different kinds of modest dresses?
>
> I ended up getting my nieces some razanne dolls cuz they really wanted the Barbie ones but im [sic] like look at how they're dressed, not the kind you want to impress with your kids [sic] so I got them the razanne dolls which they love.[105]

Alimagirl2004 adds later: "I think that razanne dolls r o.k., i have one with a pink kurta shilwar, [...] it does come in modest dresses and its chest does not show as openly as Barbie dolls."[106]

On the site *The Islamic Garden*, an anonymous mother published a piece entitled "Barbie Converts to Islam," in which she recounts the story of her three-year-old daughter who received her first Barbie. After the girl's older brother asked, "Where is the doll's hijab?" the mother made a hijab for Barbie. With her new Muslim outfit, the mother notes that Barbie's "chest was no longer exposed and suddenly Barbie had a completely different look." Her daughter renamed Barbie to Muslima Fatimah and loved the doll. The

---

[103] 13 December 2003.
[104] 19 December 2003.
[105] 19 December 2003.
[106] 24 January 2004.

author concludes that "it is important to make sure that a girl's dolls reflect the values which are being taught at home because dolls are used in intense pretend-play which include role-playing." She concludes "others are ahead of me in the desire to give Muslim girls an Islamic alternative to Barbie, check out the Razanne Doll."[107] "Al-Muhajabah" similarly adds in a blog debate that "it's good for young Muslim girls in particular to have dolls that look like how their moms and big sisters dress and how they may choose to dress when they are older." She adds that this is especially important for diaspora Muslim women who by wearing the *hijab* might become the target of "petty harassment, discrimination and more." It is therefore helpful to create a strong Muslim self-confidence in girls.[108] In the same blog a non-Muslim participant, Jonathan Edelstein, notes that he would prefer Razanne to Barbie anyway because of her more realistic looks. Situating Razanne in the context of liberal Western society, he sees her as an educational tool for diversity and tolerance among non-Muslims: "Of course, socialization works both ways. I'd buy my daughter a Razanne. Women in hijab are a common enough site in my neighborhood, so I doubt they'd seem alien to her, but a Razanne as part of her doll collection might "normalize" them further."[109]

At the *Muslim Village Forums*, discussants were less concerned about the theological correctness of the dolls (Fulla and Razanne). Instead, participants exchanged notes on where to buy them in different countries. The tone on this site is celebratory. Hanan Oum Medina notes about Fulla:

> Wow, they're so cute. I love the jilbab wearing ones and the prayer clothes in white. I'm going to pick up a few for my girl (...) better then the overexposed Barbie she currently has. I hate Barbie .... Go Fulla![110]

Ambernath responded, "we have Fulla & Razanne now ... No need for Barbie!"[111]

Some non-Muslim reactions to Razanne and Fulla illustrate the dolls' cultural and political significance. Largely written in response to newspaper articles about Fulla or Razanne, some observers vaguely object to the dolls' existence and purpose. Under the somewhat ironic title "Nobody will quickly take off the headscarf of the Muslim-Barbie," Michaela Simon

---

[107] "Barbie Converts to Islam," *The Islamic Garden* (2005, http://www.islamicgarden.com/article1018.html, accessed 31 August 2005).
[108] The Head Heeb, 3 October 2003.
[109] 3 October 2003.
[110] 6 June 2005.
[111] 7 June 2005.

writes in Germany that Razanne teaches the core virtues to Muslim girls, among them "submissiveness."[112] Nowhere in Razanne's marketing is this word used, instead it is reflective of the writer's prejudices. One commentator on a debate mediated by the German magazine *Stern* responds to the news brief about Razanne with the short sarcastic question: "German Barbie with a Pils in the hand and Sauerkraut on the plate ?[sic]," signifiying bewilderment and ridicule.[113] On another German site "Dexter" responds to Razanne with a simple "Ach du meine Fresse!" (vulgar pronouncement of surprise).[114] "Fano" in turn suggests the production of a menstruation Barbie.[115] Another contributor, "YKC" is surprised at the unexpected existence of the dolls: "I am out of words."[116] While ultimately fairly irrelevant, such commentaries illustrate how uncomfortable the idea of a "Muslim Barbie" is to some. It is interesting to note that the fault lines in these voices between "us" and "them" become curiously pronounced when Barbie (one of us), who is often controversial within Western culture, all of a sudden becomes something to be defended in a cultural "conflict." Barbie is "normal," the Muslim doll, however, seems excessive and transcends this oddly defined "normality."

The political nature of Fulla and Razanne is illustrated by a news item in *Reason Magazine*, published by the conservative/libertarian Reason Foundation. In August 2002, Charles Paul Freund writes about the Iranian doll Sara: Designed to promote "traditional value[s]," as Freund notes, she is designed to fend off Western influences, such as drinking alcohol, immodest dress, and "close relationships with a man." The defense of drinking alcohol as a virtue is ironic. Freund calls Sara an "enforced 'national doll'" and compares her to the enforced former Soviet music scene.[117] Yet Sara is a possibility and no must in Iran: She is not enforced upon consumers there. Muslim dolls tend to provoke a surprising resentment among Europeans and Americans, because many of them cannot imagine that Muslim women would wear a hijab of their own free will. To use a doll as an educational tool to help socialize girls so they become proper Muslim women strikes many as absurd at best, and as an act of oppression at worst. It is

---

[112] Michaela Simon, "Der Muslim Barbie zieht so schnell keiner das Kopftuch aus," *Telepolis* (15 November 2003, www.heise.de/tp/r4/artikel/16/16087/1.html, accessed 2 August 2009). Translations from German are my own.
[113] Die fahne, *Stern shortnews*, 10 October 2003.
[114] *Telefon-Treff.de*, 26 November 2004.
[115] *Telefon-Treff.de*, 26 November 2004.
[116] *Telefon-Treff.de*, 26 November 2004.
[117] Charles Paul Freund, "Dolled Up: Authoritarian Regimes Play Make-Belief – Artifact," *Reason* (August 2002, http://www.findarticles.com/p/articles/mi_m1568/is_4_34/ai_8938930 4/print, accessed 9 September 2005).

particularly interesting that in these debates Barbie, who has been severely criticized by feminists and others, is suddenly almost passionately defended.

And They Lived Happily Ever After ...

Barbie, Razanne, Fulla, Fulona, and Fulah co-exist in a complicated world of intersecting economic, cultural and religious dynamics. They are made and remade by articulations of these dynamics. Clearly, the existence of Razanne, Fulla, and Fulah is firmly rooted in Barbie's existence. Barbie produced or foreshadowed her Muslim sisters, as her existence in a globalizing and culturally aware world almost necessitated the emergence of similar ethnic dolls. And since *one single* Muslim market or culture does not exist, it is not surprising that several dolls emerged, each catering to a different niche. Razanne is a pious, largely expatriate Muslim girl, who speaks to her sisters in North America and Europe. She wants to teach, guide, and accommodate play that fosters pious and community-oriented characteristics. Due to the conviction of her producers, and also to her particular market niche, she is not marketed very actively; she benefits instead from word of mouth and communal networks. Razanne has little presence in the media and no colorful store displays. Razanne benefits from a growing critical consciousness of (Western) middle-class parents with regard to toys, their quality and educational uses. She thrives on parents' objections (which transcend the Muslim community) to the sexualized nature of fashion dolls. Razanne is a critical commentary on the sexualized and commercialized nature of the toy market. She adds a religio-cultural perspective as she points to the ethnocentric nature of Barbie's supposedly global appeal. Razanne suggests different ideals for Muslim girls: pious, studious, civically or communally minded, and modest in her consumption habits. Ultimately, of course, it is up to the young owners what they do with their dolls; nonetheless the scripts of Barbie and Razanne both provide vague frameworks and worldviews for girls to reflect upon.

Fulla is a modestly but fashionably dressed upper-middle class girl, at home in a cosmopolitan world of travel (Fulla with airport luggage cart) and fashion. She is modest about her dress but less so regarding the size of her wardrobe and play accessories. She translates global fashion trends into modest Muslim outfits. Like Barbie she delights in her overloaded closet and is a dedicated consumer. Her broad range of accessories and other toys suggests that her owners might quickly learn to copy her consumption habits and accumulate more products. Fulla's presence in malls and upscale stores fares well with her image. She is a mall kind of girl. Fulla clearly swims on the wave of Barbie, cashes in on Barbie's success, and uses similar concepts and strategies. Fulla symbolizes the extension of globalized consumerism into elite Arab/Muslim contexts. With the emergence of a culturally sensitive capitalism, Fulla thrives on Middle Eastern markets because she speaks to local culture and values. In the face of ongoing West-Islam conflict, Fulla represents the oddly peaceful side of capitalism. While unrest flares up on the streets of Paris, Damascus, Copenhagen, and Cairo, Fulla splendidly combines globalized consumerism and Muslim sensitivities. Fulla succeeds, producing both profit and religio-cultural approval.

Fulah's (the "fake" sister) presence in the stores of Sharia El Muski is fitting her characteristics as a lookalike or wannabe. In the midst of household items, clothes, and other toys, she appeals to those who are excluded from upscale consumerism but are familiar with its products as advertised on TV. Fulah exemplifies the attraction and simultaneous remoteness of the upscale market. Yet, Fulah does not need to worry about the fine points of cultural appropriateness and commentary that mark Fulla as different from Barbie, hence her bright blond hair. Fulah's headscarf is too narrow to cover her hair. Fulah, with no marketing of her own, simply swims on the waves of Fulla. Her name underscores this. Eliana and her nondescript friends are for those who cannot afford anything else, hence her appearance (exposed or covered body parts) is irrelevant as long as it is reminiscent of some sort of fashion doll. Her price is her marketing.

The tale of Barbie and her Muslim sisters is a global story of culture, religion, and most importantly the globalized economy. It is a complex tale of dolls that conquer parts of the globe with their beauty, modesty, and consumption habits. They are part of larger movements that stake out new ethnic markets, create wealth, and influence communities, debates, and controversies. Razanne and Fulla illustrate two broad trends: (1) the fine-tuned construction of meaningful long-term Muslim identities in the United States and Europe; (2) dramatic and dynamic changes in Arab/Muslim societies with regard to the emergence of new popular and media cultures (anywhere from malls to TV stations) that on one hand are firmly rooted in global models, but at the same time rework these models to religio-culturally appropriate articulations.

Figure 10.5: Razanne, Singing Fulls, Outdoor Fulla, and Fulah (white and black dress)

Bibliography

Abaza, Mona. "Brave New Mall." *Al-Ahram Weekly* (16–22 September 2004).
———. "Shopping Malls, Consumer Culture and the Reshaping of Pubic Space in Egypt." *Theory, Culture and Society* 18, no. 5 (2001): 97–122.
Abidin, Fawaz. *Private Communication*. E-mail: 11 September 2005; 3 October 2005; 7 October 2005.
Abu-Nasr, Donna. "Kuwait Debates U.S.-Islamic Life." *Dailynews.yahoo.com* (29 Nov 2001, http://dailynews.yahoo.com/h/ap/20011129/wl/islamic_dilemmas_1.html, accessed 7 September 2005).
"Barbie—or Jezebel?" *St. Petersburg Times* (11 September 2003, http://www.sptimes.com/2003/09/11/Worldandnation/Barbieor_Jezebel.shtml, accessed 7 September 2005).
"Barbie Converts to Islam." *The Islamic Garden* (2005, http://www.islamicgarden.com/article1018.html, accessed 31 August 2005).
"Barbie Loses Out to Veiled Rival." *BBC News* (12 Jan 2006, http://www.bbc.co.uk/go/pr/fr/\bibrangedash/2/hi/middel_east/4605334.stm, accessed 13 January 2006).

Bennett, David. "Getting the Id to Go Shopping: Psychoanalysis, Advertising, Barbie Dolls, and the Invention of the Consumer Unconscious." *Public Culture* 17, no. 1 (2005): 1–26.

Cook, Daniel Thomas. *The Commodification of Childhood: Personhood, the Children's Wear Industry and the Rise of the Child-Consumer 1917–1962*. Durham NC: Duke University Press, 2004.

Davila, Arlene. *Latinos Inc. The Marketing and Making of a People*. Berkeley: The University of California Press, 2001.

Del Valle, Elena, ed. *Hispanic Marketing and Public Relations*. Boca Raton: Poyeen Publishing, 2005.

Eltahawy, Mona. "Barbie Faces Rival for Arab Affections." *The Guardian* (8 June 1999, http://www.guardian.couk/interantional/story/o,,292295,00.html, accessed 26 August 2005).

Fennick, Janine. *The Collectible Barbie Doll*. Philadelphia: Courage Books, 1999.

Freund, Charles Paul. "Dolled Up: Authoritarian Regimes Play Make-Belief – Artifact." *Reason* (August 2002, http://www.findarticles.com/p/articles/mi_m1568/is_4_34/ai_89389304/print, accessed 9 September 2005).

Halter, Marilyn. *Shopping for Identity. The Marketing of Ethnicity*. New York: Schocken Books, 2000.

Huus, Kari. "Quest for the Muslim Market Niche." *MSNBC* (3 October 2003, http://msnbc.msn.com/id/3130288/print/1/displaymode/1098/, accessed 5 September 2005).

Jehl, Douglas. "It's Barbie vs. Laila and Sara in Mideast Culture War." *New York Times* (2 June 1999): A4.

Kuppinger, Petra. "Exclusive Greenery: New Gated Communities in Cairo." *City and Society* 16, no. 2 (2004): 35–61.

———. "Pyramids and Alleys: Global Dynamics and Local Strategies in Giza." In *Cairo Cosmopolitan: Urban Structure, Spaces and Identities in the New Middle East*, edited by Diane Singerman and Paul Amar, 313–344. Cairo: American University in Cairo Press, 2006.

"Lamcy Plaza to Host Barbie Wonderland." *Strategiy.com* (19 April 2005, http://www.strategiy.com/inews.asp?id=20050419155902, accessed 17 August 2005).

Linn, Susan. *Consuming Kids. The Hostile Takeover of Childhood*. New York: The New Press, 2004.

Lord, M.G. *Forever Barbie. The Unauthorized Biography of a Real Doll*. New York: Avon Books, 1995.

Mafi, Ali. "Sara and Dara Are Here!" *TehranAvenue.com* (April 2002, http://tehranavenue.com/print.php?IN=en&id=212, accessed 7 September 2005).

Martin, Paul. "Religious Police Take After Barbie." *The Washington Times* (2 January 2004, http://washintongtime.com/world/20040102\bibrangedash112738\bibrangedash9433r.htm, accessed 5 September 2005).

Martin, Susan Taylor. "Call It the Fulla Phenomenon." *Chicago Tribune* (25 May 2005).

———. "Coverup Girl." *St. Petersburg Times* (12 January 2004, http://www.sptime.com/2004/01/12/Floridian/Coverup_girl.shtml, accessed 26 August 2005).

———. "The Doll That Has Everything—Almost." *St. Petersburg Times* (15 May 2005, http://www.sptimes.com/2005/05/15/Floridian/The_doll_that_has_eve.shtml, accessed 26 August 2005).

McDonough, Yona Zeldis. *The Barbie Chronicles. A Living Doll Turns Forty*. New York: Touchstone Books, 1999.

Mitchell, Timothy. "Dreamland. The Neoliberalism of Your Desires." *Middle East Report*, no. 210 (1999): 28–33.

Nomani, Asra. "Hijab Chic. How Retailers Are Marketing to Fashion-Conscious Muslim Women." *Washingtonpost/Newsweek Interactive Co./slate.com* (2005, http://www.slate.com/toolbar.aspx?action=print&id=2129906.Accessed29.4.20062005.http://www.slate.com/toolbar.aspx?action=print&id=2129906, accessed 29 April 2006).

Noorart.com. *Who We Are!* 2003, http://noorart.com/whoweare.shtml, accessed 9 September 2005.

Pires, Guilherme Dias, and John Stanton. *Ethnic Marketing*. Florence KY: Cengage Learning Business Press, 2005.

Pomeranz, Dorothy. "The Barbie Bust." *Forbes* (3 March 2005, http://www.forbes.com/business/forbes/2005/0328/064a.html, accessed 5 September 2005).

Qamaruzzaman, Mariem. "Lease of Faith." *Islamic Horizons* (March/April 2006): 48–49.

Quart, Alissa. *Branded. The Buying and Selling of Teenagers*. New York: Basis Books, 2004.

Rice, Gillian, and Mohammed Al-Mossawi. "The Implications of Islam for Advertising Messages: The Middle Eastern Context." *Journal of Euromarketing* 11, no. 3 (2002): http://www.haworthpressinc.com/store/product.asp?sku=J037.

Saadeh, Noor. *Private Communication*. E-mail: 3 October 2005.

Salem, Mohammed Ahmed. "Stores Cashing in on Back-to-School Fever." *The Peninsula* (29 August 2005, http://thepeninsulaqata.com/Display_news.asp?section=Local_news&subsection=, accessed 7 September 2005).

"Saudi Ban in Female Doll Imports." *Guardian Newspapers* (18 December 2003, http://buzzle.com/editorials/text12\bibrangedash18\bibrangedash2003\bibrangedash48740.asp, accessed 5 September 2005).

"Saudi Police Say Barbie Doll a Threat to Morality." *CNN* (10 September 2003, http://cnn.com/2003/WORLD/meast/09/10/saudibarbie.ap/index.html, accessed 10 September 2003).

Schor, Juliet. *Born to Buy*. New York: Scribner, 2004.

Schreiber, Alfred. *Multicultural Marketing. Selling to the New America*. Lincolnwood IL: NTC Business Books, 2001.

Show News. Toy Fair 2005, http:\\www.toyfairdubai.com, accessed 5 September 2005.

Simon, Michaela. "Der Muslim Barbie zieht so schnell keiner das Kopftuch aus." *Telepolis* (15 November 2003, www.heise.de/tp/r4/artikel/16/16087/1.html, accessed 2 August 2009).

Steinberg, Shirley, and Joe Kincheloe. *Kinderculture: The Corporate Construction of Childhood*. Boulder: Westview Press, 2004.

Tdc.trade.com. *New Cars and Hand-Made Stars at Middle Eastern Toy Jamboreee*. Report from Toy Fair 2003, Dubai, 29 May 2003, http://tdctrade.com/imn/03052905/tradefairs006.htm, accessed 5 September 2005.

Tosa, Marco. *Barbie. Four Decades of Fashion, Fantasy and Fun*. New York: Harry N. Abrams, Inc., Publishers, 1998.

Utmaster Import & Export Co., Ltd. 2005, http://alibaba.com/catalog/111008636Muslim_Dolls.html, accessed 26 August 2005.

Utmaster Import & Export Co., Ltd. *Offer Muslim Toys and Muslim Ornaments*. 25 August 2005, www.alibaba.com/manufacturer/12425002/Offer_Muslim_Toys_Muslim_Orna..com, accessed 9 September 2005.

Valle, Francisco J., and Judy M. Mandel. *How to Win the Hispanic Gold Rush*. New York: iUniverse, 2003.

Vitali, Alessandra. "Velo, pudore e un piccolo Corano e Razanne, la Barbie musulmana." *La Repubblica* (31 October 2003, http://www.repubblica.it/2003/j/sezioni/esteri/Barbie,usul/barbiemusul/barbiemusul.html, accessed 9 September 2005).

Yifeng Imp. & Exp. Trading Co., Ltd. 2005, http://yifengtrading.en.alibaba.com/product/0/50268590/Doll__4_Arabia_dresses/sho..., accessed 26 August 2005.

Newspapers and Magazines
Bidoun
Islamica
Islamic Horizon

Web discussion sites
alt.muslim
http://www.altmuslim.com/perm.php?id=1077_0_26_0_C25
Accessed 7 September2005.

Muslim Village Forums
http://forums.muslimsvillage.net/lofiversion/index.php/t12715.html
Accessed 17 August 2005.

Net Muslims Message Board
http://netmuslims.com/bboards/ultimatebb.cgi?ubb=get_topic;f=2;t=000135
Accessed 17 August 2005.

Stern shortnews
http://shortnews.stern.de/start_ppp.cfm?id=480645&free_id=1&rubrik1=frei-zeit
Accessed 1 September 2005.

Swaramuslim.com
http://swaramuslim.com/ISLAM/more.php?id=790_0_4_0_M
Accessed 17 August 2005.
Telefon-Treff.de
http://www.telefon-treff.de/showthread.php?s=&threaded=143773
Accessed 31 August 2005.

The Head Heeb
http://headheeb.blogmosis.com/archives/016498.html
Accessed 9 September 2005.

Company Websites
Alibaba.com (on Utmaster Import and Export Co., Ltd)
Citystars.com.eg
Halalplaza.com
Ilham.fcpages.com
Iqra4kids.com.au
Islamicbookstore.com

IslamicCity.com
Mctoy.com.hk
Noorart.com
New-boy.com
Onlineislamicstore.com
Smoby.fr
Soundvision.com
Soundvisioncanada.com

CHAPTER ELEVEN

ISLAMIZING THE MARKET? ADVERTISING, PRODUCTS, AND CONSUMPTION IN AN ISLAMIC FRAMEWORK IN SYRIA

ALINA KOKOSCHKA

The phenomenon of (re-)Islamization,[1] also often referred to as the resurgence, revitalization, or revival of Islam, has been thoroughly researched over the last few years. But due to its predominant perception as a political topic it is seldom looked at in economic terms. While Islamic banking is studied in great detail, connections between the market and the Islamization of society are often overlooked. In this paper, I will discuss the relations and interdependency between the Syrian economic opening, Islamization, and identity formation, using selected consumer goods and advertisements targeted at Muslims. Most of the material was collected as part of my fieldwork in Damascus in 2006.[2]

According to Müller, Islamization can be described as a phenomenon in which Islam affects more and more aspects of society: Institutions as well as individuals increasingly invoke Islam as a source of legitimacy and significance in all areas of life.[3] Schulze's definition adds a useful perspective on agency.[4] He does not consider Islamization to be a political process but

---

[1] While upveiling and the growing of Islamically correct beards (*liḥya*) can be referred to as re-Islamization, i.e. the return to existing Islamic traditions, the phenomena discussed in this article are newly Islamized.

[2] This paper is designed to raise questions and formulate ideas rather than to provide answers. Further questions about motivations and interests of consumers will be answered in future extended fieldwork.

[3] Joachim Müller, *Islamischer Weg und islamistische Sackgasse: Die Debatte um Islam, islamische Wirtschaft und moderne Gesellschaft in Ägypten* (Göttingen: Lit Verlag, 1993), 3–9.

[4] Schulze as cited in ibid., 9.

rather one that is expressed in forms of acting and discourse which define everyday culture in Islamic communities. One of these forms, I argue, is consumer behavior.

In Syria in 2006, the stores and stalls of Suq al-Hamidiyya, Sha‛lan, and Suq Saruja offered an increasing variety of "Islamized" goods that fit neither into the category of halal products (such as correctly slaughtered meat) nor what are traditionally called Muslim goods (such as headscarves or the *siwāk* stick that Mohammad is said to have used for dental hygiene).

What is found on jammed shelves in Midan, as well as on carriages in front of Sayyida Ruqayya-Mosque, is evidence of a new Muslim target group—be it Muslim family, child, or housewife—with special needs and desires. The design of these Muslim-targeted products supports the mainstream trend toward public piety and the definition of identity via consumption. What Maha Abdelrahman detects for Egyptian society has to be taken into account for the Syrian case as well: "The transformation of the Islamic project, from a collective, political[ly] organized movement to one of fragmented individuality steeped in material fulfilment, fits well with the increasing integration of Egyptian society into a global market economy."[5]

While, for example, the Indonesian or Malaysian market[6] offers a huge range of products targeted at Muslims, Syria currently is in a tense situation between deregulation and sticking to the ideals and rules of a socialist state, which includes a ban on certain international companies. In addition, Syria is essentially a secular state, so there is no official support for products aimed at Muslims. The present status of the market reflects this "reduced" form of capitalism: society is not differentiated into countless subcultures and there is an absence of corporate identities. In the midst of this economic and political tension, the market for Islamized products is growing explosively, and Muslim consumers in turn use these products as a new way to express their Muslim identity and to indicate their social status.

Functions of Public Piety

In religious societies, such as Syria, a pious life serves as a role model by embodying the moral values of virtuousness, righteousness, veracity, modesty, discipline, and adherence to norms. Within the relevant social fabric this lifestyle is equivalent to a certain prestige, which forms Symbolic Capital in Bourdieu's sense. The usual factors that define one's position

---

[5] Annelies Moors, "Muslim Fashions – Fashionable Muslims," *ISIM Review*, no. 16 (2005): 59.

[6] See Firly Annisa and Ragnar K. Willer, chapters 13 and 14 of this volume.

in society—socio-economic differences, ancestry, and level of education—are, in the case of Islamization, accompanied by a new source of identity and most notably status: public piety. The interesting thing about public piety in this context is that it can be acquired independently of economic capital. It has the potential to disturb and adjust the value system and legitimize new values held by segments of society that would otherwise have no access to influential positions.[7] Symbolic power, based on Symbolic Capital has "a power to 'consecrate,' to render the sacred."[8]

In other words, in a society that accepts piety as Symbolic Capital, people with a pious lifestyle get—at least partially—to interpret or decide what constitutes a religious symbol. These assumptions lead to questions about consumption: Do religious commodities that suggest the buyer or owner has a pious lifestyle increase Symbolic Capital? Might they even enable people to be seen as pious Muslims who do not pursue a corresponding lifestyle? Might this lead to a reciprocal process of "sacralization" between customer and commodity?

In Syrian society "the acquisition of adab"[9] [decency] has to be constantly renewed through moral performance, as Pinto has shown. I argue that buying and showing products with "Islamic messages"[10] is part of a materialized moral performance. Islam as a main source of identity and meaning is also a condition for affiliation. Confessing an Islamic identity provides "individuals with both collective support and moral justification for their social practices."[11] When the use and display of Islamic products is tightly interwoven with belief and piety, it can facilitate mechanisms of identity, affiliation, distinction, and exclusion.

Buying and owning commodities that convey an Islamic message are an expression of distinction in Bourdieu's sense. Via distinction identity is formated and strengthened, and it preserves (or develops) a hierarchy of values in relation to the relevant reference group. Individuals as well as groups or institutions use a pool of qualities that are supposed to be accepted in the societal fabric. The question is, how does the self-classifying person relate to the existing hierarchy of goods and objects? It might be in terms

---

[7] This can be found in Egyptian society. Wise gives an account of the development of the hijab from a lower-middle-class movement toward an elite accessory; cf. Lindsay Wise, *Words from the Heart: New Forms of Islamic Preaching in Egypt* (Oxford: University of Oxford, 2003), 69.

[8] David Swartz, *Culture and Power: The Sociology of Pierre Bourdieu* (Chicago: University of Chicago Press, 1997), 47.

[9] Paulo G. Pinto, "Embodied Morality and Social Practice in Syria," *ISIM Review*, no. 17 (2006): 15.

[10] This useful term was coined by Gregory Starrett; cf. Gregory Starrett, "The Political Economy of Religious Commodities in Cairo," *American Anthropologist* 97, no. 1 (1995): 92.

[11] Pinto, "Embodied Morality and Social Practice in Syria," 14.

228 Chapter Eleven

of imitation—aiming at assimilation—or negation of established legitimate goods, aiming at constructing new cultural goods and objects. Regarding the above questions, in Syria individuals can distinguish themselves from other faiths, the official party line, social classes, and cultures, namely the "West." When analyzing the products and advertising below, the central question is: Do the products work as an agent of distinction in the formation of a Muslim identity, and if so, to what degree? Which elements of a possible Muslim identity do they emphasize? My intention here is to highlight significant examples of symbols and allusions that are used for "Muslim products."

Promoting Allah: Advertising for Muslims

Advertising in public spaces is a very effective way to communicate Islamic imagery: the size of the images makes them hard to ignore. Moreover, the combination between an object of need or even desire—i.e. the advertised good—and moral values communicated via religious symbols makes the advertising of Islamized commodities a delicate issue. This way Islamic symbols are actualized in use as well as part of the desire or ideal that the observer is intended to feel. The recipient, though, is not to be thought of as passive. Images presented in advertisements are generated realities that are being adapted by the recipient. What advertising does, however, is create an anonymous "peer group," i.e., a relevant reference group. Through purchase decisions the recipient positions himself or herself within this group either by distinction or assimilation. Finally, it needs to be pointed out that although Syria was an almost advertisement-free society for a long time, due to the socialist part of the Ba^{c}th-ideology, it is a society that is used to viewing and decoding visual language in public displays. The presence of large-size likenesses of Hafiz al-Asad and his sons paved the way for the now omnipresent billboard advertisements.

Let us consider the first two images; they are perfect examples of how different images of piety and modern lifestyle can be combined.

Dima: Saudi-American Cookies?

The Saudi biscuit company Dima created the slogan *Dīmata allāhu yadīma* ("Dima, may God sustain them") to suggest that its chocolate-cream-filled biscuits are precious. From a grammatical and an orthographic perspective, this slogan is incorrect. What is meant, however, is the colloquial *Dīma allāhu yadīma*.[12] This way the slogan plays with the homophones *Dīma*,

---

[12] In standard language (*fuṣḥā*) there would be a suffix *hā: yadīmahā*.

the name of the brand, and the verb *dāma, yadīmu* combined with the colloquial feminine singular possessive, the *ā* in the end being an *alif*. What is remarkable here is the use of the name of God in a context as banal as an advertisement. Even though God's name is frequently used in colloquial Arabic without any particularly religious connotations—like in the English expressions "Oh my God" or "Thank God"—this colloquial usage is usually not transferred to print ads. Besides, in the Dima advertisement, the word *Allāh* is printed in the signal color red and thus particularly highlighted. Apparently, the company tries to distinguish their product by making it appear as blessed. The name of God is being alienated for commercial ends by a Saudi company, which is most likely rated by Syrian consumers as a company being mindful of religious values and sensitivities of believers. At the same time it might well be thought that by using a religious but everyday phrase the company tries to connect to the everyday Muslim who does not feel offended by it because Islam is touching everything in his daily routine, even his selection of cookies.

Figure 11.1: Advertisement for Dima cookies seen in Lattakia, Syria

Owing to Saudi Arabia's rank as a prosperous country that produces value products, the purchaser thinks of Dima biscuits as a quality product. Dima biscuits are available all over Syria but are more expensive than the Syrian products, which are sold at the same places. The image of the "better cookie" is emphasized by a design that does not remind the viewer of the typical Arab date-cookies but rather recalls the image of American cookies like "Oreos." This impression is reinforced by the fact that the name of the product is written in English. This gives rise to the assumption that the buyer is attracted by this delicate mixture of American style, which makes it a chic product, and the trustworthiness that only an Arab product can offer: "The Saudi cookie."[13] Thereby the purchaser opens up for a modern snack, but distinguishes himself at the same time from those not paying attention to the righteous background of the goods they buy. This is especially relevant with regard to the calls for boycotting Danish and other products suspected of being involved in the 2005 cartoon controversy. In conclusion, the Dima campaign serves as an example of how Muslim consumers can position themselves in two ways: moral-religiously and moral-politically.

"Ultra Mudhish:" *Ultra Modern*

Berger argues that successful advertisements must "trade on the average recipient's traditional upbringing."[14] The detergent advert shown below grabs the viewer's attention exactly at this point on both the visual and the linguistic level.

Figure 11.2: Detergent ad placed on top of a building in Midan Square, Damascus

---

[13] *al-biskwīt al-saʿūdī.*
[14] John Berger, *Sehen: Das Bild in der Welt der Bilderwelt* (Rowohlt: Reinbek, 1974), 126.

Stretching across two-thirds of a banner that is several meters long, the slogan reads: "'Wonderful' Ultra – A new generation deeply rooted in the past."[15] Let us take a closer look at it. The name of a detergent or cleaning agent that promises marvelous results is also a common feature of German and American advertisements. One of the biggest German washing agents, "Ariel," even borrows its name from the Bible. Using the superlative for intensification is nothing new. The slogan only becomes "Muslim" in the second part. Besides the added appeal that the words "new generation" have to a young audience and their suggestion that the product is the result of the latest research and improved effectiveness, the words also have an Islamic connotation—*al-jīl al-awwal*,[16] point of reference for every Muslim; *jīl jadīd*, the promising new generation that unites its powers in the name of God. Thus, the slogan embraces modernity by referring to the golden ages. The last part, *li-māḍin ʿarīqin*, does not directly refer to a religious expression, but suggests a wide range of Arabic expressions and metaphors linked to questions of descent (*aṣl*) and roots (*ʿirq*). *Māḍī* means not only "past" but also "efficient," which helps viewers remember the product. The visual level works in an analog way. The observer is guided from a black-and-white past of hard work and rigorous dress code directly to a warm and modern life in which the washing machine saves time and the housewife dresses modestly but attractively with a fashionable veil. Grey is replaced by a classy beige. The suggested ideal of a clever housewife harkens back, in terms of aesthetics, values, and gender roles, to Germany in the 1950s and its various detergent ads. It must be added that in 2008, detergent advertisements often still supported the same patriarchal gender roles, updated only in style. However, one feature makes this advertisement typically Syrian or even Damascene: the floating blossoms of jasmine are the symbol of Damascus, *al-Fāʾiḥa*, "the odoriferous," which is commemorated every year with a campaign to plant jasmine trees. By this the company refers to its Damascene background and establishes a connection with the consumer who is Muslim, or rather Muslima, and Damascene, or would like to be.[17]

Since the only remarkable differences between Syrian and Western detergent ads seem to be the veil and certain religious allusions in the slogan, we can conclude first of all that regarding housework there is not much difference between the gender stereotypes pictured in Western and Syrian advertising. In the Syrian context, however, we find a code for "the proper

---

[15] *ultra mudhish—jīl jadīd li-māḍin ʿarīq*.
[16] Among others see Sayyid Quṭb, *Maʿālim fī al-ṭarīq* (1964), 14 ff.
[17] As Salamandra has shown, "Damasceneness" is an important pillar of Syrian Symbolic and Social Capital. Cf. Christa Salamandra, *A New Old Damascus: Authenticity and Distinction in Urban Syria* (Bloomington: Indiana University Press, 2004).

housewife"—the veil. Various household products are often illustrated with pictures using that code. Promoting this code might enforce pro-veil arguments since a lot of girls only decide during their studies to wear a headscarf, keeping clearly in mind that it is time to find a valuable marriage partner. The process of assimilation might well be encouraged or supported by buying the product advertised. By purchasing goods that stand for a spotlessly kept household, the consumer also buys part of the image. Still, the example implies that the target group for this billboard is not predominantly Muslim; it is captured by a confrontation between "tradition"—which is shared by both Muslims and Christians, or other confessions in general—and progressiveness, which results in a hybrid product image.

Positioning Oneself: Accessories with a Message

Many Islamized products combine practical benefits with a decorative design, e.g., clocks with suras on them, lamps or housewares with pictures of the Ka{}^cba. Accessories that have no practical use but feature a striking Islamic design constitute another big section. The fact that they can be removed easily, and with it their message, makes this kind of adornment interesting to consider. On the one hand, these accessories convey a clear message: "Look, I am Muslim and I want you to know;" they can help their owner to become a role model or to affiliate with people of the same kind. On the other hand, they can be quickly added to or removed from the outfit and do not require a final commitment, whereas growing a beard or wearing a headscarf requires a final or at least long-term decision.

Accessories are worn on the body and in public. Accessories communicate both the value of the object worn and the value one attaches to oneself. Pinto speaks about "embodied morality," which seems to be a suitable term with respect to the examples discussed below.[18]

Do Islamic Wallpaper Images on a Mobile Phone Bless the Owner's Communications?

The growing importance of mobile phones is as much a Syrian phenomenon as it is a global one. However, in Syria mobile phones are more important as a status symbol than they are in Germany. Young people, in particular, treat their mobiles with the same importance that other cultures might reserve for a car. Many times I learned in conversation with students that they had been saving for months to be able to buy their desired cell phone. Mobile phones not only enable them to communicate with a person who is not there,

---

[18] Pinto, "Embodied Morality and Social Practice in Syria."

but also send non-verbal messages about their owner, whether the device is displayed on the table in a cafe or played around with in public. Messages are being sent first and foremost by tiny trinkets tied to the phone and by the background or wallpaper images on the phone.

Background or wallpaper images, displayed on the screen of the mobile phone, represent a huge market. There are more than a thousand wallpapers with Islamic content on offer for Nokia phones alone. Who produces those images is an open question yet to be researched. These screen-filling images allow a relatively complex message to be displayed, and only people who are physically near the phone can see the image, i.e., members of the peer group. By using religious symbols, pictures, or even short quotations, the user signals the reach of his faith. Even his or her communications on the mobile—perhaps the biggest secrets that an unwed Syrian has—are still under Allah's control, because they are morally faultless. A further-reaching interpretation might be that by using Islamic images as wallpaper, all the conversations on that phone are blessed.

Pictures of Mecca and the Dome of the Rock are very popular, as well as quotations from the Qur'an, which are mostly too small to read, even for people close to the mobile. So regarding questions of public piety, the discussion below is of even greater interest.

"Remember Allah"

This wallpaper (figure 11.3) works as a direct call to the user and people nearby. The slogan *Udhkur Allāh* can be found in hectically scribbled graffiti all over walls and doors in Damascus, but here it appears in a neat script with a pink heart design that is most likely aimed at young girls. The deeply religious call is being loosened. Is this meant to remind us of God in terms of love and friendship? Or might it be understood as a request to submit to God not only by tongue but within the heart? In this case it would stand for a kind of piety that is less about puritanical austerity and more about a spiritual, emotional way of living Islam.

Here is a more classical way of communicating piety (figure 11.4): The Qurʾan as a "companion,"[19] always there for advice, words of consolation as well as rejoicing. The Qurʾan can be seen as a friend, with the emphasis on the function of Islam as a source of affiliation.

---

[19] *rafīq al-darb.*

234 Chapter Eleven

Figure 11.3: Wallpaper for sale in a mobile shop in Old Damascus

Figure 11.4: Wallpaper for sale in a mobile shop in Old Damascus

Nike, Playboy, Islam: Being Male and Muslim

Syrian shops offer a specific type of bracelet—silver for prosperity with solid links that imply strength—that is clearly a male accessory.[20] Islamic symbols often co-exist with non-religious designs on these bracelets. Next to simple ornaments reminiscent of tribal tattoos, we might find references to Nike (a U.S. manufacturer of popular sports equipment) and the logo of the soft-porn magazine *Playboy* (a rabbit with a bow tie).[21]

Hidden between these double symbols of Western culture is the two-pronged sword, the zulfikar (*dhū al-faqar*), given by Muhammad to ᶜAli b. Abi Talib at the Battle of Badr. Might it be taken as simply one symbol among others standing for a youth culture that's trying to be cool? According to this interpretation, the sword has been reinterpreted as a code for masculinity but is meaningless from a religious perspective. This might have been the designer's perspective, but it is also conceivable that young people have added a new dimension to Islam: Islam as a belief that is fashionable and up-to-date.

Guiding Children: Early Ties in Play

Toys of countless kinds are available in specialized shops as well as from street vendors. Even though there is obviously a trend towards serving typical role models—war games for boys, kitchen and beauty accessories for girls—the variety is too big to be covered in this paper. However, toys designed to lead children to pious behavior can be easily categorized. For one thing there are products that are just a variation of conventional teaching

---

[20] In the Syrian market there are few comparable goods made for a male consumer.
[21] The fact that very different designs exist makes it seem likely that the producers do not explicitly put forward Muslim matters. This is in contrast to the Muslim producers analyzed by Gökariksel and Secor in chapter 2 of this volume.

Figure 11.5: A typical range of bracelets for men

material, e.g., an educational computer that teaches suras and basic rules of conduct.[22] This example shows again that these pious aims are combined with a very modern look, in imitation of Apple's MacBook.

For another thing, there are commodities that also serve the intention to guide children, but do so in a more subtle and perhaps unexpected way. Fulla is probably the most well known of these products. The considerable range of Fulla accessories plays a big part in the dominant role of Islamized toys for girls. Fulla is more or less a copy of Barbie, but she has dark hair and various veils she can wear when she goes outside her Fulla home.[23] Fulla is a high-end toy and therefore very prestigious, but there are various replicas

---

[22] Cf. Vítš isler's contribution, chapter 12 of this volume.
[23] In order to get an impression, see "Barbie Fulla," http://www.youtube.com/watch?v= 6WqmCAzxUxI, accessed 27 August 2008.

236   Chapter Eleven

Figure 11.6: Educational computer in the style of an Apple Macintosh laptop

as well that can be purchased on a shoestring. But also on a moral level Fulla conveys Symbolic Capital due to her pious image, which is being attributed to the purchaser, i.e., to mother and child. Due to her obvious American roots, Fulla communicates on the cultural level, too, resulting in an arbitrary amalgam of meanings. In order to bring young girls in contact with Islamic dress codes and to show them an alternative version of American culture, this doll has an adult body like Barbie. But Barbie is accompanied by Ken, her boyfriend, one important indication of her being an adult. Fulla, in contrast, has no male equivalent. Does that indicate that giving her an adult body has the predominant use of showing reasons and necessity for veiling? A toy that has been sexualized to show the danger of sexuality but at the same time excludes sexuality from the play? Or does the fact that she has no boyfriend just put more emphasis on Fulla as a confident, autonomous woman? The girl plays her own grown-up self going to work, to prayer, or shopping, rather than playing "mother" as she would with a baby doll. This way, however, girls become familiar with the idea of sexual segregation from a very young age. They come into intimate contact with strict interpretations of a pious life. Since the Syrian "Barbie" herself has already become a topic of lively scholarly debate,[24] I will instead focus on Fulla's accessories.

Fulla Prayer Set

For a Muslim child's parents, Fulla's prayer set (made to be worn by the child, not by the doll) has a very practical use. It makes praying fun and an enjoyable part of the daily routine. Whereas prayer cloaks for women are mostly white and made from simple cotton, the Fulla Prayer Set consists of a smooth rose-colored cloth. The set comes with a prayer mat in pink satin, and all the accessories fit in a Fulla bag, which is made from the same pink satin as the mat. Satin stands for a certain noblesse and the color surely attracts attention in the mosque against the background of red woven carpets. The owner signals her wealth and maybe also a hint of criticism at the more traditional ways of practicing Islam. It is also worth observing that the accessories bag, with its big Fulla logo, introduces something that is both profane and purchasable to a sacred act. Even during prayers, the girl is promoting Fulla. The question arises, to what extent does this conflict with certain Islamic views on luxurious goods, which are thought to be incompatible with a pious lifestyle? But once again, this contradiction can be viewed in a constructive way. By having their own religious accessories, children might be able to invent their own personal relationship to religious duties and can maybe even claim a more child-oriented way of expressing their religion.

Fulla Coloring Book: Fulla Outside, Barbie Inside

The Fulla coloring book is accessible to nearly every child, even in its original branded, non-generic version, because it costs so little. It serves as an example of contradictory messages of Islamic products, especially in children's commodities.

The cover design suggests that the book contains at least as many images of the pious Fulla to color as of the cool and sporty Fulla without the scarf. Inside the book, however, the child is confronted without exception with pictures of Fulla in a classical Barbie-style, i.e., sexy and emphasizing feminine charms, especially her long flowing hair.

Little details, like a bird or a handbag, clearly signal that the scenes in the coloring book occur in a public sphere—and Fulla is not wearing a hijab. This discrepancy between expectation and content, and between the colored

---

[24] Cf. Petra Kuppinger's contribution, chapter 10 of this volume.

Figure 11.7: Pink for prayer

world and the real world in a pious family, will most likely be confusing to the child. Admittedly, children playing with Barbie will also never look like her or live like her, but Muslim kids playing with Fulla will not only not look like a non-veiled Fulla, they could also violate taboos if they try to imitate her. The idea of Fulla, to make the hijab something attractive, does not contradict the wish to be a "hip" young girl; in this product, however, it seems to be of marginal importance.

Conclusion

In this paper, we have seen that the range of symbols and allusions used to mark products as Islamic is limited and predictable. However, the meaning of these symbols and the allusions they suggest are manifold. The veil can function as a code for the ideal housewife. In contrast, the veiled Syrian Barbie, "Fulla," provides subtle lessons in religious education. The sword of Ali is just one symbol among other, non-Islamic ones; when the sword

Figure 11.8: Coloring Fulla's world

hangs next to the Nike logo and the Playboy rabbit on a man's bracelet, all three symbols represent potency, masculinity, and coolness. Being athletic, a womanizer, and a Muslim are put on the same level. On second thought, the *zulfikar* sword also might denote a much closer connection between these aspects, i.e., that its owner is assertive because of, and not in spite of, his belief. All of the examples fuse tradition with modernity, the latter in form of up-to-date looks respectively techniques. Many times we find designs that reference American products. These are often misinterpreted as mere copies. A more fertile way of reading these phenomena is to see them as hybrid products of a creative and critical examination of different influences, adapting them to the local context. Purchasing decisions reveal more than just lifestyle and status preferences, they can also indirectly reveal political choices, especially against the background of Syrian society and the government's repressive politics.

Despite these varieties in meaning, the products shown above all send out Islamic messages via the owner or buyer. They create a new kind of Muslim peer group, the consuming Muslim, who has style and a sound grasp of contemporary developments. Moreover, Islamic products that are not part of the halal category and are predominantly decorative tell us that the possessor is able to spend money on nonessentials. The consuming Muslim is the alternative version of the austere, strict Muslim. He is most likely young, since he is familiar with Western products and designs. Probably the Muslim consumer is also unmarried. All these little accessories can help to form an outward identity, which at the very least might be useful for finding a virtuous spouse in an anonymous urban surrounding.

Islamization of the market might at first sight appear less significant than upveiling or praying in public. But the Islamized products underscore the importance of public displays of piety, and by this, they add another aspect of reproducing Islamic symbols and ideals to the process of Islamization. Especially in the Syrian case, the market dynamics in this regard seem to have been underestimated so far. In reality, the market has a great potential to support Islamization in Syria, last but not least because of the seductive power of the relatively newly opened economy.

In the end, one question is left unanswered. The market has gained a new element, the Islamic sector; Islam has left its trace on the newly liberalised consumer market. But what about the reverse trend? How does the discovery of the "Muslim" target group influence the religious field? Does Islam in Syria benefit from being perceived as a fashion trend? One could argue that Muslim identity is undergoing a process of differentiation, and this makes it more attractive to the young generation. As a matter of fact, it could even lead to a new interpretation of being Muslim in this generation. Yet we can conclude that the religious sphere is partly becoming commoditized, consumable. It is being "economized," and piety might thereby lose in value.

Bibliography

Berger, John. *Sehen: Das Bild in der Welt der Bilderwelt*. Rowohlt: Reinbek, 1974.
Moors, Annelies. "Muslim Fashions – Fashionable Muslims." *ISIM Review*, no. 16 (2005): 59.
Müller, Joachim. *Islamischer Weg und islamistische Sackgasse: Die Debatte um Islam, islamische Wirtschaft und moderne Gesellschaft in Ägypten*. Göttingen: Lit Verlag, 1993.
Pinto, Paulo G. "Embodied Morality and Social Practice in Syria." *ISIM Review*, no. 17 (2006): 14–15.
Quṭb, Sayyid. *Maʿālim fī al-ṭarīq*. 1964.
Salamandra, Christa. *A New Old Damascus: Authenticity and Distinction in Urban Syria*. Bloomington: Indiana University Press, 2004.
Starrett, Gregory. "The Political Economy of Religious Commodities in Cairo." *American Anthropologist* 97, no. 1 (1995): 51–68.
Swartz, David. *Culture and Power: The Sociology of Pierre Bourdieu*. Chicago: University of Chicago Press, 1997.
Wise, Lindsay. *Words from the Heart: New Forms of Islamic Preaching in Egypt*. Oxford: University of Oxford, 2003.

CHAPTER TWELVE

VIDEO GAMES, VIDEO CLIPS, AND ISLAM: NEW MEDIA AND THE COMMUNICATION OF VALUES

VÍT ŠISLER[1]

Most academic research on Islam has, until now, been deeply entrenched in the Western cultural heritage of scholarship based on written materials rather than on oral tradition, despite the important role the latter plays in many Muslim communities. This paradigm prevails not only in our preferences and evaluations of primary sources—where something that is "written" can be quoted and put into a bibliography, i.e., included in the academic rituals—but also in the very way we understand cultural transmission and its methods. As Allievi says, "We often read Islam through the literature it produces, and from this we deduce Muslims, using a procedure that appears 'natural' to us or which is at any rate habitual for us, whilst it is only 'cultural.'"[2] These habitual mechanisms have to be taken into account, particularly when it comes to research on information and communication technology (ICT) and the new patterns of media production and consumption.

This chapter analyzes video games and video clips with an Islamic emphasis and the various levels at which they convey ethical and moral values. Both video games and video clips have been neglected and marginalized by the academy, albeit to varying degrees. Given their pervasiveness, especially

---

[1] This chapter is based on a research project on Islam, the Middle East, and digital media (digitalislam.eu). The project is funded by the research grants "GAUK 125408" and "GRANTY/2008/547," financed by the Faculty of Philosophy and Arts and Grant Agency of Charles University in Prague (GAUK).

[2] Stefano Allievi, "Islam in the Public Space: Social Networks, Media and Neocommunities," in *Muslim Networks and Transnational Communities in and across Europe*, ed. Stefano Allievi and Jørgen Nielsen (Leiden: Brill, 2003), 15.

among Middle Eastern youth, we are in crucial need today of critical understanding of the different ways these media articulate Islam and communicate it to consumers. This chapter in particular discusses the appropriation of games by various private Islamic companies, operating in the broader religious and cultural context of the Islamic revival and piety movement, for educational purposes. It does not address the political and propagandistic video games of Islamist Jihadi movements. Analysis of the latter can be found in other works by the author.[3] Finally, this chapter discusses how Islamic game production and, more generally, the public discourse of the Islamic piety movement are shaping mainstream video game production targeted at Muslim audiences and the marketing strategies of game production companies.

Debates related to ICT and Islam focus mainly on websites with written normative content, namely fatwas (legal recommendations) and *khuṭab* (Friday sermons).[4] Recently, a systematic research exercise analyzing weblogs and their potential role in decision-making processes in Muslim societies has emerged.[5] At the same time, non-written digital media—video games, video clips, audio sermons, etc.—and its role in the articulation of Islam and the reproduction of Islamic culture remain profoundly understudied, despite their arguably important social and cultural impact. This has led Reichmuth and Werning to introduce an umbrella term "neglected media," which encompasses a broad variety of popular and pervasive media systematically omitted by academia. According to their definition:

> Neglected media exhibit strong popular appeal and economic relevance, contrasted by lack of cultural prestige and scientific coverage. Often, they have a profound impact on the collective imagination, although this so-called passive knowledge is seldom accepted as culturally relevant.[6]

---

[3] E.g., Vít Š isler, "Neglected Media and Their Role in Shaping Muslim Identities" (Paper presented at the conference Science, Technology and Entrepreneurship in the Muslim World, 5–8 September 2007, in Lund, Sweden); Vít Š isler, "Digital Arabs: Representation in Video Games," *European Journal of Cultural Studies* 11, no. 2 (2008): 203–220.

[4] E.g., Gary R. Bunt, *Virtually Islamic* (Cardiff: University of Wales Press, 2000); Gary R. Bunt, *Islam in the Digital Age: E-jihad, Online Fatwas and Cyber Islamic Environments* (London: Pluto Press, 2003); Matthias Brückner, "Der Mufti im Netz," in *Islam im Internet, Neue Formen der Religion im Cyberspace*, ed. Rüdiger Lohlker (Hamburg: Deutsches Orient-Institut, 2001); Jon W. Anderson, "Globalizing Politics and Religion in the Muslim World," *Journal of Electronic Publishing* 3, no. 1 (1997); Dale F. Eickelman and Jon W. Anderson, *New Media in the Muslim World* (Bloomington: Indiana University Press, 2003).

[5] Gary R. Bunt, *iMuslims: Rewiring the House of Islam* (Chapel Hill: University of North Carolina Press, 2009).

[6] Philipp Reichmuth and Stefan Werning, "Pixel Pashas, Digital Djinns," *ISIM Review*, no. 18 (2006): 47.

Although Reichmuth and Werning have used the concept of neglected media primarily as a theoretical framework for the study of racial schematizations of Arabs and Muslims in video games, the term also encompasses video clips, audio clips, comic strips, board games, etc. The list of neglected media is by definition an open one, as new forms of popular (particularly digital) media emerge almost overnight (e.g., podcasting, modding, *machinimas*, etc). To transcend the media-centric logic, neglected media are not defined by any specific form, but rather by their pervasiveness, social relevance, and academic marginalization.

Video games and video clips stand for emblematic examples of neglected media. Both constitute a popular leisure time activity for a substantial part of Middle Eastern youth. At the same time, they are increasingly gaining economic and social relevance within the fabric of Middle Eastern consumer culture. Helal Saeed Almarri, general director of Dubai World Trade Centre, has recently stated that digital gaming has turned out to be a very important market in the Middle East, with not only the young population of the region, but also a wider adult audience increasingly investing a higher proportion of its disposable income in specialized hardware and software.[7]

However, the rising video game culture is not limited to only the wealthy Gulf states. The growing emergence of cyber cafés facilitates wide access by consumers in many Muslim countries to the latest game industry products.[8] As Abdulla reports in her survey, there is currently a huge number of internet cafes in Egypt: even in the most rural and poorest areas of the country.[9] Especially in *sha^cbī* (popular) quarters of Middle Eastern cities, one can find plenty of specialized cyber cafés dedicated to gaming. They are equipped with networked computers and occupied till late at night by a predominantly young, male audience—playing games, commenting on how others play, and socializing around these activities. Thus, the consumption of games is by no means only a passive process, but rather it is a dynamic interaction between production and fulfillment of expectations, meanings, and messages.

Conversely, video and audio clips have had a presence in the region for a long time and have already established themselves as important conveyors of religious, cultural, and political messages. Anyone who has carried

---

[7] Mufaddal Fakhrudin, "Dubai World Trade Centre Launches Gitex Digital Game World," *Middle East Gamers* (20 May 2008, http://www.megamers.com/pc/news.php?game_category=2&article_id=2825, accessed 9 October 2008).

[8] Ines Braune, "Youth in Morocco," in *Youth and Youth Culture in the Contemporary Middle East*, ed. Jørgen B. Simonsen (Aarhus: Aarhus University Press, 2005), 128–139.

[9] Rasha A. Abdulla, *The Internet in the Arab World: Egypt and Beyond* (New York: Peter Lang Publishing, 2007).

out fieldwork research in the Middle East has most likely noticed the overwhelming number of audiocassettes, CDs, DVDs, and VCDs with music, movies, lectures, sermons, and other content that are available on every street corner. These media pervade much of society and play an important role in the reproduction of culture. Most popular Islamic lay preachers make sure that their lectures are available both in print and in audio format.[10]

As has been stated above, several researchers have already expressed concern that written materials are not necessarily representative in relation to contemporary Islam and media.[11] This claim pertains particularly to the articulations of Islam within the Arab language sphere. As Amin and Gher put it:

> Arabic cultural heritage must be considered when trying to evaluate the impact of digital communications in the Arab world. Primary among many cultural issues is the fact that the oral tradition is the preferred mode of communication among Arabic peoples.[12]

As early as 1982, Ong coined the term "secondary orality" to describe the tendency of electronic media to echo the communication patterns of oral cultures.[13] His work seems especially prescient in light of recent ICT developments, which have enabled new forms of audiovisual communication, social networking, and non-written individual expression (e.g., video blogging, posting on YouTube, etc.). In the linguistic and cultural context of the Arab world, the notion of oral tradition reveals two important facts. First, given generally lower literacy rates, it has to be taken into account that Modern Standard Arabic (MSA) is not the primary communication mode for most of the Arab public.[14] On the contrary, non-written popular media are produced in various linguistic modes, usually combining MSA with a local variation of colloquial Arabic. Second, spoken Arabic offers greater space for structural and semantic repetition, which ensures both linguistic cohesion and rhetorical force. In the Arabic language and the Arab-Islamic

---

[10] Susanne Olsson, "Islamic Revival in Urban Egypt: The Preaching of Amr Khaled" (Paper presented at the conference Science, Technology and entrepreneurship in the Muslim World, September 5–8 2007), 8.

[11] Allievi, "Islam in the Public Space: Social Networks, Media and Neocommunities."

[12] Hussein Y. Amin and Leo A. Gher, "Digital Communications in the Arab World Entering the 21st Century," in *Civic Discourse and Digital Age Communications in the Middle East*, ed. Leo A. Gher and Hussein Y. Amin (Stamford, Conn.: Ablex Pub. Corp, 2000), 136.

[13] Walter J. Ong, *Orality and Literacy: The Technologizing of the Word* (London: New Accents Series, 1982).

[14] At the same time, the written sources studied by Western academia are almost exclusively in MSA.

cultural tradition, repetition is often used for creating rhetorical presence, which enhances the persuasive potential of the discourse.[15] As I will demonstrate below, the concept of orality is significant both to Islamic video clips and video games, and particularly to their instructive and educational content.

Theoretical and Methodological Framework

Video games as cultural artifacts and their social connotations are being studied within the framework of game studies. Unlike film or other audiovisual media, video games are interactive, which implies that any content analysis has to cover three intertwined levels: audiovisual features, narrative structure, and game play, which is the rule system governing a player's interaction with the game. On all these levels educational messages or values can be communicated to the players. As Frasca puts it:

> Video games not only represent reality, but also model it through simulations. This form of representation is based on rules that mimic the behavior of the simulated systems. However, unlike narrative authors, simulation authors do not represent a particular event, but a set of potential events. Because of this, we have to think about their objects as systems and consider what laws govern their behaviors.[16]

These rules cannot be described using classical audiovisual methods like segmentation into sequences and shot-by-shot analysis. Several methodological approaches exist for the description of non-determinist structures in game narration. For this paper's purposes I have utilized Finite State Machines and Petri Nets analysis for game description[17] and segmentation and shot-by-shot analysis for video clip description.[18]

The materials for this research were gathered during fieldwork in Syria (2005), Lebanon (2005), Egypt (2006–2008), and the UK (2007). A significant number of games and clips have been downloaded from freely accessi-

---

[15] Barbara Johnstone, *Repetition in Arabic Discourse: Paradigms, Syntagms, and the Ecology of Language* (Amsterdam: J. Benjamins Publishing, 1991).

[16] Gonzalo Frasca, "Videogames of the Oppressed: Critical Thinking, Education, Tolerance, and Other Trivial Issues," in *First Person: New Media as Story, Performance, and Game*, ed. Noah Wardrip-Fruin and Pat Harrigan (Cambridge: MA: The MIT Press, 2004), 21.

[17] Stéphane Natkin and Liliana Vega, "Petri Net Modelling for the Analysis of the Ordering of Actions in Computer Games," in *Proceedings of Game-ON* (London: Eurosis, 2003), 82–92; Cyril Brom and Adam Abonyi, "Petri-Nets for Game Plot," *Proceedings of AISB—Artificial Intelligence and Simulation Behaviour Convention 3* 3 (2006): 6–13.

[18] Francis Vanoye and Anne Goliot-Lété, *Précis d'analyse filmique* (Paris: Nathan, 2001).

ble websites, such as You Tube, Islamic Torrents, etc. The materials include more than 120 video games and video clips (mostly in Arabic and English), other para-textual materials related thereto (booklets, manuals, and websites), and interviews with designers and producers.[19]

Islamic Revival and Youth Consumer Culture

The term "Islamic revival" has been commonly used as an umbrella term, referring to various contemporary Islamic movements and their emerging presence in the public space in recent decades. Lapidus defines "Islamic revival" as both a response to the conditions of modernity—to the centralization of state power and the development of capitalist economies—and a cultural expression of modernity. The revivalist movements emphasize Islamic values and strive to cope with contemporary problems through a renewed commitment to the basic principles, though not the historical details, of Islam.[20] Mahmood recognizes three important components that make up the Islamic revival: state-oriented political groups and parties, militant Islamists, and a network of socio-religious, non-profit organizations that provide charitable services to the poor and perform the work of proselytizing. At the same time, she stresses that the term refers not only to the activities of state-oriented political groups, but also more broadly to a religious ethos or sensibility that has developed within contemporary Muslim communities. According to her, this sensibility manifests itself, among other ways, in marked displays of religious sociability, including adoption of the hijab (veil) or brisk consumption and production of religious media and literature.[21]

In this chapter, I use the term "Islamic revival" in its broader sense of Islamization of the socio-cultural landscape of media and society. This refers specifically to the growing role Islam and Islamic piety play in the public space, which is visible and audible through books, music, clothes, and new media.[22] At the same time, most media analyzed within this chapter are targeted to younger generations. Given the fact that due to recent demographic developments, some 50 percent of the total population in the Middle East is

---

[19] A comprehensive database with references to most of the material analyzed in this chapter can be found on the website Digital Islam: http://www.digitalislam.eu/.

[20] Ira M. Lapidus, "Islamic Revival and Modernity: The Contemporary Movements and the Historical Paradigms," *Journal of the Economic and Social History of the Orient* 40, no. 4 (1997): 444–460.

[21] Saba Mahmood, *Politics of Piety: The Islamic Revival and the Feminist Subject* (Princeton: Princeton University Press, 2005).

[22] Olsson, "Islamic Revival in Urban Egypt: The Preaching of Amr Khaled."

18 years of age or younger,[23] youth, as a social group, and youth consumer culture are of growing importance in the region. Similarly, young people constitute a large and creative part of the Islamic revival.[24] They consume new technologies and are innovative, when it comes to new political organizations and social movements, including social networks enabled by ICT. Media producers are well aware of this fact and therefore Islamic video games and video clips are designed with the youth consumer base in mind and tend to incorporate and reflect its tastes, fantasies, and expectations. Abaza describes similar linkages as "a happy marriage between religion and consumer culture in the making."[25] This phenomenon, which Haenni calls "market Islam,"[26] is by no means limited to the realm of new media. It is also becoming increasingly visible in other segments of popular culture as well, such as markets for toys,[27] for women's fashion,[28] for management literature, or for rap music.[29] The fact that culture and religion are increasingly becoming a market issue prevents clear distinction of the religious, educational, and economic motivations among media producers—if such a thing were ever possible. As I will demonstrate below, the Islamic educational media market is open to various subjects with significantly different backgrounds, motivations, and agendas.

Video Games, Education, and the Communication of Values

As Piaget argues, play is a crucial method through which we test ideas, develop new skills, and participate in new social roles.[30] In this respect early video games raised various expectations about their educational value. Given the fact that motivation is regarded as a key aspect of effective learning, the popularity of games among younger generations has inspired many educators. Indeed, early research on arcade-style games has demonstrated that games create intrinsic motivation through fantasy, control, challenge,

---

[23] Jørgen B. Simonsen, *Youth and Youth Culture in the Contemporary Middle East* (Aarhus: Aarhus University Press, 2005).

[24] Lila Abu-Lughod, *Remaking Women: Feminism and Modernity in the Middle East*, ed.1998 (Princeton: Princeton University Press, 1998).

[25] Mona Abaza, "Today's Consumption in Egypt," *ISIM Review* 15 (2005): 39.

[26] Patrick Haenni, *L'islam de marché. L'autre révolution conservatrice* (Paris: Seuil, 2005).

[27] See Kuppinger and Kokoschka, chapters 10 and 11 of this volume.

[28] See Firly Annisa and Gökarıksel/Secor, chapters 13 and 2 of this volume.

[29] Samy H. Alim, "A New Research Agenda: Exploring the Transglobal Hip Hop Umma," in *Muslims Networks: From Hajj to Hiphop*, ed. Miriam Cook and Bruce B. Lawrence (Chapel Hill: University of North Carolina Press, 2005), 264–174.

[30] Jean Piaget, *Play, Dreams and Imitation in Childhood* (New York: Norton, 1962).

curiosity, and competition.[31] Bogost argues that video games open a new domain for persuasion and instruction, thanks to their core representational mode, procedurality. He calls this new form "procedural rhetoric" and defines it as the art of persuasion through rule-based representations and interactions, rather than the spoken word, writing, images, or moving pictures. As Bogost explains:

> 'This type of persuasion is tied to the core affordances of the computer: computers run processes, they execute calculations and rule-based symbolic manipulations. [...] Among computer software, I want to suggest that videogames have unique persuasive power. [...] In addition to becoming instrumental tools for institutional goals, video games can also disrupt and change fundamental attitudes and beliefs about the world, leading to potentially significant long-term social change.[32]

The high popularity and consumption of games has even led some authors to suggest that children of the "video game generation" do not respond to traditional instruction, and developing educational games is thus a necessity.[33] Several Middle Eastern game designers, including Radwan Kasmiya, CEO of the Syrian company Afkar Media, have actually expressed the same concern. They have stated that young Arabs "do not read any more," so video games are needed to teach them about the history of Islamic civilization.[34]

The majority of educational games with an Islamic emphasis, produced either in the West or in the Middle East, fall into the category of so-called edutainment (i.e., educational entertainment). Most edutainment products are designed according to a behaviorist paradigm, exposing players to educational content, testing them (via quizzes and puzzles), and finally allowing them to play the game as a reward. As recent research suggests, the high expectations that early edutainment would enhance learning have not been achieved. The reasons mentioned in this regard are that such tools were poorly designed, simplistic, repetitious, and did not allow players any active exploration opportunities.[35] Nevertheless, despite their simplicity, the Is-

---

[31] Thomas W. Malone, "Toward a Theory of Intrinsically Motivating Instruction," *Cognitive Science* 4 (1982): 333–369.

[32] Ian Bogost, *Persuasive Games: The Expressive Power of Videogames* (Cambridge: MA: The MIT Press, 2007), ix.

[33] Marc Prensky, *Digital Game-Based Learning* (New York: McGraw Hill, 2001).

[34] Vítš isler, "In Videogames You Shoot Arabs or Aliens—Interview with Radwan Kasmiya," *Umělec/International* 10, no. 1 (2006): 77.

[35] S. Egenfeldt-Nielsen, "Beyond Edutainment: Exploring the Educational Potential of Computer Games" (PhD diss., University of Copenhagen, 2005).

lamic edutainment games seem to be quite successful economically, at least from their increasing presence in the market. Their marketing strategies usually target parents, offering them "safe" entertainment for their children, more or less connected with education on the basic tenets of Islam. The following advertisement by the company Islam Games represents a generic example:

> Our goal is to provide you with quality, Islamic entertainment for both you and your children. Thanks to high levels of interaction, video games are actually a great learning tool. Yet, unfortunately, many games available on the market address issues contrary to the teachings of Islam. This results in our children tending to identify with secular values and concepts more than with those of Islam. By providing an alternative to mainstream video games, we can help our children, in a subtle way, learn to identify with Islamic values, and thereby become more closely attuned to the teachings of Islam.[36]

Typical products of Islamic edutainment are CDs and DVDs, with a set of simple games, puzzles, and quizzes aimed at teaching the hadith (sayings and deeds of the prophet, Muhammad), verses of the Qur'an, prescriptions for ritual ablution and prayer, etc. Besides games, they often contain short, animated video clips with educational or moral messages, e.g., Syrian educational CD *Ta‘līm al-ṣalawāt* (Fig. 12.1). The video clips follow a typified narrative structure, usually exposing the main character to a temptation that he or she overcomes with the help of the teaching of Islam. In the end the reference to the corresponding hadith or Qur'anic verse is included. Other educational products (e.g., Egyptian *Arkān al-Islām*) simply instruct children how to behave in particular situations, like giving thanks before meals, proper Islamic greetings, etc. If a game is intended to communicate Muslim values to the player, it reflects the same patterns using basic interactive elements, like choosing the right (*ṣaḥīḥ*) scenario from among various options (e.g., the Egyptian game *Al-Muslim al-ṣaghīr*, Fig. 12.2), putting together Qur'anic verses from Arabic letters, or adventure games focused on searching for collections of hadith (e.g., the U.K. game *Abu Isas, Quest for Knowledge*, Abu Isas Games, 2006).

Close examination of the above-mentioned advertisement by the company Islam Games reveals that the text is in fact marketing two different things to parents. First, the obvious Islamic educational content, and second, the educational potential of video games per se. In most cases, how-

---

[36] http://www.islamgames.com, accessed 20 July 2005.

Figure 12.1: *Taʿlīm al-ṣalawāt*   Figure 12.2: *Al-Muslim al-ṣaghīr* (Safeer)

ever, the game and the educational content constitute two separate elements. Oftentimes, an educational video clip is followed by a classic video game without any Islamic emphasis, serving only as a possible reward and motivating factor for the children (e.g., Egyptian *al-Mughāmirūn*). Given the high popularity of video games among youth, they are often used for promotional purposes.[37] In 2007, a number of U.S. churches used the commercially successful, first-person shooter game *Halo 3* for so-called LAN parties to attract young to people to the church.[38] A similar strategy, i.e., including games on their websites, was recommended to internet evangelists.[39] Many Islamic websites dedicated to *daʿwa* (invitation to Islam) have been actually using the same concept for years—e.g., *NetMuslims.com*. In this context, the games themselves have no educational or proselytizing content—they are purely fun and a vehicle for peaking interest in the web-page content. In some cases, the economic motives behind the production of so-called "Islamic" games seem to be more relevant than the religious ones. For instance, the U.K. game *Abu Isa's A New Dawn: Learn Asma-ul-Husna* (Abu Isas Games, 2006) is a classic action game that places the player in the role of spaceship pilot and is allegedly aimed at the teaching of *al-asmāʾ al-ḥusnā* (The 99 Most Beautiful Names of God). As the package labeling says: "Battle your way through enemy planets while learning the names and

---

[37] Vít Šisler, "Videogames and Politics," in *EnterMultimediale 2: International Festival of Art and New Technologies*, ed. Denisa Kera and Pavel Sedlák (Prague: CIANT, 2005), 38–40.
[38] Matt Richtel, "Thou Shalt Not Kill, Except in a Popular Video Game at Church," *New York Times* (7 October 2007).
[39] "By offering a range of fun games to play, an evangelistic website can become more sticky—i.e. encourage return visits and enhance the perceived value of the site. In this context, the games themselves have no evangelistic content—they are purely ethical fun." http://guide.gospelcom.net/resources/games.php, accessed 21 September 2008.

attributes of your Creator." The educational aspect of the game manifests itself only via the display of a random "Name of God" on the screen every time the player scores.

Despite the fact that markets in many Middle Eastern cities seem to be flooded by such Islamic edutainment products and a substantial number of these are produced also by American and European companies, simple games and animated video clips seem to satisfy mainly younger kids (6–10 years old). For older audiences, these games pale in technological and conceptual comparison with mainstream game production. As a reviewer noted about the Islamic educational game *Maze of Destiny*, produced by Islam Games: "Not at all what we expected, far too boring for children by today's gaming standards." (Samina Saeed)[40] Similar observations have been made regarding edutainment products in general—simple educational games do not easily attract teenagers.[41]

Immersive Learning Environments: Virtual Muslim Worlds

As early as 1993, McDonnell stated that "education, including religious education, has on the whole been comfortable with the language of print and the logical, sequential mode of thinking that print favors. Now, religious education has to find ways to understand and appreciate the non-linear, associative mode of making sense of the world."[42] This observation relates noticeably to the above-mentioned Islamic edutainment products, which do not really utilize the fundamental features of video games—i.e., interactivity, immersion, and exploration. A recent trend in game-based learning is built on the concept of so-called "immersive worlds." De Freitas defines immersive worlds as given environments, which may be explored in a non-linear way by learners. They include artifacts and objects and allow users to learn by exploring the environment and its objects in a relatively open-ended way.[43]

Probably the first game with an Islamic emphasis that has to some extent utilized the concept of immersive worlds is *Quraysh*, created by the Syrian company Afkar Media in 2005 (Fig. 12.3). This real-time, strategy

---

[40] http://simplyislam.com/iteminfo.asp?item=54854, accessed 21 September 2008.

[41] Egenfeldt-Nielsen, "Beyond Edutainment: Exploring the Educational Potential of Computer Games."

[42] Jim McDonnell, "Religion, Education and Communication of Values," in *Religion and the Media: An Introductory Reader*, ed. Chris Artur (Cardiff: University of Wales Press, 1993), 98.

[43] Sara de Freitas, *Learning in Immersive Worlds: A Review of Game-Based Learning*, Joint Informational Systems Committee (JISC) 2006, http://www.jisc.ac.uk/media/documents/programmes/elearninginnovation/gamingreport_v3.pdf, accessed 21 September 2008.

252   Chapter Twelve

game takes place in pre-Islamic and early Islamic periods and deals with the origin and spread of Islam. It allows the player to control four different nations, i.e., pagan Bedouins, Muslim Arabs, Zoroastrian Persians, and Christian Romans, and presents him or her with the various perceptions of Islam that these nations possess. *Quraysh* in particular meets the abovementioned claim of Arab oral culture heritage, as every mission starts with an unusually long and well-developed introductory story narrated in classical Arabic. Through these introductions and the unfolding game narrative, the players are taught about pre-Islamic Arab culture and early Islamic history. During the particular missions, the player takes part in many real historical events (e.g., the war between the Ghassanids and the Lakhmids) and visits places like Hira, Ukaz, or Medina, whose topographies seem to be based on available historical descriptions. By situating the player inside a simulated world, the game arguably develops a deeper understanding of the broader geographical, social, and economic processes determining the historical spread of Islam. At the same time, game play communicates Islamic moral and ethical values to the player.[44] Unlike previous educational games, Afkar Media products cannot be simply lumped into the framework of the Islamic revival, since their mission is more educational and cultural in nature. Radwan Kasmyia, CEO of Afkar Media, explains that he refuses the concept of *da^cwa* in video games and perceives the games rather as a cutting-edge venue for cultural dialogue.[45]

In January 2008 the release of a new Islamic educational game was announced. The game, which was conceived in Saudi Arabia and is supposed to be developed in Europe, looks to help children learn about the Hajj pilgrimage. Players will supposedly be able to lead pilgrims through the different stages of Hajj by acting as security guards, first-aid workers, or other service providers. According to the authors, educational bodies and psychologists from Saudi Arabia will oversee the game's development. The Hajj game aims to provide a positive learning experience for children, a feature that is arguably missing in popular video games. As Amer bin Mohamed Al-Mutawa, one of the designers, says:

> Most video games available on the local market today do not contribute to increasing the skills or the intellectual capacities of consumers and do not encourage good deeds among children. Furthermore, these games rely heavily on the concept of "survival of the fittest" through theft, kidnapping, murder,

---

[44] Šisler, "Neglected Media and Their Role in Shaping Muslim Identities."
[45] Šisler, "In Videogames You Shoot Arabs or Aliens—Interview with Radwan Kasmiya."

Figure 12.3: *Quraysh*, Afkar Media, 2005

destruction, and the creation and manipulation, for example, of mafia groups in order to win the game.[46]

The Hajj game is clearly morally and religiously focused, in a way similar to the educational games mentioned above. Nevertheless, the concept of immersive 3D virtual environment, which allows players to engage directly in the organization of the Hajj, transcends the simple framework of edutainment.

The most-developed example of an Islamic learning immersive environment to date represents a re-creation of the city of Mecca and the Hajj pilgrimage in *Second Life*, a user-created virtual world originally developed by Linden Lab in 2003 (Fig. 12.4). The simulation of the Hajj and Mecca is sponsored by *Islam Online*, a popular and comprehensive Islamic website loosely associated with the Egyptian scholar Yusuf al-Qaradawi.[47] The Mecca simulation was released in December 2007, just prior to the 2007–2008 Hajj season, with the purpose of educating Muslims about how to

---

[46] http://www.asharq-e.com/news.asp?section=7&id=11393, accessed 21 September 2008.
[47] http://www.islamonline.net//english/index.shtml, accessed 21 September 2008.

participate in the Hajj and non-Muslims about the important ritual and the various steps that pilgrims take therein. In the simulation, all parts of Mecca relevant to the Hajj are recreated, together with clearly defined paths marked by large, chronologically ordered numbers placed throughout. These numbers, once "touched," activate a note card that gives the virtual pilgrims specific information about their present station, and any instructions for that station.[48] The project designers say the degree of interactivity in the 3D virtual world allows participants the ultimate step-by-step guide to the Hajj:

> The Second Life Hajj project is exceptional in that it breaks all the traditional limits of training. It allows the trainees to actually interact and be part of the program, in addition to providing them all the textual material they may need.[49]

Figure 12.4: *Second Life*, Linden Lab, 2003. Courtesy of Krystina Derrickson.

---

[48] Krystina Derrickson, "Second Life and The Sacred: Islamic Space in a Virtual World," *Digital Islam* (13 September 2008, http://www.digitalislam.eu/article.do?articleId=1877, accessed 21 September 2008).

[49] http://www.islamonline.net/servlet/Satellite?c=Article_C&pagename=Zone-English-News/NWELayout&cid=1196786035497, accessed 21 September 2008.

The game *Quraysh*, the virtual Hajj in *Second Life*, and the planned Hajj Saudi game all represent a fundamental change in the realm of Islamic educational media. Instead of exposing consumers to Islamic, "halal," or religious instructive content, which is the case with video clips and most other edutainment, these games situate the players in immersive environments and encourage them to experience various situations and processes firsthand. These games in particular meet the above-mentioned claim by Bogost on procedural rhetoric and specific persuasive potential based on core affordances of the computer. The imprint from any instruction and education in a well-designed, immersive environment is, according to Egenfeldt-Nielsen, deeper and arguably produces better learning effects than do traditional methods of instruction.[50] This applies particularly to the understanding of certain key principles of given topics, mainly when dealing with complicated and multifaceted issues that are hard to comprehend through factual knowledge only. As Gee puts it, a large body of facts that resist out-of-context memorization becomes easier to assimilate if learners are immersed in activities and experiences that use these facts for plans, goals, and purposes within a coherent knowledge domain.[51]

However, academic research findings suggest that it is extremely difficult to prove a direct causal link between the messages disseminated by the mass media and changes in people's behavior.[52] By the same token, I argue that Islamic educational games can be particularly successful in instructing children how to pray (like *Ta^{c}līm al-ṣalawāt*), developing gamers' understanding of the historical background of the spread of Islam (*Quraysh*), and explaining step-by-step Hajj rituals (Mecca simulation in *Second Life*). Yet, given the ambiguous results of research on media's influence on people's behavior in general, it seems to us that it is hard to prove how these games influence users' personalities, beliefs, and motivations. Given that communication of values arguably constitutes an important part of Islamic educational games, such questions are of significant importance and raise issues for further research. Nevertheless, the increasing production of such materials suggests that both producers and consumers (or, in the case of Islamic edutainment, the parents) consider the educational impact relevant. Be this as it may, immersive virtual worlds could possibly well indicate the future shape of what Bunt calls "cyber Islamic environments," moving

---

[50] Egenfeldt-Nielsen, "Beyond Edutainment: Exploring the Educational Potential of Computer Games."

[51] Jim P. Gee, "What Would a State of the Art Instructional Video Game Look Like?" *Innovate* 1, no. 6 (August/September 2005, http://www.innovateonline.info/index.php?view=article&id=80, accessed 6 June 2007).

[52] McDonnell, "Religion, Education and Communication of Values."

toward creatively connecting gaming technologies, social networking, and Islamic values.[53]

Video Blogging for Islam

The use of ICT for education and communication of values within the sphere of popular youth culture is not limited only to educational video games or video clips distributed on CDs, VCDs, and DVDs. Recent surveys show that young people in the Middle East increasingly utilize the internet for entertainment, research, socializing, and social networking.[54] One specific format that seems to be popular among Muslim youth is video blogging—posting short video clips created by individual users on the internet, mainly through public venues such as You Tube or on individual blogs. Many of these video blogs share the same agenda as the games discussed above—i.e., "halal" entertainment, education, and the spread of the Islamic message; for example, Ummah Films[55] or Dawah Works.[56] The latter's mission statement is again generic for a broader group of blogs:

> We at Dawah Works are not professional filmmakers, but we will attempt to bring halal entertainment and information to Muslims and non-Muslims. With the popularity of other film groups we realized that the medium of video blogs can aid us (Inshallah) in promoting Islam. We would like to interact with and initiate thought among Muslims & non-Muslims.[57]

Most of the clips posted on such video blogs feature the authors expressing their beliefs, commenting on various social topics (e.g., wearing hijab, drinking alcohol, smoking, dating) and sharing their perspectives on Islam with others. Often they post materials borrowed from satellite channels and other websites they find interesting. A symbolic example of the latter is the series *Shayṭān: Video Blog from the Devil* [in Arabic language], originally broadcast by the *Al-Resalah* channel and then posted on You Tube by a user called KnowledgeIsLight27.[58] The series soon appeared on many

---

[53] Bunt, *Islam in the Digital Age: E-jihad, Online Fatwas and Cyber Islamic Environments*.
[54] Braune, "Youth in Morocco"; Albrecht Hofheinz, "Arab Internet Use: Popular Trends and Public Impact," in *Arab Media and Political Renewal*, ed. Naomi Sakr (London: I.B. Tauris, 2007), 56–79; Abdulla, *The Internet in the Arab World: Egypt and Beyond*.
[55] http://www.ummahfilms.com/home.html, accessed 21 September 2008.
[56] http://dawahworks.com/, accessed 21 September 2008.
[57] http://dawahworks.com/, accessed 21 September 2008.
[58] http://www.youtube.com/watch?v=QUS0ZeGRkEY, accessed 21 September 2008.

other sites and provoked heavy comment and discussion by other users. Table 12.1 shows a transcript of the popular Hijab episode:

Table 12.1: Transcript of *Shayṭān*: Video Blog from the Devil—Hijab episode

Bedroom. Probably evening. A dim lamp is switched on. A girl in a modest plain abaya is adjusting her hijab in front of a mirror.	
Suddenly she hears the voice of the devil.	Devil (in colloquial Arabic): "Are you going out like that?"
The devil (dressed as a young man in black) appears in the mirror.	"What would people say?"
They both closely inspect the girl's face in the mirror.	"Your face looks so pale…"
The girl starts to seem uneasy. She touches her face.	"… and your eyes are swollen as if you have just got out of bed."
	"No, no…"
Close up of girl's face. She examines herself with growing disaffection.	"You must at least wear some makeup! Just a little, no one will notice."
The devil teases her.	"Are you going to a funeral?"
He walks around her in pretentious dismay.	"Oh my God, what are you wearing?! It makes you look like a black bag."
The devil stands behind the girl and looks directly into her eyes in the mirror.	(in a serious voice) "Do you want your friends to make fun of you? What do you want them to say about you?"
	(in an ironic voice) "You couldn't find anything to wear except to wear your mom's abaya?! You must pick a cool abaya that suits you!"
The girl slowly unties her hijab… The devil has a satisfied look on his face.	"Who told you that you must cover all your hair? Loosen it a bit!"
Cut. The devil hides himself in a wardrobe and closes the door behind him. On the other side of the door is a mirror.	"The guys won't bite you!"

We can see the girl in this mirror. She has makeup on, her loose hijab revealing her hair and decorated abaya.	"Now you look so cool and beautiful and your hijab is just the same..."
Phone rings. The girl answers. Camera slowly moves around her body. Fade out.	Girl: "Yalla, yalla, I'm coming." (We can hear the devil breathing.)
Cut. The head of another devil appears surrounded by darkness.	Second devil: "Hijab you say, huh?"
A Qurʾanic [Q 24:31] verse appears on the screen.	Narrator (in MSA): "And say to the believing women that they should lower their gaze and guard their modesty: that they should not display their beauty and ornaments except what (must ordinarily) appear there of."

The narrative structure of the *Shayṭān* video clips follows the same pattern as the above-mentioned animated videos for children, although its target audience is considerably older. The actors in the clips face temptations, which they can resist with the help of the teachings of Islam, or alternatively they give in to them. Sometimes viewers see both options and their subsequent results. In the end, there is always a reference to the particular rule of law, i.e., Qurʾan or hadith. The important and novel aspect of video blogging is that it effectively creates a space for discussion, exchange of opinions, and self-expression, as is demonstrated in many commentaries posted under the video, e.g.:

wow! someone actually feels the same as i do?! amazing, ALLAH HAFIZ to all muslimahs! (cabwhisperer)[59]

"Thank you KnowledgeIsLight27. I love your creativity you show thru your videos. Very interesting. I wasnt a religious person (altho i never smoke, never drink, never clubbing & partying, etc) but i was very lazy when it came to Solat. Sometimes i did, sometimes not. Thanks to YouTube, i regained Hidayah from Allah. Praise to Allah the Most Merciful. He still loved me, and He wanted me to change, to be a better person. I love you, ya Allah! Give me more of your Hidayah and Light!" (ladynox200)[60]

---

[59] Ibid.
[60] http://www.youtube.com/watch?v=bto0xikkcW4&feature=related, accessed 21 September 2008.

Given the global character of the internet, video blogging in fact effectively creates a specific manifestation of what Eickelman and Anderson call the Muslim "transnational public sphere."[61] The audio-visual character of the medium, as well as the chat-like nature of the subsequent commentaries both exemplify Ong's concept of second orality, with its participatory, interactive, and communal aspects. At the same time, the non-hierarchical and do-it-yourself character of the blogging culture appeals to youth and provides them a space for construction and representation of their individual identities. The combination of entertainment, youth consumer culture, and Islamic piety echoes the above-mentioned examples of video games. By utilizing various mainstream media, the video and game producers, in fact, transcend confinement to Islamic movements and generally promote a more religious, rather than cultural, concept of Muslim identity. As I will demonstrate, this concept has started to be slowly, albeit increasingly, accepted by the mainstream media.

Targeting New Audiences: Religious Sensitivity in Mainstream Game Production

Generally speaking, until recently the global video game industry seemed to show little, if any, cultural and religious sensitivity toward Muslim (and Middle Eastern) audiences. The vast majority of Western games featuring Arabs and Muslims (or taking place in Middle Eastern settings) represent them in either an Orientalist manner or within a conflict framework, exploiting concepts that stereotype religious fundamentalism and/or terrorism. Racial stereotypes regarding Arabs and Muslims seem to be more overt and explicit in video games (more so than in any other media), particularly because of the lack of media critique and academic coverage.[62] However, with the rising self-awareness of Muslim audiences and the emerging Middle Eastern game industry, this paradigm is about to change. This also draws attention to the economic reasons for the time-dominant modes of representation used thus far. As Western game companies start entering Middle Eastern markets, they have to increasingly target Muslim audiences and pay attention to their religious beliefs and concerns.

The game *Hitman 2: Silent Assassin,* produced by IO Interactive in 2002, most likely sets a precedent for game designers' awareness of religious sensitivity. The player in this first-person shooter represents a high-target hitman, working for an international contractor, whose task is to assassinate

---

[61] Eickelman and Anderson, *New Media in the Muslim World.*
[62] Šisler, "Digital Arabs: Representation in Video Games"; Reichmuth and Werning, "Pixel Pashas, Digital Djinns."

a leader of a global terrorist sect. However, the visual signifiers depicting the members of this terrorist group resemble those of Sikhism. One of the missions takes place in a shrine, which corresponds architecturally with the Harimandir Sahib (Golden Temple), the spiritual and cultural center of the Sikh religion, located in the city of Amritsar in Punjab, India. After a massive campaign, led predominantly by Sikh minorities living in Europe and the United States, the developer of the game, Eidos Company, promised to remove all offensive elements from any future releases of this game. At the same time, Eidos stated that it had learned from the debacle, and would "observe and respect cultural, religious and ethical sensitivities in its future products."[63]

A similar religious and cultural sensitivity is increasingly becoming part of contemporary popular media productions, whose target audiences could possibly include Muslims. In 2007 Ubisoft released a game called *Assassin's Creed* (figure 12.5), which deals with the Nizari branch of the Isma𝑐iliyya, commonly called *Ḥashīshiyya* or Assassins, and is situated in the Holy Land during the Third Crusade (approximately 1191 C.E.). The player assumes the role of Altair, an elite assassin, whose task is to eliminate nine Crusader and Saracen leaders. The authors' intention to avoid possible controversies arising from the game's religious and political connotations is clear from the beginning. The game itself starts with a disclaimer: "This work of fiction was designed, developed, and produced by a multicultural team of various faiths and beliefs." The following narrative states that Altair comes from a mixed Christian-Muslim background, leaving his personal religious convictions open. His violent mission is defined by the somehow broad, ethical context of stopping the atrocities committed by both sides in the conflict. As Corey May, the game scriptwriter, sums it up:

> As the Saracens and Crusaders battle one another for control, the assassins are working to find a way to end the hostilities. They see the war as pointless. [...] The assassins are not allied with either side of the conflict, nor are they driven by a desire for profit or power. They are also not interested in furthering a religious agenda. In fact, they are generally opposed to most

---

[63] http://www.theregister.co.uk/2002/11/13/eidos_settles_hitman_sikh_dispute, accessed 21 September 2008. A similar concept of religious and cultural sensitivity can also increasingly be observed in relation to Islam. Recently, the Council on American-Islamic Relations (CAIR) announced that the phrase "Allahu Akbar" will be removed from the upcoming game *Zack & Wiki* developed by Capcom. This is because the Council had found the in-game context of the phrase offensive. http://www.gamedaily.com/articles/news/islamic-phrase-removed-from-capcoms-zack-and-wiki/17735/?biz=1, accessed 21 September 2008.

forms of organized religion. [...] The assassins are fighting to end the Third Crusade.[64]

This discrepancy between the game narrative and the real, historical background of the *Ḥashīshiyya* could actually serve a marketing purpose. Depicting the assassins as being outside both the religious and conflict frameworks gives consumers the opportunity to identify themselves with the hero, regardless of their geographical or religious origin. Positive reception of the game by Muslim players on the internet in fact proves the correctness of this strategy, e.g.:

> I love [this game]. It makes Muslims look really cool. (Simba, Sunni Muslim)[65]

> "Did anyone know that Altair from Assassin's Creed is a Muslim? Wow, I am a Muslim. I can finally relate my self to videogames." (furqan2006)[66]

Paradoxically, another marketing strategy capitalizes on the game's alleged accuracy in terms of architecture and depiction of daily life in the medieval cities of Damascus, Jerusalem, and Acre. In a promotional video, producer Jade Raymond says: "We have recreated these Middle Eastern cities exactly as they were in 1191 A.D. We have worked with historians in order to find all existing documents and materials."[67] Given the fact that most games until now have constructed the Middle East mostly in quasi-historical or fantasy manner,[68] the proclaimed authenticity of *Assassin's Creed* could be of relevance to the Muslim public—e.g.:

> It is the only game my parents pay attention to when I'm playing, as they always want to see the mosque and Jerusalem and other Muslim icons like Prophet Solomon's grave. (joshF2295)[69]

Important factors that have an impact on the growing interest of video game producers in the Middle Eastern markets are, first, slowly improving

---

[64] http://www.1up.com/do/previewPage?cId=3154208, accessed 21 September 2008.
[65] http://muslimonline.org/forum/index.php?s=b323a113b26682f37683f45ea382cc78&showtopic=3833&pid=49872&st=0&#entry49872, accessed 21 September 2008.
[66] http://www.gamespot.com/pages/forums/show_msgs.php?topic_id=26053507, accessed 21 September 2008.
[67] http://assassinscreed.uk.ubi.com/home.php#/devdiary/, accessed 21 September 2008.
[68] Šisler, "Digital Arabs: Representation in Video Games."
[69] http://www.gamespot.com/pages/forums/show_msgs.php?topic_id=26053507, accessed 21 September 2008.

262   Chapter Twelve

Figure 12.5: *Quraysh*, Afkar Media, 2005

copyright law enforcement in the Middle East, and, second, the growing economic relevance of the Middle Eastern consumer culture, especially as it relates to youth. As Jens Hilgers, CEO of Turtle Entertainment, says: "The business potential of electronic gaming is enormous, and the market in the Middle East is proving incredibly receptive to new games."[70]

Unlike the above-discussed case of *Assassin's Creed*, in which the sensitivity toward religion shown in the design of its game play and narrative constitutes rather a pragmatic step aimed at easing acceptance of the product by global Muslim audiences, some video games are exclusively designed for Middle Eastern markets. This is the case with *Arabian Lords* (*Sādat alṣaḥrāʾ*), a real-time strategy game developed in 2007 as part of a cooperative effort between the U.S. company BreakAway Games and the Jordanian studio Quirkat (figure 12.6.). According to the authors' statement, their goal was to create a fun, exciting strategy game that would appeal to Middle Eastern gamers:

---

[70] Fakhruddin, "Dubai World Trade Centre Launches Gitex Digital Game World."

With this product historical accuracy and cultural relevance became important guiding factors. We knew that, on a cultural level, religion played a major role during the time span covered in the game, and that it still does today. We wanted to make sure to include this in a way that would honor its significance, while being sensitive to all religious and cultural concerns.[71]

Figure 12.6: *Arabian Lords*, BreakAway Games, 2007

The *Arabian Lords* game enables the player to assume the role of a medieval Muslim merchant, and its game play involves building cities, municipal politics, diplomacy, espionage, etc. It includes many distinguishing features of early Islamic civilization, such as poetry contests, camel markets, etc. Nevertheless, regarding all levels of the game—including narrative, game play, and visual signifiers—designers have paid attention to the delicate subject of representing Islam, e.g., in the role of imam in the game. *Arabian Lords* is available in both English and Arabic, and, according to the producers, the game "was an instant success in the Arab world."[72] As a result, Quirkat and BreakAway Games are preparing a new project based

---
[71] http://www.arabianlords.com/Public/public_master.aspx?Site_Id=2&Page_Id=424&Path=66, accessed 21 September 2008.
[72] http://www.breakawaygames.com/entertainment/feature/, accessed 21 September 2008.

on Arab mythology, which is again designed primarily for Arab markets—a trading-card game called *Mythic Palace* (*Qaṣr al-asāṭīr*).[73]

With the growing importance of the Middle Eastern marketplace, we can expect more culturally and religiously "localized" projects to follow. Therefore, based on the concerns of global media producers, the emerging Muslim consumer culture is shaping global patterns of production and consumption. Moreover, the present public discourse of Islamic revival and the piety movement, both audible and visible in various Islamic media production, reconfigures the generally accepted concept of Muslim identity itself.

Conclusions

This chapter has analyzed how Islam is articulated and how Islamic values are communicated to consumers in two emerging forms of non-written digital media—video games and video clips. The analysis has covered a broad range of examples, originating from both Muslim majority and Muslim minority settings in the Middle East, Europe, and the United States respectively.

The underlying logic behind all the examples analyzed emphasizes private Islamic piety and individual self-determination. The consumer is usually addressed as an individual who has the chance to change his life, repent, and strive to be a better Muslim. The trope is centered on topics of personal piety—e.g., wearing the hijab, respecting one's parents, praying, doing good deeds, etc. In this sense, most of the video clips and games are engaging and educational. However, we can hardly find any "call for action" in the sense of direct social or political involvement. This represents a substantial difference from games with an agenda produced in the West, which are often used for straightforward social or political activism. Exceptions are the already-mentioned games and clips with an Islamist agenda, ranging from Jihadi videos posted on You Tube to the virtual re-creation of battles by the Lebanese Hezbollah movement, whose aims are promotional and propagandistic.[74]

Conversely, most of the Islamic clips and games actually strive to promote "positive" or "family" values, deliberately distinguishing themselves from mainstream game production, which is labeled as "morally corrupt," "violent," or simply "not promoting the good values." As such, these products are marketed to a broader audience, which does not necessarily have

---

[73] http://www.mythicpalacegame.com/, accessed 21 September 2008.
[74] Šisler, "Neglected Media and Their Role in Shaping Muslim Identities"; Šisler, "Digital Arabs: Representation in Video Games."

to be Muslim. For example, the animated characters of the Egyptian educational series *Al-Muttaḥidūn* (New Way Group) are advertised as "the good heroes, who at all times strive for justice and promote good and kindness." The key underlying message for parents is that the product is safe to buy. This strategy resembles the advertising campaigns of the so-called "Barbie non-Barbie dolls," Razanne and Fulla, which are reportedly also being bought by Christian families who are dissatisfied with the explicit sexuality of Barbie.[75]

Another important aspect is that most of the Islamic video games and clips are produced by private companies or individuals. This needs to be considered, within the broader framework of the above-mentioned Islamic revival or piety movement, as an ongoing privatization of Islamic knowledge production. As Patrick Haenni points out in his interview with Ursula Lindsey:

> When we speak of Islamic revival, we always focus on politically-organized groups intent on gaining power. But "private religious entrepreneurs" are just as important a phenomenon. These entrepreneurs target the upper middle class, and focus on personal enlightenment rather than political engagement. They're socially conservative and opposed to what they see as the decadence of much of Western culture. But they want to benefit from Western science, education, and progress, and they condemn violence and extremism. [...] They fully use all the means of mass culture, [like] chats on the Net, chat shows on TV, Islamic rap in the West.[76]

The cultural appropriation of originally "foreign" media—as is the case with video games or video blogs—together with the new persuasive strategies these media possess, like the immersion of players in virtual environments or the viral dissemination of clips through the blogosphere, constitutes a fundamental change in the communication of religious values. The new strategy capitalizes on the consumers' self-action and engagement, as well as on the appeal these new media have for the younger generation. At the same time, this appropriation of Western media has occurred mainly on a symbolic level; whereas, on a structural level, the product remains mostly unchanged. For example, in most cases, Islamic video games adopt the patterns, i.e. game play and narrative structure, of Western established genres, like edutainment, real-time strategy games, or first-person shooters. A

---

[75] See Kuppinger, chapter 10 of this volume.
[76] Ursula Lindsey, "The New Muslim TV: Media-Savvy, Modern, and Moderate," *Christian Science Monitor* (May 2006, http://www.csmonitor.com/2006/0502/p01s04\bibrangedashwome.html, accessed 21 September 2008).

similar phenomenon is actually the case with the well-known example of "Islamic soft drinks," such as Mecca Cola or Cola Turka:[77] both capitalize on the Coca-Cola concept.

Last but not least, the increasing manifestation of Islamic values in the public sphere influences mainstream media production aimed at Muslim audiences or Middle Eastern markets. This is an important phenomenon, particularly in the realm of video games, where religious and cultural sensitivity has until recently been a non-existent concept.

Bibliography

Abaza, Mona. "Today's Consumption in Egypt." *ISIM Review* 15 (2005): 38–39.
Abdulla, Rasha A. *The Internet in the Arab World: Egypt and Beyond.* New York: Peter Lang Publishing, 2007.
Abu-Lughod, Lila. *Remaking Women: Feminism and Modernity in the Middle East.* Ed.1998. Princeton: Princeton University Press, 1998.
Alim, Samy H. "A New Research Agenda: Exploring the Transglobal Hip Hop Umma." In *Muslims Networks: From Hajj to Hiphop*, edited by Miriam Cook and Bruce B. Lawrence, 264–174. Chapel Hill: University of North Carolina Press, 2005.
Allievi, Stefano. "Islam in the Public Space: Social Networks, Media and Neocommunities." In *Muslim Networks and Transnational Communities in and across Europe*, edited by Stefano Allievi and Jørgen Nielsen, 1–27. Leiden: Brill, 2003.
Amin, Hussein Y., and Leo A. Gher. "Digital Communications in the Arab World Entering the 21st Century." In *Civic Discourse and Digital Age Communications in the Middle East*, edited by Leo A. Gher and Hussein Y. Amin, 109–140. Stamford, Conn.: Ablex Pub. Corp, 2000.
Anderson, Jon W. "Globalizing Politics and Religion in the Muslim World." *Journal of Electronic Publishing* 3, no. 1 (1997).
Bogost, Ian. *Persuasive Games: The Expressive Power of Videogames.* Cambridge: MA: The MIT Press, 2007.
Braune, Ines. "Youth in Morocco." In *Youth and Youth Culture in the Contemporary Middle East*, edited by Jørgen B. Simonsen, 128–139. Aarhus: Aarhus University Press, 2005.
Brom, Cyril, and Adam Abonyi. "Petri-Nets for Game Plot." *Proceedings of AISB—Artificial Intelligence and Simulation Behaviour Convention 3* 3 (2006): 6–13.

---

[77] Cf. Mutlu, chapter 6 of this volume.

Brückner, Matthias. "Der Mufti im Netz." In *Islam im Internet, Neue Formen der Religion im Cyberspace*, edited by Rüdiger Lohlker. Hamburg: Deutsches Orient-Institut, 2001.

Bunt, Gary R. *iMuslims: Rewiring the House of Islam*. Chapel Hill: University of North Carolina Press, 2009.

———. *Islam in the Digital Age: E-jihad, Online Fatwas and Cyber Islamic Environments*. London: Pluto Press, 2003.

———. *Virtually Islamic*. Cardiff: University of Wales Press, 2000.

Derrickson, Krystina. "Second Life and The Sacred: Islamic Space in a Virtual World." *Digital Islam* (13 September 2008, http://www.digitalislam.eu/article.do?articleId=1877, accessed 21 September 2008).

Egenfeldt-Nielsen, S. "Beyond Edutainment: Exploring the Educational Potential of Computer Games." PhD diss., University of Copenhagen, 2005.

Eickelman, Dale F., and Jon W. Anderson. *New Media in the Muslim World*. Bloomington: Indiana University Press, 2003.

Fakhruddin, Mufaddal. "Dubai World Trade Centre Launches Gitex Digital Game World." *Middle East Gamers* (20 May 2008, http://www.megamers.com/pc/news.php?game_category=2&article_id=2825, accessed 9 October 2008).

Frasca, Gonzalo. "Videogames of the Oppressed: Critical Thinking, Education, Tolerance, and Other Trivial Issues." In *First Person: New Media as Story, Performance, and Game*, edited by Noah Wardrip-Fruin and Pat Harrigan, 85–94. Cambridge: MA: The MIT Press, 2004.

Freitas, Sara de. *Learning in Immersive Worlds: A Review of Game-Based Learning*. Joint Informational Systems Committee (JISC) 2006, http://www.jisc.ac.uk/media/documents/programmes/elearninginnovation/gamingreport_v3.pdf, accessed 21 September 2008.

Gee, Jim P. "What Would a State of the Art Instructional Video Game Look Like?" *Innovate* 1, no. 6 (August/September 2005, http://www.innovateonline.info/index.php?view=article&id=80, accessed 6 June 2007).

Haenni, Patrick. *L'islam de marché. L'autre révolution conservatrice*. Paris: Seuil, 2005.

Hofheinz, Albrecht. "Arab Internet Use: Popular Trends and Public Impact." In *Arab Media and Political Renewal*, edited by Naomi Sakr, 56–79. London: I.B. Tauris, 2007.

Johnstone, Barbara. *Repetition in Arabic Discourse: Paradigms, Syntagms, and the Ecology of Language*. Amsterdam: J. Benjamins Publishing, 1991.

Lapidus, Ira M. "Islamic Revival and Modernity: The Contemporary Movements and the Historical Paradigms." *Journal of the Economic and Social History of the Orient* 40, no. 4 (1997): 444–460.

Lindsey, Ursula. "The New Muslim TV: Media-Savvy, Modern, and Moderate." *Christian Science Monitor* (May 2006, http://www.csmonitor.com / 2006 / 0502 / p01s04 \ bibrangedashwome . html, accessed 21 September 2008).

Mahmood, Saba. *Politics of Piety: The Islamic Revival and the Feminist Subject*. Princeton: Princeton University Press, 2005.

Malone, Thomas W. "Toward a Theory of Intrinsically Motivating Instruction." *Cognitive Science* 4 (1982): 333–369.

McDonnell, Jim. "Religion, Education and Communication of Values." In *Religion and the Media: An Introductory Reader*, edited by Chris Artur, 89–100. Cardiff: University of Wales Press, 1993.

Natkin, Stéphane, and Liliana Vega. "Petri Net Modelling for the Analysis of the Ordering of Actions in Computer Games." In *Proceedings of Game-ON*, 82–92. London: Eurosis, 2003.

Olsson, Susanne. "Islamic Revival in Urban Egypt: The Preaching of Amr Khaled." Paper presented at the conference Science, Technology and entrepreneurship in the Muslim World, September 5–8 2007.

Ong, Walter J. *Orality and Literacy: The Technologizing of the Word*. London: New Accents Series, 1982.

Piaget, Jean. *Play, Dreams and Imitation in Childhood*. New York: Norton, 1962.

Prensky, Marc. *Digital Game-Based Learning*. New York: McGraw Hill, 2001.

Reichmuth, Philipp, and Stefan Werning. "Pixel Pashas, Digital Djinns." *ISIM Review*, no. 18 (2006): 46–47.

Richtel, Matt. "Thou Shalt Not Kill, Except in a Popular Video Game at Church." *New York Times* (7 October 2007).

Simonsen, Jørgen B. *Youth and Youth Culture in the Contemporary Middle East*. Aarhus: Aarhus University Press, 2005.

Vanoye, Francis, and Anne Goliot-Lété. *Précis d'analyse filmique*. Paris: Nathan, 2001.

Šisler, Vít. "Digital Arabs: Representation in Video Games." *European Journal of Cultural Studies* 11, no. 2 (2008): 203–220.

———. "In Videogames You Shoot Arabs or Aliens—Interview with Radwan Kasmiya." *Umělec/International* 10, no. 1 (2006): 77–81.

———. "Neglected Media and Their Role in Shaping Muslim Identities." Paper presented at the conference Science, Technology and En-

trepreneurship in the Muslim World, 5–8 September 2007, in Lund, Sweden.
———. "Videogames and Politics." In *EnterMultimediale 2: International Festival of Art and New Technologies*, edited by Denisa Kera and Pavel Sedlák, 38–40. Prague: CIANT, 2005.

CHAPTER THIRTEEN

REPRESENTATION OF FASHION AS MUSLIMA IDENTITY IN *Paras* MAGAZINE

FIRLY ANNISA

Introduction

In 2001, the Indonesian government relaxed constraints on all forms of media, thereby effecting a great improvement in the publishing industry. A large variety of magazines resulted from this greater freedom to produce and publish. Based on reader segmentation according to age, sex, and economic status, publishers created a wide variety of products to suit the market. Women were a preferred target group of these marketing strategies—a fact that arguably contributed to their exploitation by a male-dominated society, for an analysis of the content of women magazines shows that they are dominated by fashion, recipes, and tips for couples to improve their love lives.

The most popular magazines focus on lifestyle issues, e.g., how to look more beautiful, be sexy, be successful in a career, become a better cook, and how couples can enjoy greater pleasures. Fashion and beauty products figure prominently in the magazines, which attract an increasing audience among women. Thus, the magazines suggest that buying the right products can improve their readers' personal life and social status.

Croteau and Hoynes argue as follows:

> The women's magazine is one medium that is particularly advertising-oriented and consistently promotes the ideology of consumerism. [...] More generally, the magazines promote the consumer lifestyle by showing how beauty, sexuality, career success, culinary skill and social status can be *bought* in the

consumer marketplace. [...] Women's magazines, in addressing a specific social group, identify women as a consumer category with special product needs.[1]

Market segmentation, as it was constructed by publishers, was, at first, mainly based on sex, income and age; later, however, a religious dimension was added. It is an interesting phenomenon in the Indonesian women's magazine industry that there are now women's magazines that claim to be Islamic. *Anggun* and *Paras* magazines especially feature articles that discuss things to do with Muslim marriage and Muslima lifestyle. Thus, *Paras* magazine is capable of "selling" the Islamic religion and attracting a large number of consumers.

The fact that Indonesia has the largest Muslim population in the world makes the increasing Muslim self-awareness a golden opportunity for marketing. Even the premier issue of a magazine that labels itself "Islamic" in title or content tends to be very successful. From its market launch in 2003, the publishers of *Paras* magazine had a clear vision of its potential readers. This is evident from the fact that every single edition of the magazine specifically addresses Muslim women. It presents what is fashionable and trendy to a Muslima and promotes the idea that using halal cosmetics and wearing a veil are not a barrier to looking beautiful in any situation, making such new ideas acceptable to Indonesian society.

If we analyze the content of the articles in *Paras* magazine, we find that almost all the articles present fashion, mostly in a rather loose and vague connection with Islamic values. Discussions about fashion, tips on wearing a trendy veil, mixing and matching clothes for the office and workplace, and how to look attractive at a party are all part of the magazine. Of course, the fashion items it promotes are accompanied by advertisements with the magic words "Must Buy!" Behind all such articles are messages from the sponsors, such as, "Use Wardah cosmetics that are guaranteed halal."[2] Another example is the article "Beauty Consultation," which discusses cosmetics that are labeled halal and Islamic.[3] The article gives Muslimas advice on how to handle aging, pockmarks on the face, getting rid of acne, and avoiding skin blemishes caused by wearing the veil. It features a famous Indonesian artist who wears the veil while acting as a beauty consultant and brand ambassador.

---

[1] David R. Croteau and William H. Hoynes, *Media/Society: Industries, Images, and Audiences*, 2nd ed. (California: Pine Forge Press, 2000), 185.
[2] See Wardah advertisment in *Paras*, 5, no. 56 (May 2008).
[3] *Paras*, 5, no. 49 (October 2007), 136.

The Muslima identity presented on the pages of *Paras* magazine—which labels itself "the Foremost Muslima's Magazine"— is striking. The typical Muslima is consistently portrayed as slim, modern, and fashionable, which is no different from the identity construction shown in any other women's magazine that is not specifically aimed at the Muslim women market.

Semiotics—Understanding the Meaning

Budiman defined semiotics as "the term given to a method of communication in which signs and symbols are used as coded system to present messages (codes and messages), without ignoring the context and the audience."[4] This paper uses semiotics as a method of interpreting the hidden meaning behind the text in the magazine.

Sobur wrote that "semiotics analyzes text in terms of signs codified in a system. Therefore, semiotics can be used to analyze all varieties and genre of text, including news, film, advertising, fashion, fiction, poetry, and drama."[5] The signs used in such a unitary system are able to indicate how people organize their lives because signs relate very closely to people's lives. To observe and understand the sign system Budiman found, Saussure put it in a human communications context, suggesting two classifications: the signifier and the signified. *Signifiers* refer to the material aspects which can potentially be subjected to censorship, while *signified* refers to the mental aspects.[6]

Representation of Muslimas in the Magazine

The media's representation of women is based on stereotypes. For example, there is an article in *Paras* magazine[7] entitled "Intimacy." It discusses the importance of maintaining the intimacy of the husband-wife relationship. In that article it appears that women bear the sole responsibility for ensuring intimacy within their marriage. It is the woman's role to make her husband happy. The article deliberately fits women into the stereotypes that are created by Indonesian capitalist mass media. I argue that there is no difference at all between the function of women in the Islamic magazine and in non-Islamic magazines.

---

[4] Kris Budiman, *Semiotika Visual* (Yogyakarta: Yayasan Cemeti, 2003), 12.
[5] Alex Sobur, *Analisis Teks Media, Suatu Pengantar untuk Analisis Wacana Analisis Semiotik dan Analisis Framing*. (Bandung: Remaja Rosda Karya, 2001), 123.
[6] Ibid., 123.
[7] *Paras*, 5, no. 50 (November 2007), 34.

In a patriarchal system women are automatically assigned a specific role and identity that are not to their advantage. In this context, textual analysis of media such as films and advertisements can reveal the media's ideology and the real intention behind what is presented by those who produce the media. As stated by Strinati:

> The capacity of the mass media to reflect the reality of women's lives in patriarchal, capitalist societies is something which is important to the liberal feminist viewpoint, and can clearly be examined by a content analysis methodology. Content analysis can be used to show how cultural representation of women, say in advertising, distorts the reality of women's lives, portraying a fantasy world rather than one women actually live in. But as we have already indicated, feminists have questioned this view by asking who is to define the objective reality the media have to represent? They have pointed out that some cultural stereotypes may have their social equivalents or at least elements of them in the "real" world (some advertisers, for example, aim their products at women because they are the main consumers of certain products), and have criticised the contention that cultural representations must either be real or unreal (the representations of women in soap operas, for example, might be difficult to understand if they are thought to be purely fictitious).[8]

Thus, it is evident that when the media create a construct of women's lives, this construct may be quite different from reality. There might be not only exaggerations, but even complete fabrications that contradict reality. What is published depends on its potential for maximizing the media companies' profits.

A "construct" is the making of a representation, an image of things or characters as the media choose to depict them. The women shown in *Paras* magazine are closer to such a construct or representation than they are to real women. They are inevitably active and dynamic. This is shown in a special edition of *Paras* magazine,[9] where *Paras* presents women dressed for a career in the public arena. The pictures bear titles such as: "Fashionable in the Office," "Sophisticated Glam," and "Dynamic Personality." *Paras* magazine has a powerful motivation to describe its readers as women who are fashionable in public life and working in an office.

---

[8] Dominic Strinati, *An Introduction to Theories of Popular Culture* (London: Routledge, 1995), 196.
[9] *Paras*, Special edition: "Special Collection of Dressing for Work; Simplicity Parade, Collection 2," 2008.

In Pilliang's terminology, the global system of capitalism exposes sexuality and passion as a commodity that could be called *Passionate Capitalism*.[10] Women use their bodies and appear in a variety of Muslim commodities, such as dress, veil, and other items that are identified with Islam, and these are communicated and sold by being representative signs in women's magazines. In other words, women are the tools that capitalistic agencies, such as the media, producers, and advertisers, use to sell their products. Historically, the depiction of women's bodies in the media has created an entrapment for women.

This is so in *Paras* magazine, where the bodies of the women used as models, though wearing Muslim clothing, still appear exhibitionist. Never are the women on the *Paras* magazine cover large or overweight. The woman model on the cover of *Paras* magazine's October 2007 edition[11] acts as a *signifier* that appeals to women, and is signified by the model wearing Muslima clothing with a colorful veil in the media. The focus is on the model's beautiful face, her veil, and her fashionable Muslima clothes. *Paras* presents itself as the fashion trendsetter for Muslimas.

The magazine never fails to depict a beautiful woman's figure in a pose that suggests a sexy, sensual, beautiful body. Female sexuality is very rich in signs representing a sexual image intended to raise the passions of the target audience. Originally, the religious function of the veil as a piece of finery worn by women is to cover the *aurat* (hair and neck). Producers have capitalized on this religious obligation. However, its social function in the media is to portray a woman as belonging to a specific social class. The veil can be *signified* and *signifier* at the same time. Fashion produces a representation system that has a *signifier* effect on the consumer society, a fashion signifier of the post-modern era.

While identity or self-actualization processes in modern society were commonly driven by processes of production (working, making something, creating something), in post-modern society, it is the practice of consumption (buying something, using something, wearing something) that plays the most prominent role in processes of identity making and self-actualization, creating the image of "Who I Am" and what it is to be "She." An advertisement in *Paras* shows the "Novie Collection" of veils, bearing the tagline "Veils for Modern Women," as representative of the modern woman's identity that can be materialized in a totem. Modern women will identify with the product used in the advertisement. At this point the marketing technique is masked in religion, and thus has an extraordinary influence.

---

[10] Yasraf A. Libidonomics Pilliang, *"Ekonomi Pasar Bebas Libido" dalam Sebuah Dunia Yang Dilipat* (Bandung: Pustaka Mizan, 1999).

[11] *Paras*, 5, no. 49 (October 2007).

Tips on tying the veil in order to be a fashionable Muslima are also presented in *Paras*. The media have thus created what could be referred to as an identity that can be modified according to the user's preferences. As a part of modernity, the power of religion has become something that can be constructed as well as deconstructed—i.e., women can mix and match clothes based on personal preference.

Images that continue to emerge in the media suggest that religion can be created and reproduced based solely on the motivation of market capitalism. With the addition of flowers and jewellery, the veil can be a colorful cover for the hair according to the wearer's choice. "Religion"— i.e., the veil as a marker of religious identity—has become a set of commodities ready to choose or to buy. It has become flexible based on preferences that can be created, remade, or even bought and sold, and the media have become its Scripture.

Ideal Muslima vs. Consumerism

In a voyeuristic society, women have a dominant function as image makers and as signifiers of a variety of commodities. But the images and signs that present a woman's body are used to sell a commodity, or in other words, the body itself has become the commodity. This function has been deliberately created by producers with the sole aim of making a financial profit. It has caused the shaping of images and signs in the media that make the audience look at a woman's body in terms of monetary value. The original biological function of the body has been transformed into economic and political function. This explains the fact that, even though *Paras* magazine labels itself *Islamic*, it always displays slim and tall women's bodies to advertise its products. Commodities such as clothes, handbags, and cosmetics are shown in *Paras* to promote Muslima fashions; the women's bodies as well as the products are for sale. The images of Muslimas that are displayed in the magazine are consistently of good quality, exclusive and expensive, based on the financial capacity of the upper middle class Muslim consumer society. It is a form of *Islamic capitalism* that uses women as sales objects as well as consumer targets.

Articles that feature designer names, shop addresses, and the prices of products are aimed at women readers who are considered to be a soft target for consumerism. Furthermore, women's magazines today act like shop display windows that feature products ready for consumers who can afford to buy, but those who cannot are satisfied just to view them: It is as if they were just window-shopping.

As stated previously, media content can be a "constructed reality," created by the media to produce a financial profit. In Islamic magazines it is highly likely that this *constructed* reality is much different from the *actual* reality. Supposedly Islamic values and ideology are, in reality, constructed by the media, built into their magazines, and given a religious label—and laden with sponsors' messages in the background. Members of the Muslima target group of *Paras* magazine are more inclined to focus on fashions and modern lifestyle than on religion.

The media can have a strong influence, close to hegemony, on consumers' minds; they have the capacity to produce and spread the ideology of consumerism. As the media spreads its ideology through the use of signs that they try to create, it is likely that in consumerist media products like *Paras*, every message is a tool to maximize financial profit.

Muslima Identity

> Let's go party with good make-up and dress up to show who you are. (*Paras* magazine)

Clothes can signify the group to which a person belongs and be a method to differentiate one group from another. Celia Lury notes, following anthropologist Marshall Sahlins, that

> modern society has substituted scientific objects and species for factory-made products, and clothes can become a totem which communicates a person's membership of a social group. Clothes can be an expression of individuality for men and women from both the upper middle class and the lower middle class, and can also indicate differences in attitude between these groups. Clothes can communicate what could be termed "softness" for women and "strength" for men. They may be seen to signify "politeness" in the upper middle class and even "coarseness" in the lower middle class.[12]

In the article "Mix and Match, It's Party Time" in *Paras*, a Barbie doll, dressed to go to a party, is used as a model.[13] As a *signifier*, Barbie appears as a substitute object for a female model who displays various possibilities for mixing and matching clothing that can be worn to a party. As a *signified*, Barbie has the image of a modern Muslima, wearing a veil on her head

---
[12] Celia Lury, *Budaya Konsumen* (Jakarta: Yayasan Obor Indonesia, 1998), 22.
[13] *Paras*, 5, no. 57 (July 2008), 110–111.

to indicate a Muslima identity. *Paras* magazine used the Barbie image to represent Muslimas from the upper middle class segment of society. Barbie comes from the modern era and has "rights"; she is an icon of modern life with her dress and her image as a white-skinnned, sophisticated upper middle class woman.

In conclusion, post-modern society gives identity to every individual based on the totems they choose to use. These can include the style of clothing, the color of the clothes, the veil, or a touch of makeup color. The deliberate intention of *Paras* in the "Party" article previously cited was to present a woman as an object designed for pleasurable times, with clothes suggesting softness, and an image of sexuality and passion displayed on her body. David Gauntiet explains:

> As Giddens puts it, "Modernity opens up the projects of the self, but under conditions strongly influenced by the standardising effects of commodity capitalism ...." The stuff we can buy to "express" ourselves inevitably has an impact upon the projection of the self.[14]

According to Barnard, "identity can be expressed through different representations that we ourselves and other people understand. Identity is in essence what we signal through indicators, such as preferences, beliefs, attitudes and life style."[15] Identity can be easily reshaped and even change its form. Likewise, Muslima identity can change depending on whether a woman is out in society or in her own home taking care of her husband and children. She can be made up to go into the public arena using a new identity as a professional or be a fashionable individual at a party. It is this image that the media continually produce and reproduce, and *Paras* magazine is no exception.

Bibliography

Barnard, Malcolm. *Fashion sebagai komunikasi: Cara Mengkomunikasikan Identitas Sosial, Seksual, Kelas, dan Gender*. Yogyakarta: Jalasutra, 1996.

Budiman, Kris. *Semiotika Visual*. Yogyakarta: Yayasan Cemeti, 2003.

---

[14] David Gauntiet, *Media Gender, and Identity: An Introduction* (New York: Routledge, 2002), 102.

[15] Malcolm Barnard, *Fashion sebagai komunikasi: Cara Mengkomunikasikan Identitas Sosial, Seksual, Kelas, dan Gender* (Yogyakarta: Jalasutra, 1996), 218.

Croteau, David R., and William H. Hoynes. *Media/Society: Industries, Images, and Audiences*. 2nd ed. California: Pine Forge Press, 2000.
Gauntiet, David. *Media Gender, and Identity: An Introduction*. New York: Routledge, 2002.
Lury, Celia. *Budaya Konsumen*. Jakarta: Yayasan Obor Indonesia, 1998.
Paras. 5, no. 56 (May 2008).
Paras. 5, no. 49 (October 2007).
Paras. 5, no. 50 (November 2007).
Paras. 5, no. 57 (July 2008).
Paras. Special edition: "Special Collection of Dressing for Work; Simplicity Parade, Collection 2," 2008.
Pilliang, Yasraf A. Libidonomics. *"Ekonomi Pasar Bebas Libido" dalam Sebuah Dunia Yang Dilipat*. Bandung: Pustaka Mizan, 1999.
Sobur, Alex. *Analisis Teks Media, Suatu Pengantar untuk Analisis Wacana Analisis Semiotik dan Analisis Framing*. Bandung: Remaja Rosda Karya, 2001.
Strinati, Dominic. *An Introduction to Theories of Popular Culture*. London: Routledge, 1995.

CHAPTER FOURTEEN

THE RE-SPIRITUALIZATION
OF CONSUMPTION OR THE
COMMERCIALIZATION OF RELIGION:
CREATIVITY, RESPONSIBILITY,
AND HOPE
*The Case of Sunsilk Clean and Fresh
in Indonesia*

RAGNAR K. WILLER

Gone are the old and rigid meanings of "religion" and "politics," as well as the clear boundaries that separate them from "lifestyle". In today's Islam in Indonesia, old familiar images have been replaced by new ones. The associations of Islam with rural poverty, religious dogmatism, the Middle East, anti-Chinese, anti-Western sentiments, and fundamentalists seeking to establish an Islamic state are juxtaposed with new images. Now Islam is also associated with television talk shows, name cards with Ph.D.s from prominent Western schools, erudite intellectual debates, mobile phones and consumption of *ketupat*[1] during Ramadan at McDonald's.[2]

Sunsilk helps me to follow the Islamic rules as well as possible.[3]

---

[1] *Editor's note*: A kind of rice dumpling typically eaten on festive occasions.
[2] Ariel Heryanto, "The Years of Living Luxuriously," in *Culture and Privilege in Capitalist Asia*, ed. Micheal Pinches (London: Routledge, 1999), 176.
[3] Indonesian interviewee, 2005

Globalization and Religion

At the beginning of the 21st century, religion seems to play a considerable role in the construction of identity in a hyper-mobile "globalized" world with its collective temporary experiences of vulnerability, displacement, and alienation. Increased religiosity is apparent, for example, in the growing number of members of Pentecostal communities in the United States, South America, South Korea, and Singapore; the media coverage of underground religions in China, such as Falun Gong; the metamorphosis of Pope Benedict XVI into a celebrated pop-culture phenomenon; and the larger public role that Islam plays in societies once considered on the fringe of the Islamic world, such as Indonesia and Malaysia. In these countries Muslim consumers have been discovered as a culturally and economically relevant target group for testing consumer goods geared at a Muslim public. It seems that Francis Fukuyama's 1999 prediction that religion would become a source of new rituals in many societies has become true. The processes of modernization and rationalization do not seem to lead to a diminished significance of religion as originally expected.[4] In fact, today an increasing number of people from all social echelons are turning to religion,[5] and this is also reflected in their consumer behavioral patterns. A renaissance of religion is apparent in Indonesia, too, and has been widely discussed.[6] This change seems to be

---

[4] Hans-Dieter Evers and Sharon Siddique, "Religious Revivalism in Southeast Asia: An Introduction," *SOJOURN: Journal of Social Issues in Southeast Asia*, February 1993, no. 1, 1–10; Raymond L. M. Lee, "The Globalization of Religious Markets: International Innovations, Malaysian Consumption," *SOJOURN: Journal of Social Issues in Southeast Asia* 8, no. 1 (1993): 35–61; Christian Kiem, "Re-Islamization among Muslim Youth in Ternate Town, Eastern Indonesia," *SOJOURN: Journal of Social Issues in Southeast Asia* 8, no. 1 (1993): 92–127; Nils Mulder, *Inside Indonesian Society. An Interpretation of Cultural Change in Java* (Bangkok: Editions Duang Kamol, 1994), 184–194.

[5] Ahmed Akbar and Donnan Hastings, *Islam, Globalization and Postmodernity* (New York: Routledge, 1994); Aziz Al-Azmeh, *Islams and Modernities* (London: Verso Books, 1993); Jürgen Stark, *Kebangkitan Islam. Islamische Entwicklungsprozesse in Malaysia von 1981 bis 1995* (Hamburg: Abera Verlag, 1999).

[6] Evers and Siddique, "Religious Revivalism in Southeast Asia: An Introduction," 1; Robert W. Hefner, *Civil Islam: Muslims and Democratization in Indonesia* (Princeton: Princeton University Press, 2000), 1–40; Dawan M. Rahardjo, "Perceptions of Culture in the Islamic Movement: An Indonesian Perspective," *SOJOURN: Journal of Social Issues in Southeast Asia* 7, no. 2 (1992): 248–273; Klaus H. Schreiner, "Mehrheit mit Minderwertigkeitskomplex? Der Islam in Indonesien," in *Islam in Asien*, ed. Klaus H. Schreiner (Bad Honnef: Horlemann, 2001), 157–179; Georg Stauth, *Globalization, Modernity, Islam* (Bielefeld: Working Paper no. 249, Universität Bielefeld, Fakultät für Soziologie, Forschungsschwerpunkt Entwicklungssoziologie, 1999), 7–9; Andreas Ufen, "Islam und Politik in Südostasien: Neuere Entwicklungen in Malaysia und Indonesien," *Aus Politik und Zeitgeschichte. Beilage zur Wochenzeitung Das Parlament*, 2004, no. B21–22, 15–21.

closely related to the process of globalization.[7] Thus in Indonesia during the process of globalization, neither the cultural imperialism of the West nor a decline in religiosity can be observed.

This paper seeks to contribute a novel perspective to the field of consumer studies by presenting a consumer product that bridges the hopes and ideals of Indonesian Muslim women and tries to close the gap between "real" and "ideal" in social life. This paper demonstrates how rapidly crises can lead to religious transformations, which then are reflected in consumer culture. With the help of a case study, it explores the societal conditions that led to changes in the consumer attitudes of the Muslim majority in Indonesia and the issues involved in developing and advertising a product for a female Muslim target group. It argues that in Indonesia, identity construction—as it relates to products perceived as Muslim—is an ongoing process that is affected by global and local changes. This case study shows how the central aspects of consumer culture—such as needs, choice, identity, status, alienation, objects, and culture[8]—have dramatically changed in just a few years in Indonesia. Research was conducted using ethnographic methods.[9]

Consumer Society and the Search for Identity

Consumer society is defined as the modern period of mass consumption, based on mass production.[10] In the modern world, it has become a cliché to suggest that one inhabits, or is a victim of, a "consumer society,"[11] as seen by the Frankfurt School.[12] Consumer goods have a significance that

---

[7] Arjun Appadurai, "Introduction: Commodities and the Politics of Value," in *The Social Life of Things: Commodities in Cultural Perspective*, ed. Arjun Appadurai (New York: Cambridge University Press, 1996), 7.

[8] Don Slater, *Consumer Culture and Modernity* (Oxford: Polity Press, 1997).

[9] As described in Ragnar K. Willer, "Dispelling the Myth of a Global Consumer: Indonesian Consumer Behavior Researched by Means of an Analytical Diagram for Intercultural Marketing. With a Case Study of Sunsilk Shampoo for the Veiled Woman" (Dissertation, Humboldt Universität, 2006), http://edoc.hu-berlin.de/dissertationen/willer-ragnar-karl-2006-07-19/HTML.

[10] See, for example, William Westley and Margaret Westley, *The Emerging Worker: Equality and Conflict in the Mass Consumption Society* (Montreal: McGill-Queen's University Press, 1971), 14; John Alt, "Beyond Class: The Decline of Industrial Labour and Leisure," *Telos*, Summer 1976, no. 28, 72–80; Ben Fine and Ellen Leopold, "Consumerism and the Industrial Revolution," *Social History* 15, no. 2 (1990): 151–179; Ben Fine and Ellen Leopold, *The World of Consumption* (London: Routledge, 1993); Kenneth Hudson, *The Archaeology of the Consumer Society: The Second Industrial Revolution in Britain* (London: Heinemann, 1983).

[11] Ben Fine, *The World of Consumption. The Material and Cultural Revisited*, 2nd (London: Routledge, 2002), 155.

[12] See, for example, Herbert Marcuse, *Der eindimensionale Mensch: Studien zur Ideologie der fortgeschrittenen Industriegesellschaft* (Frankfurt/Main: Suhrkamp, 1989), 24–28.

goes beyond their utilitarian character and commercial value. This significance is derived largely from their ability to carry and communicate cultural meaning.[13] A diverse body of scholars has made the cultural significance of consumer goods the focus of renewed academic study.[14] Their work has established a subfield within the social sciences that devotes itself with increasing clarity and thoroughness to the study of person-object relations.[15]

The modern search for identity is based to a great extent on the acquisition of cultural codes. Identity can be defined as the subjective concept (or representation) that a person holds of himself or herself.[16] To view consumption as communication also implies that consumers use consumption to express to others who and what they are, or to put it another way, that social differentiation is constantly maintained through practices that consciously utilize the symbolic nature of material goods.[17] For example, the possession of goods (or the wearing of clothing that signifies a particular status or allegiance) also implies the existence of a group for whom a particular commodity has a particular meaning. In certain situations, there is little doubt that possessions and goods, even the most apparently banal, can be used as "markers" of identity.[18] Yet it can be acknowledged that the same material object might have many different and contradictory messages other

---

[13] Mary Douglas and Baron Isherwood, *The World of Goods* (New York: Basic Books, 1979).

[14] See, for example, Eric J. Arnould and Richard Wilk, "Why Do the Natives Wear Adidas?" *Advances in Consumer Research* 11 (1984): 748–752; Jean Baudrillard, *The Consumer Society: Myths and Structures* (London: Sage, 1998); Russell Belk, *Collecting in a Consumer Society* (London: Routledge, 1995); Simon Bronner, "Visible Proofs: Material Culture Study in American Folkloristics," *American Quarterly* 35, no. 3 (1983): 316–338; Marcus Felson, "The Differentiation of Material Life Styles: 1925 to 1966," *Social Indicator Research* 3 (1976): 397–421; Lita Furby, "Possessions: Towards a Theory of Their Meaning and Function Throughout the Life Cycle," in "Lifespan Development and Behaviour: A Critial Review," *Journal of Consumer Research* 11 (1994): 927–938; Carl F. Graumann, "Psychology and the World of Things," *Journal of Phenomenological Psychology* 4, no. 1 (1974–75): 389–404; Rebecca Holman, "Product Use as Communication: A Fresh Appraisal of a Venerable Topic," in *Review of Marketing*, ed. Ben M. Enis and Kenneth J. Roering (Chicago: American Marketing Association, 1980), 250–272; Martin Krampen, "Survey of Current Work on the Semiology of Objects," in *A Semiotic Landscape: Proceedings of the First Congress of the International Association for Semiotic Studies*, ed. Seymour Chatman, Umberto Eco, and Jean-Marie Klinkenberg (The Hague: Mouton Press, 1979), 158–168.

[15] For an overview, see Michael Jäckel, *Einführung in die Konsumsoziologie. Fragestellungen, Kontroversen, Beispieltexte* (Wiesbaden: VS Verlag für Sozialwissenschaften, 2006), 23–66.

[16] Helga Dittmar, *Consumer Culture, Identity and Well-Being: The Search for the Good Life and Body Perfect* (East Sussex: Psychology Press, 2008).

[17] Pierre Bourdieu, *Distinction: A Social Critique of the Judgment of Taste* (Cambridge: Harvard University Press, 1984).

[18] Bourdieu, *Distinction: A Social Critique of the Judgment of Taste*; Belk, *Collecting in a Consumer Society*; Michael Hitchcock and Ken Teague, *Souvenirs: The Material Culture of Tourism* (London: Ashgate, 2000).

than that intended, if indeed any message was consciously intended in the first place.[19] Consumerism seemingly provides the opportunity to create a new "self," but it is not all about unfettered individualism and identity. Although consumption is a means by which self-identities can be defined and maintained,[20] it is not the only one. Factors such as gender, ethnicity, kinship, age, and religion, for example, might be more salient ways to express identity or to mediate patterns and forms of consumption.[21] In fact, consumption might simply be a vehicle through which more significant aspects of identity are expressed. Due to a surge in the global supply of symbols that serve as substituting signifiers, which are reinforced by the constant simulation through the media, the consumer creates for himself or herself a patchwork identity, made up of fragments stemming from a host of different cultures. Yet decorating the self with code elements does not mean that culture-specific societal references have been internalized to the point that the consumer feels a commitment to a given culture. One example of this insight is the trend toward the Islamization of consumer products in Indonesia, where consumption has played an increasing role in identity formation since the early 1990s.

Turbulence in Times of Change

A study of consumer culture involves more than simply the study of texts and textuality, of individual choice and consciousness, of wants and desires, but rather the study of such things in the context of social relations, structures, institutions, and systems. For Slater, "it is the study of social conditions under which personal and social wants and the organization of social resources define each other."[22] The explanations that follow present a kaleidoscope of the social conditions that have contributed to a re-spiritualization of public life in Indonesia.

Spread across a chain of thousands of islands between Asia and Australia, Indonesia has the world's largest Muslim population. Ethnically it

---

[19] Colin Campbell, "When the Meaning Is Not a Message: A Critique of the Consumption as Communication Thesis," in *Buy This Book: Studies on Advertising and Consumption*, ed. Andrew Blake, Mica Nava, and Barry Richards (London: Routledge, 1997), 114–116.
[20] See, for example, Harriet Friedmann, "Premature Rigour: Can Ben Fine Have His Contingency and Eat It, Too?" *Review of International Political Economy* 1, no. 3 (1994): 103.
[21] Stephen Edgell and Kevin Hetherington, "Consumption Matters," in *Consumption Matters. The Production and Experience of Consumption*, ed. Stephen Edgell, Kevin Hetherington, and Alan Warde (Oxford: Blackwell Publishing, 1997), 1–10; Yasser Mattar, "Habituation and Choice in the Process of Consumption: A Case Study of Popular Music in Singapore," *Asia Studies Review* 27, no. 4 (2003): 443–461.
[22] Slater, *Consumer Culture and Modernity*, 2.

is highly diverse, with more than 300 local languages. The people range from rural hunter-gatherers to a modern urban elite. In recent years Indonesia has experienced enormous turmoil, including the Asian financial crisis, the fall of President Suharto after 32 years in office, the first free elections since the 1960s, the loss of East Timor, independence demands from restive provinces, bloody ethnic and religious conflict, and devastating natural catastrophes. The country faces demands for independence in several provinces, where secessionists have been encouraged by East Timor's 1999 success in breaking away after 25 years of occupation. Militant Islamic groups have flexed their muscles over the past few years. Some have been accused of having links with Osama bin Laden's al-Qaeda organization, including the group blamed for the 2002 and 2005 Bali bombings and the violent attacks on foreign property in the capital city of Jakarta.

A Boulevard of Broken Dreams

In 1998 Indonesia and its citizens overnight saw themselves in the middle of a multidimensional crisis. The Asian financial crisis, which started in Thailand in 1997, floored Indonesia's banking system and led to an economic crisis that turned many of the former winners of globalization into losers who could no longer afford basic commodities, such as baby milk powder. In just two years, the level of poverty in the country returned to the level of the 1960s. Particularly affected by this crisis were members of a social group often described as the "New Rich in Asia"—or "bourgeoisie" or "middle class"—which had benefited from the economic transformation and had aroused the interest of various scholars, starting in the 1990s.[23] During

---

[23] See, for example, Bert Becker, Jürgen Rüland, and Nikolaus Werz, *Mythos Mittelschichten* (Bonn: Bouvier, 1999); Solvay Gerke, *Symbolic Consumption and the Indonesian Middle Class* (Bielefeld: Working Paper no. 233, Universität Bielefeld, Fakultät für Soziologie, Forschungsschwerpunkt Entwicklungssoziologie, 1995); Solvay Gerke, "Global Lifestyles under Local Conditions: The New Indonesian Middle Class," in *Consumption in Asia. Lifestyles and Identities*, ed. Beng-Huat Chua (London: Routledge, 2000), 135–158; Hans-Dieter Evers and Solvay Gerke, *Globale Märkte und symbolischer Konsum: Visionen von Modernität in Südostasien* (Bielefeld: Working Paper no. 314, Southeast Asia Programme, Universität Bielefeld, Fakultät für Soziologie, 1995); Alexander Horstmann, *Hybrid Processes of Modernization and Globalization: The Making of Consumers in South Thailand* (Bielefeld: Working Paper, no. 283, Universität Bielefeld, Fakultät für Soziologie, 1997); Robert Robison, *The Emergence of the Middle Class in Southeast Asia* (Perth: Working Paper no. 57, Asia Research Center, Murdoch University, 1995); Krishna Sen and Maila Stivens, *Gender and Power in Affluent Asia* (London: Routledge, 1998); Robert Robison and David S. G. Goodman, *The New Rich in Asia: Mobile Phones, McDonald's and Middle-Class Revolution* (London: Routledge, 1996); Beng-Huat Chua, "Consuming Asians: Ideas and Issues," in *Consumption in Asia. Lifestyles and Identities*, ed. Beng-Huat Chua (Routledge: Routledge, 2000), 1–34; Beng-Huat Chua, *Life is Not Complete without shopping. Consumption Culture in Singapore* (Singapore: Singapore University

this period Indonesians found themselves in the midst of radical transformation processes, which were caused by high economic growth and its accompanying changes (employment structure, level of urbanization).[24] The wealth created was apparent, for example, in the construction of luxurious apartment buildings and huge shopping centers,[25] as well as in the increasing registration figures for motorbikes and automobiles.[26] As a result of the economic upturn and the social transformations it induced, various means of creating an identity emerged in the 1990s. But in the wake of the economic, political, and social crises that began in 1998 in Indonesia, religion and religious symbols began to play a greater role in the construction of identity.[27]

Loss of Identity

Those layers of Indonesian society that had used the consumption of imported goods as symbols of belonging and positioned themselves as members of the urban middle class by a certain type of house, furniture, clothing, car, etc. were massively affected by the escalating crisis in 1998. The crisis increased uncertainty and destroyed the financial basis of the new middle class.[28] Booth explains: "The middle-classes in urban areas had taken the brunt of the crisis, and the young, relatively well-educated workers had suffered far greater income declines than the least educated and poorest work-

---

Press, 2003); Francis Loh, "Modernität in Malaysia. Konsumorientierung, Selbstbezogenheit und Apathie in den 90er Jahren," *Südostasien*, no. 1 (1998): 46–50; Michael Pinches, "Cultural Relations, Class and the New Rich of Asia," in *Culture and Privilege in Capitalist Asia*, ed. Michael Pinches (London: Routledge, 1999), 1–55; Richard Tanter and Kenneth Young, eds., *The Politics of Middle Class Indonesia* (Clayton: Centre of Southeast Asian Studies, Monash University, 1990); Aris Ananta, "What Do We Learn from the Crisis?" In *The Indonesian Crisis. A Human Development Perspective*, ed. Aris Ananta (Singapore: Institute of Southeast Asian Studies, 2000), 2–27.

[24] Kian Wee Thee, "The Soeharto Era and After: Stability, Development and Crisis, 1966–2000," in *The Emergence of a National Economy: An Economic History of Indonesia, 1800–2000*, ed. Howard Dick et al., ASAA Southeast Asia Publications Series (Honolulu: Allen & Unwin / University of Hawaii Press, 2002), 194–242; Robison, *The Emergence of the Middle Class in Southeast Asia*, 79.

[25] Nirwan Dewanto, "Icarus-Coming Soon to Jakarta," *Tempo* (8 December 2003): 52–53.

[26] Robison, *The Emergence of the Middle Class in Southeast Asia*, 80.

[27] Azyumardi Azra, "The Islamic Factor in Post-Soeharto Indonesia," in *Indonesia in Transition: Social Aspects of Reformasi and Crisis*, ed. Chris Manning and Peter Van Diermen (Singapore: Institute of Southeast Asian Studies, 2000), 3–26.

[28] Chris Manning and Peter van Diermen, *Indonesia in Transition: Social Aspects of Reformasi and Crisis* (Singapore: Institute of Southeast Asian Studies, 2000), 143–144; John Strauss et al., "Evidence from the Indonesia Family Life Survey," in (Singapore: ISEAS, 2004), chap. Indonesian Living Standards: Before and after the Crisis.

ers in rural areas."[29] Booth goes on: "By mid 1998, it was frequently being asserted that *krismon* (Indonesian: monetary crisis) was primarily a crisis affecting urban Java, ... the outer Islands ... were actually benefiting from the effects of massive Rupiah devaluation."[30]

The university-educated middle class often did not have the option of returning to their villages and looking for agricultural employment, as did the less-educated migrant laborers who had become unemployed during the crisis.[31] Jellinek states: "While the lower middle classes in Depok are unable to feed their children, rubbish recyclers are still able to feed themselves and save money to send back to their children in the village."[32] During the crisis, the new middle class realized the increasing volatility of its circumstances as a result of social, political, and economic events that were difficult to predict.

Jellinek explains: "The new middle classes who have lost their jobs in advertising agencies and mega-malls are copying the survival strategies of the poor."[33] In the end, the former winners of globalization—i.e., the members of the new middle class—became the victims of globalization. They were robbed of their material clout. Jellinek adds: "Good solid houses, once stocked with consumer goods, are now empty. Most possessions have been sold."[34] In losing these objects, they also lost part of their identity.

Signatures of Chaos: Nostalgia and Despair

During these turbulent economic and political times the young multiethnic democracy was threatened, both internally and externally by the international economic system (Vatikiotis 1999, pp. 218–232; Simanjuntak 2000, pp. 58–75; Johnson 2000, pp. 77–86). The sense of community constructed under Suharto slipped away, and Indonesians experienced the fragility of their existence as domestic bombings, radical Islamist demands, and rowdy street demonstrations created distrust in the multiethnic population and undermined their democracy (Manning and van Diermen 2000, pp. 1–11). Natural disasters—such as droughts caused by El Nino, numerous earth-

---

[29] Anne Booth, "The Impact of the Indonesian Crisis on Welfare: What Do We Know Two Years On?" In *Indonesia in Transition: Social Aspects of Reformasi and Crisis*, ed. Chris Manning and Peter van Diermen (Singapore: Institute of Southeast Asian Studies, 2000), 147.
[30] Ibid., 154.
[31] Lea Jellinek, "The New Poor," *Inside Indonesia*, January–March 1999, http://www.insideindonesia.org/edit57/lea.html, no. 57, 2, 6.
[32] Ibid., 2.
[33] Ibid., 6.
[34] Ibid., 2.

quakes, and a tsunami—brought suffering and despair to the nation. The spread of diseases (including SARS and bird flu) as well as natural forces that caused numerous air traffic disasters led to confusion, frustration, and disbelief. Yearning for better times, Indonesians searched for new structures to compensate for their loss of control. Political leaders with integrity seemed scarce, even as religious leaders, presenting their teachings in the media (which had previously been state-controlled but was now free) became popular (Azra 2006, pp. 27–36; 179–198).

Images of hope and reminiscences about the past were prevalent in advertising and on soap operas as the nation struggled through an identity crisis. Advertisements presented traditional settings, often portraits of landscapes with indigenous spiritual meanings. Additionally manifestations of Islam were more visible in public, and the answers to the questions "Who am I?" and "Who are we?" increasingly hinged on religion. Islam appeared to play a far greater role in many areas of life (Azra 2000, pp. 307–318). The economically marginalized middle class started to inoculate itself via an idealized lifestyle against social transformation processes with the aid of religion. Evers (1991, p. 99) points out that religious renaissance is often a mechanism to reduce the fears provoked as a result of the social and economic pressure and distress originating in modernization.

The new middle class gravitated toward Islam and transformed its lifestyle into a Muslim way of life, mainly expressed though consumption as soon as their financial situation allowed them to do so. Islam had already become an identity indicator for upper and upper-middle class Indonesians (Heryanto 1999, pp. 173–176), a phenomenon that was avidly followed by the Indonesian press. Heryanto (p. 175) reports: "Collective prayers, Ramadan-dining in fancy restaurants and Islamic education among top business executives, state bureaucrats, rock singers, movie stars and other celebrities have become regular cover stories in today's media industry." The Asian crisis, with its accompanying scarcity of material means necessary for consumption, led the middle class to turn increasingly to other symbols.

Crisis Experience and Social Change

The urge for significance and a sense of purpose is apparent in times of crisis. When social, moral, and cognitive structures break down, people are forced to confront their helplessness and impotence. Riesebrodt summarizes it thus: "Crises pose a major impetus to carry out religious work."[35]

---

[35] Martin Riesebrodt, *Die Rückkehr der Religionen: Fundamentalismus und der "Kampf der Kulturen"* (Munich: Beck, 2001), 47.

Religious armor allows one to cope with life's disappointments in an unknown, modern, pluralistic world, when everyday control is removed, and thus supra-human power is required.

Indicators of social change in Indonesia between 1998 and 2006 include an increase in the number of mosques, madrasah, and hajj pilgrimages, but first and foremost, Islamization was visible in the world of consumption. Goods that respect Islamic teachings were being bought to a greater degree (halal food), and Islamic services (such as banking and insurance) were heavily requested. The demand for goods that reflect and document one's own (partly new) religious piety is on the rise. Among the objects of desire are Muslim fashion (*Busana Muslim*);[36] Muslim lifestyle magazines, such as *Noor* and *Ummi*; Muslim beer brands; Islam-customized products; and hajj travel programs.[37] Mobile phones equipped with software specially designed for Muslims, with prayer reminder tones and electronic compasses, are enjoying great popularity.[38] Architects who design shopping centers and residential complexes are including more Arabic stylistic elements.[39]

Identity-Seeking: Busana Muslim

Islamization is especially apparent in the choice of clothing.[40] The *jilbab* (Indonesian name for the Islamic veil worn by women) has spawned a whole fashion industry since the revival of Islam. Interviewee AS explains: "The *jilbab*, the most visible part of a complete Muslim outfit, is a relatively recent phenomenon in Indonesia." Stereotypical images of Muslim women covered from head to toe in black, as one might know them from Arab countries, have been replaced in Indonesia by images of fashionable ladies clad in bright, opulent colors.

In Indonesia, Islamic clothing is considered by the urban middle class to be chic. Indonesian women, especially members of the urban middle class, are starting to choose to complement their apparel by wearing a veil or a tunic.[41] These clothing styles are colorful, in vogue, and frequently very

---

[36] Elizabeth Raleigh, "Busana Muslim dan Kebudayaan Populer di Indonesia: Pengaruh dan Persepsi" (Unpublished research paper, Universitas Muhammadiyah, Malang, 2004).

[37] Jeremy Wallach, "Dangdut Trendy," *Inside Indonesia*, April–June 2004, 30.

[38] Jeremy Wagstaff, "Mecca for Gadget Makers," *Far Eastern Economic Review* (5 August 2004): 32–34; "SMS Takes Over the Place of Traditional Idul Fitri Cards," *The Jakarta Post* (7 November 2005): 1.

[39] Hari Kurniawan, "An Afternoon at Plaza Indonesia," *The Jakarta Post* (March 2005): 8.

[40] Interviewee AS, November 2004.

[41] "Baju Lebaran. Bisa Paket atau 'Mix&Match' Sendiri," in "Halaman Khusus Anka Muda," *Kompas* (5 November 2004): 56.

figure-hugging. Many expensive stores (i.e., Pasaraya Grande and Blok M) reserve whole departments for fashionable, Muslim-evocative clothing, and they offer a wide range of veils and matching clothing, which are celebrated as *le dernier cri* thanks to fashion magazines such as *Noor* and *Ummi*.[42] Wearing a *jilbab* seems to be situation-dependent, selective, and is not only an expression of religion but also of taste, style, and a way of positioning oneself in society. In fairness this fashion trend reflects not just genuinely religious motives but also motives of style, class, and fashion.

Interestingly, until the beginning of the 1990s wearing a *jilbab* was forbidden in Indonesia and often considered backward and associated with the Iranian Revolution. The attitude toward the *jilbab* was changed by members of Indonesia's political elite, most notably the Suharto family, who aimed to counter criticism of their materialist, immoral, and un-Islamic lifestyle by transforming their appearance into faithful Muslims. Van Leeuwen once famously summarized this behavior as: "The polished surface is more important than the content. The state of existence and the state of appearance is something totally different in Indonesia."[43] Soon the *jilbab* was no longer associated with rural backwardness but with urban modernity and success. However, until the beginning of the crisis of 1998, the *jilbab* and Muslim fashion in general remained the domain of Indonesia's elite, whose female members covered themselves in veils adorned with pearls and gemstones to distance themselves from the new middle classes, which surrounded themselves with goods that were perceived as Western.

The Case of Sunsilk Segar dan Bersih

Contrary to popular opinion, brands and their products differ widely. In an attempt to distinguish their brands from their competitors', companies give their brands certain attributes with the help of so-called branding strategies.[44] The corporate world even refers to the "magic of branding." Brands act as symbols in the individual or social communication process, and sat-

---

[42] Tutut Handayani and Henri T. Soelaeman, "Inspirasi Bisnis dari Kaum Berjilbab," *SWA*, 17 Februar –2 March 2005, no. 04/XXI, 18.

[43] Lizzy van Leeuwen, "Being Rich in Jakarta, 1994: A Mother and Two Daughters," in *Outward Appearances. Dressing and State in Indonesia*, ed. Henk S. Nordholdt (Leiden: KITLV, 1997), 341.

[44] Franz-Rudolf Esch, *Moderne Markenführung. Grundlagen, Innovative Ansätze, Praktische Umsetzungen* (Wiesbaden: Gabler Verlag, 2001), 6; Heribert Meffert, Christoph Burman, and Martin Koers, *Markenmanagement. Grundfragen der identitätsorientierten Markenführung* (Wiesbaden: Gabler, 2002), 6–7.

isfy the needs for self-fulfillment, social distinction, and recognition.[45] The identity-endowing effect of brands is the focus here, i.e., the person purchasing the branded goods receives the attributes of the product himself or herself and defines his or her self-image through it.[46] Especially in today's stressful world of mistrust and trouble, people are looking for an escape. A brand ought to provide orientation and guidance, as well as the feeling that the consumer is wanted, belongs, and is cared for during these times.

Originally launched in the Netherlands in 1956, Sunsilk provides hair care solutions in 80 countries around the globe. Whether it is hair relaxers in Africa or combing creams in Brazil, or special treatments for limp, flat hair in Europe, Sunsilk addresses, according to its parent company Unilever, the needs of local consumers. It brings happiness to beauty—helping women to feel good, look good, and get more out of life wherever they live. The Sunsilk brand distinguishes itself with recognizable elements such as name, package design, and imagery.

Obviously, the ideals of fashion and taste had changed since the beginning of the crisis. As Islamic fashion became increasingly popular, a new image of Muslim beauty emerged in Indonesia. Unilever argued that a woman's hair under the *jilbab* would have little contact with light and air, and therefore women would need a special hair care product to keep their hair healthy. Unilever decided to tap into this trend and develop a shampoo for veiled women. It was considered dangerous for a global company to target a Muslim audience, and women in particular. However Sunsilk's brand managers identified strategic and operational goals, such as the brand being regarded as respectful towards Islam, unique, and local, thereby increasing market share and sales. It was argued that as it is Sunsilk's brand promise to help women feel good, look good, and get more out of life wherever they live, the brand would need to get in touch again with consumers whose attitude toward religion, lifestyle, and beauty had changed.

It was decided that the product should not be directly linked to Arab countries. Indonesian women interpreted Muslim fashion as modern and not as a backward and intolerant symbol of male domination. Focusing on Indonesian consumer behavior, a corresponding product and marketing strategy was generated locally with the intention to develop a shampoo targeted at Muslim women who wear a veil and who take pride in their appearance. There were already four shampoos under the umbrella brand name Sunsilk on the Indonesian market prior to Sunsilk's "Segar dan Bersih" (Clean and

---

[45] Meffert, Burman, and Koers, *Markenmanagement. Grundfragen der identitätsorientierten Markenführung*, 348.
[46] Esch, *Moderne Markenführung. Grundlagen, Innovative Ansätze, Praktische Umsetzungen*, 111.

Fresh). But not a single shampoo from either Unilever or its competitors catered to veiled Muslim women and their hair care matters.

Sunsilk perceived this as a huge opportunity. The brand image was designed to be approachable, inviting, and to radiate warmth, especially to the target group. The women featured in the endorsements were not supposed to look introverted or old-fashioned. Since a shampoo for veiled women was being advertised, no hair would be shown, which was something of a novelty in a shampoo advertisement.

Rebranding Sunsilk with a Reinvented Inneke Koesherawati

By choosing Inneke Koesherawati, a former actress who achieved fame as a model and entrepreneur in Indonesia, for the initial campaigns, Unilever managed a feat. Inneke Koesherawati had opted to wear a veil only since 2001, and prior to that she had always been considered somewhat irreligious. Many marketing professionals in Indonesia regard Inneke Koesherawati's transformation as one of the most successful rebrandings in Indonesia. She transformed herself into a female Muslim icon at a time when she had to think about a strategy of how to be still relevant and in demand as actress and model when Indonesian high fashion became Muslim fashion. In the Indonesian press Inneke Koesherawati was described: "From sex bomb to cosmo-Muslim. Even glamour models are embracing Muslim clothes. Inneke Koesherawati, a former pin-up girl who once posed for racy photographs for a glossy men's magazine, recalled the day she decided to cover up. 'I just came back from the Hajj and my body just didn't feel comfortable any more without being covered,' said Koesherawati, whose past movies such as *Metropolitan Girls, Naughty Desires,* and *The Stained Bed* had left little to the imagination. Now she insists those days are long gone. 'I don't feel old-fashioned, in fact I feel more cosmopolitan,' she says."[47]

Today Inneke Koesherawati is revered as a "cosmo-Muslim"—a modern, self-assured, successful Muslim, who lives her faith overtly. She is known all over Indonesia as one of the best-dressed women. Inneke continuously presents herself as a good Muslim and uses every opportunity to communicate her belief. During a Sunsilk event she said, "Women should not forget God's will; and while conducting business, must also continue to pray."[48]

Today, together with Ratih Sanggarwati, Inneke Koesherawati is regarded as one of the most popular and successful female entrepreneurs in Indonesia. Inneke Koesherawati oversees a conglomerate of Muslim fashion houses,

---

[47] Toni Soetjipto, "Islam's All-Enveloping Hijab Is Hip in Indonesia," *Reuters* (18 December 2003).
[48] Interviewee RS, 2006.

modeling schools and agencies, and spreads her pieces of wisdom through her TV shows and magazine publications.

The Launch

In October 2004 the product was finally launched as "Sunsilk Segar dan Bersih" (Sunsilk Clean and Fresh) during the time of Ramadan, when women prepare a lot of traditional food, presents are exchanged, and the overall mood is particularly festive and emotional. An Indonesian lifestyle magazine once described Ramadan as "the time of the year when we need to stylishly cover up ourselves" to share "the timeless and divine tradition of breaking the fast."[49]

Excursus: A Gender Perspective

Advertisements present the Sunsilk consumer as modern, free, educated, and independent from old stereotypes. The Sunsilk young woman is not a woman who seeks shelter in a man's shadow. Rather she declares herself as independent, is open to others, and wishes to establish social relations. Sunsilk reflects an Indonesian social reality as an increasing number of women are acquiring more responsibility and power, such as Inneke Koesherawati, Ratih Sanggarwati, and many other female celebrities and entrepreneurs. Senior Brand Manager of Sunsilk, Ade, explains: "Sunsilk wants to take a step into the lives of women in relation to the development of their performance and potential. We want to give inspiration to Indonesian women to continuously develop their potential to work, perform and enhance the quality of their lives. ... Therefore Sunsilk has set up the Melati foundation to provide Indonesian women with training and educational opportunities."[50] Sunsilk combines Islam, modernity, and empowerment, and symbolizes the current state of Indonesian lifestyles.[51]

Beyond the Shampoo

"Sunsilk Segar dan Bersih" and its transformation into a pop-cultural phenomenon seem to support the hypothesis that the symbolic meaning of a

---

[49] "Jilbab Gaul," *Latitudes*, no. 46 (November 2004): 14–23.
[50] Interviewee AS, 2005.
[51] Advertising videos of Sunsilk may be found at: http://www.youtube.com/watch?v=excxIZ4wUvg and http://www.youtube.com/watch?v=LwTHZi0eo2s, accessed 24 August 2008.

commodity is not dictated by its producers. Producers of commodities actually have little or no control, despite the rhetoric of marketing and advertising, over their deployment and use of their products. Therefore one should not fall into the naive fallacy of assuming that the "intentions" of the producers are simply absorbed whole and unmediated by the unsuspecting and passive "consumer" in whatever social or cultural milieu they are located. Although Unilever did not have a religious mission, "Sunsilk Segar dan Bersih" has become a modern talisman, providing spiritual peace of mind to some consumers.

During interviews in Jakarta in 2004 and 2005, consumers of "Sunsilk Segar dan Bersih" stated that they bought Sunsilk to compensate for wrong doings or because they wanted to be transformed just as Sunsilk had transformed Inneke Koesherawarti. Others argued that they believed that being a good Muslim meant that they should use Sunsilk, or that Sunsilk would help them to be a good Muslim. Sunsilk and its world of images became a curriculum for Muslim women who learn to be independent and fashionable. For many, buying Sunsilk meant "belonging" and not "purchasing." Although Sunsilk never directly encouraged consumers to believe that the consumption of "Sunsilk Segar dan Bersih" is enough to understand Islam, this seems to be the general belief among the brand's most loyal customers. Using "Sunsilk Segar dan Bersih" is interpreted as a guarantee of paradise by numerous Indonesian consumers. Extraordinary marketing campaigns helped Sunsilk achieve the cult status of a "holy" product.

Selected notable statements by consumers during interviews in 2004 and 2005:

> I find it very important to buy Sunsilk, although I do not follow other religious prescriptions.

> 'Sunsilk helps me to follow the Islamic rules as well as possible.

> Washing my hair is now a quasi-religious act.

These statements arouse suspicion that decorating oneself with code elements does not mean that one has fully internalized or feels fully committed to a cultural phenomenon. Looking back at the strategically chosen dates of the market launch and the marketing campaigns with their huge billboard advertisements which converted the notion of popular and obvious via the religious revelation of Inneke Koesherawati's conversion to an Islam conforming lifestyle (she is depicted enveloped in a silky green veil and looking expectantly), Unilever appears not only to have intended to satisfy consumers, but rather to tempt and enchant them, as if the consumer were shouting: "Transform me the way Inneke Koesherawati has transformed herself!" Unilever is, of course, not directly responsible for Inneke Koesherawati's life metamorphosis, but this is indirectly implied, as if to say: "I'm a good Muslim woman and I use Sunsilk. Sunsilk helps me to be a good Muslim." The religiously charged brand has, in this case, become a means of transforming consumers. Whether you buy Sunsilk or Nivea is no longer a question of taste but rather a question of world philosophy. In this way Indonesian consumers resemble Bolz's "post-material consumers"[52] who do not merely purchase goods. Instead they purchase stories, feelings, dreams, and values. The more modern (or differentiated) a society is, the more labor is divided, the more confused society becomes, the greater the yearning for unity and entirety.

The case of "Sunsilk Segar dan Bersih" shows that consumers construct a sense of who and what they want to be based on local and temporary conditions and that they use a product as a raw material for everyday creativity. By indirectly linking itself to Islam, Sunsilk successfully rebranded itself and subverted its non-Indonesian and non-Muslim global brand heritage. Sunsilk's success is also tied to the particular moment in time when "Segar dan Bersih" launched: consumers were searching for hope and responsibility. Their increased religiosity in daily life was reflected in the form of Muslim consumer goods. With the launch of "Sunsilk Segar dan Bersih," Unilever Indonesia has aroused continued interest in its products and established an emotional rapport. Unilever has also managed to increase identification with the brand and to make sure Sunsilk stays relevant. Sunsilk has become a feminine Muslim brand with a profile and character that women can identify with. Sunsilk geared relevance along with credibility and the brand was helped to its unique position.[53]

Sunsilk and Muslim fashion can be seen as symbols of an individualized multi-option society where the self is a wandering dune and not a rock. Additionally, it shows how "being modern" and "cosmopolitan" are interpreted by young Indonesian women—i.e., by wearing the *jilbab* and surrounding oneself with objects of Muslim (consumer) culture. As Miller notes, although consumption may be globalized, it can also act as a way for local groups to both create and maintain a sense of difference.[54]

---

[52] Norbert Bolz, *Das konsumistische Manifest* (Munich: Wilhelm Fink Verlag, 2000), 108.
[53] *SWA*, "Merek-merek terbaik 2004," 22 July–4 August 2004, 9–10.
[54] Daniel Miller, *Worlds Apart: Modernism through the Prism of the Local* (London: Routledge, 1995), 41.

Conclusion

This paper demonstrates that advertising, materialism, and consumption are not just central aspects of contemporary Western culture. In Indonesia, too, consumer culture is a means of expressing and seeking identity, which is an ongoing, constantly negotiated process. Ample evidence has been provided, in the case of Indonesia, for the hypothesis that religion influences consumer attitudes and behavior in general, despite the secularization thesis that argues for a weakening of the role of religion. From observations made during a visit to Indonesia in 2008, it is apparent that identity projects continually evolve over time and produce new hybrid identities. Sunsilk seems to have served as an opportunity for discourse, both within the innovative group and between the innovative group and the larger society, during the nation's most difficult times. Today, in Indonesia, the veil is increasingly put aside and new fashions are selectively adapted. After globalization had produced an increased religiosity, it currently seems to encourage a revaluation of the local ethnic culture. Now, it is batik that's hip, much more than the *jilbab*. This development seems to prove the idea that the meaning of consumer goods is constantly changing. Meaning, as McCracken describes it, is constantly flowing to and from its several locations in the social world, aided by the collective and individual efforts of designers, producers, advertisers, and consumers.[55] It is clear that in this world individuals have enormous freedom with respect to the meaning they seek to draw from goods as one can learn from the case of "Sunsilk Segar dan Bersih." Indeed, consumers are engaged in an ongoing enterprise of self-creation. "Sunsilk Segar dan Bersih" was and is used as an object whose purpose it is to complete the self. It supplies individuals with the cultural materials to realize their various and changing ideas of what it is to be a modern Muslim women in Indonesia.

Bibliography

Akbar, Ahmed, and Donnan Hastings. *Islam, Globalization and Postmodernity*. New York: Routledge, 1994.
Al-Azmeh, Aziz. *Islams and Modernities*. London: Verso Books, 1993.
Alt, John. "Beyond Class: The Decline of Industrial Labour and Leisure." *Telos*, Summer 1976, no. 28, 55–80.

---

[55] Grant McCracken, "Culture and Consumption: A Theoretical Account of the Structure and Movement of the Cultural Meaning of Consumer Goods," *Journal of Consumer Research* 13 (1986): 71.

Ananta, Aris. "What Do We Learn from the Crisis?" In *The Indonesian Crisis. A Human Development Perspective*, edited by Aris Ananta, 2–27. Singapore: Institute of Southeast Asian Studies, 2000.

Appadurai, Arjun. "Introduction: Commodities and the Politics of Value." In *The Social Life of Things: Commodities in Cultural Perspective*, edited by Arjun Appadurai. New York: Cambridge University Press, 1996.

Arnould, Eric J., and Richard Wilk. "Why Do the Natives Wear Adidas?" *Advances in Consumer Research* 11 (1984): 748–752.

Azra, Azyumardi. "The Islamic Factor in Post-Soeharto Indonesia." In *Indonesia in Transition: Social Aspects of Reformasi and Crisis*, edited by Chris Manning and Peter Van Diermen, 307–318. Singapore: Institute of Southeast Asian Studies, 2000.

"Baju Lebaran. Bisa Paket atau 'Mix&Match' Sendiri." In "Halaman Khusus Anka Muda." *Kompas* (5 November 2004): 56.

Baudrillard, Jean. *The Consumer Society: Myths and Structures*. London: Sage, 1998.

Becker, Bert, Jürgen Rüland, and Nikolaus Werz. *Mythos Mittelschichten*. Bonn: Bouvier, 1999.

Belk, Russell. *Collecting in a Consumer Society*. London: Routledge, 1995.

Bolz, Norbert. *Das konsumistische Manifest*. Munich: Wilhelm Fink Verlag, 2000.

Booth, Anne. "The Impact of the Indonesian Crisis on Welfare: What Do We Know Two Years On?" In *Indonesia in Transition: Social Aspects of Reformasi and Crisis*, edited by Chris Manning and Peter van Diermen, 145–162. Singapore: Institute of Southeast Asian Studies, 2000.

Bourdieu, Pierre. *Distinction: A Social Critique of the Judgment of Taste*. Cambridge: Harvard University Press, 1984.

Bronner, Simon. "Visible Proofs: Material Culture Study in American Folkloristics." *American Quarterly* 35, no. 3 (1983): 316–338.

Campbell, Colin. "When the Meaning Is Not a Message: A Critique of the Consumption as Communication Thesis." In *Buy This Book: Studies on Advertising and Consumption*, edited by Andrew Blake, Mica Nava, and Barry Richards, 340–352. London: Routledge, 1997.

Chua, Beng-Huat. "Consuming Asians: Ideas and Issues." In *Consumption in Asia. Lifestyles and Identities*, edited by Beng-Huat Chua, 1–34. Routledge: Routledge, 2000.

———. *Life is Not Complete without shopping. Consumption Culture in Singapore*. Singapore: Singapore University Press, 2003.

Dewanto, Nirwan. "Icarus-Coming Soon to Jakarta." *Tempo* (8 December 2003): 52–53.

Dittmar, Helga. *Consumer Culture, Identity and Well-Being: The Search for the Good Life and Body Perfect*. East Sussex: Psychology Press, 2008.
Douglas, Mary, and Baron Isherwood. *The World of Goods*. New York: Basic Books, 1979.
Edgell, Stephen, and Kevin Hetherington. "Consumption Matters." In *Consumption Matters. The Production and Experience of Consumption*, edited by Stephen Edgell, Kevin Hetherington, and Alan Warde, 1–10. Oxford: Blackwell Publishing, 1997.
Esch, Franz-Rudolf. *Moderne Markenführung. Grundlagen, Innovative Ansätze, Praktische Umsetzungen*. Wiesbaden: Gabler Verlag, 2001.
Evers, Hans-Dieter, and Solvay Gerke. *Globale Märkte und symbolischer Konsum: Visionen von Modernität in Südostasien*. Bielefeld: Working Paper no. 314, Southeast Asia Programme, Universität Bielefeld, Fakultät für Soziologie, 1995.
Evers, Hans-Dieter, and Sharon Siddique. "Religious Revivalism in Southeast Asia: An Introduction." *SOJOURN: Journal of Social Issues in Southeast Asia*, February 1993, no. 1, 1–10.
Felson, Marcus. "The Differentiation of Material Life Styles: 1925 to 1966." *Social Indicator Research* 3 (1976): 397–421.
Fine, Ben. *The World of Consumption. The Material and Cultural Revisited*. 2nd. London: Routledge, 2002.
Fine, Ben, and Ellen Leopold. "Consumerism and the Industrial Revolution." *Social History* 15, no. 2 (1990): 151–179.
———. *The World of Consumption*. London: Routledge, 1993.
Friedmann, Harriet. "Premature Rigour: Can Ben Fine Have His Contingency and Eat It, Too?" *Review of International Political Economy* 1, no. 3 (1994): 553–561.
Furby, Lita. "Possessions: Towards a Theory of Their Meaning and Function Throughout the Life Cycle." In "Lifespan Development and Behaviour: A Critial Review." *Journal of Consumer Research* 11 (1994): 927–938.
Gerke, Solvay. "Global Lifestyles under Local Conditions: The New Indonesian Middle Class." In *Consumption in Asia. Lifestyles and Identities*, edited by Beng-Huat Chua, 135–158. London: Routledge, 2000.
———. *Symbolic Consumption and the Indonesian Middle Class*. Bielefeld: Working Paper no. 233, Universität Bielefeld, Fakultät für Soziologie, Forschungsschwerpunkt Entwicklungssoziologie, 1995.
Graumann, Carl F. "Psychology and the World of Things." *Journal of Phenomenological Psychology* 4, no. 1 (1974–75): 389–404.
Handayani, Tutut, and Henri T. Soelaeman. "Inspirasi Bisnis dari Kaum Berjilbab." *SWA*, 17 Februar –2 March 2005, no. 04/XXI, 18.

Hefner, Robert W. *Civil Islam: Muslims and Democratization in Indonesia.* Princeton: Princeton University Press, 2000.
Heryanto, Ariel. "The Years of Living Luxuriously." In *Culture and Privilege in Capitalist Asia*, edited by Micheal Pinches, 159–187. London: Routledge, 1999.
Hitchcock, Michael, and Ken Teague. *Souvenirs: The Material Culture of Tourism.* London: Ashgate, 2000.
Holman, Rebecca. "Product Use as Communication: A Fresh Appraisal of a Venerable Topic." In *Review of Marketing*, edited by Ben M. Enis and Kenneth J. Roering, 250–272. Chicago: American Marketing Association, 1980.
Horstmann, Alexander. *Hybrid Processes of Modernization and Globalization: The Making of Consumers in South Thailand.* Bielefeld: Working Paper, no. 283, Universität Bielefeld, Fakultät für Soziologie, 1997.
Hudson, Kenneth. *The Archaeology of the Consumer Society: The Second Industrial Revolution in Britain.* London: Heinemann, 1983.
Jäckel, Michael. *Einführung in die Konsumsoziologie. Fragestellungen, Kontroversen, Beispieltexte.* Wiesbaden: VS Verlag für Sozialwissenschaften, 2006.
Jellinek, Lea. "The New Poor." *Inside Indonesia*, January–March 1999, http://www.insideindonesia.org/edit57/lea.html, no. 57.
"Jilbab Gaul." *Latitudes*, no. 46 (November 2004): 14–23.
Kiem, Christian. "Re-Islamization among Muslim Youth in Ternate Town, Eastern Indonesia." *SOJOURN: Journal of Social Issues in Southeast Asia* 8, no. 1 (1993): 92–127.
Krampen, Martin. "Survey of Current Work on the Semiology of Objects." In *A Semiotic Landscape: Proceedings of the First Congress of the International Association for Semiotic Studies*, edited by Seymour Chatman, Umberto Eco, and Jean-Marie Klinkenberg, 158–168. The Hague: Mouton Press, 1979.
Kurniawan, Hari. "An Afternoon at Plaza Indonesia." *The Jakarta Post* (March 2005): 8.
Lee, Raymond L. M. "The Globalization of Religious Markets: International Innovations, Malaysian Consumption." *SOJOURN: Journal of Social Issues in Southeast Asia* 8, no. 1 (1993): 25–61.
Leeuwen, Lizzy van. "Being Rich in Jakarta, 1994: A Mother and Two Daughters." In *Outward Appearances. Dressing and State in Indonesia*, edited by Henk S. Nordholdt, 339–359. Leiden: KITLV, 1997.
Loh, Francis. "Modernität in Malaysia. Konsumorientierung, Selbstbezogenheit und Apathie in den 90er Jahren." *Südostasien*, no. 1 (1998): 46–50.

Manning, Chris, and Peter van Diermen. *Indonesia in Transition: Social Aspects of Reformasi and Crisis*. Singapore: Institute of Southeast Asian Studies, 2000.
Marcuse, Herbert. *Der eindimensionale Mensch: Studien zur Ideologie der fortgeschrittenen Industriegesellschaft*. Frankfurt/Main: Suhrkamp, 1989.
Mattar, Yasser. "Habituation and Choice in the Process of Consumption: A Case Study of Popular Music in Singapore." *Asia Studies Review* 27, no. 4 (2003): 443–461.
McCracken, Grant. "Culture and Consumption: A Theoretical Account of the Structure and Movement of the Cultural Meaning of Consumer Goods." *Journal of Consumer Research* 13 (1986): 71–84.
Meffert, Heribert, Christoph Burman, and Martin Koers. *Markenmanagement. Grundfragen der identitätsorientierten Markenführung*. Wiesbaden: Gabler, 2002.
SWA. "Merek-merek terbaik 2004." 22 July–4 August 2004, 9–10.
Miller, Daniel. *Worlds Apart: Modernism through the Prism of the Local*. London: Routledge, 1995.
Mulder, Nils. *Inside Indonesian Society. An Interpretation of Cultural Change in Java*. Bangkok: Editions Duang Kamol, 1994.
Pinches, Michael. "Cultural Relations, Class and the New Rich of Asia." In *Culture and Privilege in Capitalist Asia*, edited by Michael Pinches, 1–55. London: Routledge, 1999.
Rahardjo, Dawan M. "Perceptions of Culture in the Islamic Movement: An Indonesian Perspective." *SOJOURN: Journal of Social Issues in Southeast Asia* 7, no. 2 (1992): 248–273.
Raleigh, Elizabeth. "Busana Muslim dan Kebudayaan Populer di Indonesia: Pengaruh dan Persepsi." Unpublished research paper, Universitas Muhammadiyah, Malang, 2004.
Riesebrodt, Martin. *Die Rückkehr der Religionen: Fundamentalismus und der "Kampf der Kulturen."* Munich: Beck, 2001.
Robison, Robert. *The Emergence of the Middle Class in Southeast Asia*. Perth: Working Paper no. 57, Asia Research Center, Murdoch University, 1995.
Robison, Robert, and David S. G. Goodman. *The New Rich in Asia: Mobile Phones, McDonald's and Middle-Class Revolution*. London: Routledge, 1996.
Schreiner, Klaus H. "Mehrheit mit Minderwertigkeitskomplex? Der Islam in Indonesien." In *Islam in Asien*, edited by Klaus H. Schreiner, 157–179. Bad Honnef: Horlemann, 2001.

Sen, Krishna, and Maila Stivens. *Gender and Power in Affluent Asia.* London: Routledge, 1998.
Slater, Don. *Consumer Culture and Modernity.* Oxford: Polity Press, 1997.
"SMS Takes Over the Place of Traditional Idul Fitri Cards." *The Jakarta Post* (7 November 2005): 1.
Soetjipto, Toni. "Islam's All-Enveloping Hijab Is Hip in Indonesia." *Reuters* (18 December 2003).
Stark, Jürgen. *Kebangkitan Islam. Islamische Entwicklungsprozesse in Malaysia von 1981 bis 1995.* Hamburg: Abera Verlag, 1999.
Stauth, Georg. *Globalization, Modernity, Islam.* Bielefeld: Working Paper no. 249, Universität Bielefeld, Fakultät für Sozilogie, Forschungsschwerpunkt Entwicklungssoziologie, 1999.
Strauss, John, et al. "Evidence from the Indonesia Family Life Survey." Chap. Indonesian Living Standards: Before and after the Crisis in. Singapore: ISEAS, 2004.
Tanter, Richard, and Kenneth Young, eds. *The Politics of Middle Class Indonesia.* Clayton: Centre of Southeast Asian Studies, Monash University, 1990.
Thee, Kian Wee. "The Soeharto Era and After: Stability, Development and Crisis, 1966–2000." In *The Emergence of a National Economy: An Economic History of Indonesia, 1800–2000*, edited by Howard Dick et al., 194–243. ASAA Southeast Asia Publications Series. Honolulu: Allen & Unwin / University of Hawaii Press, 2002.
Ufen, Andreas. "Islam und Politik in Südostasien: Neuere Entwicklungen in Malaysia und Indonesien." *Aus Politik und Zeitgeschichte. Beilage zur Wochenzeitung Das Parlament*, 2004, no. B21–22, 15–21.
Wagstaff, Jeremy. "Mecca for Gadget Makers." *Far Eastern Economic Review* (5 August 2004): 32–34.
Wallach, Jeremy. "Dangdut Trendy." *Inside Indonesia*, April–June 2004, 30.
Westley, William, and Magaret Westley. *The Emerging Worker: Equality and Conflict in the Mass Consumption Society.* Montreal: McGill-Queen's University Press, 1971.
Willer, Ragnar K. "Dispelling the Myth of a Global Consumer: Indonesian Consumer Behavior Researched by Means of an Analytical Diagram for Intercultural Marketing. With a Case Study of Sunsilk Shampoo for the Veiled Woman." Dissertation, Humboldt Universität, 2006. http://edoc.hu-berlin.de/dissertationen/willer-ragnar-karl-2006-07-19/HTML.

CHAPTER FIFTEEN

AMERICAN-MUSLIM IDENTITY: ADVERTISING, MASS MEDIA + NEW MEDIA

MICHAEL HASTINGS-BLACK

> I've seen plenty of things making FUN of us [...] We would love to be part of a general marketing campaign if the media world would accept Muslims as a common part of the North American diaspora. (Amethyst, creator of *Ninjabi*[1])

> It is impossible for media to recognize the emergence of the Black Nerd as a lifestyle when the media on a whole chooses not to look at [sic] Black Males directly in the eye [...]. I'm glad that popular culture is [now] recognizing us, if only to use that recognition to sell us more bullshit. (Dallas Penn, Blogger[2])

Introduction

Advertising in the United States has often influenced the pop-culture identities of religious and ethnic minorities. To be targeted by marketers serves as an invitation to join in the national narrative of capitalism. To shop is to be an American.

While this act of inclusion has merit, it has also fostered myopic marketing campaigns. Rather than diversity being, well, diverse, minority-targeted

---
[1] Personal interview, 25 June 2008.
[2] Dallas Penn, *Black Nerds*, http://desedo.com/blog/black-nerds/comment-2419, accessed 1 September 2008.

advertising often traffics in reductive stereotypes of soul claps and sombreros. While some of this is due to those creating content, it is also the fault of mass media, a distribution model based upon "few senders and many receivers."[3]

But this is slowly changing. In 2008, with the new media environment of blogs, video and social networks, we are beginning to see a more accurate depiction of minority groups. Why? Because there is now more content being created by them, not just about them. Dialogue is supplanting monologue.

In the coming years, the U.S. market will likely begin to recognize and court the $170 billion purchasing power of American-Muslims.[4] To date, pop-culture representations of Islam are either cloaked in evil or infused with pathos. But as Hallmark, Wal-Mart, and 20th Century Fox begin creating content geared toward this demographic, it will slowly help to prove that American-Muslims are not only "as boring as the rest of us [Americans]" but also, as Amethyst states above, "a common part of the North American diaspora."[5] This is a process of "becoming American."

When considering this slow embrace of the Islamic consumer, our analysis must acknowledge the point made by legal scholar Leti Volpp:

> September 11 facilitated the consolidation of a new identity category that groups together persons who appear "Middle Eastern, Arab, or Muslim." This consolidation reflects a racialization wherein members of this group are identified as terrorists and disidentified as citizens.[6]

With this in mind, we will look at Islamic identity within American advertising, film, mass media and new media. We will examine how each of these media spaces engages and represents American-Muslims in terms of cultural citizenship and the process of "being/becoming American."

---

[3] Jon Anderson, "New Media, New Publics: Reconfiguring the Public Sphere of Islam," *New School for Social Research* 70, no. 3 (2003): 893.

[4] Marian Salzman, "Marketing to Muslims," *AdWeek* (30 April 2007, http://www.adweek. com/aw/content_display/community/columns/marian\bibrangedashsalzman/e3i36f550df45 cfda974c50e4b12f5838cc, accessed 1 September 2008).

[5] Andrea Useem, *American Muslims are so American they are ... boring?* http://www. religionwriter.com/reviews/books/american-muslims-are-so-american-they-areboring/, accessed 1 September 2008.

[6] Leti Volpp, "The Citizen and the Terrorist," *UCLA Law Review* 49 (2002): 1575.

Sources and Style

I was invited to contribute not as an academic, but as a working member of the American advertising industry—one that often avoids engaging the nuances of race, religion, and ethnicity, instead opting for code works like 'urban'[7] or window dressing for the idea of diversity.[8] Since the advertising industry spends billions of dollars annually, this lack of open engagement is not just feckless, it is a missed market opportunity. Money is being left on the table. I write this paper with the hope that it might be read by both academics and members of the advertising industry. Most of my source material is drawn from blogs, newspapers, and interviews. My goal is to situate and frame various voices that speak about Muslim identity, as it is produced, expressed, and consumed in America. It is an ongoing and living document.

Framing the Inquiry

Let us first examine the ways mass media in the United States constructs the identities of "Islam" and "America:"

Islam

- Understanding Volpp's (2002) point about the "consolidation [of people into] 'Middle Eastern, Arab, or Muslim' that are identified as terrorists and disidentified as citizens,"[9] it is important to note that American-Muslims are targets of both the U.S. "War on Terror" and the "War on Illegal Immigration."[10]

- On the cover of the *New Yorker* magazine, Democratic presidential candidate Barack Obama was portrayed as an anti-American terrorist Muslim (flag burning in fireplace, portrait of Osama bin Laden) and his wife, Michelle, was portrayed as the black nationalist Angela Davis, a woman who was once on the FBI Most Wanted List and politically aligned with the Black Panthers. This picture captures (and

---

[7] Michael Hastings-Black, *Urban*, http://desedo.com/blog/urban, accessed 1 September 2008.

[8] Ken Wheaton, "Agencies Have Funny Way of Showing 'Commitment' to Diversity," *Advertising Age* (7 August 2008, http://adage.com/bigtent/post?article_id=128219, accessed 1 September 2008).

[9] Volpp, "The Citizen and the Terrorist," 1575.

[10] Sunaina Maira, "Youth Culture, Citizenship and Globalization: South Asian Muslim Youth in the United States after September 11th," *Comparative Studies of South Asia, Africa and the Middle East* 24, no. 1 (2004): 221–235.

attempts to satirize) the idea held by some that the Obamas are Muslim and ergo threatening terrorist/non-citizens.

- During the civil rights movement in the 1960s, Dr. Martin Luther King Jr. was a Christian and Malcolm X a Muslim. Malcolm's most famous statement is:

> We declare our right on this earth to be a man, to be a human being, to be respected as a human being, to be given the rights of a human being in this society, on this earth, in this day, which we intend to bring into existence *by any means necessary*.

In 1968 this was perceived as a stark threat to the physical and financial comfort of White America. The current leader of the Nation of Islam, Minister Louis Farrakhan, is situated within mass media as anti-Semitic/anti-American, furthering the "threat" of Islam.

- The U.S. government's pro-Israel policy is conversely anti-Palestine, and is thus imbued with and interpreted as having an anti-Islam stance.[11]

America

- "Is America Ready for a Black President?" The mass media has been asking this question since Obama first declared his candidacy. The question truly means, and mass-media dodged this fact until Fall 2008: Is (White) America Ready for a Black President?[12] This question, when considered along with racial hyphens and prefixes (African-, Hispanic-, Asian-, etc.), creates the impression that the only "true" Americans are of Anglo-Saxon descent.[13] And let us not forget that

---

[11] Ali Alarabi, *Arab/Muslim Americans should NOT vote for Barak Obama*, http://www.mideastyouth.com/2008/09/03/arabmuslim-americans-should-not-vote-for-barak-obama/, accessed 1 September 2008.

[12] Average Bro, *Is America Finally Ready for a Black President?* http://www.averagebro.com/2008/01/is-america-ready-for-black-president.html, accessed 1 September 2008.

[13] "... post-September 11, a national identity has consolidated that is both strongly patriotic and multiracial. The multiracial consolidation of what it means to be American was represented in a cartoon, whereby various persons marked on their T-shirts as African American, Irish American, and Asian American dropped the hyphenated identities, so that all in the second frame had become 'American.' [Fn29] This expansion of who is welcomed as American has occurred through its opposition to the new construction, the putative terrorist who 'looks Middle Eastern.' Other people of color have become 'American' through the process of en-

the American promise of "life, liberty and the pursuit of happiness" was accorded only to property-owning European men.[14]

- In interviews for both this paper and other Desedo Films research projects, many non-white interviewees saw the idea/ideal of "America" as something that both overtly and covertly aims to exclude them from the national narrative. This is part of the representational politics of a country that is 68 percent white, with a House of Representatives that's 83.5 percent white, and a Senate that's 94 percent white.

- If one is a U.S. citizen of the hyphenate class, his or her supposedly inalienable rights are often imperiled. Middle-aged Hispanic-Americans in Texas are having to prove their legal citizenship.[15] Nineteen states have proposed laws to re-prove citizenship in order to vote, which will primarily disenfranchise poor and/or minority Americans who do not have adequate paperwork.[16] These are the same folks who were prevented from voting in the contested 2000 presidential race.[17] And of course there are the hundreds of thousands of Middle Eastern, Arabian, South Indian people who have been denied due process and the supposed rights of American citizenry post-9/11.

- In the days after 9/11, the Ad Council of America created a Public Service Announcement (PSA) called "I Am an American," in "direct response to the hundreds of hate crimes committed against Arabs, Muslims and Sikhs."[18] The goal was to paint a unified yet diverse portrait of America to prevent any further attacks. Yet, shockingly,

---

dorsing racial profiling. Whites, African Americans, East Asian Americans, and Latinas/os are now deemed safe and not required to prove their allegiance." Volpp, "The Citizen and the Terrorist," 1584.

[14] And integral to our economy are millions of un-documented/non-citizen Latinos, who provide labor, but are afforded none of the rights of citizens. Historically, non-whites were not seen as having any purchasing power, or therefore any true participatory/empowered/actual agency in the participation and shaping of the American Economy. They were not subjects, but objects.

[15] Miriam Jordan, "They Say They Were Born in the USA, The State Department Says Prove Ithe State Department Says Prove It," *Wall Street Journal* (11 August 2008, http://online.wsj.com/article/SB121842058533028907.html, accessed 1 September 2008).

[16] Ian Urbina, "Voter ID Battle Shifts to Proof of Citizenship," *New York Times* (12 May 2008, http://www.nytimes.com/2008/05/12/us/politics/12vote.html_r=2&scp=10&sq=must\ %20prove\%20born\%20in\%20the\%20US&st=cse&oref=slogin&oref=slogin, accessed 1 September 2008).

[17] Gregory Palast, "Florida's 'Disappeared Voters': Disfranchised by the GOP," *The Nation* (18 January 2001, http://www.thenation.com/doc/20010205/palast, accessed 1 September 2008).

[18] Evelyn Alsultany, "Selling American Diversity and Muslim American Identity through Non-Profit Advertising Post 9/11," *American Quarterly* 59, no. 3 (2007): 596.

within this framework "... and despite seeking to deconstruct the binary between the citizen and the terrorist, Arabs, Muslims, and Sikhs are not specifically included in this diverse display. There are no visible markers of anything Arab, Muslim, or Sikh in the ads—no veil, no mosque, no turban, no beard, no ... clothing [or] accent."[19] These people are not "American."

- In June 2008, Barack Obama was giving a speech in Detroit, Michigan, when two hijabis were asked to not stand behind him while he spoke. Their hijabs were visual signifiers of their Muslim religion, and thus un-American. Had they not been wearing hijabs, they might not have been "identified" as Muslims, and likely would not have been excluded from the diverse background tapestry that all political candidates seek. Interestingly enough, I posit that had a Republican candidate been on stage, he or she might have courted this "background." Within American politics, both parties often play to the center in pursuit of votes—Republicans not wanting to appear too white and Democrats not wanting to appear too diverse.[20]

Cultural Citizenship: Advertising

Given the vagaries of legal citizenship, the importance of cultural citizenship comes to the fore. Our national narrative is marked by acts and activities that are tied to an occasionally abstract idea of "America"—sports such as baseball or football, food like Thanksgiving Dinner, Apple Pie, McDonald's, activities like Boy Scouts, PTA, Church, etc. ... Like much of Brand America, these activities are seen as virtuous and "from the heartland." In the post-9/11 space, the Council on American-Islamic Relations (CAIR) released a series of ads entitled "I am an American Muslim" in an effort to place Islam within this narrative.[21]

While via CAIR American-Muslims have advertised themselves within the Brand America, the reverse has not yet happened: American brands are not yet reaching out to American-Muslims. Why might this be important? Let us not forget that President George W. Bush urged Americans to express

---

[19] Alsultany, "Selling American Diversity and Muslim American Identity through Non-Profit Advertising Post 9/11," 597.

[20] Andrea Elliot, "Muslim Voters Detect a Snub from Obama," *New York Times* (24 June 2008, http://www.nytimes.com/2008/06/24/us/politics/24muslim.html?hp, accessed 1 September 2008); Ben Smith, "Muslims barred from picture at Obama event," *Politico* (18 June 2008, http://www.politico.com/news/stories/0608/11168.html, accessed 1 September 2008).

[21] Alsultany, "Selling American Diversity and Muslim American Identity through Non-Profit Advertising Post 9/11."

their patriotism through the act of purchasing in the aftermath of 9/11, and that we are a capitalist country that cleaves to shopping on national and religious holidays.
As noted in a study by the ad agency JWT:

> Almas Abbasi, a radiologist in Long Island [...] said she would be grateful for advertising that included Muslims. "If Ramadan starts, and you see an ad in the newspaper saying, 'Happy Ramadan, here's a special in our store,' everyone will run to that store," she said.[22]

Now American brands indeed do this within primarily Muslim countries: Burger King in UAE, HP in Bangladesh, Oreos in Indonesia, etc. It's pretty mundane. But to date, no Muslim holidays are seized as a sales opportunity within the U.S., except perhaps in Dearborn, Michigan, the city with the highest concentration of Muslims and Middle Eastern folks in America. Wal-Mart, the largest retailer and (private) employer of Americans in 2008, has opened a store in Dearborn designed specifically for Muslim and Middle Eastern consumers:

> Wal-Mart offers its standard fare, plus 550 items targeted at Middle Eastern shoppers. [...] To fit into this bastion of ethnic tradition, Wal-Mart started two years ago to meet with imams and moms, conducting focus groups at Middle Eastern restaurants.
>   Walk through the front door of the 200,000-square-foot supercenter and instead of rows of checkout counters, you find a scene akin to a farmers market in Beirut. Twenty-two tables are stacked high with fresh produce like kusa and batenjan, squash and eggplant used in Middle Eastern dishes. Rimming the produce department are shelves filled with Arab favorites like mango juice from Egypt and vine leaves from Turkey used to make mehshi, or stuffed grape leaves. A walled-off section of the butcher case is devoted to halal meats [...] in the freezer case, you'll find frozen falafel. You can also pick up a CD from Lebanese pop singer Ragheb Alama or buy Muslim greeting cards.[23]

Ikea has taken similar, but smaller, measures to court Dearborn shoppers and the local McDonald's and KFC serve halal. On the national scale,

---

[22] Louise Story, "Rewriting the Ad Rules for Muslim-Americans," *New York Times* (28 April 2007, http://www.nytimes.com/2007/04/28/business/28muslim.html?pagewanted=1&_r=1, accessed 1 September 2008): par. 20.
[23] Ken Naughton, "Arab-America's Store," *Newsweek* (10 March 2008, http://www.newsweek.com/id/117835, accessed 1 September 2008): par. 2.

Hallmark carries Eid cards and the United States Postal Service issued an Eid stamp in 2001 (though there was a backlash after 9/11 when people attempted to boycott the stamp because Eid spelled backwards is "Die").[24] But that's about it, except, of course, "in advertisements for universities to emphasize their 'diversity.'"[25]

Now while tailoring stores to reach this consumer base is one important step for retailers, they should not forget that "the average Muslim consumer is much like the average American consumer, with wants and needs mainly dictated by her income, education, and type of family. Their socioeconomic status dictates their spending habits more than their religious affiliation."[26] When speaking about Saatchi & Saatchi's strategic "Lovemarks" with Dilara Hafiz, co-author of *The American Muslim Teenager Handbook*, she mused, "[...] wow—it would be great if they saw a whole new field of Muslim consumers just eager to purchase products due to their amazing ads ☺ Seriously—there's a lot of untapped buying potential amongst all these doctors & engineers."[27] And as noted by Sara in her blog "Muslim Canvas:"

> I guess the value I see in this marketing stuff is the effect it'll have on the American psyche, rather than the Muslim psyche necessarily. An image of a hijabi mom spreading Jif peanut butter on her son's sandwich, or of a long-bearded man answering the door on a Domino's commercial, could go a long way for our "image."[28]

But this is not yet happening for several reasons. The first of which is that "part of the problem is that it is difficult for ad execs to create an advertising profile for Muslims as a whole, because [they] come from many diverse backgrounds and believe many different things."[29] Advertising is an industry that operates by committee, with many rounds of approval and risk management: there is an institutional aversion to engaging a seemingly complex demographic—one where there is the chance of "getting it wrong."[30] While

---

[24] *Eid Stamp Controversy – Articles*, University of West Florida Counter-Terrorism Research, http://www.uwf.edu/counterterrorism/topics/EID_Stamp/EIDStampArticles.html, accessed 1 September 2008.
[25] Amethyst, personal interview, 25 June 2008.
[26] Y. Hafiz, personal interview, 12 June 12 2008.
[27] Personal interview, 30 July 2008.
[28] Sara, *Advertising for the Muslim Demographic*, http://muslimcanvass.blogspot.com/2007/04/advertising-for-muslim-demographic.html, accessed 1 September 2008.
[29] Y. Hafiz, personal interview, 12 June 12 2008.
[30] Robert, personal interview, 7 September 2008.

Sara's point above on "Muslim Canvas" is wholly correct, on the flip side there is the issue that

> portraying "Islam" could fall into stereotypical depictions of women in headscarves and guys with long dishdashas and beards [...] in reality, any of the people in [any] commercial could be a Muslim, but unless they wear their faith in their clothing, it's not something that will be obvious.[31]

There is in fact a history of missteps by American businesses within the context of advertising and Islam—oddly enough none of them were borne out of an effort to reach the consumer demographic, but from using Islam as a backdrop or subtext for general market adverts.[32] There is also an unspoken fear about engaging a supposedly "controversial" consumer group—remember "terrorist/non-citizen."

In a Spring 2008 campaign for Dunkin' Donuts, spokeswoman Rachel Ray wore a scarf that looked like a keffiyeh. Conservative blogger and Fox analyst Michelle Malkin chided Ray for wearing a "jihadi chic" garment.[33] In the ensuing media maelstrom Dunkin' Donuts dropped the advert. While I am certain that any brand considering this space will be aware of the inflammatory anti-Muslim backlash that foments in the blogosphere, I posit that this may be similar to the hurdles faced when marketers first reached out to gay and lesbian consumers in the U.S.[34] As Saad Ahmad, the 20-

---

[31] Fakhraie, personal interview, 12 June 2008.

[32] "Protests from the Muslim community have resulted in a change in DoubleTree Hotels Corporation's recent television advertising campaign, according to the Council on American-Islamic Relations (CAIR). The ads emphasized hotel staff's quality of service by showing men wearing 'Arabian' clothing prostrating themselves to guests in the same way Muslims perform their prayers. Greg Malark, an official with the Phoenix, AZ-based hotel chain, told CAIR the ad 'has been revised' in response to Muslim concerns." See Greg Noakes, "Ad Campaigns Altered," *Washington Report* (April/May 1995, http://www.washington\bibrangedashreport.org/backissues/0495/9504073.htm). CAIR recently has responded to a number of advertisements deemed offensive to Muslims. Anheuser-Busch apologized to the Muslim community for a December ad which featured a model wearing a tank-top decorated with Islamic calligraphy; Timeslips Corporation redesigned a print ad in which business executives kneeled on prayer rugs to "worship" a box of computer software; and the Seagram's distillery recently pulled an ad for an alcoholic beverage which featured the Taj Mahal, a classic example of Muslim architecture from India's Moghul dynasty. See Mai Abdul Rahman, "Bell, Boeing and TM Advertising Blame Others for Their Tasteless Ad," *Washington Report* (December 2005, http://www.washington\bibrangedashreport.org/archives/December_2005/0512058.html).

[33] Michelle Malkin, *The Keffiyeh Kerfuffle*, http://michellemalkin.com/2008/05/28/the-keffiyeh-kerfuffle/, accessed 1 September 2008, par. 1.

[34] Note that GLBT targeted ads (or those featuring a member of that demo) still rarely run in general market. "Jaguar, Land Rover ads halted in gay media, Ford confirms," *TheAdvo-*

year-old author of the blog *Chill Yo, Islam Yo*, pointed out: "Seeing that we live in a capitalist society [including Islam] in advertising is really just an economic issue."[35] If there is money to be made, this will indeed happen. So soon come the adverts.

Cultural Citizenship: Film and TV

It is common knowledge in the U.S. that the onscreen portrayals of Muslims/Middle Eastern/Arab/Desi are often not a positive experience. *Chicago Tribune* reporter Kiran Ansari notes that in the book *Guilty: Hollywood's Verdict on Arabs after 9/11*

> [...] author Jack Shaheen states that in the hundred new movies he reviewed about Arab characters in the post-9/11 period, 1 out of 4 are not even set in the Middle East, yet they have a dubious Arab character thrown in. And although I realize that no one should rely on Hollywood as a source of information, a misrepresentation of any issue or minority group can trickle down to become public perception.[36]

While there may actually be an upswing in positive portrayals within small independent films, there is also the danger of falling into the same reductive typecasting that created the Hollywood stock character of the Magic Negro: African-American characters that "exist because most Hollywood screenwriters don't know much about black people ... so instead of getting life histories or love interests, they get magical powers" that ultimately serve to benefit the white protagonists.[37] Similarly, in the 2007 CW series *Aliens in America*, the character Raja, a Pakistani-Muslim exchange student in Wisconsin, serves as a vessel for the other characters to become more enlightened about the world. As noted by the blog *Ultrabrown* in an extensive review of the show's place within our national narrative, it "gives a middle-class Pakistani kid a kurta, a fakey accent and a higher Allah-per-sentence ratio than a Wahhabi cleric. So last night's premiere was, of course, a big hit

---

cate.com (3 December 2005, http://www.advocate.com/news_detail_ektid23064.asp, accessed 1 September 2008).

[35] Ahmad, personal interview, 24 July 2008.

[36] Kiran Ansari, "Muslims Moving beyond Stereotypes on Screen," *Chicago Tribune* (http://www.chicagotribune.com/news/opinion/chi\bibrangedashmovies\bibrangedashmuslims\bibrangedashperspective,0,7678614.story, accessed 1 September 2008): par. 3.

[37] Christopher John Farley, "That Old Black Magic," *Time* (27 November 2000, http://www.time.com/time/magazine/article/0,9171,998604,00.html, accessed 1 September 2008): par. 1.

with the mainstream media."[38] The Magical Muslim is a "'comical' friendly 'terrorist' [who] can win the hearts of a white community and an American viewership."[39]

Again keeping Volpp's identity conflation in mind, I think a more exciting moment occurred in the 2005 film *Harold and Kumar Go to White Castle*. The brilliance of this film is that it is the first Hollywood feature to portray an Indian-American and a Korean-American as red-blooded American males. Like millions of other American men in the 18–34 demographic, Harold and Kumar's prime objective is a holy trinity of bong hits, breasts, and burgers. Their race and culture are ever-present, but instead of being mined as tropes for pathos, the exotic, or education, they are well employed as one of many narrative and comic elements.

Many loved *Harold and Kumar* as the first bawdy blockbuster that spoke to their same-but-different status as hyphenated Americans. While the character Kumar, played by Kal Penn, is not tied to any religion, there are multiple times in the film when White Americans engage him as if he were Muslim/terrorist/non-citizen. The film was popular enough at the box office to spawn the 2008 sequel *Harold and Kumar Escape From Guantanamo Bay*, which was a commercial success, but critical failure. However, cultural critic Oliver Wang points out that it's "an achievement of a kind too, proof that Asian Americans have made it far enough into the Hollywood machine that they can make perfectly mediocre mainstream fare as much as the next folks. Woo hoo, the promised land."[40] Boring as the rest of us—welcome to America.

What's next? Hollywood studio 20th Century Fox has acquired the U.S. rights to develop a version of the popular Canadian CBC TV show *Little Mosque on the Prairie* (Surette 2008). Having a sitcom that centers on an ethnic, religious, racial, or social group is another American rite of passage. While many of these shows fall into reductive stereotypes, some, like *The Cosby Show*, become historic—heralded by the mass media for "its help in improving race relations by projecting universal values that both Whites and Blacks could identify with, using the tried and true format of the television sitcom."[41]

---

[38] Manish Vij, *The Magical Muslim*, http://www.ultrabrown.com/posts/the-magic-muslim, accessed 1 September 2008, par. 2.

[39] Manish Vij, *Aliens in America: Stereotyping for Fun and Profit*, http://www.racialicious.com/2007/08/01/aliens-in-america-stereotyping-for-fun-and-profit/, accessed 1 September 2008, par. 1.

[40] Oliver Wang, *Harold and Kumar: Up in Smoke Again*, http://poplicks.com/2008/04/harold-and-kumar-up-in-smoke-again.html, accessed 1 September 2008, par. 5.

[41] Joe R. Feagin and Leslie B. Inniss, "The Cosby Show: The View from the Black Middle Class," *Journal of Black Studies* 25, no. 6 (1995): 692–711.

Will *Little Mosque* have such a profound effect? If nothing else, it will make waves as the first of its kind in the U.S., a space in which lines like: "It's a perfect Muslim solution—nobody is happy" are not pernicious but funny.[42] The blog *Muslimah Media Watch* has done a brilliant job in parsing the first two seasons of CBC's *Little Mosque* and the writer Sobia reminds us that it "portrays a certain group of Muslims who follow Islam in a certain way. Although many Muslims may agree with most of the message, the message is still a conservative one."[43] Sobia also points out that even within this conservative rubric, we see "husband and wife characters Yaser and Sarah ... showing affection toward one another in public."[44] Some viewers have questioned:

> How dare she touch her husband's ass in public? If Muslims are being depicted on television, they damn well better be behaving like "good," "pure," and "proper" Muslims.

Sobia replies:

> A bit preachy if you ask me—and not to mention unrealistic! In my opinion, depicting Muslims engaging in lusty or affectionate behaviour [...] aides in the process of "normalizing" us. After all, is this not how we behave? Do Muslim couples not show affection toward each other in public? [...] Or must we portray this façade of "virginal purity" and display our modesty at all times? [...] Why must we shove morality, or at least one particular version of it, in everyone's face?[45]

It will be interesting to see how the mass media receives *Little Mosque* and reports on the subsequent public responses. Will there be product placement? In the Fall 2008 season of the CBC version, the massive Canadian insurance provider Cooperators was integrated in the narrative.[46] Will the U.S. version show Jif or Domino's in the kitchen? This could indeed help

---

[42] Zaib Shaikh (actor), *Little Mosque on the Prairie*, Television Series Episode. Z. Hawaz (Producer), The Barrier. Toronto, CBC, 17 January 2007.
[43] Sobia, *I have a crush on a boy in my Qur'an class*, http://muslimahmediawatch.org/2008/01/17/i-have-a-crush-on-a-boy-in-my-quran-class-2/, accessed 1 September 2008.
[44] Sobia, *What are they trying to tell us*, http://muslimahmediawatch.org/2007/12/06/what-are-they-trying-to-tell-us-2/, accessed 1 September 2008.
[45] Ibid.
[46] M. Darling, personal interview, 22 August 2008.

achieve comedian Maz Jobrani's dream in which Americans begin to understand that Iranians bake cookies too—sans explosives.[47]

It is indeed comedy that most often breaks down barriers between cultures, and at the vanguard of this is often standup comedy, which marks an "assimilat[ion] into the American way of self-lampooning or satirizing, which is part of the society [Murphy, 2004]. Predating 20th Century Fox's option on *Little Mosque* are two U.S. comedy tours that have since made it onscreen—*Axis of Evil* and *Allah Made Me Funny*. As the producer of *Axis* said:

> [...] this is the last stereotype to be broken down. In the same way you look back at Dick Gregory [black] or Latinos[48] or gays, it's very much a moment. There is always a moment in time when society was not ready to confront stereotypes. For people of Middle Eastern descent, [other] people aren't quite ready to confront those stereotypes.[49]

Although both the film and the tour of *Allah Made Me Funny* feature all Muslim comedians, only one of the four comedians in *Axis of Evil* is a Muslim. *Axis*, which has played to wide audiences on Comedy Central as has a special called *The Watch List*, engages the issue of conflation. In fact, comedian Dean Obeidallah, who is half-Italian/half-Arabian, said that before 9/11, he "was just a white guy."[50] Since then, he has become more acutely aware of his Arabic identity, first in response to how others define it and then how he could "try to do something to define who we are, the right way . . . it's up to us to go out there and do that."[51]

Mass media recognizing both the social and market value of this comic vein is priceless, but Maz Jobrani reminds us that it is not about waiting for this to happen within mass media—it is about taking control as an individual author. When I interviewed him on June 11, 2008, Jobrani said:

---

[47] Yoshie, *NEWS: Iranian Bakes Cookie*, http://montages.blogspot.com/2007/12/news-iranian-bakes-cookie.html, accessed 1 September 2008.

[48] The Latino demographic as a target for advertising has become so mainstream such that it can take the next step of being satirized. See "Latino Community Empowered by Coke Ad," *The Onion* (13 October 2004, http://www.theonion.com/content/node/30744).

[49] Felicia Lee, "Comedians as Activists, Challenging Prejudice," *New York Times* (10 March 2007, http://www.nytimes.com/2007/03/10/arts/television/10evil.html?ex=1331179200&en=138364304065e9a0&ei=5088&partner=rssnyt&emc=rss, accessed 1 September 2008).

[50] Dean Obeidallah (interviewee), *Stand Up: Muslim American Comics Come of Age*, Television Series Episode. G. Baker (Producer), America At A Crossroads. New York, PBS, 11 May 2008.

[51] Ibid.

People write to me and say, "Hey Maz, why don't you do this or talk about that?" And my response is "No. Better yet, YOU can do this. With the tools of new media, I am not the only mouthpiece of Iranian comics. *You, too,* can make these jokes and get them out there to the masses." And this is a great thing.

Cultural Citizenship: New Media

Jobrani's support of young comics to create and distribute their own content is consistent with what I think is the most important act within the arena of "becoming" American—authorship. Obeidallah chooses to define himself in response to the identity that others have foisted upon him. Ali Ardekani has created the YouTube world of Baba Ali. *The American Muslim Teenage Handbook* was borne from the idea that "there is no single head of Islam ... why not define ourselves?"[52]

This definition of self is inherently difficult within mass media, due to the "few senders and many receivers" model. Minority groups often have only one or two examples of self that supposedly stand in for millions. *Little Mosque* will play that role soon within the American prime time TV space (likely a welcome replacement to the conflated villains in *24* and *Sleeper Cell*).

New media offers the greatest opportunity for expression of self, as the space serves to "multiply rather than reduce the number and range of message producers and [is] far more interactive, not only in the minimal sense of an increased range of choice, than mass media."[53] Fatemeh Fakhraie, editor-in-chief of *Muslimah Media Watch*, which is both an analysis of mass media and an access point for other Muslimah bloggers, started the blog "because I didn't see any representation of Muslim women in either mainstream or feminist publications. We weren't given a voice; we are only talked about."[54]

While we are looking at this identity construction within the space of Islam, over the last 10 years there have been many hyphenated Americans who, within the new media space, have been able to remix their identity in public space—and in turn secured for themselves a more powerful and complex voice within mass media. Three quick examples of note:

---

[52] Esther Agbaje, *A Teenager's View of Islam in America*, 7 July 2008, http://www.america.gov/st/diversity-english/2008/July/20080707155320eahcny10.3362543.html?CP.rss=true, accessed 1 September 2008.
[53] Anderson, "New Media, New Publics: Reconfiguring the Public Sphere of Islam."
[54] Fakhraie, personal interview, 12 June 2008.

Black Nerds

Over the last few years across the media, we have seen an increase in black skateboarders, black rockers, black videogamers, and a new strain of hip-hop, which runs counter to the standard mass media image of the black man as athlete/rapper/criminal. Why? In 2007 director Raafi Rivero suggested:

> [T]he proliferation of media voices and sources enabled by the internet has allowed a more nuanced and less-gangster voice of young black America to emerge, untempered by market concerns and sensationalism [...] because of our more democratized communication tools we are beginning to see a more accurate depiction of black america. Mainly because, you know, that media is actually being created by, ahem, black people.[55]

Gay/Lesbian

I recently interviewed a peer who had been struggling with his gay identity at the turn of the century—he knew that he was gay—but did not want to partake in the public ritual of attending gay bars/clubs.[56] Nor did he want to "declare" himself gay for fear that to do so was fraught with signifiers and would cause others (both hetero- and homo-) to reduce him to a stereotype. But via the internet he was able to find likeminded men who, while their sexual inclinations were gay, did not fit the mass media portrayal of homosexuality. By becoming empowered through this online space, he, and many of his friends decided to come out of the closet—a trend that we have seen manifested in the "gay population explosion" over the past 10 years.[57] With an increased public presence, there is in turn a greater diversity of voices at the table.

Sex Workers

The current trend of sexually forward and tart-tongued heroines in major films and TV shows (*Juno, Washingtonienne, Secret Diary of a Call Girl*) is rooted in sex-worker literature—the majority of which began in the blogosphere. Via authoring and distributing their own stories, sex workers are

---

[55] Raafi Rivero, *Weak Rappers Need to Step Off*, http://desedo.com/blog/weak-rappers-need-to-step-off/, accessed 1 September 2008.

[56] M.A., personal interview, 29 July 2008.

[57] Paul Varnell, "A Gay Population Explosion?" *Chicago Free Press* (14 November 2007, http://www.indegayforum.org/news/show/31407.html, accessed 1 September 2008).

now newly "revealed" to be, of course, nuanced and complex human beings, boring as the rest of us, not simply "Hooker With a Heart of Gold" or a "Dumb Tramp."[58]

Islam?

Where might new media take Islamic Identity in the United States? Well even with the advent of comedy, sitcoms and Wal-Mart, Fatemeh of *Muslimah Media Watch* notes that:

> Islam's presence in [mass media] is increasingly religious, ... things like beards, keffiyehs, terrorism, niqabs, and strict gender segregation and other "rules" are often what gets aired in the [mass media], and thus that's what people think of when they hear Islam.[59]

Offsetting this narrow scope, new media is the space within which one can tease out different aspects of his or her personality by being a creater/consumer or viewer/user. A young man can more easily be a Pious Mulim/Skater/Fan of *Batman*/Blogger all at once. Rather than waiting for mass media to say OMG look at the soccer-playing hijabi, that teen, for whom this multiplicity is normal, will be likely be online accessing/authoring those different parts of herself. And of course there is a robust Muslim blogosphere.
What is so unique to online? It is

> a sphere of creole discourse and creole journeys, an intermediate sphere between more private worlds and those of public rituals; it is part of a continuum between those along which social actors can move. Viewed statically, as languages, creoles appear mixed; but viewed dynamically, as speech communities, they look more like intermediate points on a continuum of activities and encounters that people enter and leave.[60]

It is the easiest space in which to be American, to be Muslim, to be both and beyond.
It is indeed these young folks who will likely be at the vanguard of change in America. While the runway chic of Balenciaga, Raf Simons, and TSE

---

[58] Michael Hastings-Black, *Juno, Sex Workers and Mapquest*, http://desedo.com/blog/juno-sex-workers-mapquest/, accessed 1 September 2008.
[59] Personal interview with Fakhraie on 12 June 2008.
[60] Anderson, "New Media, New Publics: Reconfiguring the Public Sphere of Islam."

have been mining the visual language of hijabs and keffiyehs, far more important is the young Dutch design collective MSLM that remixes Islam with hip-hop style in Rotterdam. Fashion blogs like Hijab Style and We Love Hijab. The U.S. teen magazine *Muslim Girl*, small-press hipster T-shirts that celebrate Ramadan and Hijabman's tweaking of an old Irish saying: "Frisk Me, I'm Muslim."[61] All of this content is disseminated, consumed, and remixed by others online and authored by and for young Muslims.

Online we see the comic strip *Ninjabi*, authored by a young woman in New Jersey, "something for the new generation of muslim girls to look up to ... a character cross between then popular powerpuff girls, and a somewhat devout muslim who cares for human rights, taking a hidden ninja lifestyle to help others."[62] And then another hijabi in Texas started another comic of the same name. Soon there will be a third.

As media scholar Faris Yakob points out in his thesis *I Believe the Children Are Our Future:*

> If we look to those under 25, we see not incremental but qualitative shifts in behaviour. The generation gap has never been wider, because kids can control their own experiences of ideas in a way the generations that grew up before never could.[63]

It is these digital natives who truly understand duality. They are the first generation who can bifurcate themselves, not with the negative connotations usually ascribed to such cleavage, but in a way that actually makes them more holistic. They can likely slide between the terrorist/non-citizen label and be both American and Muslim—not "become" American as mass media may be waiting to see happen—but simply be, as they already are. It is this new media space that will feed "new" identity politics to advertising, film, and mass media. It is this authorship that hopefully will define the Muslim consumer space within America.

---

[61] For more, see these sites: http://andreiacosta.nl/mslm-magazine.htm; http://www.muslimgirlworld.com/; http://hijabstyle.blogspot.com/; http://www.chillyoislamyo.com/category/gear/; http://www.hijabman.com/.
[62] Amethyst, personal interview, 25 June 2008.
[63] Faris Yakob, *I Believe the Children Are Our Future*, http://farisyakob.typepad.com/blog/2007/11/i-believe-the-c.html, accessed 1 September 2008, 8.

Bibliography

Agbaje, Esther. *A Teenager's View of Islam in America.* 7 July 2008, http://www.america.gov/st/diversity-english/2008/July/20080707155320eahcnyl0.3362543.html?CP.rss=true, accessed 1 September 2008.

Alarabi, Ali. *Arab/Muslim Americans should NOT vote for Barak Obama.* http://www.mideastyouth.com/2008/09/03/arabmuslim-americans-should-not-vote-for-barak-obama/, accessed 1 September 2008.

Alsultany, Evelyn. "Selling American Diversity and Muslim American Identity through Non-Profit Advertising Post 9/11." *American Quarterly* 59, no. 3 (2007): 593–622.

Anderson, Jon. "New Media, New Publics: Reconfiguring the Public Sphere of Islam." *New School for Social Research* 70, no. 3 (2003): 887–906.

Ansari, Kiran. "Muslims Moving beyond Stereotypes on Screen." *Chicago Tribune* (http://www.chicagotribune.com/news/opinion/chi\bibrangedashmovies\bibrangedashmuslims\bibrangedashperspective, 0,7678614.story, accessed 1 September 2008).

Bro, Average. *Is America Finally Ready for a Black President?* http://www.averagebro.com/2008/01/is-america-ready-for-black-president.html, accessed 1 September 2008.

Eid Stamp Controversy – Articles. University of West Florida Counter-Terrorism Research, http://www.uwf.edu/counterterrorism/topics/EID_Stamp/EIDStampArticles.html, accessed 1 September 2008.

Elliot, Andrea. "Muslim Voters Detect a Snub from Obama." *New York Times* (24 June 2008, http://www.nytimes.com/2008/06/24/us/politics/24muslim.html?hp, accessed 1 September 2008).

Farley, Christopher John. "That Old Black Magic." *Time* (27 November 2000, http://www.time.com/time/magazine/article/0,9171,998604,00.html, accessed 1 September 2008).

Feagin, Joe R., and Leslie B. Inniss. "The Cosby Show: The View from the Black Middle Class." *Journal of Black Studies* 25, no. 6 (1995): 692–711.

Hastings-Black, Michael. *Juno, Sex Workers and Mapquest.* http://desedo.com/blog/juno-sex-workers-mapquest/, accessed 1 September 2008.

———. *Urban.* http://desedo.com/blog/urban, accessed 1 September 2008.

"Jaguar, Land Rover ads halted in gay media, Ford confirms." *TheAdvocate.com* (3 December 2005, http://www.advocate.com/news_detail_ektid23064.asp, accessed 1 September 2008).

Jordan, Miriam. "They Say They Were Born in the USA, The State Department Says Prove Ithe State Department Says Prove It." *Wall*

Street Journal (11 August 2008, http://online.wsj.com/article/
SB121842058533028907.html, accessed 1 September 2008).
"Latino Community Empowered by Coke Ad." *The Onion* (13 October 2004, http://www.theonion.com/content/node/30744).
Lee, Felicia. "Comedians as Activists, Challenging Prejudice." *New York Times* (10 March 2007, http://www.nytimes.com/2007/03/10/arts/television/10evil.html?ex=1331179200&en=138364304065e9a0&ei=5088&partner=rssnyt&emc=rss, accessed 1 September 2008).
Maira, Sunaina. "Youth Culture, Citizenship and Globalization: South Asian Muslim Youth in the United States after September 11th." *Comparative Studies of South Asia, Africa and the Middle East* 24, no. 1 (2004): 221–235.
Malkin, Michelle. *The Keffiyeh Kerfuffle*. http://michellemalkin.com/2008/05/28/the-keffiyeh-kerfuffle/, accessed 1 September 2008.
Naughton, Ken. "Arab-America's Store." *Newsweek* (10 March 2008, http://www.newsweek.com/id/117835, accessed 1 September 2008).
Noakes, Greg. "Ad Campaigns Altered." *Washington Report* (April/May 1995, http://www.washington\bibrangedashreport.org/backissues/0495/9504073.htm).
Obeidallah, Dean (Interviewee). *Stand Up: Muslim American Comics Come of Age*. Television Series Episode. G. Baker (Producer), America At A Crossroads. New York, PBS, 11 May 2008.
Palast, Gregory. "Florida's 'Disappeared Voters': Disfranchised by the GOP." *The Nation* (18 January 2001, http://www.thenation.com/doc/20010205/palast, accessed 1 September 2008).
Penn, Dallas. *Black Nerds*. http://desedo.com/blog/black-nerds/comment-2419, accessed 1 September 2008.
Rahman, Mai Abdul. "Bell, Boeing and TM Advertising Blame Others for Their Tasteless Ad." *Washington Report* (December 2005, http://www.washington\bibrangedashreport.org/archives/December_2005/0512058.html).
Rivero, Raafi. *Weak Rappers Need to Step Off*. http://desedo.com/blog/weak-rappers-need-to-step-off/, accessed 1 September 2008.
Salzman, Marian. "Marketing to Muslims." *AdWeek* (30 April 2007, http://www.adweek.com/aw/content_display/community/columns/marian\bibrangedashsalzman/e3i36f550df45cfda974c50e4b12f5838cc, accessed 1 September 2008).
Sara. *Advertising for the Muslim Demographic*. http://muslimcanvass.blogspot.com/2007/04/advertising-for-muslim-demographic.html, accessed 1 September 2008.

Shaikh, Zaib (Actor). *Little Mosque on the Prairie*. Television Series Episode. Z. Hawaz (Producer), The Barrier. Toronto, CBC, 17 January 2007.

Smith, Ben. "Muslims barred from picture at Obama event." *Politico* (18 June 2008, http://www.politico.com/news/stories/0608/11168.html, accessed 1 September 2008).

Sobia. *I have a crush on a boy in my Qur'an class*. http://muslimahmediawatch.org/2008/01/17/i-have-a-crush-on-a-boy-in-my-quran-class-2/, accessed 1 September 2008.

———. *What are they trying to tell us*. http://muslimahmediawatch.org/2007/12/06/what-are-they-trying-to-tell-us-2/, accessed 1 September 2008.

Story, Louise. "Rewriting the Ad Rules for Muslim-Americans." *New York Times* (28 April 2007, http://www.nytimes.com/2007/04/28/business/28muslim.html?pagewanted=1&_r=1, accessed 1 September 2008).

Urbina, Ian. "Voter ID Battle Shifts to Proof of Citizenship." *New York Times* (12 May 2008, http://www.nytimes.com/2008/05/12/us/politics/12vote.html_r=2&scp=10&sq=must\%20prove\%20born\%20in\%20the\%20US&st=cse&oref=slogin&oref=slogin, accessed 1 September 2008).

Useem, Andrea. *American Muslims are so American they are ... boring?* http://www.religionwriter.com/reviews/books/american-muslims-are-so-american-they-areboring/, accessed 1 September 2008.

Varnell, Paul. "A Gay Population Explosion?" *Chicago Free Press* (14 November 2007, http://www.indegayforum.org/news/show/31407.html, accessed 1 September 2008).

Vij, Manish. *Aliens in America: Stereotyping for Fun and Profit*. http://www.racialicious.com/2007/08/01/aliens-in-america-stereotyping-for-fun-and-profit/, accessed 1 September 2008.

———. *The Magical Muslim*. http://www.ultrabrown.com/posts/the-magic-muslim, accessed 1 September 2008.

Volpp, Leti. "The Citizen and the Terrorist." *UCLA Law Review* 49 (2002): 1575–1600.

Wang, Oliver. *Harold and Kumar: Up in Smoke Again*. http://poplicks.com/2008/04/harold-and-kumar-up-in-smoke-again.html, accessed 1 September 2008.

Wheaton, Ken. "Agencies Have Funny Way of Showing 'Commitment' to Diversity." *Advertising Age* (7 August 2008, http://adage.com/bigtent/post?article_id=128219, accessed 1 September 2008).

Yakob, Faris. *I Believe the Children Are Our Future.* http://farisyakob.typepad.com/blog/2007/11/i-believe-the-c.html, accessed 1 September 2008.

Yoshie. *NEWS: Iranian Bakes Cookie.* http://montages.blogspot.com/2007/12/news-iranian-bakes-cookie.html, accessed 1 September 2008.

Part IV

Epilogue

CHAPTER SIXTEEN

THE ECONOMIC POLITICS OF MUSLIM CONSUMPTION

PATRICK HAENNI

The political economics of Muslim consumption[1] is in full boom, from the explosion of U.S.-inspired malls full of global brands and symbols intended to appeal to a growing bourgeois (and often pious) consumer class, to the upsurge in Islamic-derived products—such as the Muslim Barbies Razanne and Fulla, as well as halal rum, beer, champagne, and whiskies.[2] "Islamic coaching"[3] has even emerged as a form of elite therapy. Competition between local brands has developed as some brandish an anti-imperialist, consumerist message: Muslim-Up has a religious tone, while Arab-Cola and Cola Turka have a more nationalistic fervor. So-called "green leisure" has emerged, including the Caprice Hotel on the Aegean coast, which is the first hotel whose services comply with Islamic moral codes. Turkish green serials and "clean art" (*fann naẓīf*) from Egypt[4] have transformed the relationship to religious references. For the halal, the licit, in these cases tends to associate conformity with not only interdictions but also a certain ethic deriving from religiosity and other aspects that range from individual health concerns to the ethics of fair trade.

---

[1] By this term, I mean the consumption behavior or marketing techniques borrowed from international consumption practices but framed in one way or another with references to Islam.

[2] These are the names of the unfermented drinks on the menu of the Grand Hyatt of Cairo. They taste vaguely like their namesakes and are sold during Oriental dance parties as a substitute for alcoholic beverages. The hotel owner, Saudi Shaykh ᶜAbd al-ᶜAzīz Ibrahim, who is known for his religious fervor, decided in May 2008 to serve drinks that respect Muslim precepts. However, his beliefs do not prevent him from allowing belly dancing, which is still part of the hotel's attractions.

[3] The market for personal success literature touted by management experts close to—or members of—the Muslim Brotherhood is very much in this vein.

[4] On the de-politicization of politically committed art by consumerism, see Patrick Haenni and Husam Tammam, "De retour dans les rythmes du monde: Une petite histoire du chant (ex)islamiste en Egypte," *Vingtième siècle. Revue d'histoire* 82 (2004): 91–102.

The intersection of Islamic references and consumer culture is laden with tension. Consumerism has always been associated with the expansion of the market and a liberal, Western ideology, whereas the fundamentalist discourse has always been in open conflict with these values. For the militant Islamist, for example, wearing the hijab is not just a response to religious injunctions; it is also a way to contest certain aspects of Western culture. The same logic applies to the promotion and perception of Razanne (the Islamic Barbie) and derisively to Cola Turka, to cite only two examples.

Liberal modernity, as revealed by consumerist society, is disseminated based on the logic of cultural domination for some (this postulate underlies catch phrases such as Coca-colonization and McDonaldization), conflict for others (an Islamized modernity founded in opposition to the West[5], or through non-confrontational mixing.[6]

Beyond their divergences, these views about how liberal modernity is exported hinge on the connections between the various forms of a peripheral construction of modernity and the initial Western model (exporting, reversal, and transfiguration of this model). They have little interest in understanding how these cultural productions are constructed within the social and political dynamics of societies that are receptive to the Western model.

I will concentrate here on this latter notion. I maintain that a Muslim consumerist society is emerging, which, locally, is taking form from the confluence of four factors. First, it is born of the constitution of a cosmopolitan and conservative bourgeois class. Second, it is implicitly participating in the mutation of religiosity towards market-friendly, individualistic beliefs that are hedonistic and open to cultural extroversion because this new religiosity is based on class. This market-driven belief can, however, support a revival of religious discipline. Third, the struggle between this discipline and hedonism is giving birth to a pluralization of lifestyles, which, in turn, is generating a Muslim consumerist society. Fourth, because this culture is derived from an explicit ideology, it plays into the hands of the dominant discourse, which is Salafi.[7] This creates a new source of tension that is not

---

[5] In reference to the Islamist project "The Islamization of Modernity" on which Shaykh ᶜAbd al-Salam Yasin will present a book.

[6] Jean-Claude Guillebaud, *Le commencement d'un monde. Vers une modernité métisse* (Paris: Seuil, 2008).

[7] Olivier Roy clearly shows how the Salafi message can be considered an ideology of the globalization of meaning, where promoting a "pure" Islam can only conflict with local cultures that have appropriated the religious. It is part of a de-territorialization process of the religious. Cf. Olivier Roy, *L'islam mondialisé* (Paris: Seuil, 2002). On the progressive imposition of a Salafi era, see Husam Tammam, *Asᵓila al-zaman al-salafī*, http://www.chihab.net/modules.php?name=News&file=print&sid=1825.

Patrick Haenni: Economic Politics of Muslim Consumption   329

defined by the relationship with the West but is defined in terms of mixing—whereby the Muslim world seeks to become part of economic modernity.

Figure 16.1: This McDonald's advertisement, displayed during Ramadan, proves that it's not always a clash of civilizations when Western mass culture collides with Islam.

Consumption therefore becomes an important political tool, mirroring the relationship with the West, mirroring, above all, Muslim societies' view of themselves, as well as the identity transformations that affect them. Finally, this consumption is a prism through which we can analyze the meaning of what we call re-Islamization.

From Ethnic Marketing to Islamic Business: The Identity Cat-and-Mouse Game of Cultural Communication

The terms of political economics surrounding Muslim consumption are set in the marketing and cultural communication stages, well before the act of consumption.

How should Muslim consumers in general, and Muslim minority markets in particular, be courted? Two distinct choices are possible: culture or religion, origin or faith, the East or Islam. In the context of an increasingly ideological Muslim identity, culture goes over better—i.e., it is easier for the majority to accept societies that still have deep misgivings about Muslim references.[8]

This is clearly the cultural approach that Wal-Mart chose when the retail giant decided to open a store specifically catering to a "Muslim and Middle Eastern" clientele in Dearborn, Michigan. The goal is to become a "bastion of ethnic traditions,"[9] with everything under its roof being equal: Islamic-referencing and evocations of the Middle East are associated with halal meat but also with decidedly un-Islamic things, such as falafel and Arab pop music from Lebanon.[10] The same thing was done by Ülker with the launch of Cola Turka, even though, given its Islamic reputation,[11] we might have expected to see the company favor the religious instead of the roots angle. In various advertisements, everyday American WASPs are seen gulping down the precious Cola Turka and being transformed by it. They start singing folklore and are reborn in a family with hybrid values—they kiss their elders out of respect, they display traditional piety, and they sport moustaches. Such derision thwarts American imperialism by replacing it with a traditional Turkish way of life instead of an Islamic alternative. This is a lightweight cultural war, not a clash of religions.

In the West, however, ethnic marketing does not have much of a future. "Roots"-targeted marketing loses traction as integration in European societies advances. Christian Johannsman[12] notes, it is becoming increasingly difficult to differentiate young Turks from young Germans, thus making it more difficult to use identity-based references to sell products. In the end, it is not ethnic business (for which the sacred is merely one factor) that will take off, but rather Islamic business (for which Islam is everything, but not quite everything . . .).

---

[8] Michael Hastings Black observes in chapter 15 that in the United States, despite the melting pot, it remains controversial from a marketing point of view to target minorities using their own symbols. He cites the controversy surrounding the appearance of Rachel Ray with a Palestinian scarf on a Dunkin Donuts poster as one such example. This "jihadist garment," as it was described by bloggers, drew criticism from certain conservative media outlets, including Fox News. Dunkin Donuts was eventually forced to pull the ad campaign.

[9] Keith Naughton, "Arab American stores," *Newsweek* (10 March 2008).

[10] Female Lebanese singers are considered scandalous in the region.

[11] On the Turkish question and the Islamic reference, see Marie-Élisabeth Maigre, "Turquie: l'émergence d'une éthique musulmane dans le monde des affaires - Autour de l'évolution du MÜSIAD et des communautés religieuses," *Religioscope* (9 May 2005, http://religion.info/french/articles/article_170.shtml). See also chapter 6 of this volume.

[12] Christian Johannsmann, "Anthropological Perspectives on Ethnic Marketing in Germany" (Paper presented at the Conference "Contemporary Muslim Consumer Cultures," Berlin, 24–27 September 2008).

To Euphemize or to Stress Difference: Tensions in Islamic Business Surrounding the Identity Question

Islamic business is soaring in the West: restaurants such as Halal Fried Chicken and "Beurger King"[13] have led to a boom in Muslim fast food; in the area of clothing, beyond the headscarf, Islamic street wear has taken off, as have music and leisure activities. While ethnic marketing focuses on one's culture or origins, Islamic business targets one's religious beliefs. There again, however, which Islam are we talking about?

Two conceptions of identity are in conflict, even if the products—more Islamized than Islamic[14]—are products of globalization and mass culture. One of these conceptions asserts its difference and refuses all compromise, while the other seeks to normalize identity. These different approaches to identity foster distinctly different forms of religiosity.

As such, the universe of meaning that surrounds the world of Islamic Barbies is clearly differentiating, as is evident in the advertisements that promote them. Chatrooms that sing the praises of Islamic Barbie try to outdo one another in conservatism as they celebrate the victory of Muslim culture over the nakedness of Barbie. At the same time, it comes as no surprise that Fulla, the latest Islamic doll,[15] is perceived by Islamophobic bloggers as a "threat" that spreads a culture of female submission.

In the same vein, the market for identity-based soft drinks, such as Mecca Cola, Muslim Up, Arab Cola, and Zam Zam Cola, following the lead of Cola Turka, seeks to "capitalize on the anti-American feelings that have grown since the Iraqi invasion," observes Dilek Kaya Mutlu.[16] These soft drinks call for people to be "committed" when they drink, playing off the fact that in Arabic, *iltizām* means both commitment and religious devotion.

However, there exist numerous inclusive responses founded on attempts to normalize the Muslim identity. First among the inclusive responses are the English-speaking productions that put a humorous spin on radical perceptions of Muslims—including *Allah Made Me Funn;* the *Axis of Evil*

---

[13] A reference to the "beurs," which is a term for the French community of North African origin.

[14] I make a distinction between Islamic products and Islamized products, which is based on Alina Kokoschka's terminology; see chapter 11 of this volume. My perception of this is that Islamic products are compliant with Muslim norms (halal meat, the headscarf) and Islamized products are identity-based imitations of Western products—e.g., halal fashion, halal music, Islamic soft drinks—though not necessarily in compliance with the Islamic norm.

[15] The advertisement is available on YouTube: http://fr.youtube.com/watch?v=6WqmCAzxUxI.

[16] See chapter 6 of this volume.

Comedy Tour; and multiethnic television shows, such as *Little Mosque on the Prairie*. The typical sequence of the normalization of the Muslim identity via consumerism begins when an economic player designs a marketing strategy that targets the minority group. If this strategy has some success, the economic player might be tempted to broaden his or her market by opening the product up to the majority group. To accomplish this, in the event that the relationship between the two groups is strained (as was the case with the ill-fated Dunkin' Donuts poster[17]), a marketing strategy must take a euphemistic approach to the minority identity—i.e., keep the initial symbol but make the reference to the controversial group allegorical, or play on a hidden meaning known only to the minority group. One such example is MBN for "Muslims By Nature." Arabic-speakers will appreciate the reference to the term *fiṭra* ("of a natural and intuitive religiosity"). EJR plays on the double entendre: on one hand it means "Elegance, *Jeunesse* [youth], Respect;" on the other hand, when the acronym is pronounced in French, it sounds like *hijra*, the start of the Muslim calendar, which can also mean, to some, a departure from impious lands (Europe) and a return to *Dār al- Islām* (Muslim lands). Likewise, *Dawahwear* is a clothing brand whose name in Arabic signifies the call to Islam, and the number 610, which features prominently on the label's clothing, refers to the year of the first revelation of the Koran.

Increasingly, Muslim identity uses aesthetic labeling and a process of syncretism (Islamic rap, Islamic streetwear). An inclusive dialogue is developing, which is based on ethics, not moral standards (in the universe of clothing, Islam is the headscarf, the headscarf is modesty).

The ethical approach includes the Islamic reference in a secular context that does not contradict Muslim moral codes. It is about inserting the Islamic reference in a discourse based on a notion of social justice[18] and respect for women (i.e., it refuses to view women as "objects" or to see them as a temptation). This posture seeks differentiation without being exclusive. As the founder of the brand EJR stated:

> The ethics are Muslim but also non-Muslim, meaning they can be shared by non-Muslims, non-believers, Christians. It is less about exclusion, which allows us to get out of our Arab-Islamic confines and reach more people who have the same needs.

---

[17] Cf. footnote 8.
[18] For further information, see Patrick Haenni, *L'islam de marché. L'autre révolution conservatrice* (Paris: Seuil, 2005).

Patrick Haenni: Economic Politics of Muslim Consumption 333

Figure 16.2: Dawahwear: An American pop culture take on Muslim identity

The same dynamic is at play in the world of Islamic soft drinks. The references are obviously religious (Mecca-Cola, Muslim Up, Qibla Cola[19]), but in an effort to tap into the mainstream market they use the religious reference in a moderate way with a preference for inclusive ethical dialogue that shifts away from a strategy that divides consumers based on identity. Muslim Up, in fact, aims to be "the drink of a new generation defending peace and love and not a clash of civilizations." In Indonesia, Qulbo Cola makes reference to the physiological and affective heart: wishy-washy consumerist ethics thus replace affirmations of identity.

---

[19] Cola Turka and Arab Cola are exceptions that play on nationalistic and cultural sentiments.

Did You Say "Halal"? The Rupture between Symbol and Meaning as a Religious Figure of Secularization

The reference to halal, an emblematic example of ethnic business that was a forerunner of Islamized products, is also changing through consumerism and its re-Islamization. This standard has been traditionally associated with a product, but it is increasingly becoming a synonym of piety. However, this platform for piety is becoming increasingly hybridized because of globalization, marketing, and Islamization.

Figure 16.3: A scene from a bazaar in Le Bourget, Paris: Ethnic business or Muslim identity embedded in Western culture?

The widespread boom of halal butchers[20] has led to an increasing need for certification. At the same time, however, the fact that it is practically impossible to be certain that products are certified by the few accredited organizations in the Malay neighborhoods of London, together with the numerous scandals that have rocked halal distributors, have sometimes caused customers to seek halal products not so much by looking for a certified butcher but by seeking out the distributors with the strongest Islamic credentials.

---

[20] Halal butchers are now in the majority in France.

Johan Fischer cites an example of an imam who refused to buy meat from a butcher wearing a gold ring.[21] The Islamic credentials of an establishment can compensate for the lack of a guarantee from the certification organizations.

Halal is therefore becoming more a question of the general feeling of an establishment and less a matter of standards. The semantics surrounding the word *halal* are also changing.

Fischer, who has observed halal markets in the Malaysian districts of London, has noted a significant repositioning of the discourse since September 11.[22] Where it was once exclusively restricted to a series of religious conditions that included not eating pork and slaughtering livestock by slitting their throats while reciting religious rites, the discourse has expanded to encompass extrinsic standards, which despite not being originally associated with halal, are anchored in hygienic and health-conscious attitudes. These inclusive qualities reflect a new, more mobile, global philosophy of food that touches on various issues, including the rejection of junk food, reference to Islam, and fair trade. There is, therefore, secularization in the sense that reference to religion is verified by a certification process with numerous criteria that for many define a global ethic founded on worldly considerations; justice and health are not exclusively Muslim.[23]

Secularization here does not mean that religious influences have receded, and it is not a contradiction with the processes linked to re-Islamization. It harks back to the disassociation of the religious symbol and the structure of meaning in which the symbol resided. The book *Halal Drinks: Great Recipes to Entertain, Relax and Rejuvenate*[24] reflects a globalized health ideal and a hedonistic world, but not compliance with a norm. It does not, however, contradict such norms, which leaves the opportunity of an Islamic perspective on this book.

A degree of tension with religious standards or the dominant discourse can add an extra layer of meaning. Consider an Indonesian advertisement for Sunsilk: it shows a woman who, although wearing a veil, wears jeans and a tight sweater, which clearly conveys a message of emancipation. Thanks to her shampoo, her hair no longer stands in the way of her desire to play

---

[21] Gold, like silk, is considered by orthodox Muslims to be something that men are forbidden from wearing.

[22] Cf. chapter 1 of this volume.

[22] See Jumaatun Azmi, *Halal Food: A Guide to Good Eating—London* (Kuala Lumpur: KasehDia Sdn. Bhd, 2003). In Ramadan, television programs offering advice during the fast are very much of the same vein.

[23] They are, however, perceived to be Islamic criteria by many Muslims.

[24] Jumaatun Azmi, *Halal Drinks. Great Recipes to Entertain, Relax and Rejuvenate* (Kuala Lumpur: KasehDia, 2004).

football, which the ad reminds us is not just a male sport. She substitutes for an injured teammate and ends up scoring the winning goal.[25] In another advertisement for the same brand, an introverted student finds the confidence to talk to the boy of her dreams, thanks to her shampoo.

In these two videos, the vision of women as capable of taking initiative where men fail, clearly flips gender roles where initiative—in flirting and football—is traditionally in the male realm. This reversal legitimizes flirting when it occurs in an environment in which Muslim morals are respected.

These advertisements exist at the junction of the re-Islamization process. They revolve around a religious symbol (the hijab, and respect its associated rules—e.g., the interdiction to show one's hair[26]) and a pluralization of lifestyle choices (feminization of football, more initiative granted to women in the area of flirting), which is promoted by the instruments of consumerism (i.e., advertising) that religious norms frown upon but do not prohibit.

At first glance, it is tempting to conclude that hedonism—i.e., free market culture—has triumphed over Muslim culture, or at least to subscribe to the idea that the latter has entered a relativist postmodernism, where everything can be put on the table and come together without a hitch.

Merging cultures, however, have never shied from balance-of-power conflicts; they are in fact their battlefields of choice, and Muslim consumerism is no exception. More than that, the affirmation of a Muslim hedonistic ethos has produced an opposite trend ruled by rigor.

Muslim consumerism makes it possible to decrypt the dialectic game working at the heart of the re-Islamization process, where mix-and-match moral standards play into the hands of the Salafis, who monopolize the discourse, whereas hedonism's cunning yet makeshift approach lacks explicit legitimacy.

Four Expressions of Muslim Consumerism

Let us turn to Uri Ram's affirmation, which unlike postmodern theses, has the merit of considering the balance of power as an integral part of mixing. Ram argues that

---

[25] The advertisement is available, with an English translation, on http://fr.youtube.com/watch?v=LwTHZi0eo2s. For a discussion of the Sunsilk campaign in Indonesia, see Ragnar K. Willer's analysis in chapter 14 of this volume.

[26] During the ad, the hair remains out of sight, hidden either by the headscarf or by the shampoo itself.

Figure 16.4: Islamic fashion: birth of a modest hedonism as seen on the cover of a magazine devoted to veiled women

Mecca Cola achieves the opposite of what it declares it does: it dispenses the Muslim idiom into vessels of commodified American culture. While 'Mecca' wins symbolically, 'Cola' wins structurally.[27]

Uri Ram does set the terms of the problem. However, his statement contains two serious methodological problems. First, if "Coca" wins, it is difficult to see what he is referring to: Is it the West? But to which West is he referring? There is the idea of domination, yet it is not clear who is doing the dominating. Second, such a statement presents the symbol and the structure as independent variables. It orders them, saying that the former is a mere veneer, while the latter would deeply affect society in some fashion. Mixing, from this perspective, would only be a lure, and the reference to Islam, a ruse by the dominating Western culture. Opposing this argument,

---

[27] Uri Ram, "Liquid Identities: Mecca Cola versus Coca-Cola," *European Journal of Cultural Studies* 10, no. 4 (2007): 465–484, quoted by Dilek Kaya Mutlu in chapter 6 of this volume.

Marco Moreira, a manager at Coca-Cola, sees soda not as an active structure but rather an indecisive object that only takes on the meaning that the appropriation process gives it. Moreira states: "I do not think that Coca-Cola projects; I think that it reflects."[28] A strong statement that is applicable to the export of all liberal consumerist modernity, whether it is indexed to Islam or not. It remains to be defined what Muslim consumerism reflects. And that is where, in contrast with a viewpoint defined by cultural domination, it is necessary to return to the situation at the local level.

I will now expand on the four "expressions," as defined by Moreira's "reflets," of Muslim consumerism.

First, Muslim consumerism is part of the creation of a bourgeois, conservative class, which is changing the re-Islamization of the Muslim world. These are the Egyptian *infitāḥiyīn*, having made their pious comeback, notably because of their immigration to the Gulf countries where they accumulated significant personal wealth, thanks to the economic policies of President Sadat, who rehabilitated the opening of the economy (*infitāḥ*, hence their name) as much as Islamization.

In Turkey, this is the "Islamic high society" that is "conservative in values but avant-garde in consumption practices,"[29] which benefited from the export-friendly policies of the 1980s as they rehabilitated both Islam and small- and medium-size enterprises to the detriment of the secular elite at the heads of large conglomerates in Istanbul and Ankara. In Indonesia, the "indigenous" merchant class benefited from economic reforms in the 1980s by Suharto, who boosted exports while simultaneously allying himself with modernist Islamic forces. The emergence of a "beurgeoisie"[30] is not to be overlooked. Part of a pious immigration, they are ambitious and ostentatious; they seek to disassociate themselves from the label of "losers from the suburban housing projects" by working hard and succeeding both financially and socially.

These are the target markets, though they are not the only ones, for new Islamic products. Razanne sells well in the Cairo markets, despite a price that is out of reach for many. Sami Youssef, icon of halal music, performed in a five-star hotel for his first appearance in Egypt. The Hotel Caprice has high prices and targets the elite. In the Islamic cafés of Istanbul, like at the

---

[28] Quoted in Jean-François Bayart, *L'illusion identitaire* (Paris: Fayard, 1996), 24.
[29] On the Islamic cafés of Istanbul, see Ugur Kömeçoğlu, "New Sociabilities: Islamic Cafes in Istanbul," in *Islam in Public: Turkey, Iran and Europe*, ed. Nilüfer Göle and Ludwig Ammann (Istanbul: Istanbul Bilgi University Press, 2006).
[30] Again, a reference to the French "beurs" of North African origin.

Dilruba, one expects the clientele to be pious, but they are also sophisticated and refined.[31]

The bourgeois clique is also confirmed by a new message that values wealth in a similar way to American Pentecostals or the elite culture that can be seen in the widening bourgeois circles and personal fulfillment books that highlight the religious aspect within an individualistic and bourgeois self. This has been demonstrated by the growing success of Islamic coaching, at least in the English-speaking world.

The second expression of Muslim consumerism lies in the rise of a market-friendly religiosity that is hedonistic, individualistic, and open to cultural extroversion. This is symbolized by the liberal veiled woman clad in Western brands, who flirts in Sunsilk adverts in Indonesia and who can also be seen on the sidewalks of Teheran, where she draws the ire of fundamentalists and clerics in Egypt. This hedonistic religiosity is promoted by certain imams, such as the Egyptian Amr Khaled, who offers a less-restrictive model of religiosity to facilitate repentance and bring parishioners back to the fold. It is also prominent in the blogs of the young Islamist brotherhood in Egypt—like ᶜAmr, who with his blog has given himself the goal of

> showing my way of life, showing that I am Islamist but that I like Fayrouz and Mohamed Mounir. I wanted to show a different face of Islamists, one in stark contrast to the images given, on the one hand, by the media and, on the other, by fundamentalist Muslims.[32]

Hedonism is also found in changes to militant songs (*nashīd*), which, by becoming more commercial, have lost their edge, becoming an instrument, softening their message and opening themselves to new genres and themes. One such example is the Islamic *nashīd* group in Brussels that has adopted gospel music. Muslim wear, as we have seen, has taken on this point of view, where syncretism and cultural extroversion dominate. Ramadan has become a consumerist tribute to a faith absorbed by globalization. This is also seen in advertisements for globalized brands during Ramadan.

However—and this is my third observation—the rise of this hedonism is sparking resistance, which sometimes uses the same methods. Conservatives of all stripes, encouraged by the progression of Islamization but also stung by its hedonistic excesses, are venting their discontent not only at non-veiled women but also at the poorly veiled, known as *bad hejabi* in Iran, or

---

[31] Quoted in Patrick Haenni, "Egypte: la blogosphère islamiste – miroir d'un nouveau militantisme et facteur de tensions internes au sein des Frères musulmans," *Religioscope* (24 September 2008, http://religion.info/french/articles/article_394.shtml).

[32] Quoted in ibid.

muḥajjaba mutaḥarrira, "liberal veiled women," in Cairo. Campaigns denouncing the "liberal veiled women" are expressed in Friday sermons and also in commercial messages. In an advertisement on the *al-Risala* channel, Satan, with requisite horns and speaking in a Lebanese accent,[33] pushes a veiled young woman into deviance (wearing makeup and going out with her friends), which is no longer equivalent to removing one's veil, but is similar to the "libertine" headscarf promoted by Sunsilk.[34] Fulla is also part of a very puritan vision of women: the doll lives in a clear division of space, and her wardrobe, extremely conservative on the outside, is also, unsurprisingly, the result of frenetic consumerist behavior.

Everything in the sphere of Muslim consumerism is resolutely modern (both hedonism and rigor are forms that go beyond tradition), but these forms of modernity are also "mixed" in the Guillebaud sense of the lifestyles they portray. For Fulla, cultural mixing is consumerism, modesty, and anorexia; for Cola Turka, it is family values; and for Sunsilk, it is the headscarf of female emancipation. For Muslim wear, it is all about popular culture and ethics. In other words, the Islamic reference, in the language of consumerism, is not carried by a single "structure" (neither Western cultural domination nor the triumph of Islam) that serves as its backbone. The pluralism of the ways of life dominates the invocation of the reference to Islam.

The fourth reflection can be understood only by contrasting the Sunsilk ads with the ad in which Satan tempts the liberal veiled woman into deviance. Each advert carries the message of the moral Muslim girl, the headscarf omnipresent, but each girl also demonstrates a lifestyle choice. One extols the belief that the sexes are equal (the veiled football player, the student taking the initiative to flirt), while the other advocates for a dichotomy of the public and private spheres. They show, therefore, that the spread of a reference does not have any bearing on the interpretation that we can tell. However, the stark difference between the two is that the advert that portrays Satan is structured around a discourse. Its conclusion is a quotation from the Qurʾan[35] that reminds women of the importance of modesty.

Pluralization of ways of life does not imply that the discourses that give them meaning will become more diverse. On the contrary, "the Salafist matrix," as coined by Olivier Roy, is increasingly dominating all of the postures of the multiplicity of lifestyles that refer to Islam and that participate

---

[33] Without a doubt, but I'm speculating, in reference to the media's suggestive correlation between the Lebanese dialect and the Lebanese singer cited.

[34] The ad is available on YouTube: http://fr.youtube.com/watch?v=6WqmCAzxUxI.

[35] Q 24:31 "And say to the believing women that they should lower their gaze and guard their modesty; that they should not display their beauty and ornaments except what (must ordinarily) appear thereof." Source of translation: http://quran.al-islam.com/.

Figure 16.5: Ramadan—a consumerist homage to a faith that is absorbed by globalization. Advertisements for global brands during Ramadan

in Islamization. For contesting the content of a norm affirms, at the same time, the pertinence of this norm and, by extension, serves as promotion of the dominant message that defines it. There can be no temptation by Satan without the girl with the liberal veil. Yet the dominant message is, today, salafist. As, paradoxically, it is salafism that best ideologically formalizes the realities of globalization and Islamic consumerism. Salafism, as a radical doctrine of pure origins, is in effect anti-culture (culture being conceived as deviance), and implicitly positions itself as an apologue of de-territorialization from which globalization comes forth.[36] It theologically formalizes, in this respect, the dynamics of globalization (notably by valuing uprooting which can be seen as an opportunity to purify Islam).[37] Salafism also operates as an ideology that discourages collective questions and promotes turning inward. It therefore religiously formalizes individualism, the "implicit ideology" (as defined by Maxime Rodinson) of contemporary consumerism.

In other words, the "consumerization" of the religious does not in any way imply its requisite loosening, because, far from freely floating in a semantic vacuum, the symbols interact with the much more ideological sphere of the discourse. The smile of the veiled, football-playing Sunsilk flirt, as brilliant as it might be, in the conflict of Muslim modernity—which opposes it to Razanne—is the corollary of a postmodern trend toward re-Islamization.

---

[36] See footnote 7.
[37] See Olivier Roy, *La divine ignorance, le temps de la religion sans culture* (Paris: Seuil, 2008).

Confronted with the reactions she provokes, the girl has only the imperfect charm of her silence in her favor.

Bibliography

Azmi, Jumaatun. *Halal Drinks. Great Recipes to Entertain, Relax and Rejuvenate.* Kuala Lumpur: KasehDia, 2004.
———. *Halal Food: A Guide to Good Eating—London.* Kuala Lumpur: KasehDia Sdn. Bhd, 2003.
Bayart, Jean-François. *L'illusion identitaire.* Paris: Fayard, 1996.
Guillebaud, Jean-Claude. *Le commencement d'un monde. Vers une modernité métisse.* Paris: Seuil, 2008.
Haenni, Patrick. "Egypte: la blogosphère islamiste – miroir d'un nouveau militantisme et facteur de tensions internes au sein des Frères musulmans." *Religioscope* (24 September 2008, http://religion.info/french/articles/article_394.shtml).
———. *L'islam de marché. L'autre révolution conservatrice.* Paris: Seuil, 2005.
Haenni, Patrick, and Husam Tammam. "De retour dans les rythmes du monde: Une petite histoire du chant (ex)islamiste en Egypte." *Vingtième siècle. Revue d'histoire* 82 (2004): 91–102.
Johannsmann, Christian. "Anthropological Perspectives on Ethnic Marketing in Germany." Paper presented at the Conference "Contemporary Muslim Consumer Cultures," Berlin, 24–27 September 2008.
Kömeçoğlu, Ugur. "New Sociabilities: Islamic Cafes in Istanbul." In *Islam in Public: Turkey, Iran and Europe,* edited by Nilüfer Göle and Ludwig Ammann. Istanbul: Istanbul Bilgi University Press, 2006.
Maigre, Marie-Élisabeth. "Turquie: l'émergence d'une éthique musulmane dans le monde des affaires - Autour de l'évolution du MÜSIAD et des communautés religieuses." *Religioscope* (9 May 2005, http://religion.info/french/articles/article_170.shtml).
Naughton, Keith. "Arab American stores." *Newsweek* (10 March 2008).
Ram, Uri. "Liquid Identities: Mecca Cola versus Coca-Cola." *European Journal of Cultural Studies* 10, no. 4 (2007): 465–484.
Roy, Olivier. *La divine ignorance, le temps de la religion sans culture.* Paris: Seuil, 2008.
———. *L'islam mondialisé.* Paris: Seuil, 2002.
Tammam, Husam. *Asʾila al-zaman al-salafī.* http://www.chihab.net/modules.php?name=News&file=print&sid=1825.

LIST OF CONTRIBUTORS

Aksu Akçaoğlu is currently a Ph.D. candidate and research assistant in the Sociology Department of the Middle East Technical University in Ankara, Turkey. His main area of interest is the sociology of consumption. In his master's thesis, he examined "The Mallification of Urban Life in Ankara: The Case of ANKAmall."

Firly Annisa is a graduate student in the communications program at Muhammadiyah University of Yogyakarta. She is also an assistant lecturer at the university where she got received her B.A. Her research centers on gender issues in the media and Muslim identity; "The Deconstruction of Women in the Cartoon Film 'Dora the Explorer'" is one of her topics. In 2007 she joined the media group Rumah Sinema as a volunteer to work on audience education.

Ayhan Erol is Associate Professor of Musicology at Dokuz Eylül University in İzmir, Turkey, where he teaches courses on theory of ethnomusicology, cultural studies, sociology of music, music history, and popular music studies. He holds a Ph.D. in ethnomusicology (2000) from Dokuz Eylül University. His research interests include Turkish popular music history, cultural identity and music, folk music revivals, Islamic [pop] music, and Alevi music. He is the author of two books: *Popüler Müziği Anlamak* (Istanbul: Bağlam Yayınları, 2002) and *Müzik Üzerine Düşünmek* (2009). His work has appeared in renowned scholarly journals, including *Journal of Interdisciplinary Music Studies*, *Middle Eastern Studies*, *European Meetings in Ethnomusicology*, *Tarih ve Toplum*, *Folklor ve Edebiyat* and *Toplum ve Bilim*. He has also contributed to several published English volumes on popular music and the Alevi musical culture.

Johan Fischer is an Associate Professor in the Department of Society and Globalisation, Roskilde University, Denmark. His work focuses on modern Islam and consumer culture in Southeast Asia and Europe. A central focus in his research is the theoretical and empirical focus on the proliferation of halal commodities on a global scale. He is presently working on a monograph with the provisional title "On the Halal Frontier: Consuming

Malays in London" that explores ways in which modern halal is formative for emerging Islamic identities; the fusion of religion and consumption; novel approaches to an anthropology of the state; and diasporic material culture as well as forms of capitalism in the new millennium.

Banu Gökarıksel is Assistant Professor of Geography at the University of North Carolina, Chapel Hill. Her research engages in a critical re-assessment of neoliberal globalization, dimensions of public space, and identity-formation through contemporary everyday Islamic and secular practices and ideologies in Turkey. She has been doing ethnographic fieldwork research in Istanbul since 1996. Her primary research questions have examined competing and contested secular and Islamic visions and practices of contingent modernity in mall spaces, cultural politics of dress, and consumer capitalism. Her publications have appeared in the journals *Area*, *Global Networks* and *Social & Cultural Geography*, and in Ghazi Falah and Caroline Nagel, eds., *Geographies of Muslim Women: Gender, Religion and Space* (New York: Guilford Press, 2005). She currently is working on a NSF-funded project with Anna Secor on the transnational veiling-fashion industry based in Turkey.

Katarzyna Górak-Sosnowska has a Ph.D. in economics and is an Assistant Professor in the Department of Sociology at the Warsaw School of Economics. She is a board member of the ARABIA.pl Association and editor of its internet portal. She is also a lecturer and trainer. Her research interests include socio-economic problems of the contemporary Arab world and Islam in Europe, as well as intercultural education. Górak-Sosnowska is the author of *Świat arabski wobec globalizacji* [*The Arab World and Globalisation*], 2007, and *Perspektywy świata arabskiego w kontekście Milenijnych Celów Rozwoju* [*Prospects of the Arab World Through the Lens of the Millennium Development Goals*], 2007. She is also the co-author of a textbook for teachers *W kręgu kultury islamu* [*Meet the World of Islam*] 2007), and the associate editor of *Bliski Wschód* [*Middle East*] yearly.

Patrick Haenni is a senior researcher at the Religioscope Foundation and co-director of Polarities, a think tank for Middle East religious affairs based in Geneva. Previously, Haenni was a senior analyst for the International Crisis Group in Beirut, Lebanon. He was also a researcher at the French CEDEJ in Cairo. Haenni has written several books on the Middle East and the Islamic World, most recently Patrick Haenni, *L'islam de marché. L'autre révolution conservatrice* (Paris: Seuil, 2005). He is working on a new book for the same publisher, entitled *Islamism and Equity: Is a Leftist Islamism Possible?*

List of Contributors 345

Michael Hastings-Black is the co-founder of Desedo, an advertising agency that specializes in New Media + Minority Markets. Prior to Desedo, he worked as an urban planner. He has a B.A. in English from Bowdoin College.

Alina Kokoschka studies Islamic studies, philosophy, and political science at the Free University of Berlin and is preparing her Masters thesis at the Institute for Islamic Studies. She spent 10 months in Damascus from 2004 to 2005 and returned in 2006, conducting the fieldwork presented in her paper. Her research interests include visual anthropology, economy and gender, urban changes and subcultures. She works as a student assistant at the Centre of Modern Oriental Studies (ZMO) in Berlin.

Petra Kuppinger is Associate Professor of Anthropology at Monmouth College in Monmouth, Illinois. Her research interests include issues of space, power, and popular and consumer cultures in the Middle East, especially Cairo, Egypt. More recently she has been working on a project on Islam, piety and participation in Stuttgart, Germany. Her publications include: "Factories, Office Suites, Defunct and Marginal Spaces: Mosques in Stuttgart, Germany," in *Mobility and the Transformation of Built Form*, ed. Michael Guggenheim and Ola Söderström (Routledge, in press); "Entertainment and Control: Social Life in Colonial Cairo," in *The Discipline of Leisure: Embodying Cultures of "Recreation,"* ed. Simon Coleman and Tamara Kohn (Oxford and New York: Berghahn Books, 2007), 149–170; "Pyramids and Alleys: Global Dynamics and Local Strategies in Giza," in *Cairo Cosmopolitan: Urban Structure, Spaces and Identities in the New Middle East*, ed. Diane Singerman and Paul Amar (Cairo: American University in Cairo Press, 2006), 313–344; and "Globalization and Exterritoriality in Metropolitan Cairo," in "Special Issue on New Geographies of the Middle East," ed. Dona J. Stewart, *The Geographical Review* 95, no. 3 (2006): 348–372.

Michał Łyszczarz, a sociologist and political scientist, is a Ph.D. candidate at the Institute of Sociology at the University of Silesia in Katowice in Poland. He is interested in the sociology of ethnic minorities, in particular the Polish Tatar community. His research focuses on the sociology of culture and religion, especially the religious dialogue between Christianity and Islam.

Dilek Kaya Mutlu is an Assistant Professor and teaches popular culture and media reception at Bilkent University, in Ankara, Turkey. She has published essays on the history of Turkish cinema, Turkish melodramas of the

1960s and 1970s, and the exhibition and censorship of American films in Turkey. She is the author of *The Midnight Express Phenomenon: The International Reception of the Film Midnight Express* (Istanbul: The Isis Press, 2005).

Johanna Pink is a lecturer at the Institute for Islamic Studies, Free University of Berlin. She holds a Ph.D. in Islamic Studies from the University of Bonn and has worked on a wide range of topics concerning contemporary forms of religious expression and debate in Muslim societies. Major publications deal with the status of religious minorities in the Arab World; politics of religion in Egypt; and contemporary Qurʾanic exegesis in the Arab World, Indonesia, and Turkey. She is the author of *Neue Religionsgemeinschaften in Ägypten. Minderheiten im Spannungsfeld von Glaubensfreiheit, öffentlicher Ordnung und Islam [New Religious Communities in Egypt. Minorities between Freedom of Belief, Public Order and Islam]* (Würzburg: Ergon, 2003); a monograph on recent Sunni Qurʾanic commentaries is forthcoming.

Anna Secor is an Associate Professor of Geography and Director of the Committee on Social Theory at the University of Kentucky. Her research on Turkey, Islam, civil society, and veiling fashion (the latter in collaboration with Banu Gökarıksel) has been funded by the National Science Foundation. Her work has appeared in journals such as the *Annals of the Association of American Geographers, Antipode, Environment and Planning D: Society and Space, Political Geography,* and *Transactions of the Institute of British Geography*.

Relli Shechter is Senior Lecturer and Chair of the Department of Middle East Studies, Ben-Gurion University, Israel. Among his recent publications are: "Glocal Mediators: Marketing in Egypt during the Open-Door Era (*infitah*)," *Enterprise and Society* 9, no. 4 (2008): 762–787; "The Cultural Economy of Development in Egypt: Economic Nationalism, Hidden Economy and the Emergence of Mass Consumer Society during Sadat's *infitah*," *Middle Eastern Studies* 44, no. 4 (2008): 571–583; *Smoking, Culture and Economy in the Middle East: The Egyptian Tobacco Market 1850–2000* (London: I.B. Tauris Publishers / AUC Press, 2006); and Hillary Cooperman and Relli Shechter, "Branding the Riders: 'Marlboro Country' and the Formation of a New Middle Class in Egypt, Saudi Arabia, and Turkey," *New Global Studies* 2, no. 3 (2008): article 1.

Vít Šisler is a visiting Fulbright scholar at the Buffett Center for International and Comparative Studies at Northwestern University and a Ph.D.

candidate at Charles University in Prague, where he is finishing his thesis on new media, the internet, and the production of contemporary Islamic knowledge.Š isler is also engaged in research on contemporary Islamic law, the relation between Islam and digital media, and the social and political aspects of video games. He is founder and editor-in-chief of Digital Islam, a compound research project on Islam, the Middle East, and digital media (digitalislam.eu). Among his recent publications are "Digital Arabs: Representation in Video Games," *European Journal of Cultural Studies* 11, no. 2 (2008): 203–220 and "European Courts' Authority Contested? The Case of Marriage and Divorce Fatwas On-line," *Masaryk University Journal of Law and Technology* 3, no. 1 (2009): 51–78.

Ulrike Stohrer has studied anthropology, history, and media studies at the Johann Wolfgang Goethe-University in Frankfurt/Main, where she received her Ph.D. in anthropology in 2004. She teaches anthropology of the Middle East in Frankfurt and Marburg. Her main research interests are ritual, performance, and processes of identity building in the Middle East. She has conducted extensive fieldwork in Yemen and published several articles on Yemenite culture. Currently, she is starting a research project on clothing, consumerism, and identity in Yemen. Among her recent publications are "Gegenwärtige Modetrends in Sana," in *Töchter des Jemen*, ed. Museum für Völkerkunde, Ausstellungskatalog Museum für Völkerkunde zu Leipzig (Leipzig, 2005), 15–21; "Mapping the Nation through Performance in Yemen: Sanaa as 'the Capital of the Present, the History and the Unity'," in *Nationalism, Historiography and the (Re) Construction of the Past*, ed. Claire Norton (Washington: New Academia Press, 2007), 115–125; "Keeping Stability in an Unstable World: Ritual, Performance, and Identity in Yemen," in *Rituals in an Unstable World. Contingency - Hybridity - Embodiment*, ed. Alexander Henn and Klaus-Peter Köpping (Frankfurt/Main: Lang, 2008), 31–45; and *Barᶜa. Rituelle Performance, Identität und Kulturpolitik im Jemen* (Berlin: Klaus Schwarz Verlag, 2009).

Tanfer Emin Tunç is an Assistant Professor in the Department of American Culture and Literature at Hacettepe University, Ankara, Turkey. She received her B.A., M.A. and Ph.D. from the State University of New York at Stony Brook in the social and cultural history of the United States, and specializes in women's history/literature; gender, sexuality, and reproduction; and feminist/cultural theory. The recipient of her fields most prestigious grants and fellowships (including awards from the National Science Foundation, the Woodrow Wilson Foundation of Princeton University, Rockefeller University, Duke University, the University of Michigan, Smith College, the American Historical Association, and the National Women's Studies Association), Dr. Tunç has presented her research at conferences all over the world. She has also published dozens of articles, many of which have appeared in internationally renowned journals such as *Rethinking History*, *Asian Journal of Women's Studies* and *Foreign Literature Studies*. Her books include *Technologies of Choice: A History of Abortion Techniques in the United States, 1850–1980* (Saarbrücken: VDM, 2008); *The Globetrotting Shopaholic: Consumer Spaces, Products, and their Cultural Places*, ed. Tanfer Emin Tunç and Annessa Ann Babic (Cambridge Scholars Publishing, 2008); and *The Theme of Cultural Adaptation in American History, Literature, and Film: Cases When the Discourse Changed* (Lewiston: Edwin Mellen Press, forthcoming).

Ragnar K. Willer, a specialist on Southeast Asia, has trained at Passau University, LSE, and INSEAD, and received his Ph.D. from Humboldt University, Berlin. He is an independent consultant, researcher, and writer; his work focuses on sociocultural change, glocalization processes, and consumer culture. His current research topics are strategic consumption, green lifestyles, and popular religions and their effects on consumer behavior. He welcomes your comments and discussion via (email) rw@oceo-consult.com, (web) www.oceo-consult.com, (blog) www.konsumkulturconsumerculture.com, (Twitter) www.twitter.com/oceoconsult.